The Stuff of Spectatorship

The publisher and the University of California Press Foundation gratefully acknowledge the generous support of the Robert and Meryl Selig Endowment Fund in Film Studies, established in memory of Robert W. Selig.

The Stuff of Spectatorship

Material Cultures of Film and Television

Caetlin Benson-Allott

UNIVERSITY OF CALIFORNIA PRESS

University of California Press
Oakland, California

© 2021 by Caetlin Benson-Allott

Library of Congress Cataloging-in-Publication Data

Names: Benson-Allott, Caetlin Anne, author.
Title: The stuff of spectatorship : material cultures of film
    and television / Caetlin Benson-Allott.
Description: Oakland, California : University of
    California Press, [2021] | Includes bibliographical
    references and index.
Identifiers: LCCN 2020037054 (print) | LCCN 2020037055
    (ebook) | ISBN 9780520300408 (cloth) |
    ISBN 9780520300415 (paperback) |
    ISBN 9780520971820 (epub)
Subjects: LCSH: Motion pictures—Social aspects.
Classification: LCC PN1995.9.S6 B46 2021 (print) |
    LCC PN1995.9.S6 (ebook) | DDC 302.230973—dc23
LC record available at https://lccn.loc.gov/2020037054
LC ebook record available at https://lccn.loc.gov
    /2020037055

Manufactured in the United States of America

29 28 27 26 25 24 23 22 21
10 9 8 7 6 5 4 3 2 1

For Seth, always

Contents

Figures

Acknowledgments

This book argues that film and television spectatorship are informed by material objects and forces whose influence typically goes unacknowledged. The same can be said of film and television criticism. I am grateful for the opportunity to recognize some of the people and institutions that helped make this book a thing in the world.

I want to thank Georgetown University and its English Department for supplying grants and fellowships that made this project possible and the Georgetown Film and Media Studies Program for hosting visiting speakers who advanced my research. Working at Georgetown, I have benefitted from exchanging ideas with truly gifted colleagues and students, including Harry Burson, Katherine Chandler, Cara Dickason, Nathan Hensley, Brian Hochman, Sherry Linkon, Dana Luciano, Cóilín Parsons, Amanda Phillips, Nicole Rizzuto, Sky Sitney, Matthew Tinkcom, and Elizabeth Crowley Webber. I am particularly grateful to Melissa Jones, reference librarian extraordinaire, and the talented Georgetown research assistants who contributed to this project: Katherine McCain, Grace Foster, Susan Long, and Julia Yaeger. Georgetown made it possible for me to interview the many film exhibitors, television executives, and other industry professionals whose insights enrich this work; they include Vanessa Theme Ament, David Cabrera, Phil Contrino, Steven Denker, Jennifer Dorian, James Duffy, Richard L. Edwards, Greg Godbout, Greg Julian, Lydia Kim, Justin LaLiberty, Genevieve McGillicuddy, Fred Schoenfeld, Stephanie Thames, and Kristen Welch. Thank you all for sharing your time and wisdom with me. Although he was not an official interview subject, Coleman Breland facilitated this project in myriad ways, including introducing me to his wonderful team at Turner Classic Movies; thanks again, Coleman!

While writing *The Stuff of Spectatorship*, I also had the honor of editing *JCMS*—formerly *Cinema Journal*—with a truly amazing team of selfless, dedicated scholars; thank you, dream team, for inspiring me and making this book possible. I was privileged to present portions of this manuscript at Amherst College, Boston University, Emerson College, Emory University, King's College London, Rowan University, University of Rochester, University of Wisconsin–Milwaukee, and Yale University. Their faculty and students buoyed me with enthusiasm and challenged me with probing questions; I remain grateful for their support. A previous version of chapter 2 appeared in *Feminist Media Histories*, while previous versions of chapter 6 were published in *FLOW: A Critical Forum of Television and Media Culture* and Richard Grusin and Jocelyn Szczepaniak-Gillece's anthology *Ends of Cinema*. I also had the opportunity to work through some of my ideas for chapters 4 and 5 in my column for *Film Quarterly*, although those essays should be considered companion pieces to this volume rather than excerpts from it.

Many friends and colleagues generously pitched in to help me develop these ideas; without their generosity, I doubt I would have persevered. Thank you, in particular, to Neta Alexander, Neda Atanasoski, Courtney Baker, Sara Bakerman, Miranda Banks, Jeremy Berlin, Jacob Brogan, Francesco Casetti, David Church, J.D. Connor, Beth Corzo-Duchardt, Shane Denson, Ramzi Fawaz, Racquel Gates, Christine Geraghty, Michael Gillespie, Hollis Griffin, Richard Grusin, Danielle Hacque, Amelie Hastie, Daniel Herbert, Lucas Hilderbrand, Julia Himberg, Chris Holmlund, Tanya Horeck, Eric Hoyt, Brian Jacobson, Sarah Keller, Kara Keeling, Amanda Ann Klein, Chuck Kleinhans, Barbara Klinger, Regina Longo, Jennifer Malkowski, Carla Marcantonio, Alfred L. Martin Jr., Paula Massood, Ross Melnick, Jeff Menne, Jessica Metzler, Jason Middleton, Jason Mittell, Colleen Montgomery, Paul Monticone, Karla Oeler, Jessica Pavone, Brian Price, Zachary Price, Masha Raskolnikov, Anthony Reed, Angelo Restivo, Daniel Reynolds, B. Ruby Rich, Scott Richmond, Ariel Rogers, Nick Salvato, Jeff Scheible, Jane Shattuc, Samantha Sheppard, Vivian Sobchack, Janet Staiger, Shelley Stamp, Jacqueline Stewart, Jocelyn Szczepaniak-Gillece, Neda Ulaby, Kristen Warner, Madeline Whittle, Brian Winston, and Greg Zinman. You've all supplied advice and contacts, talked through concepts, read drafts, and provided invaluable feedback. I am eternally grateful for your insight and kindness. Extra-special thanks are due, as always, to Amy Villarejo. Amy, I am grateful beyond words for your friendship, wit, and critical acumen. I don't get enough opportunities to say thank you, so I'm doing it again here.

I have had the good fortune to work with two amazing editors on this project. Laura Portwood-Stacer of Manuscript Works read every single word in this book and helped me articulate the through line when I feared none existed (save my own eccentricity). Raina Polivka of the University of California Press greeted this project with enthusiasm and provided sage council—and superlative reader reports—that improved it immeasurably. The entire UC Press team has enhanced this project with their professional insight and zeal; thank you all!

Most of all, I want to thank my wonderful and supportive family, who have humored my peculiar obsessions for decades now. John and Lynne Benson; Liz and Mark Rodrigo; Earl, Leslie, Pat, and Sarah Silbert; David and Joan Perlow; Dara and Sam Matthew; and Mimi Stevens: You've put up with me working on countless holidays and vacations and smiled each time I said it would be the last time. Thank you for your patience and for watching movies with me under all the various conditions in which I insisted I needed to watch them. And Seth Perlow: you've assuaged more writing-related breakdowns than anyone should have to, especially for a book that involved going on an international cruise. You too read every word in this book (sometimes multiple times) except for these: Thank you for the pep talks and the tough love, the flowers and the triage, for believing in me and this book even when we drove you insane. Since this is the first book of mine you cannot claim to have named, this one's for you.

Introduction

Material Meditations

Film and television create worlds, but they are also of a world—the real world, for lack of a better term. This world is eminently, although not exclusively, material. It is made up of stuff, to which humans attach meaning. We encounter movies and television series through some kinds of stuff (projectors, monitors, speakers, and other exhibition technology) and are ourselves stuff: material objects that react to and affect other material objects. But audiovisual componentry and human bodies are not the only stuff mediating our experiences of film and television. Think of the last time you watched a movie: the chair you sat in, the home snacks or concessions you ate, the other viewers and their belongings, maybe the beer or joint you consumed to help you unwind. This book is about all those things and their unacknowledged influence on film and television spectatorship. The material culture around film and television changes how we make sense of their content, not to mention the very concepts *film* and *television*. But while scholars have spent decades studying how human identities, human bodies, and various technologies influence media reception, little attention has been paid to the material culture *around* viewers and their screens.[1]

Theorists and historians of film and television have spent decades analyzing exhibition technologies and spaces—how the "apparatus" of the movie theater or the design of television sets conveys ideological cues that guide viewers' perceptions.[2] More recently, some scholars have become interested in how viewers' bodies and specific sites of media consumption shape their encounters with film and television.[3] Others analyze the infrastructures that make media distribution possible.[4] However, scholars rarely consider the panoply of media reception, the commodities and comestibles that surround viewers, and the impact those objects have on viewers' relation to media content or one another. In *Stuff*, anthropologist Daniel Miller observes that "much of what makes us what we are exists, not through our consciousness or body, but as an exterior environment that habituates and prompts us."[5] Material culture rarely gets credit for its epistemological significance, however, because it is "familiar and taken for granted." Its ability to disappear is evidence of how significant material culture actually is, however. As Miller explains, "Objects are important, not because they are evident and physically constrain or enable, but quite the opposite. It is often precisely because we do not *see* them. The less we are aware of them, the more powerfully they can determine our expectations."[6] Miller's observation reveals unacknowledged material complexities within "the scene of the screen," an evocative phrase I borrow from Vivian Sobchack. In her essay of that title, Sobchack argues that "as materialities of human communication," film and television have radically reoriented human experiences of time and space, not to mention people's "bodily sense of existential 'presence.'"[7] While media technologies have changed who we are, the scene of their intervention includes not just screens, speakers, and bodies but food, drugs, branded merchandise—even physical violence. These material forces radically alter viewers' sense of themselves, their media, and their world.

Material culture is always shot through with social politics, with messages about class, race, gender, and other social divisions. This is especially true of material media cultures, which also shape cultural memory and the terms for cultural participation. Take my early childhood introduction to television culture and class politics, *TV Guide*. The physical presence of that little digest in my friends' living rooms taught me that not everyone watched TV the same way, that it was a material culture suffused with class distinction. My family did not subscribe to *TV Guide*; instead, we had *TV Week*, the television listing supplement that came free with the Sunday *Boston Globe*. *TV Week* was a utilitarian catalog of upcoming broadcasts, published on inexpensive newsprint. *TV Guide*, by contrast, featured glossy coated paper and contained feature articles, editorial content, and reviews as well as broadcast schedules. *TV Guide* taught me about the power of conspicuous consumption: that in certain contexts, function was less important than presentation and packaging.

I was fascinated by my friends' *TV Guide*s; I couldn't believe that their parents bought things to help them watch TV.[8] I knew my friends weren't watching better shows than I was—we all followed the same series—but *TV Guide* suggested that they might belong to a better class of television viewer. It was like the difference between owning a vacuum cleaner and hiring someone to do your vacuuming for you; folks who could afford the latter had things a little easier than the rest of us (and a lot easier than folks using a dustbin and broom).

TV Guide's influence extended far beyond the social dynamics of suburban Massachusetts, thanks in no small part to its unique design. In 1948, *TV Guide* began as *The TeleVision Guide*, a small circular that covered programming for the New York City area. Walter Annenberg bought *The TeleVision Guide* in 1953, along with several similar regional weeklies. He began publishing these magazines under one title, *TV Guide*, and "putting a national wrap around them": the aforementioned articles, reviews, and recommendations, not to mention name-brand advertisements.[9] Annenberg's first *TV Guide* was published on April 3, 1953, with a cover story about Desi Arnaz Jr., "Lucy's $50,000,000 Baby!" At fifteen cents per issue, it sold just over 1.5 million copies at newsstands—not bad, considering that its regional editions only covered ten cities.[10] Circulation tumbled that summer, but the national "Fall Preview" wrap excited consumer interest and brought circulation back to almost 1.75 million. It kept climbing.[11] During the 1960s, *TV Guide* "became indigenous in the American household," according to Michael Dann, a former director of programming for NBC.[12] By 1967, one in every five television households in the United States subscribed to *TV Guide* (12.5 million out of 57 million).[13] Consequently, the national networks began timing their programming decisions around *TV Guide*'s deadlines. The mechanics of print publication now set the schedule for broadcasters, suggesting that television's companion had become its master.

TV Guide had an equally significant effect on viewers. As Dann recalls, "It was one of the great media feats in publishing history. You could almost count on so many viewers if you got a cover."[14] By 1988—when I was most attentive to which of my friends' families subscribed—*TV Guide*'s circulation exceeded seventeen million, making it the most profitable and popular magazine in the United States.[15] During this era, *TV Guide* and weekly newspaper television inserts like *TV Week* were the presiding material manifestations of television culture and physical tokens of the industry's message of consumer plenty. Through their design and material ubiquity, *TV Week* and *TV Guide* both affirmed an ideology

FIGURE I. Covers of the *Chicago Tribune*'s *TV Week* and *TV Guide* for the third week of September 1978. Photo by author.

that British cultural critic Brian Winston calls "the television of abundance."[16] After all, a terrain must be sufficiently complex for it to require a *Guide*. Differences in their contents, layout, and design impute class distinctions between their readerships, however. *TV Guide*'s original digest-sized format was slightly smaller than a paperback book in its height, width, depth, and weight. This resemblance bestowed cultural capital to both the journal and its subject, making the publication seem more learned than it was. Most newspaper supplements, by contrast, were 8½ × 11 inches—about the size of a traditional newsstand magazine— but very thin and light. Some sported logos suspiciously similar to *TV Guide*'s. Most used full-color covers, yet their derivative iconography, material modesty, and even their name signaled their ephemerality and disposability (figure 1).

For while *TV Guide* also printed its local television listings on newsprint, they were bookended by that full-color "national wrap" on two dozen pages of high-gloss coated paper. Although less informative than the local programming pages, these introductory materials helped establish a veneer of quality and respectability for the magazine. Their national advertisements, for instance, reinforced *TV Guide*'s cultural authority; ads for iconic brands such as Marlboro, Oscar Mayer, and Atari bolstered the magazine's commercial prominence through a kind of eminence by association. Additionally, their polished graphics improved the overall look of the magazine. The patina of the national wrap was very important, because the black and white regional listings were visually stultifying. Their two-column layout created a graphic uniformity that local and series ads could only do so much to interrupt (figure 2). *TV Week*, by contrast, was printed entirely on newsprint, with only its front and back cover in color, although the larger pages allowed for a four-column layout and a larger font size, which made its listings more readable than those of *TV Guide* (figure 3). *TV Week* rarely contained national ad campaigns, however; its ads were typically for local businesses. A 1978 issue of the *Chicago Tribune*'s *TV Week* featured promotions for local hair-loss clinics, personal loan providers, and hardware and furniture outlets, as well as specific television shows. These ads enforce a provincial sense of identity, as befits a regional newspaper publication. By contrast, *TV Guide* physically encloses the regional in the national, offering its readers a more cosmopolitan frame for their television viewing.

In sum, *TV Guide* and *TV Week* provided their readers with materially and culturally distinct experiences of television, even as both showcased, and profited from, US television's ideology of abundance. *TV Guide* encouraged viewers to approach television as a national pastime worthy of informed engagement. Its presence in viewers' living rooms bespoke sufficient leisure time and disposable income to enrich one's television experience through consumer goods. Importantly, I refer here to the impression created by the object itself, not its intellectual contributions (which were meager). *TV Week*, on the other hand, affirmed the regional specificity and ephemerality of television. As a newspaper insert, it was fundamentally supplemental; no one bought *TV Week* per se, however much they might have used it. Its cheap materials and spartan design affirm its pragmatic goal: to convey what's on when, as accurately as possible. Other scholars have observed *TV Guide*'s significance as a "cultural mediator"; I argue that its social and industrial power were directly related to its material presentation.[17] Growing up in a *TV Week* household, I envied my friends their *TV Guides*. The sleek little digest connoted an investment in entertainment that I correlated with wealth and privilege. As an adult, I realize that this correlation is less

FIGURES 2 and 3. Interiors of *TV Guide* (left) and the *Chicago Tribune's TV Week* (right) for the third week of September 1978. Photos by author.

direct than I assumed it was then, but I also recognize that *TV Guide* was designed to connote prosperity, taste, and national cultural literacy. Sometimes the objects we consume while we are consuming media impact our understanding of media cultures as much as the media itself.

TV Guide and *TV Week* show that film culture and television culture are also material cultures, that how we read and live with the objects associated with film and television are instrumental to our understanding of them. These periodicals demonstrate that objects considered ephemeral to film and television culture are in fact constitutive of it. For scholars, this means that material culture provides new perspective on and rationale for textual analysis, as it invites us to rethink how media content becomes invested with meaning. As this book argues, the material culture of film and television includes objects that viewers carry into screenings as well as substances they ingest there. It includes networks' branded merchandise and the video packaging that frames television and film history for many consumers. Indeed, the material culture around film and television is much more heterogeneous than one might assume. When planning this book, I chose diverse case studies to demonstrate the broad political scope of material media cultures and how they intervene in the messages that film and television deliver about

race, gender, class, and sexuality. I wanted to show that material paratexts intervene in our interpretation of film, television, and, through
them, one another. Scholars have long argued that film and television
influence these and other socially constructed identity categories, but
they have not considered how material cultures mediate that power.

While some consumers and producers still consider television and
film separate genres, there is no rationale for studying their current
material cultures separately. In my first book, *Killer Tapes and Shattered Screens*, I argue that film has lost its medium specificity, meaning
that the genre and its original technology are no longer co-constitu-
tive.[18] The same could be said of television. For that reason, *The Stuff of
Spectatorship* considers congruences between media cultures and genres
even as some individual chapters focus on television or cinema. Television and film were not always as convergent as they are now, of course,
which is why *The Stuff of Spectatorship* explores media spectatorship
since 1975: the year that the first VCRs were introduced in the United
States and the year that the Duffy Brothers opened the first Cinema 'N'
Drafthouse outside Orlando, Florida. (The implications of these events
are explored further in chapters 1 and 4.) Since the 1970s, movies and
television have increasingly permeated one another's milieus. Before the
TV series *Battlestar Galactica* "premiered" on ABC on September 17,
1978, for instance, its pilot was distributed as a feature film to cinemas
abroad. As a television series and film, *Battlestar Galactica* was embedded in material culture, through toys, T-shirts, bed sheets, and various
video releases. Such material media histories are especially important
now that digital distribution platforms obfuscate the material substrates
behind media, making movies and television feel ever more ethereal and
incorporeal—no more tangible than a cloud. But "the cloud" is material too, as Tung-Hui Hu has shown.[19] Contemporary media are as
embedded in material culture as legacy media, not just in their production, distribution, and exhibition but in the ways that consumers make
sense of them and incorporate them into their lives.

In making these arguments for the historiographic and political
power of material media cultures, however, I find myself at odds with
several of the academic fields that shaped my research. You might say
that *The Stuff of Spectatorship* emerges from a Venn diagram of media
industry studies, reception studies, new cinema history, and materiality
and material culture studies. All four open up new ways of thinking
about how media are produced and consumed, as objects and as discourses, and how they participate in a wider world. However, my claims

for the political significance of material media cultures also run counter to constitutive trends in each of these fields. In what follows, I will outline how each field informs my argument that material forces (like physical violence) and material objects (like cannabis) condition film and television spectatorship and reception. Each field asks questions apposite to this study but also defines its area of inquiry in ways that preclude important issues I want to address.

MEDIA INDUSTRY STUDIES

Media industry studies cohered in the early twenty-first century as an interdisciplinary enterprise focused "on scholarship that holds together economic, political, and cultural dimensions of media" production, distribution, and exhibition.[20] The field traces its lineage to anthropology, business studies, economics, mass communications, political economy, and sociology as well as cultural studies, film studies, and television studies, while the industries it analyzes include film, television, radio, digital media, music, book publishing, and sometimes advertising and telecommunications. As Timothy Havens, Amanda Lotz, and Serra Tinic argue in an inceptive 2009 mission statement, media industry scholars explore everything from localized production cultures to "structural issues of regulatory regimes, concentration of media ownership, historical change, and their larger connection to capital interests."[21] Their work addresses circulations of power within and between different industrial organizations, as scholars scale their research across micro-, middle, and macro-levels of industry practice, from on-set negotiations between individual executives and artists to specific studio hierarchies to globalized media conglomerates.

Media industry research focuses on the people, institutions, and—to a lesser extent—objects involved in bringing media to their audiences. Media industry scholars also provide important insight into media infrastructures, both administrative and physical, showing how they shape our consumer experience.[22] Much of the work concentrates on media production and production cultures, however, although lately some scholars have begun pushing the field toward considering media retail and merchandizing as well.[23] Such work complements film and television scholarship focused on advertising and merchandizing, such as Jonathan Gray's *Show Sold Separately: Promos, Spoilers, and Other Media Paratexts*. While not always considered a part of media industry studies, merchandizing research like Gray's shows that promotion and branding are crucial elements of the media business. Gray's approach to "off-screen studies" has inspired others (myself included) to analyze how licensing agreements, consumer merchandise, and retailing influence viewers' understanding of film and television.[24] Hence, this book analyzes the material culture of industries that deliver (and thus mediate) content for media consumers. Consumption is, after all, a crucial component of media circulation, one that corporations spend lots of time and money to control.

Despite Gray's provocation, however, human labor still overshadows material culture in much industry studies research. Put another way, the field tends to be more interested in workers (and organizations) than in the things they work with or on. While multiple introductions to media industry studies emphasize how it can enrich textual analyses of media, none consider how it might itself be enriched by widening its scope to include nonhuman agents.[25] Such priorities may reflect scholarly genealogy; given the field's roots in sociology and anthropology, ethnography remains a privileged methodology in media industry studies. The field's connections to business studies and political economy likewise direct scholars toward questions of corporate organization, ownership, and regulation. Of course, media industry studies also owes much to the Frankfurt School and Birmingham models of cultural studies, both of which inform its connection to film and television studies. These antecedents suggest that media industry studies can be helpful for thinking about how material culture shapes the social circulation of film and television. In this book, I consider how different corporately administered material cultures condition viewers' responses to film and television. These include the economies of scale in DVD distribution that affect which films are chosen for rerelease (chapter 2) and the branded merchandise and travel that transformed a television network into a lifestyle brand (chapter 3). As it turns out, material culture studies and media industry studies have a lot to say to one another, as the material world is no less important in media production than it is in media reception.

SPECTATORSHIP AND RECEPTION STUDIES

In many ways, spectatorship and reception studies are as old as film studies itself, but they coalesced into different subfields in the 1970s and 1980s. In the 1970s, a wave of film theorists deployed poststructuralist, Marxist, and psychoanalytic theory to explain how the cinematic apparatus interpellates an individual viewer as spectator. The spectator is the subject position created by the apparatus; it is thus a function of ideology, which is why apparatus theorists sought to expose and contest it. However, their descriptions of the cinematic apparatus were all, to varying degrees, transhistorical and universalizing; they rarely accounted for how real people respond to cinematic interpellation. Reception historians seized on this shortcoming to argue that individuals are never wholly subservient to the movies' ideological manipulation, that they bring their personal histories to bear in every encounter with film (and other media). Strongly informed by the Birmingham model of cultural studies—particularly Stuart Hall's theory of negotiated reading—reception scholars use ethnography and archival research to analyze how specific groups of viewers respond to spectatorial subject positioning.[26] They do not dispute the ideological function of the cinematic or any other media apparatus; they are just more interested in how people respond to interpellation than in interpellation itself.

While I do engage in some auto-ethnographic explorations of material media cultures in this book, *The Stuff of Spectatorship* mostly continues in the vein of spectatorship theory. Specifically, it expands the notion of the apparatus to include the material culture around film and television and investigates how that culture influences spectatorial subject positioning. I agree that 1970s apparatus theorists largely focused on or simply assumed a white, able-bodied, bourgeois, heterosexual male spectator. However, many argued that movies and the apparatus of the movie theater privileged precisely that sort of viewer and forced all others to conform to his normative gaze. Similar hegemonic positioning occurs in material media cultures today. However, *The Stuff of Spectatorship* resists universalizing its claims about material media cultures by firmly locating its case studies in their historical moments and relevant reception practices. Hence chapter 4 draws on regional histories of American moviegoing—usually considered the purview of reception studies—to investigate how adult concessions have changed the ways that US cinemas interpellate their customers. Interviews with theater owners and other industry professionals maintain the book's focus on the construction of material culture, however, rather than viewers' subjective experiences.

Focusing on viewers' experience leads some reception scholars to overlook the significant role that material culture plays in how viewers relate to various media technologies and texts. To expand on Stuart Hall's formulation, I suggest that negotiated readings are not just negotiated between viewer and text; they also include the scene of spectatorship and everything in it, all the devices, snacks, furniture, people, and consumer goods in the room. That is why, for example, I negotiated a very different relationship with *Shirley Valentine* (Lewis Gilbert, 1989) while watching it with a glass of wine in a corporate hotel room after a conference than I did after renting it on VHS with my mother and my sister when I was ten years old. Whereas once Gilbert's film occupied the center of a feminist family ritual (despite its dubious depiction of female friendship), the last time I saw it, my exhaustion (and my drink) caused me to identify with Valentine's melancholy and suspect relationship to alcohol. Aging certainly played a role in my new relation to Gilbert's film, but the material scene around the screen did too. Too often reception studies focus on human agents at the expense of the inanimate forces around them.

Even though *The Stuff of Spectatorship* focuses on spectatorship over reception, it shares reception studies' political commitment to inclusive historiography. In many ways, reception studies emerged in response to the prior erasure of minority viewers from media history and theory. To that end, many reception historians focus on how particular identity categories shape viewer experience, how specific racial, gender, class, and ethnic groups participate in film or television cultures at various points in time. But all reception studies require a boundary—a frame, if you will—to organize their archives and foreground their arguments. Tight framing bespeaks reception historians' commitment to deep understandings of specific sites of cultural negotiation: Pittsburgh film culture between 1905 and 1929, for instance, or the role of newspapers in establishing the norms of US film culture between 1913 and 1916.[27] Hence *The Stuff of Spectatorship* focuses on material cultures of US film and television since 1975, but it explores national trends rather than specific regional experiences. These trends are deeply tied to issues of race, class, sexuality, and gender—issues that were overlooked in much 1970s spectatorship theory but are now central to any responsible inquiry into human-media encounters.

NEW CINEMA HISTORY

Reception studies partly inspired the third—and newest—field in the critical Venn diagram that informs *The Stuff of Spectatorship*: new cinema history, which investigates cinema "as a sociocultural institution" rather than film as an artform.[28] Whereas "film history has predominantly been a history of production, producers, authorship and films," new cinema history "focuses on the circulation and consumption of film and . . . the history of cinema audiences, exhibition and reception."[29] In this regard, new cinema history owes a lot to both media industry and reception studies, but its disciples typically analyze "the commercial activities of film distribution and exhibition, the legal and political discourses that craft cinema's profile in public life, and the social and cultural histories of specific cinema audiences," rather than production cultures, organizational hierarchies, negotiated readings, or fan communities.[30]

Many new cinema historians rely on archival research, but the field further supports memory studies and computational approaches to historiography, since all three can shed light on how cinemas operate in the world.[31] Also central to its project are exhibition histories, including Douglas Gomery's *Shared Pleasures: A History of Movie Presentation in the United States* and more recent studies of theater architecture by Ross Melnick, Andreas Fuchs, and Jocelyn Szczepaniak-Gillece.[32] Szczepaniak-Gillece's special issue of *Film History* on "Objects, Exhibition, and the Spectator" (coedited with Stephen Groening) expands the remit of new cinema history to encompass not just spaces of film exhibition but the objects that fill them: from hats to headphones, cigarettes to seat buzzers. In their afterword, Szczepaniak-Gillece and Groening "insist that the tangible matter of history inflects the elusiveness of film experience . . . that objects themselves are not only part of larger media discourses but in fact aid in shaping them." Although material culture is not (yet) a major component of new cinema history, Szczepaniak-Gillece and Groening argue that it should be. Hence they assert that "we can extrapolate what exhibitors, theater patrons, and film producers thought spectatorship should, could, or might be" from different objects in the viewing environment and industrial responses to them.[33] *The Stuff of Spectatorship* embraces this observation as a mandate, because it pushes new cinema history toward further ideological analysis.

What spectatorship should, could, or might be is inherently political, after all, because it involves prescripts about who goes to the movies and how they behave there. Yet many new cinema historians downplay the ideological functions of exhibition. The field's privileged methods and sources tend to produce highly specific case studies that affirm the importance of cultural, economic, and geopolitical context for understanding any cinema history. Attention to detail does not preclude political critique, of course, but the field has not (yet) championed such work (by showcasing it in book series or anthologies). In contrast, *The Stuff of Spectatorship* uses its case studies to illuminate widespread social practices and political inequalities. Hence chapter 6 surveys dozens of incidents of cinema violence rather than focusing on the particularities of one event. This methodology allows me to make broader observations about how racism fuels panicked reception cultures on some occasions but not others, to develop a theory while also building a record.

The Stuff of Spectatorship also pushes new cinema history to reconsider its singular focus on theatrical exhibition. Many new cinema historians acknowledge and celebrate similar work being done in television studies, but they do so without questioning the medium specificity of either field. Cinema is a material practice enmeshed in a network of other legal, economic, cultural, and discursive institutions as well as media ecologies that include television, radio, and digital media. For all its commitment to enworlding cinemas and cinema audiences, new cinema history isolates its subject from other genres and platforms that directly influence(d) it. Medium specificity can be a convenient fiction in certain circumstances, but it is always—and only—an expedient elision of a more complicated story.[34] I am interested in what happens when scholars try to write media history without that fiction, when they embrace the messiness of media convergence.

MATERIAL CULTURE STUDIES AND NEW MATERIALISMS

New cinema history is part of a larger material turn that has been sweeping the humanities and social sciences since the 1990s. At that time, excitement around digital culture was leading scholars to speculate optimistically about the imminent dematerialization of human consciousness and connection.[35] To reassert the importance of materiality in their disciplines, humanities scholars borrowed theories from anthropology, art history, and science studies. These approaches coalesced into a set of "new materialisms" that champion the radical otherness of objects, things, and stuff.[36] There are important differences between object-oriented ontology, thing theory, and the other branches of new materialism, but they all challenge the anthropocentrism of traditional humanities scholarship. Each in their own way, they assert a broader, even planetary, perspective on nonhuman agency that relativizes the importance of human subjectivity. This iconoclasm helped new materialisms become quite trendy, until they overshadowed older materialist modes of thinking, such as cultural materialism and material culture studies, the latter of which explores intersections of human ideology and the physical world.[37]

Scholars of material culture examine how the things of the world shape and reflect human perceptions of the world. Contra new materialisms, material culture studies maintains that "meanings are not in the materiality of things, but rather in how things are constructed as meaningful in social practices of representation."[38] The meaning of a kernel of popcorn, for example, depends both on its material properties and on when, where, and how one encounters it. Thanks to its economy of production, stable shelf life, and caloric density, popcorn has been a staple of American diets and helped shape Americans' perceptions of one another. In 1785, Benjamin Franklin noted popcorn as a convenient nutriment carried by indigenous Americans while traveling.[39] In the 1840s, when street peddlers began selling popcorn snacks, American elites disparaged it as a "lower-class food," because it was cheap, filling, and noisy.[40] In 2009, a minor moral panic broke out among American consumers around the caloric load of movie theater popcorn. This alarm was part of a growing alarmism about obesity in the United States.[41] As anthropologist Ian Hodder points out, "Things and society co-produce each other."[42] Popcorn enabled discrimination among Americans while Americans cultivated it as a "companion species."[43] Material culture studies analyzes precisely these sorts of complex sociohistorical dynamics, which is why it shapes *The Stuff of Spectatorship* more than new materialisms.

Given that film and television cannot be produced, distributed, exhibited, or received outside material culture, it is surprising how little attention film and media studies has paid to the stuff of media. Of course, medium theorists have long debated the specificities of different platforms. However, they focus almost exclusively on the affordances and limitations of particular media technologies.[44] Not until the twenty-first century did infrastructure and platform studies emerge as distinct, theoretically rigorous subfields. Yet, like new cinema history, both infrastructure and platform studies strongly delimit their inquiries to the material technologies used to distribute and play media content, respectively. (In this regard, they may be more closely aligned with cultural materialism than material culture studies.) *The Stuff of Spectatorship* conversely investigates an eclectic array of material cultures of film and television spectatorship that include video technologies, branded merchandise, legal and illegal inebriants, and even physical violence. Indeed, the book's eclecticism is meant to demonstrate the breadth of material objects influencing film and television reception, which exceed the materials of its production and distribution. Following Hodder, then, I argue that they are deeply "entangled" in material culture and that any attempt to understand how they create meaning for viewers must accept that both media and "human existence [are] thingly, irreducibly so."[45]

CHAPTER SUMMARIES

The six chapters of *The Stuff of Spectatorship* cumulatively argue that material culture is inextricable from contemporary film and television culture. Each chapter demonstrates that film and television spectatorship involve more than media content, viewers' identities, and the viewing apparatus. That being said, there are important ways in which the material distribution of film and television—particularly the packaging and decay of physical media—inflect our relationship to those genres. Hence, the first two chapters investigate how various video formats condition viewers' understanding of television and film history. Chapter 1 argues that the video format through which one accesses classic television series influences how one understands both television and history. Much has been written on the ways that DVD, Blu-ray, and streaming media influenced contemporaneous television poetics and reception. However, scholars have not considered how video's cultural and commercial packaging also molds audiences' perceptions of classic, or "legacy," series. I argue that a series' status as a historical document of its era and of television culture changes depending on whether one encounters it via off-the-air (OTA) recording, prerecorded videocassette, a DVD or Blu-ray season box set, or a video-on-demand platform (such as Netflix or iTunes). To illustrate this point, I examine the remediation of one show that has appeared on every major consumer video platform: the original *Battlestar Galactica* (ABC, 1978–1979). Examining the packaging and remediation of the series pilot across all four formats, I assert that the commercial—which is to say the human—framing of various video technologies changes consumers' perception of television's historical value. Whereas OTA recordings feed fantasies of historical simulation—of access to an original broadcast—prerecorded cassette packaging tends to obfuscate a show's televisual origins. DVD and Blu-ray boxsets also downplay television history in order to construct auteurist celebrations of a series' artistic significance, while video-on-demand platforms generally strip their content of historical or industrial context, encouraging what I call *transient viewing*. All video formats thus occasion and obscure historical loss by fostering material cultures that promote other frames of reference. So, while video may yet serve certain kinds of cultural memory, scholars need to attend to how different formats influence what we value when we value television, meaning both television technology and television programming.

Chapter 2 further investigates the difference that format can make through issues of material deterioration and loss. For legal and financial reasons, Richard Brooks's *Looking for Mr. Goodbar* (1977) has not been distributed on video since 1997, when its last VHS edition came out. Those tapes are decaying rapidly, and with them goes viewers' access to a controversial critique of the sexual revolution. The material availability of licensed video editions has a huge impact on which classic films get written up, studied, and taught, yet commercial distributors have their own fiscal logic for deciding which films to release and how. Chapter 2 argues that, to a genuinely alarming extent, film history is being written by corporate rationales at odds with film historians' values. To illuminate and refine those values, I bring a few different reading strategies to bear on the decaying object and reputation of *Looking for Mr. Goodbar*. I begin with what Eve Kosofsky Sedgwick calls "paranoid reading," searching for the reason Brooks's film is being allowed to disappear.[46] As Sedgwick points out, however, paranoid reading can only confirm bad news, so I turn to her alternative hermeneutic, reparative reading. VCR-assisted reparative analysis reveals latent feminism in the film's critique of the sexual revolution and its gendered double-standard. As Sedgwick avers, such reparative analysis generates hope for a better, more equitable future. Both reading strategies buoy the critic, then, yet one cannot interpret a disintegrated videotape back to operability. So I propose a new approach to decaying media that I call *sitting with*. To sit with a deteriorating media object means accepting its loss and acknowledging material transience as an intrinsic element of media reception. It also means paying attention to how material transience affects our relationship to our cultural history and our identities as media fans and scholars.

Chapter 3 turns from the materials of media consumption to the materialization of media consumption, specifically the branded merchandise and travel enterprises of Turner Classic Movies (TCM). When it premiered in 1994, TCM promised viewers a curated stream of classic films "uncut and commercial-free," twenty-four hours a day.[47] This promise restricted its revenue prospects to cable carriage fees, the money cable providers pay to networks to include them in their packages. Nevertheless, TCM built a loyal fanbase around its educated and urbane approach to cable-era cinephilia. In the twenty-first century, the network leveraged that reputation to promote a wide range of branded merchandise, subscription services, and travel enterprises. These include books, apparel, jewelry, housewares, massive open online courses, location tours, film festivals, a wine club, and even an international cruise. Each of these objects and events offers an interpretation of film history; by interpreting them, I show how TCM is using material culture to transform love of classic film into an identity asserted and maintained through commercial transactions. TCM now understands itself as a lifestyle brand, a shift that exacerbates meaningful contradictions within its brand values: between democratic principles of fan community and the idealization of glamour and exclusivity and between a cinephilic admiration for film history and licensed merchandise that exploits classic Hollywood clichés. As a network and as a lifestyle brand, TCM is in the business of taste-making; thus its products have important implications for how millions of viewers encounter, engage, appreciate, and remember film history. By exploiting an enduring American desire to evince cultural sophistication via conspicuous consumption, TCM divorces love of film from actual film spectatorship. TCM's evolution thus demonstrates how material culture establishes norms for movie spectatorship that exceed those of the movies themselves.

Material culture also informs spectatorship norms within cinemas, of course, and to that end chapter 4 investigates how "adult concessions" refashioned moviegoing in the twenty-first century. In 2014, the president of the National Association of Theater Owners hailed beer and wine as the "future" of cinema.[48] Alcoholic beverages are now on the menu at historic art-houses, community theaters, corporate megaplexes, and underground microcinemas across the country. Many of these venues rely on "adult concessions" to keep the lights on—or off, as the case may be. But alcohol also changes cinema culture, affecting who goes to the movies and what it means to them. More than any other concession, alcohol comes freighted with class associations and ethnic prejudices that exhibitors exploit to target their desired audiences. This chapter begins by expounding the history of alcohol in US cinemas, from the nickelodeon era through early beer sales at drive-ins and illicit drinking in midcentury repertory houses. Adult concessions gained prominence as an exhibition practice after 1975, the year that the Duffy brothers opened the first hardtop theater that sold beer and wine. Following in their footsteps, contemporary exhibitors now use adult concessions to brand their venues in three distinct ways. High-end cinébistros sell liquor to promote moviegoing as an upper-class entertainment, while neo-rep houses rely on alcohol service to bolster their countercultural identity. Meanwhile corporate multiplexes employ adult concessions to help them target desired audience demographics, particularly Latinx families. These case studies demonstrate that alcohol has become a material condition enabling twenty-first-century cinematic exhibition, regardless of whether any given viewer imbibes or not.

Turning from alcohol to pot, chapter 5 examines how material viewing cultures inform spectatorial poetics, specifically how certain US television series recreate characteristic effects of cannabis inebriation to entice and entertain viewers.[49] Since the 1990s, US television has gone from actively supporting the federal government's so-called War on Drugs to capitalizing on the increasing popularity of cannabis. Series as varied as *Broad City* (Comedy Central, 2014–2019), *Jersey Shore* (MTV, 2009–2012), *Breaking Bad* (AMC, 2008–2013), *High Maintenance* (HBO, 2016–), and *Atlanta* (FX, 2016–) operate as virtual intoxicants; they use stylistic and narrative strategies to interpellate a spectator who is high (or likes feeling that way). These poetics of inebriation, as I call them, allow television creators to incorporate a niche reception practice into mainstream television culture. They place viewers "under the influence" of television and thereby extend its cultural, which is to say its commercial, reach. Pot can make its users feel distracted, hyper-focused, or paranoid. So too does television, through segmentation and replays that reward intermittent attention (distraction); complex serial narratives and world-building that encourage extreme, if unproductive, engagement (enhanced focus); and hermeneutics of suspicion that invite paranoia. Race is a crucial factor in television's poetics of inebriation, moreover, and while most series align such poetics with a white gaze, shows like *Atlanta* demonstrate that poetics of inebriation also provide opportunities for antiracist critique.

In its final chapter, *The Stuff of Spectatorship* raises the stakes of its investigation to life and death by examining material violence in movie theaters, also known as cinema violence. Based on extensive archival research and discursive analysis, I show that material violence at screenings changes how films are received by the media and viewers, particularly films by and about Black men. To illustrate this claim, I analyze the panicked reception cultures around theater shootings, stabbings, and riots between 1979 and 2016, noting that whether a panic developed or not depended on the races of the assailants and victims involved and those of the characters in the associated film. Between 1979 and 2011, cinema violence only generated panicked reception cultures when the films concerned African American young men or gang members, groups largely construed as interchangeable. Starting in July 2012, a series of sensational cinema shootings by white men challenged anti-Black suppositions about cinema violence. Whereas previously reporters "blamed the movie" for attracting putatively dangerous audiences, after 2012, they began lamenting cinema violence as "random" and "tragic." Such bromides were never invoked so long as cinema violence was associated with Black viewers or Black films, suggesting that such events were regarded as the inevitable result of theatrical heterogeneity. Chronicling the reception of material violence at movie theaters reveals that many white filmmakers, audiences, and critics still idealize cinema as a racially and socioeconomically homogenous idyll for white viewers. Thus, with chapter 6, *The Stuff of Spectatorship* demonstrates that material media cultures are inseparable from social prejudice and that they must be further researched to contest racist, sexist, and classist assumptions that they perpetuate.

Finally, the brief conclusion to this volume explores how material culture opens up new approaches to media historiography and textual analysis. While technologies, texts, and viewers will always be critical elements of film and television history, they do not operate in a vacuum. Other material objects and forces also shape how people make sense of media and incorporate it into their lives (or don't). Without necessarily intending to, media scholars have drawn a line between media culture and material culture; that line has prevented us from fully recognizing how media production, distribution, and consumption operate in and affect a larger material world. Together with media industry studies and new cinema history, material culture studies also provides a new rationale and frame for textual analysis, as it invites scholars to consider how a text's composition and narratives are understood in conversation with the physical world. More attention to material culture could also resolve the decades-old rift between spectatorship theorists and reception historians, both of whom are necessary to analyze how audiovisual media interact with and become objects.

I wrote this book because I believe that material culture changes how people relate to film and television. In selecting its six case studies, I sought to illustrate the range of objects that affect our media experiences and the various ways that they shape those encounters. Acknowledging the epistemological power of material culture does not in any way disempower human actors. Rather, it highlights the complexity of our media ecologies, all the intricate ways that we involve media in our lives. Film and television are never ethereal; they always become present to us through material platforms and amid specific material conditions whose parameters we are only beginning to explore. It is my hope that this book will encourage readers to consider other material media cultures and scrutinize the complex social histories they result from and express.

Material culture is always political, as are media cultures. Thinking them together helps us recognize and contest their power.

CODA: MATERIAL MEDIA CULTURES IN THE COVID-19 ERA

I wrote *The Stuff of Spectatorship* between December 2014 and December 2019. In January 2020, a person in Washington state was diagnosed with the novel coronavirus that causes COVID-19. Within two months, all of the hardtop movie theaters in the United States had closed to help mitigate the spread of the virus. By the time I was completing final revisions on this manuscript—in May 2020—US cinema was on an indefinite hiatus. Many independent exhibitors and festivals started selling tickets to online "virtual screenings" in a desperate bid to survive the pandemic. This coda was composed in September 2020, as movie theaters slowly began to reopen in some states. At present, a minority of viewers seem eager to return to cinemagoing as usual—complete with popcorn, beer, and now hand sanitizer—while many more fear contagion within the darkened confines of a movie theater.

Air—and the bacteria and viruses that travel through it—have long been part of the material culture of cinema (and television, although television is so strongly equated with domestic spectatorship that it is rarely associated with community transmission of infectious disease). As early as 1906—within one year of "the rise of seedy, store-front 'nickelodeon' theaters" in the United States—state and municipal governments began ordering exhibitors closed to prevent the spread of airborne illnesses.[50] These included diphtheria, influenza, scarlet fever, smallpox, and whooping cough.[51] During these contagion scares, the air of the theater was understood as a medium for disease transmission as well as a material substance comprised of various unseeable gases and particles. Fears of contagion at the cinema lapsed after World War II, however, at least in the United States. Improved sanitation and ventilation soothed public anxiety, and viewers mostly stopped thinking about the air in movie theaters, unless they were dreaming of theatrical air conditioning on a hot summer day.

No one knows yet how the COVID-19 pandemic will affect cinema culture in the years to come. Rather than prognosticate, I want to emphasize that the novel coronavirus is a defining component of material media culture in the twenty-first century. It will combine with other material media cultures—such as concessions culture and cinema violence—in ways none of us can predict. It has already provided a shot in the arm (sorry, bad joke!) to television cultures and video-on-demand services, not to mention the medical and recreational cannabis industries.[52] The novel coronavirus reminds us that material cultures are not limited to objects we can see or touch, for this infective agent measures barely one-tenth of a micrometer and yet has brought US cinema culture to a stand-still. Its power confirms that there are many more material media cultures yet to be analyzed, on scales yet to be considered.

CHAPTER I

Collecting and Recollecting

Battlestar Galactica through Video's
Varied Technologies of Memory

On September 17, 1978, *Battlestar Galactica* (ABC, 1978–1979) was
supposed to be the biggest thing on television. Billed as "the most fantastic space adventure ever filmed," the three-hour series premiere was
also ABC's Sunday Night Movie of the Week, intended to capitalize on
the recent success of George Lucas's *Star Wars* (1977).[1] Television and
print advertisements built anticipation for the debut, as did stories in
Newsweek, People, TV Guide, and other magazines.[2] But the grand
premiere was interrupted. At approximately 10:00 p.m. Eastern Daylight Time, ABC temporarily cut in on their space opera with a newsflash announcing the signing of the Camp David Accords, a surprise
breakthrough in the long-term hostilities between Egypt and Israel.
Some viewers were frustrated by the intrusion, others amused by the
uncanny coincidence it created between fantasy and real-world diplomacy. For *Battlestar Galactica* begins with a peace treaty between
twelve human planetary colonies and their long-standing enemies, the
warmongering robot Cylons. As it happens, the Cylon armistice is a
ruse, designed to distract the humans while the Cylons destroy all their
colonies and most of their military. That conceit probably inclined ABC
viewers to receive the Camp David Accords ironically at best, cynically
at worst. But contemporary viewers cannot share their reaction to the
historic juxtaposition, because no off-the-air recordings of it remain.

   With those recordings, a certain relationship to television history was
also lost. *Battlestar Galactica* is still widely available—it has been

released on every major home video platform since VHS—but different video platforms facilitate different forms of cultural memory, including none at all. As opposed to personal memory, cultural memory refers to artistic, institutional, and other texts that serve as mnemonics to trigger ideas about historical events. How one accesses television history on video influences a series' relationship to both of those terms—television and history—as it can position the show as either an important facet of cultural memory or merely entertainment.

When *Battlestar Galactica* premiered, television was a genre largely understood through hermeneutics of liveness, ephemerality, and flow, but recording fixes TV as history, or rather histories.[3] All video technologies can be what Marita Sturken calls "technologies of memory," or rather memories, since each new video format generates a new history for the series distributed on it.[4] Video technologies are not self-similar technologies, in other words, and they do not offer the same kinds of access to content. Our relationship to television history and, through it, cultural history changes depending on whether we access it through off-the-air recordings, prerecorded videocassettes, DVD or Blu-ray season box sets, or digital files delivered through a video-on-demand platform. When I watch an off-the-air recording of a television program, I inevitably see traces of its broadcast history within the televisual flow of series, commercials, and news flashes, no matter how scrupulously the person who made the recording may have tried to edit out such interstices. A prerecorded videocassette of the same episode isolates it from both history and its series, compromising television's intrinsic seriality and intertextuality to create a stand-alone commodity. When I watch that episode as part of a prerecorded DVD or Blu-ray season box set, I see it through the logic and economy of the "Collector's Edition," which governs both these formats. The box set's distributor imbues their product with the ahistorical ideology of collection through auteurist bonus features that promote the artistic value of the show. These supplements are unavailable when one streams or downloads the program.[5] Video-on-demand platforms smooth out differences of production, distribution, and access, making all content available in the same way and enabling a form of shallow spectatorship that I call *transient viewing*.

By reexamining the pilot episode of *Battlestar Galactica* through each of the videographic technologies of memory outlined here, this chapter argues that *Battlestar Galactica*'s status as historical document and televisual text changes depending on its distribution technology. This is not to say that the medium is the message, however, or that "the 'content' of any medium is always another medium."[6] With all due respect to McLuhan, my argument is not so technodeterminist as his. Rather, I posit that the commodity forms—which is to say, the commercial framing—of different video formats change consumers' perception of television's historical value.[7] Video *as we've constructed it* changes what we value when we value television, meaning both television programming and television history. This distinction is especially important for legacy television, series originally broadcast on over-the-air networks or cable channels. Many scholars are examining the changes that new platforms create in television production. Fewer analyze how these changes affect legacy television, and almost none have studied the way that video-on-demand platforms affect viewers' conception of television history or its place in cultural memory.[8] Therefore this chapter takes up the crucial work of analyzing video formats not just in terms of access—perhaps the key term of video studies—but in terms of value.[9] As television historians, theorists, and fans, we must ask what it is we are being shown when we watch old television on new media.

OFF-THE-AIR RECORDING AND HISTORICAL SIMULATION

In 1978, less than 2 percent of US households had VCRs, yet the *Battlestar Galactica* premiere was one of the most video-worthy events of the emerging home video era.[10] In the 1970s, VCRs were marketed as time-shifting devices; consumers mostly used them to record television programs for later viewing. *Battlestar Galactica* was heavily promoted as an important, big-budget series and calibrated to appeal to multiple generations, genders, and racial and ethnic groups. The series boasted cutting-edge special effects by John Dykstra, who had recently won an Academy Award for Best Visual Effects for *Star Wars*. Having Dykstra and his team on board positioned *Battlestar Galactica* as the de facto sequel to Lucas's blockbuster, then the second-highest-grossing film ever made.[11] As mentioned, the series pilot, "Saga of a Star World," begins with the signing of a false truce between the twelve human planetary colonies and the Cylons (figure 4). The false truce distracts the humans while Cylons attack, destroying all their planets and all but one of their military spacecrafts. The eponymous battlestar Galactica only survives because its commander, the skeptical Adama (Lorne Greene), doubted the Cylons' intentions and the possibility for peace. Now Adama must

FIGURE 4. The Cylons of *Battlestar Galactica* (ABC, 1978–1979).

lead his crew and the few civilian survivors on a caravan for "Earth," a mythic thirteenth colony located "somewhere beyond the heavens."

This premise promised lots of extraterrestrial excitement for newly minted *Star Wars* fans, but it also offered timely commentary on earthly affairs. Diplomacy was front-page news in the 1970s, as American experiments in "ping-pong" and citizen diplomacy contributed to a thaw in the Cold War. In April 1971, the US table tennis team became the first representatives of the United States to visit the People's Republic of China (PRC) in over twenty years. Two months later, Mao Zedong (a ping-pong enthusiast) came to the United States as captain of the Chinese team. Soon thereafter President Richard Nixon became the first US president to visit the PRC since its founding in 1949. A few years later, Robert Fuller raised the public profile of citizen diplomacy by visiting the Soviet Union. Fuller was part of an international movement of private citizens contesting the continued hostilities between the United States and the Soviet Union through personal travel. Together, ping-pong and citizen diplomacy inspired new hope for a peaceful solution to the Cold War.[12] In that context, the Cylons' false truce in

Battlestar Galactica represents more than just extraterrestrial treachery; it engages contemporaneous concerns about the power of diplomacy and cynically questions the wisdom of trusting longtime enemies. In many ways, the humans' negotiations with the Cylons resembled recent thaws in the Cold War—making the Cylons' duplicity that much more disturbing. Their betrayal justifies Adama's rather hawkish insistence on active military vigilance, not to mention his scorn for pacifists like his president, whose faith in the Cylon armistice led to the destruction of the human colonies.

The show's militarist commitments provided an inauspicious frame tale for the real-world truce that interrupted its premiere in the Eastern and Central time zones: the Camp David Accords. Unbeknownst to most of the world, US president Jimmy Carter had earlier that month invited Egyptian president Anwar el-Sadat and Israeli prime minister Menachem Begin to the presidential retreat in rural Maryland for a secret summit about their countries' ongoing conflict.[13] After thirty years, both sides had finally expressed interest in ending hostilities, but neither was willing to compromise publicly. Hence their private conference at Camp David, where Carter served as mediator and go-between for Sadat and Begin, who reportedly were not on speaking terms. After thirteen days, Begin and Sadat reached two partial agreements, or accords, leading to the Israel-Egypt Peace Treaty of 1979 and a shared Nobel Peace Prize.

ABC, NBC, and CBS all interrupted their Sunday evening broadcasts with live coverage of this historic diplomatic achievement. During the signing ceremony, Carter acknowledged that "there are still great difficulties that remain" but expressed "hope that the foresight and the wisdom that have made this session a success will guide these leaders and the leaders of all nations as they continue the progress toward peace."[14] Such hope might have seemed naive to *Battlestar Galactica* viewers, as the show's Manichean universe primed them to question the power of the Accords. After all, the pilot begins with Adama's warning to his president that long-term enemies can never trust one another. As he puts it, the Cylons "hate us with every fiber of their existence. We love freedom. We love independence—to feel, to question, to resist oppression. To them, it's an alien way of existing they will never accept." When the Cylons violate their truce, Adama's cynicism seems prescient. Giving peace a chance only gives the enemy the upper hand. As Adama's speech builds on real Cold War American exceptionalist rhetoric, the Cylons' attack seems to justify that rhetoric via analogy. It also inadvertently promotes skepticism of Sadat and Begin's momentous achievement.

The Camp David interruption has become a feature of *Battlestar Galactica* trivia collections, which is how I first learned about it. Some fans remember with pleasure ABC's inadvertent juxtaposition of real-world and fantasy statecraft, but others recall only irritation. The younger the viewer at the time, the more likely they were to have been annoyed by the interruption. On multiple *Battlestar Galactica* and television fan forums, formerly juvenile viewers recollect how "at the end of hour two, ABC news broke in with the enfamous [*sic*] report" for approximately twenty minutes.[15] Many were frustrated with the unplanned suspense and afraid that their parents would not let them stay up to watch the episode's delayed conclusion. It was, after all, a school night. Blogger Bob R. recollects that he "FREAKED THE HELL OUT!!!" when ABC cut to the newsflash, while Jon Nichols, in a post to the blog *Esoteric Synaptic Events* entitled "You're a jackass, Jimmy Carter," asks sarcastically: "what did I get to see for a full hour? Not Richard Hatch as Apollo. Not Dirk Benedict as Starbuck. Not even that brat kid Boxey." Instead he was "treated" to an unprecedented breakthrough in international relations, an offence, he satirically suggests, that may have led directly to the Egyptian president's subsequent murder: "Wasn't Anwar Sadat assassinated just a few years after signing those accords in the middle of *Battlestar Galactica*? Was an incensed *Battlestar Galactica* fan involved? Coincidence? I think not."[16]

Then-adult *Battlestar Galactica* fans demonstrate more mature responses to the Accords interruption. Startrek.com writer David McDonnell appreciates the postmodernity of *Battlestar Galactica*'s historical coincidence: "Bizarrely, I recall ABC interrupting the story mid-premiere for breaking news coverage of the Middle East-Camp David Accords Signing (starring U.S. President Jimmy Carter with this episode's special guest stars Israeli Prime Minister Menachem Begin and Egyptian President Anwar el-Sadat). The juxtaposition of televised fiction and historical reality, of tomorrow's space warfare and the promise of peace on Earth today was, well, jarringly surreal to say the least."[17] Journalist and blogger Steven Hart—who was a college student in 1978—now believes that "the announcement of the accords . . . was the most memorable thing about the show," although he considers that to be the minority opinion: "Interesting, isn't it, how the thirtieth anniversary of some crappy sci-fi TV show gets more attention than the thirtieth anniversary of the Camp David Accords?"[18] Another viewer remembers watching the show at a comics convention and muses, "Looking back, I can only imagine that some who were against the peace accords must have tried to draw parallels between Israel and Egypt and the humans versus the Cylons who are about the sign a peace treaty . . . but that didn't occur to me at the time."[19] In fact, there are no records of such cultural commentary at the time, yet the intersection of science fiction and world politics certainly emphasized the conservative ideology behind TV's latest spectacle.

Viewer recollections may now be all that remain of the historical coincidence between *Battlestar Galactica*'s premiere and the signing of the Camp David Accords. There are no off-the-air recordings of "Saga of a Star World"—with or without the ABC newsflash that interrupted it—in any government, industry, or university archives. The Library of Congress possesses neither the newsflash nor the series. The UCLA Film & Television Archive and the Paley Center for Media have copies of the *Battlestar Galactica* broadcast master but not an off-the-air recording. The Vanderbilt Television News Archive only recorded regularly scheduled news programs on September 17, 1978, not news briefs, and the ABC News VideoSource likewise does not archive news break-ins.[20] The Jimmy Carter Presidential Library does not keep recordings of network news coverage, only the White House Communication Agency logs (the master footage from which network news briefs are made).[21] My inquiries to fans and on *Battlestar Galactica* message boards also failed to turn up a single off-the-air recording of the interrupted pilot in watchable condition. The few fans who have off-the-air recordings of "Saga of a Star World" edited their copies to eliminate ABC's break-in. Only one claimed to own an off-the-air recording of the episode with news flash, and unfortunately, "it hasn't held up well over the years."[22] Videotapes may be technologies of memory, as Sturken claims, but the technology is subject to elision and can also fail entirely. Like any material technology, it is vulnerable to the ravages of time, as are those who would use it to remember.

Off-the-air recording is thus a technology of contingency as much as it is a technology of memory. An off-the-air recording captures a unique intersection in television's flow—including narrative series, advertisements, news programs, station identifications, and public service announcements—made possible by a historical juncture to which the recording seems to provide access. However, it can only offer viewers a simulation of historical context, not a recreation of it, and a fantasy of televisual originality or authenticity that does not exist. Hilderbrand posits that if "an off-the-air recording includes commercials and interstitial local news promos . . . it can not only reproduce a fairly exact simulation of historical flow but also document the economic and political context for the program."[23] Perhaps, but a simulation is not a recreation. Jean Baudrillard defines simulation as a form of simulacrum, the copy replacing the original, while Gilles Deleuze further observes that such a simulacrum "places in question the very notations of copy and model."[24] An off-the-air recording may seem to reproduce its moment of historical transmission, but it actually disrupts the very logic of copying. An off-the-air recording of the premiere of "Saga of a Star World," even one that includes all the original advertisements and the Camp David Accords newsflash, only appears to recreate an original moment of transmission. It cannot do so, however, because there *was* no singular moment of original transmission.

"Saga of a Star World" actually premiered twice on September 17, 1978: once in the Eastern broadcast feed (for the Eastern and Central time zones) and once in the Pacific broadcast feed (for the Mountain and Pacific time zones). Only the former was interrupted by the signing of the Camp David Accords, yet it would be inaccurate to refer to the Eastern feed as the "real" premiere. Moreover, "Saga of a Star World" had already been released as a cinematic feature film in Australia, Canada, and some European countries before its television premiere. Although *Battlestar Galactica* was definitely produced for television, its advance theatrical remediation further confuses the issue of originality and provides an ironic counterpoint to that ubiquitous home video warning, "This film has been modified from its original version. It has been formatted to fit this screen and edited for content." Even if one wanted to argue that the Eastern broadcast feed constitutes the chronological premiere of *Battlestar Galactica* in its natal medium, the advertisements and promos that ran within it were still different from affiliate to affiliate. It would be impossible to decide which one is "the original." For all these reasons, an off-the-air recording cannot provide access to the "original" historical flow in which a show was broadcast, although it may create the impression of and desire for such an original.

Creating and watching off-the-air recordings inspires complex emotional responses for viewers. Off-the-air recording produces a paranoid relationship to televisual history, one premised on loss or the threat of loss. After all, what impulse is more paranoid, more grandiose and yet insecure in its motivation, than the desire to shift time? As Lucas Hilderbrand observes, "videotape enabled television audiences to become participatory viewers who interacted with the technology and recorded texts."[25] Media theorists often assume that participation equals pleasure, yet recording generates frustration as well, the frustration of transforming flow into record. Off-the-air taping makes television material, but in so doing it also makes the taper vulnerable to the vagaries of broadcast flow. Such vulnerability can inspire both paranoia and historical reflection, especially when the tape seems to capture a one-time event, like the intrusion of real-world drama into a high-profile television premiere.

Nevertheless, off-the-air recordings do offer their viewers a pleasing *frisson* of being in two times at once (and possibly two locations at once). Off-the-air recording facilitates a kind of nonce cultural memory. For while the content of the recording may remind its viewer of the era when it was made, it cannot provide an authoritative record of that period. Each televisual flow is a stream of coincidence, unique to the particular station that broadcast it, but it may still amuse viewers through the chance juxtapositions and accidents of history it contains. When I revisit my favorite childhood recording of *Annie* (John Huston, 1982; NBC, 1986), for instance, I laugh at the use of Beethoven to sell burgers in a McDonald's commercial. I chuckle at the frizzy perm of the newscaster entreating me to tune in for a late-night report about tomorrow's weather. I note the contouring makeup prominent among so many of the actresses in television trailers and advertisements and consider the return of contouring as a popular cosmetic effect in the 2010s, but this observation is not based on an authoritative record of women's makeup trends. The off-the-air recording does not leave the realm of the simulacrum, nor does my engagement with it provide much real historical insight. I am not, in fact, returned to 1986, even if the recording does trigger my own haphazard, idiosyncratic memories of the era. But the off-the-air recording places me in a position to reflect on the time that has passed between what-seems-like-then and now. It amuses, even if it does not reliably elucidate.

The absence of an off-the-air recording stimulates a different sort of reflection—at least, it did for me. My research assistants and I were never able to locate a watchable off-the-air recording of "Saga of a Star World." However, the past existence of such recordings inspired a certain inquisitiveness into that other time. How was September 1978 different from September 2017? How did historical conditions of reception make the *Battlestar Galactica* of September 1978 a different show from the one I watch today? The interruption of an ABC newsflash into "Saga of a Star World" reminds a twenty-first-century viewer that diplomacy could be break-in news in 1978, as it has been only occasionally since then. The break-in urges one toward historical research, and it also inspires one to consider how 1970s international relations might have influenced the extraterrestrial relations in Larson's universe. The absence of even a simulacrum of *Battlestar Galactica*'s Eastern premiere invites one to wonder—and investigate—how real-world diplomacy shaped the reception of diplomatic fictions like *Battlestar Galactica*. In sum, it encourages a historical poetics of the series, not necessarily at the expense of textual analysis but in support of better and greater interpretation. When these two things—"Saga of a Star World" and the ABC newsflash on the signing of the Camp David Accords—intersected and were brought into televisual flow by ABC broadcasters, they invited viewers to read each differently: the fiction as a historical product and the historical event as inspiration for fiction. The television space opera was temporarily more intertextually aligned with world events than with Lucas's *Star Wars*. One might even say that *Battlestar Galactica* draws Lucas's film into conversation with diplomatic history. Such interpretive possibilities still abound, even though the tapes no longer do.

Off-the-air recordings thus differ from live broadcast in their historical implications as well as their material specificity, which includes their material vulnerability. Every time a videotape is played, the material contact of the tape with the heads of the VCR distresses the magnetic oxide particles containing its signal, not to mention the plastic substrate and adhesive that make up the tape. Just sitting on the shelf can contribute to the physical degradation of videotape; long-term vertical storage can stretch or warp the substrate, distorting both sound and image. For Hilderbrand, "the distress and disappearance of the video signal . . . call attention to the tapes as copies—analog, personal copies."[26] Off-the-air recordings are personal not just in the sentimental sense but also in the sense that they were made by a person. An off-the-air recording attests to the presence of a recorder—and I do not mean the VCR. Someone created this tape, whether for a specific reason or by accident. That person's identity may be known, hidden, or lost to history, but the tape is a record of the desire to record—a desire, as Hilderbrand points out, that was created by videocassette recorders.[27]

Ethnographic research with off-the-air tapers and television collectors suggests that the paradigm shift toward a viewerly imperative to preserve fostered newly insecure relationships to television. As Kim Bjarkman has shown, videocassette recorders allowed quotidian viewers to create their own televisual archives and thus their own interpretations of television history. By interviewing US and UK collectors of off-the-air television recordings, Bjarkman learns that "they present a strikingly different account of television's legacy than more official channels . . . and they make their own case for what slices of television history deserve to be immortalized."[28] For Bjarkman, collectors' historiographic project can be understood through the "range of personas" they adopt in relation to their recordings, including the captor, the crusader, and the curator.[29] Driven by desires such as "locking light in a box" (the captor) and "civic duty" (the crusader), these television collectors experience "pleasures of acquisition, ownership, guardianship, and membership" through personal archival practice.[30] In psychoanalytic terms, their egos are affirmed by recording and stockpiling ephemeral television programs. For Bjarkman's subjects, collecting involves a deeply held but unsubstantiated belief that if they did not save these broadcasts, they would be lost. In this paranoid fantasy (which may yet correspond with reality), the fan-collector must protect the object from industrial and cultural forces that do not appreciate it.

I sympathize with their position. While trying—and failing—to locate an off-the-air recording of "Saga of a Star World" for this chapter, I could not help but imagine that a conspiracy of commercial distributors was preventing my access. How could every copy have been lost or destroyed? (Recall that there were approximately one million VCR households in the United States in September 1978.) The premiere was so widely promoted—and the thrill of recording television so new and appealing— surely one single tape must have survived. How could an event that so easily could have been saved have disappeared? Could Universal have bought up all the tapes and destroyed them, the better to sell their prerecorded episodes and (later) season box sets? The very allure of off-the-air recording—its simulacrum of television history—drives such thinking. As a technology of memory, off-the-air recording *even when inaccessible* makes its viewer a promise it cannot keep: ephemerality for posterity. Its simulation of one iteration of television's historical flow encourages the fantasy of a singular, original broadcast and, for those who choose to look, reflects the ever-receding horizon of the actual past. The specific material vulnerability of videotape and its audiovisual artifacts of physical wear also contribute to an ideology of rarity that compounds the perceived uniqueness of the recording. Hence older off-the-air recordings take on an air of coincidence: what are the odds that this particular flow should have been recorded and have survived?

That being said, off-the-air recordings also always seem like they might be the only copy. After all, how many copies can there be of an original that never existed? Whether they are quite common—such as the many off-the-air recordings of vintage episodes of *The Price Is Right* (CBS, 1972–) floating around YouTube—or rare to the point of being irrecoverable—such as the 1978 premiere of *Battlestar Galactica*—off-the-air recordings do not conquer the ephemerality of television. Rather they encourage the viewer to fetishize it, even in the Freudian sense. Like all fetish objects, off-the-air recordings exist to protect the ego of the fetishist, to screen it from the horrible revelation not that the mother has no phallus but that nothing lasts. When we record television programs off-the-air, when we archive those recordings and engage in struggle against television's ephemerality and intangibility, it is a one-sided struggle rooted in the taper's fear of impermanence. In this regard, taping satisfies what André Bazin calls the psychological ambition of art, "a defense against the passage of time."[31] While Bazin traces this "mummy complex" from ancient Egyptian burial practices through painting and the plastic arts and on to photography and film, the impulse can also be seen in taping.[32] Bazin notes that "the image helps us remember the subject and to preserve him from a second spiritual death"—which, I contend, is exactly what Bjarkman's tapers seek to do with their recordings.[33] The difference between Bazin's imperative and Bjarkman's collectors is the mortality of the subject. Bazin assumes a human, or at least animate, subject, one who can die and whose death must be conquered. But television shows are never alive, no matter how "live" they seem. Death and evanescence are not commensurate.

More to the point, *Battlestar Galactica* itself has no such awareness of its fleeting presence on this earth. Being only an inanimate television show, it does not concern itself with its legacy; that burden falls to its creators and its fans. So unlike when we paint a person's portrait, when we tape, we are not saving a subject that wants to be saved, unless that subject is the taper. It may be, however, that the uniqueness of the recording serves as a metonymy for the uniqueness of the taper, who joins the historical record by creating it with tapes.

Creating and collecting off-the-air recordings imbues the taper-collector with a material, and a seemingly concrete, connection to the past and the future, but in fact these collections manifest one specific, conditional relation to televisual contingency and cultural memory. Off-the-air recordings fetishize the ephemerality of the past and may thereby help tapers deny their own mortality. But they do not preserve the past, because they are inevitably copies without an original (as there is never a single, original broadcast). When we consider them transparent portals to history, we do ourselves a great political disservice, for we ignore the particular fantasies and fears that off-the-air taping engenders in us. The illusions we impose on these recordings can shape our understanding of history, which is inherently political, because it changes our cultural memory. Prerecorded VHS also affects viewers' relationships to television, history, and television history, but in different ways. Prerecorded cassettes elevated individual episodes to stand-alone artworks, implicitly singling them out from the mundanity of television's flows—plural—and from the series of which they were a part. Their supervening logic is not that of the television enthusiast but rather that of the distributor, who suppresses televisuality in order to create a new consumer product that scarcely acknowledges its former format.

PRERECORDED VIDEOCASSETTES AND THE TELEVISION EPISODE AS STAND-ALONE COMMODITY

There has been very little scholarship of television programming released on prerecorded videocassette, and yet television shows and television movies were regularly released on prerecorded video, just not as season box sets.[34] This should be the first hint that 1980s cassette distributors did not value—or rather did not see the market value of—seriality as such.[35] Their remediations reflect these values and suggest that television history itself is not worth preserving, even if individual episodes might be. In 1985, MCA Home Video released a 125-minute condensation of "Saga of a Star World" which it called *Battlestar Galactica* (hereafter referred to as *Battlestar Galactica—The Video* for clarity). *Battlestar Galactica—The Video* largely follows "Saga of a Star World" in its plot, despite being twelve minutes shorter, but it also contains some new footage. In 1988, MCA released a second *Battlestar Galactica* feature, *Conquest of Earth*, which was cobbled together with footage from previously broadcast episodes and *Galactica 1980* (ABC, 1980), a short-lived spin-off of the original series. Between 1990 and 1997, MCA also released video editions of the twelve telemovies that series creator Glen A. Larson fabricated for syndication from *Battlestar Galactica*'s original seventeen episodes (after those proved insufficient for licensing deals). One such telefilm, *Experiment in Terra* (Rod Holcomb, Ron Satlof, and Gene Palmer, 1996), was based on an episode from the original series but included previously unseen footage as well. In short, *Battlestar Galactica*'s prerecorded videos were only based on the television series and were not faithful reproductions of the episodes as aired. Early TV-to-videotape remediations stabilized television as a consumer good but did so at the expense of its televisuality, as they transformed episodes into stand-alone commodities rather than components in a narrative sequence. When "Saga of a Star World" became *Battlestar Galactica—The Video*, it curtailed the world-building premise of the television pilot and obscured its televisual roots in order to imitate film in its narrative structure. As this history demonstrates, then, prerecorded VHS not only removes television from its broadcast history, it also prevents viewers from understanding the show in context by divorcing the concepts of television and history.

On prerecorded VHS, television no longer offers even a simulation of liveness, its defining ethos. As Marita Sturken explains, "The essence of the television image is transmission" because "it is relentlessly in the present, immediate, simultaneous, and continuous."[36] For Sturken, this characteristic presentism leads television to narrating history through reenactments and replays. When recorded on videotape, television's characteristic repetition changes, however. For while tapes can be rewatched, there is no programming contingency involved, so their content never changes. Rewatching tapes is not same as watching television reruns, in other words, because it does not occur in the context of televisual presentism (this rerun is happening *now*) but rather in the eternal-present-that-is-never-now of prerecorded video. When prerecorded to videotape, television becomes a stable commodity by losing its association with liveness and repetition-as-historiography. Moreover, VHS releases often obscure broadcast history and represent their televisual content as filmic, as autonomous artworks to be enjoyed outside of the series narrative.

Battlestar Galactica was an ideal product for such remediation because of the remediations intrinsic to its production history. Larson originally conceived *Battlestar Galactica* as a seven-hour miniseries. ABC later decided to promote it to full series production while also marketing its pilot as a movie of the week. At that time, it was common for network television movies to appear in theaters abroad, and indeed the 125-minute version of "Saga of a Star World" was screened theatrically in Canada, Australia, and parts of Europe before the series' televisual premiere in the United States. In 1979, *Battlestar Galactica—The Film* also went to cinemas in the United States and Japan. Some US theaters exhibited the film in "Sensurround, which actually 'shook' people in the audience during appropriate moments of high action."[37] *Battlestar Galactica—The Film* made over $10 million at the domestic box office, which John Kenneth Muir notes as "an unprecedented feat considering that the production was essentially an abbreviated rerun of a story already broadcast more than once on television!"[38] But then, the television version of *Battlestar Galactica* was no longer available. Between 1980 and 2000 (when MCA/Universal Home Video released a

VHS box set of series), if one wanted to watch *Battlestar Galactica*, one had to watch it as a telemovie (or series of telemovies) on video.

Watching a television show—even a TV movie—as a remediated feature film on VHS alters its narrative structure and the spectator position it generates for the viewer. Notably, the rhythm of the show's narrative changes entirely, as do its goals. Although marketed as a telemovie, "Saga of a Star World" was also a series pilot, intended to establish a narrative universe for future storytelling and to hook viewers on characters and themes in order to create an audience for that storytelling. Thus, it follows the poetics of the scripted prime-time serial. As Michael Z. Newman explains, prime-time serials have been a dominant style of television storytelling since the commercial and critical successes of *Dallas* (CBS, 1978–1991) and *Hill Street Blues* (NBC, 1981–1987).[39] *Battlestar Galactica* premiered the same year as *Dallas* and shares many of its narrative imperatives—such as balancing episodic closure with ongoing themes and character arcs and fostering viewers' identification with and "investment in character"—that keep viewers coming back week after week, season after season.[40] Newman notes that "following a narrative is a process of accumulating information. Television writers strive to parcel out this information in such a way that it will seem urgent, surprising, and emotionally resonant."[41]

To that end, prime-time serials follow a highly regimented format to help their viewers interpret their narratives. *Battlestar Galactica* is no exception. All television series break their narratives into seasons. Each season is made up of roughly ten to twenty-four episodes, which are divided across three or four segments that each emphasize particular characters or story arcs. As Newman explains, each episode consists of four acts, which introduce, complicate, develop, and resolve a discrete problem while also incrementally advancing segment and season arcs. Each act is comprised of six to eight "beats" (moments of change within scenes) that further their act's narrative agenda: "Each beat tells us something new, something we want—need—to know, and amplifies our desire to know more."[42] "Saga of a Star World" follows this format rigidly: after the opening exposition, beat one of act one begins with establishing shots of a battlestar in space, then cuts to President Adar (Lew Ayres) toasting the humans' truce with the Cylons as "the most significant event in the history of mankind." The second beat introduces pilots Apollo (Richard Hatch), Starbuck (Dirk Benedict), and Zac (Rick Springfield) as they agree to let Zac fly in the routine patrol that will later reveal the Cylons' treachery. The rest of the episode also adheres to the narrative structure of the prime-time serial. Act 1 sets up the truce and the Cylons' violation of it. Act 2 complicates the humans' response as survivors are gathered aboard the Galactica and other vessels are organized for a caravan to the mythic planet Earth. Act 3 develops the problems the humans will face on their way to Earth when they stop for food and fuel at the resort planet Carillon. Act 4 *somewhat* resolves the issue as Apollo and Starbuck discover that Carillon is being run by the Cylons and narrowly escape their trap, a victory that allows the humans to continue on their voyage to Earth. As Newman explains, "this tight dramatic structure satisfies the audience's desire for resolution—not totally but adequately," for the episode actually ends with a final "epilogue" scene: the human traitor Baltar (John Colicos) visits a Cylon basestar and promises to help them relocate and exterminate the humans, thus extending viewers' interest in the series.[43] This epilogue completes the mission of the pilot—establishing a narrative universe for future storytelling—but would serve no purpose on video, which is probably why MCA cut it.

Battlestar Galactica—The Video was not marketed as part of a serial narrative, and accordingly it resolves its narrative differently, in a manner befitting viewer expectations for an autonomous work that is part of a series. In Battlestar Galactica—The Video, Baltar dies about halfway through the narrative, a major change from the television pilot, and the story concludes with the human victory at Carillon.[44] This leaves the happy ending open ended while still affirming it as a completed narrative event: the escape of the humans from the Cylons. Battlestar Galactica—The Video thus represents itself as a whole that can also contribute to a larger whole, rather like Star Wars. Both offer conclusion enough to strike the "kind of balance between episodic closure and serial deferment" that creates desire for future installments.[45] Lucas always intended Star Wars to be part of a larger narrative universe that would include sequels and spinoffs across various media. Hence his film offers its spectator emotional resolution but leaves its major narrative conflict open. The last scene is a medal ceremony, honoring Luke Skywalker (Mark Hamill) and Han Solo (Harrison Ford) for destroying the Death Star, and the Rebel Alliance is still at war with the Empire when the end credits roll. As fans of the franchise know, the rebels' victory was deferred for nearly forty years, although each addition to the Star Wars oeuvre always contains its own localized form of narrative resolution.

Battlestar Galactica videos offer their spectator similarly imperfect yet satisfying narrative resolutions. The humans never settle on Earth, but they always overcome the immediate obstacle to that goal. These deferments do not necessarily generate suspense, however, because while the tapes leave open the possibility for future adventures, they do not promise any. *Battlestar Galactica—The Video* does not contain trailers for any related tapes, as none were available or even planned in 1985.[46] Without any expectation of further narrative installments, the viewer's attention is directed toward the text at hand, toward its bounded pleasures. In this context, the Cylons' betrayal of the humans becomes all the more important to the narrative, if less historically suggestive. Without a televisual flow of advertisements, station identifications, and news breaks—such as the signing of the Camp David Accords—the ersatz "Saga of a Star World" moves along at a brisk pace, the Cylons' betrayal of the armistice flowing directly into their devastating attack, the humans' departure for Earth, their misadventure at Carillon, and the Cylons' defeat there. The narrative still adheres to a four-act structure, rather than the Hollywood feature's typical three-act arrangement, but this amounts to a minor deviation from convention, especially given how closely the movie hews to *Star Wars*' epic scale, special effects, and other generic precedents. Without commercial breaks, the transitions between acts would be difficult to recognize, were it not for the unique poetics of televisual editing.

Evidence of the commercial breaks in "Saga of a Star World" still remain in *Battlestar Galactica—The Video*, but they are one of viewers' only reminders that they are watching a former television show. Vestigial remnants of an occluded platform, they irritate rather than illuminate. These phenomena become quite noticeable during the discovery of the planet Carillon. To reach Carillon, the human fleet must traverse a giant star field laced with Cylon mines. Apollo, Starbuck, and Lieutenant Boomer (Herbert Jefferson Jr.) fly ahead of the fleet in fighter crafts to eliminate the threat. The heat of the star field disrupts their scanners, however, so the lieutenants must rely on navigation from the battlestar to destroy the mines. This leads to a tense and exciting scene that cuts between the Galactica's core command and the pilots until they succeed in taking out all the mines. As Apollo announces, "I think we're gonna make it," and Boomer whoops, the score surges into its signature melody, and extras in the Galactica's command center cheer loudly. Adama and his colonel grasp hands as he commands with satisfaction, "Recall the flight crews," and then . . . then the score suddenly disappears as the video cuts to an external long shot of the Galactica. The disruption is quite jarring. The viewer hears nothing but space drone for two seconds until the camera pans left toward a beige globe in the distance and

Adama intones in voiceover, "The planet Carillon. Landing operations will begin at once. Prepare to land the mineral ships." Adama's order provides explanation for the act to come and recaps the major development of the last scene, specifically the humans' arrival at Carillon. This recapping—which Newman notes is "a ubiquitous feature of television in all genres"—and abrupt disappearance of the score may nettle a VHS viewer, because they suggest clumsy remediation. They represent the poetics of another format, namely broadcast television, and serve no purpose on video except to remind the viewer that they are watching a derivative product. Moreover, *Battlestar Galactica* typically uses sound bridges to smooth transitions between scenes, so the sudden cut from score to space drone stands out. It marks an interruption in the video narrative and the loss of televisual flow. Like the Pan & Scan editing of widescreen films for video release, it reminds the viewer that something is missing, namely televisuality.

While *Battlestar Galactica*'s televisual past gets obscured in its remediation to prerecorded video, its packaging—the "paratext" that shapes viewers' expectations—actively conceals its televisuality.[47] The VHS box art for *Battlestar Galactica—The Video* features a painting of various series regulars juxtaposed against smaller images of Cylons, fighter crafts, and an alien planet. A small MCA Universal logo in the bottom right corner assures would-be viewers that this is indeed a Hollywood studio product, not a direct-to-video or B-movie knockoff (figure 5). The back-cover copy briefly summarizes the Galactica's narrative situation and notes, "The extraordinary special effects are provided by John Dykstra, an Academy Award winner for his work on *Star Wars*." To be sure, Dykstra's pedigree was always one of *Battlestar Galactica*'s selling points, but he also won an Emmy for Outstanding Individual Achievement in Creative Technical Crafts for his work on "Saga of a Star World." In other words, MCA/Universal calls attention to Dykstra's film credentials instead of the award he won for *Battlestar Galactica*. Placing *Battlestar Galactica* in a genre continuum with *Star Wars* is more important than direct acknowledgments of its quality, at least where such acknowledgments might reveal its televisual origins. Hence there are also no reviews quoted on the VHS box, since such reviews would expose the wannabe movie as a television pilot. Indeed, nothing about the box design acknowledges *Battlestar Galactica* as televisual at all.

In sum, MCA Home Video was not trying to sell *Battlestar Galactica—The Video* to fans of *Battlestar Galactica*, the television show. The back-cover summary, its reference to *Star Wars*, and its silence regarding

FIGURE 5. MCA/Universal's
VHS edition of *Battlestar
Galactica*, released in 1985.

the series of which it was a part all suggest that viewers were meant to
enjoy the tape's contents as an autonomous narrative rather than part
of a beloved series. In this *Battlestar Galactica—The Video* represents a
widespread but far from universal trend: isolating episodes from television history. VHS releases of classic series like *Star Trek* (NBC, 1966–
1969) and *I Love Lucy* (CBS, 1951–1957) openly admitted their small-
screen origins, but they are exceptions to the rule. When Paramount
began releasing *Star Trek* episodes on VHS cassettes in 1985, each of
the ten cassettes featured the name of the episodes contained below the
series title, as well as the legend "The Original and Uncut Television
Series." Their boxes even report the initial airdates of the episodes,

although this practice was highly unusual and rarely repeated, even for *Star Trek*. Yet these cassettes, too, offer their contents as autonomous masterworks; no effort is made to contextualize any given episode within the series, nor is the larger arc of the series acknowledged beyond any references to it in a given episode. VHS season box sets would not appear until 1991, when CBS Home Video finally released a box set of all the *Star Trek: The Original Series* seasons. Thus, prerecorded videocassettes made television history more accessible, but rarely as television and never as history. No prerecorded VHS cassettes I have ever found connect their contents to world events, cultural movements, or social issues beyond those mentioned in the diegesis. They cleave television from cultural memory to frame it as universal entertainment. Episodes become stand-alone commodities, laying the groundwork for television's transformation into a manufactured collectible on DVD.

SEASON BOX SETS AND COLLECTOR POLITICS

Both prerecorded episode cassettes and DVD and Blu-ray season box sets promise buyers the unobtainable, an authoritative "original" version of a show that off-the-air recordings cannot deliver. However, season box sets do so not by isolating an episode but by recontextualizing the series in nostalgic narratives of creative genius (never political, cultural, or even televisual history). Season box sets emerged at a very different moment in home video history than prerecorded episode cassettes; by 1988, prerecorded video had become the movies' dominant distribution platform, a truth that transcends the shift from videotapes and discs to video-on-demand platforms. However, television did not succeed as a video genre until the introduction of the DVD season box set in April 2000. That's when Fox released the first season of its cult series *The X-Files* (Fox, 1993–2002) as a single product, packing twenty-four episodes plus bonus materials onto a mere seven discs. Like episode cassettes, the box set contains digital, upconverted versions of series' masters, and it also has production documentaries, commentary tracks, and other bonus features. As scholars have argued, such distributor additions replace the personal trace of off-the-air recordings with illusions of insider knowledge.[48] They are not merely companion documents but framing devices, supplements that fundamentally alter the kind of cultural memory that video provides.

DVD box sets restore a sense of the televisual flow unavailable on prerecorded episode cassettes, although it is a flow organized by and within the series season rather than between different series and interstitials. Kompare shows how the DVD box set built on television's ethos of the "repeatable property" by marking it as a "collectible commodity."[49] (Saying that box sets made television a "collectible commodity" does not mean that fans did not collect television on VHS or other videotape formats; rather, DVD box sets changed distributors' attitudes toward the collectability of television.) DVD season box sets were designated as "collector's editions" from that first *X-Files* release and with a consistency unmatched among film releases. Media executives further emphasized the collectability of season box sets with special packaging. Embossing, inserts, and other special features transform mere cartons into display items; they are designed to trigger a latent "collector gene" among young people and make them more appealing as gifts.[50] There is more at stake in the collector's edition box set business plan than mere marketing, however, as the box set's features also construct its spectator as a collector. When an object becomes part of a collection, especially when it has been manufactured as a collectible, its relationship to history fundamentally changes. It becomes an expression of the collector's individual taste and part of their history of collecting, and this change in context transforms viewers' interpretation of a television show.

Season box sets quickly and effectively replaced off-the-air and prerecorded cassettes in many fans' collections and displaced off-the-air recording's fetishization of fan labor with nostalgia and auteurism. As Kompare explains, the first box sets were of shows (like *The X Files*) with dedicated fan bases: "distributors prioritized programs with particularly solid—if not necessarily 'mass'—followings—the so-called cult audiences . . . who had proven to be loyal consumers of licensed merchandise in the past."[51] Television fans historically made and traded their own off-the-air recordings, but box sets undermined the significance of such personal labors, as "the trade value of . . . off-the-air recordings diminishes the moment a program is released commercially on video or DVD."[52] Fans were complicit in this revaluation of off-the-air recordings, as they evidently found something appealing, something worth paying for, in the season box set. DVD and Blu-ray box sets do offer higher resolution in a more convenient package, and they also include bonus features that, with rare exception, reward fandom by affirming the merit of the series and venerating its producers as auteurs.[53]

Auteurism is intrinsic to the commodity form of the season box set and thus its collectability. As Karl Marx writes, "a commodity is . . . a mysterious thing, simply because in it the social character of men's labour appears to them as an objective character stamped upon the product of that labour."[54] Commodities are not just things but material stand-ins for social relations between people, as their variable exchange values mystify the labor relation between producer and consumer. Season box sets build this mystification into their very content. Their bonus features, especially those dedicated to series production, cast and crew reminiscences, and creator commentaries, present labor as entertainment; both stars and below-the-line workers become characters in the series' extended universe. The economic relation of television crews, production companies, distribution houses, and their parent corporations disappear behind amusing anecdotes from the set and insights into artists' techniques. The latter may be more interesting to fans, but any production story is incomplete without that corporate history—incomplete, in this case, by design. Watching a box set's bonus features, the viewer learns more about the work that went into making their favorite show, but the social character of that labor is effectively obfuscated when it comes to be part of the product. This is political; work becomes infotainment, surplus value that increases the exchange value of the box set.[55]

Like prerecorded videotapes, season box sets package television; they make it tangible and fungible. Unlike prerecorded videotapes, they also make television collectable: compact and affordable. Season box sets deliver their content as a complete unit within a larger series calling out for its own completion. This characteristic—location within a sequence—defines the manufactured collectible and its unique commodity fetish. Manufactured collectibles are a nineteenth-century invention: objects created to be collected, as opposed to objects collected despite or even because of some other use-value. Manufactured collectibles developed from collectable promotionals, such as cigarette cards, which were introduced in 1875 to give one tobacco brand a market advantage over another. While cigarette cards were widely collected, and some collectors may have bought cigarettes for the cards, the cards were not sold on their own.[56] Hence the first real manufactured collectible did not emerge until 1895, when publishers started advertising high-end "collector's editions" of popular and esteemed book titles. Collecting promotionals and collector's editions gained in popularity through the twentieth century. Then in 1965, the Franklin Mint started selling coins, dolls, and decorative plates as "collectibles"—commodities sold with no intended use-value other than their collection. Collector's edition books and season box sets do have use-value, in that they can be read or watched. Like other manufactured collectibles, however, their value also inheres in their capacity to expand or complete collections.

Collection is thus intrinsic to, even an intensification of, the modern fetishization of commodities. As Susan Stewart explains, "the collection furthers the process of commodification," for it "marks the space of nexus for all narratives, the place where history is transformed into space, into property."[57] Stewart is not writing about manufactured collectibles but personal treasuries of art glass, movie posters, or other objects produced with an intended function other than collection. However, her point applies equally to manufactured collectibles and prepackaged collections, including the season box set. Season box sets are both collections (of the set of episodes that comprise a season) and components in a larger collection, namely the set of seasons that make up a series and the DVDs that comprise a collector's personal archive. Collecting recordings of all the episodes from a season or a series used to require fan labor; now that labor is performed by the distributor. Box sets render valueless the labor of collecting, and they obscure the work, even the existence, of distributors by directing fan attention toward series creators and stars. Their commentary tracks and bonus documentaries provide select information about who made the show and how, but much is lost with this exclusive, exclusionary focus, such as a series' place in its network's flow of shows, ads, and promos. As Charlotte Brunsdon points out, box sets rob their viewers of "that uncontrollable time between broadcast episodes which gave temporal force to narrative inexorability, and which allows us to see something of the aesthetics of broadcast time."[58] The box set compensates for this loss with its bonus features, which also help obscure the loss as a loss. In place of television history, one finds a hermetically sealed season that disavows any story besides the one it tells about itself.

As a case in point, the first DVD box set release of *Battlestar Galactica*, *Battlestar Galactica: The Complete Epic Series* (Universal, 2004), emphasizes auteurism and diegetic completeness rather than historical situation or significance. It was released to promote an ongoing reboot of the series, and in service of the reboot it indeed encourages reparative nostalgic affection over critical analysis.[59] In addition to all twenty-four episodes, it contains voice-over commentary from three of the series' stars (Richard Hatch, Dirk Benedict, and Herbert Jefferson Jr.); deleted scenes; documentaries about the series, creator Glen A. Larson, and composer Stu Philips; and "A Sneak Peek at the New *Battlestar Galactica* Mini-Series." Such "bonuses" comprise the supplement that effectively excludes television and cultural history from this collection, as it is excluded from all collections. Jacques Derrida defines the supplement as the secondary concept or phenomenon that seems to support a primary concept or phenomenon but in fact constructs the primary phenomenon, enabling its existence (e.g., homosexuality and heterosexuality).[60] As supplements, the bonuses on *Battlestar Galactica: The Complete Epic Series* write a new history for the show that changes its meaning for the DVD viewer. They emphasize the individual genius and personal experience behind its creation rather than its place in televisual or cultural history. In this box set, *Battlestar Galactica* is no longer a cynical commentary on US diplomacy nor for that matter part of the historic revival of science-fiction storytelling in the 1970s. Rather the season is framed as a discrete media object and a collectable franchise.

The season box set does not express media history, then. Rather it manifests the distributor's logic of consumption—that is, the broadcast season. With the flow and coherence of the series season replacing the flow and coherence of ABC's programming schedule, *Battlestar Galactica* is divorced from the actual season in which it aired—that is, autumn 1978 through spring 1979. Like most season box sets, *Battlestar Galactica: The Complete Epic Series* does not acknowledge original air dates anywhere except in its copyright information. It cannot, because, as Stewart observes, the collection's "function is not the restoration of context of origin but rather the creation of a new context, a context standing in a metaphorical, rather than a contiguous, relation to the world of everyday life."[61] Hence season box sets rarely if ever comment on what else was playing on their network that season. *Battlestar Galactica: The Complete Epic Series* never mentions the series' initial programming position between *The Hardy Boys* (ABC, 1978–1979) and the *ABC Sunday Night Movie* and against *All in the Family* (CBS, 1971–1979); it never considers the way that that spot might have shaped product differentiation or the audience and their perceptions of the program. On video, "season" no longer refers to temporality but to a narrative unit, one presented as hermetically sealed: whole in itself and without need of reference to its historical and cultural origin or its narrative relation to the rest of the series. Indeed, it can be remarkably difficult to find information on any other season within a given season box set; if one wants such insights, one must collect. In sum, the collector's edition box set exists not to help consumers reconstruct a past media moment but to create a new one. Through its insularity and its insistence on the primacy of the season (a distinction that makes little sense for certain genres, such as classic sitcoms), it creates a media object that never previously existed and reifies new spectatorial systems of value.

Rejecting more expansive histories is intrinsic to the ethos of the box set and the collection more broadly; as Stewart explains, the collection's founding "impulse [is] to remove objects from their contexts of origin and production and to replace those contexts with the context of the collection."[62] Elsewhere she observes, "The collection seeks a form of self-enclosure which is possible because of its ahistoricism. The collection replaces history with *classification*."[63] As she notes, the collection's logic of classification creates a fundamental equivalence among all its objects.[64] Individual components are unique but not special. They may trigger particular memories or associations for the viewer, but so does every other component. To paraphrase Stewart, the collection manipulates, qualifies, orders, and arranges desire, a function easily observed in the careful sequence of episodes and extras within a season box set.[65] One comes to desire the commentary of Dirk Benedict or deleted scenes—that is, they become valuable, collectable, and worth collecting—by virtue of their inclusion in a collectable box set. Of course, these materials were of long-standing interest to fans, but DVDs recode such ephemera as exegesis. Their existence creates their necessity by recoding the program they purport to supplement, marking it as incomplete without them. These extras seem to bring viewers closer to one past, to scenes of creation behind *Battlestar Galactica* that they might previously have sought out by buying shooting scripts or meeting the stars at conventions. However, they actually make that past more distant by fixing the authoritative version of it. This authoritative version excludes other frames and interpretations, notably those that draw focus away from the series-commodity.

For instance, *Battlestar Galactica: The Complete Epic Series* uses its two bonus documentaries, *Remembering "Battlestar Galactica"* (Keith A. Cox, 2004) and *Inside "Battlestar Galactica"* (no director listed, 2004), to encourage viewers' nostalgic overinvestment in the show by glorifying production history and on-set bloopers over historical context and content. The longest section of *Remembering "Battlestar Galactica"* is devoted to special effects, but unlike the standard making-of featurette—which concentrates on the talents and achievements of below-the-line creators—*Remembering "Battlestar Galactica"* revels in shortcuts and shortcomings. Directors and stars bemoan the difficulty of synching actors' performances to matte recordings playing behind them, and multiple takes reveal how often the actors failed to keep up with the technology. Still, the documentary emphasizes the cast and crews' nostalgia for "compositing in the camera" and for the limited realism of practical effects, passing that nostalgia on to the viewer.[66]

Through such rhetorical devices, *Battlestar Galactica: The Complete Epic Series* stimulates spectatorial appreciation of authorial intention, of the artistic ambition behind uneven execution. Despite John Dykstra's impressive visual effects, the original *Battlestar Galactica* no longer inspires awe; bad acting, hackneyed plot lines, and silly concepts make the show seem dated (despite airdates being omitted from the box set). Yet the deleted scenes and showrunner biographies that accompany these flawed episodes add charm to their faults and teach the viewer how to find joy in the show's shortcomings. They perform a kind of television analysis focused on recuperating pleasure, a critical practice Eve Kosofsky Sedgwick called reparative reading.[67] As I'll explain in greater detail in the next chapter, reparative reading seeks to restore value to overlooked or disparaged cultural objects rather than investigate their ideological message or historical significance. In this case, it also downplays political analysis by focusing on amusing anecdotes of series production.

Thus does *Battlestar Galactica: The Complete Epic Series* draw viewers' attention to Muffit, the robotic dog played by Evie, a chimpanzee in a robot-dog suit (figure 6). Freed from historical reflection and encouraged by cast reminiscences, the spectator becomes invested in the computerized scamp, who pops up unexpectedly across the season. Muffit is introduced during the series pilot to comfort Boxey (Noah Hathaway), a little boy whose dog (or daggit, in the argot of the show) died during the Cylon attack. Apollo gives him Muffit to help acclimatize the child to his new life as a refugee, but he also serves important extradiegetic functions, such as charming young audience members. As a robot, Muffit shares a basic ontology with the Cylons, yet he is cute and loyal—that is, loveable. Boxey's affection for Muffit saves his life, and Muffit saves the lives of several other Galactica crew members in subsequent episodes. Thus, Muffit performs crucial affective labor both within the diegesis and for the narrative. Muffit provides solace for the only child character in *Battlestar Galactica*, the sole representative of human futurity. If Boxey can love Muffit, then there is a reason to continue the human quest. Together, Boxey and Muffit embody affective futurity, the promise of life worth living. Such hope is essential for *Battlestar Galactica*'s serialized narrative. If viewers were objective about the humans' chances of ever finding Earth, the series would be incomprehensibly depressing, a serialized vigil for species extinction. But Muffit changes that; he keeps Boxey's spirits up and the spectator's as well.

Rapid episode viewing—enabled by the season box set—also reveals Muffit's contributions to the series' posthuman optimism. Boxey's love

FIGURE 6. Muffit, the loveable, life-sustaining robot dog of *Battlestar Galactica* (ABC, 1978–1979).

for Muffit provides an inspiring model for human-mechanical relations for a world in which humans are no longer the dominant intelligence. As a robotic pet, Muffit is not just an extension of the human but an alternative to its traditions, indeed an alternative to animality. Whereas the human has been defined by its difference from (typically its superiority to) the animal, this robotic dog differentiates the human from both the animal and artificial intelligence. Human intellect was already matched by the Cylons; now Muffit suggests that animality too can be replaced by the mechanical. Thus does Muffit decenter the human within the show's universe by demonstrating the commutability of human corporeality and intelligence by machines. Importantly—and unlike the Cylons—Muffit renders this posthuman future nonthreatening, even adorable. Humans need not fear species obsolescence because we are going to love it—and it us! This may be why Muffit does not appear in *Battlestar Galactica*'s 2003 reboot, which rethinks the human-Cylon conflict as an experiment in skepticism. (It is also more violent, more philosophically complex, and aimed at an exclusively adult audience.) In the reboot, Cylons look and behave exactly like humans; some even have trouble distinguishing themselves from humans. Cylons have been living and working among the humans undetected for years, all the while plotting their destruction. They even infiltrate the Galactica's crew, leading to paranoia and infighting among the humans. The *Battlestar Galactica* reboot thus imagines posthuman futurity as terrible, as no future at all, even though the show is premised on hope for human survival. The original series is never so fatalistic. It still manages to imagine and embrace posthuman futurity in the form of a robotic dog played by a chimpanzee. The hermetic seal of the box set helps focus viewers' attention on such narrative details by directing them inward, toward the text, rather than outward, toward its intertexts.

Thus do box set bonus features influence the spectator, their interpretation of a series, and the pleasures they take in it. Some features can be quite overt in how they shape viewers' relation to the series, as when *Remembering "Battlestar Galactica"* ends with Richard Hatch, Herbert Jefferson Jr., and Laurette Spang all exclaiming over the continual loyalty of *Battlestar Galactica*'s allegedly ever-growing fan community. Strategically placed on the last disc in the set, this encomium solicits the viewer's identification as fan. The viewer's spectatorship is praised by the actors they just watched for keeping their art alive. The artists also hail the viewer as a part of their community, drawing them into the extended world of *Battlestar Galactica*. So how can they not also support the *Battlestar Galactica* reboot and Galacticon, a convention (and a documentary about the convention) in celebration of the show's twenty-fifth anniversary? As Matt Hills points out, the season box set educates its viewer in fandom as a process, in "building value around specific narrative worlds, characters and personalities" as opposed to political history, industry history, or industrial limitations on narrative or form.[68] For scholars, such formal myopia leads to "a scene where TV Studies (along with fandom) finds itself ever more closely integrated into the political economies and brand-valuing strategies of contemporary TV."[69] The line between scholars and brand promotors is blurring, in other words, as box sets encourage reparative reading of the televisual season as an object discrete from outside histories.

With or without historical context, season box set viewers still encounter one of the most common limitations of media analysis, namely insufficient viewing time. *Battlestar Galactica: The Complete Epic Series* contains over nineteen hours of footage; the multi-season box set for the series' 2003–2009 reboot contains almost seventy hours of footage. These are just two of the thousands of television box sets that have been released on DVD and Blu-ray. The proliferation of DVD season and series box sets creates competition for fan attention and for reparative reevaluation. As Adrian Martin argues, DVD's format and branding encourage "the nightmare of *stockage*—roughly, 'stockpiling,'" due in no small part to "proliferating special editions and boxed sets that often cloak themselves in the surplus value of scholarship."[70] Here Martin builds on Thierry Jousse's observation that DVD's "apparatus of footnotes" encourages "fetishism and reification."[71] In sum, DVD's bonus materials deemphasize the use-value of their content to impress consumers with their sheer volume. Of course, entertainment value is never lost entirely; no doubt some fans have watched all of both *Battlestar Galactica* box sets—helpfully combined by Universal Pictures Home Entertainment into one set under the title *Battlestar Galactica—The Complete Series*—not to mention the spin-off series *Galactica 1980* (ABC, 1980) and *Caprica* (SyFy, 2010). But it is not in such use that the extras' value resides. Like fancy packaging, their value inheres in appearance first, functionality second.

Many viewers stop short of watching all the extras that come with a season box set, of course, but even so, those extras are not wasted; they are still intrinsic to the appeal of box set editions. Their mere advertisement on the packaging provides a format-unique promise of completeness. That is, the quantity of extras included in a season box set simultaneously inspires and seeks to satisfy a collector's desire to know the series completely. The more *Battlestar Galactica*'s box sets offer fans in and as bonuses, the better they reinforce the fantasy of future bonuses, of still greater stores of series information. Bonus features—especially director and star commentaries, making-of documentaries, and deleted scenes—promise to reveal the story-behind-the-story and suggest that there is always more story, more to find out. They perpetuate a logic of diminishing returns by seeming to deny it, as the bonuses themselves are evidence that there is always more to know. The bigger the *Battlestar Galactica* franchise gets, the more box sets its distributors release, the more the horizon of complete knowledge recedes, creating more desire for more extras. Those extras also change what counts as knowledge or knowledge worth having about the show. The more of them one watches, the less important the series' formative event can seem. The failed diplomacy between the Cylons and the humans loses significance within the box set's ever-more recursive collection of information. Indeed, one might be forgiven for forgetting the failed truce that started the Galactica's voyage to Earth in the first place, not to mention the diplomatic history that once punctuated it.

VIDEO ON DEMAND AND TRANSIENT VIEWING

Online media platforms have radically altered DVD's "privatized museu-mification" of classic television, to borrow Adrian Martin's term for the practical and interpretive fixity that prerecorded discs and their extras exert.[72] Subscription and ad-supported video-on-demand (SVOD and AVOD) platforms such as Netflix, Hulu, and network websites bring ephemerality and contingency back to television viewing, but they do so by profoundly decontextualizing series from one another and from television history. Indeed, these services suggest a radical equivalence between all the media in their vast libraries, as do transactional video-on-demand (TVOD) services like iTunes. Importantly, SVOD, AVOD, and TVOD platforms do not typically provide the reparative framework of DVD box sets. Instead of bonus features, keywords like *classic show*, *science fiction*, and *space* become the new supplements to the series themselves, not to mention the wealth of entertainment choices lurking just off screen, ready to intercede the moment a given program fails to please. Such framing positions television as nothing but entertainment; it encourages transient enjoyment rather than deep analysis, the kind of analysis that would engage cultural, industrial, aesthetic, or political histories.

SVOD, AVOD, and TVOD platforms thus impose a new ethos and economy of access on classic television. Although most scholarship on internet-distributed television has focused on contemporary production, most of the series available through these services were previously broadcast elsewhere. As Amanda Lotz notes, "The most desired application for distributing video via internet protocol has been accessing legacy television content outside its linear delivery."[73] In 2019, the *New York Times* noted that legacy series "are how the battle lines are being drawn between the streaming services," and are in fact far more valuable to them and to many viewers than original series.[74] VOD platforms seem to make all of television history available to viewers—without the scheduling rigors of broadcasting—but that impression is misleading. The financial barriers to streaming legacy television can exceed those of prior platforms. An SVOD provider requires subscription fees (e.g., Netflix) or a cable subscription (e.g., authenticated video-on-demand sites and apps), while a TVOD service demands episode or season purchases (e.g., iTunes) and AVOD sites necessitate ad exposure (e.g., NBC.com). And every model requires consistent high-speed internet access to transmit files from servers to the viewer's device. Most legitimate online media services also employ limited-term licenses for legacy television series and pre-distributed films. These licenses are issued by copyright holders who may have had nothing to do with the creation or broadcast of the series; hence NBCUniversal now streams *Battlestar Galactica* on NBC.com even though it appeared on ABC originally, because it was produced by Universal. Voluminous streaming libraries and competing services give consumers the impression that any classic series must always be available somewhere, but the reality is that titles can disappear from libraries at any time. After Starz refused to renew its licensing contract with Netflix in February 2012, many viewers learned a hard lesson about the ephemerality of streaming media. Over eight hundred titles disappeared from the Netflix streaming library, including many popular Disney films and classics like *Scarface* (Brian De Palma, 1983) and *Young Frankenstein* (Mel Brooks, 1974). Netflix scrambled to replace disappearing Starz titles with other content, but viewers invested in specific properties quickly realized that streaming's logic of abundance did not reflect or respond to their sentimental attachments. Video-on-demand services seemed initially to eradicate the need for individual home video libraries—replacing the logics of recording and collecting with that of reaccessing—but the Starz-Netflix debacle revealed SVOD to be far less reliable that consumers assumed, bolstering the electronic sell-through market for TVOD services like iTunes. "If you love it, buy it," consumers are told, but the media experiences one purchases via electronic sell-through are not the same as those available via season box sets, prerecorded videocassettes, or off-the-air recordings, as each composes a different relation to television history.

When one streams *Battlestar Galactica* online, historical context is not compensated for but obviated entirely (figure 7). Most web-based video-on-demand interfaces use black framing, monochrome banners, and simple scrollbars to embed content within their branded platform. On NBC.com, for instance, the viewing window contains no other icons but the NBC logo, which imprints series with a network identity in lieu of other information about them. The *Battlestar Galactica* series menu page offers little more than a list of other "NBC classics" that "you may also like." Like other streaming video platforms, NBC.com fosters an impression of abundance; it seems to guarantee the unmitigated "access" that video always promised, but the terms of that access are not publicized. *Battlestar Galactica* left Netflix's streaming collection in January 2017, for instance, although it is still available via DVD rental there and streaming on NBC.com—at least as of September 2019. How long any series will

FIGURE 7. "Saga of a Star World" playing on NBC.com in June 2016.

remain on any streaming platform is unknowable for most consumers. When I stream *Battlestar Galactica*, or any other legacy series, the platform interface obscures the legal agreements and actual technologies of memory that govern those shows and deliver them to me. The "technology" seems to be the platform—for example, Netflix or NBC.com—and not their server farms. Video-on-demand media trade on the mystification of their software as well as their hardware, as both could potentially reveal the limits of their services. I do not have access to the institutional logics and practices that determine what makes *Battlestar Galactica* "classic" or makes it available as an exemplar of classic television on these platforms. As Lotz explains, the service that video-on-demand platforms provide is "to curate a collection of cultural goods such that curating involves both *compiling* content and *organizing* it in a convenient and accessible manner."[75] Through such curation, video-on-demand platforms create illusions of plenty to cover the arbitrary limits of their libraries. They also reduce the spectatorial experience to undemanding interactions of branded access and transitory viewing—by which I mean the shallow engagement created by a superabundance of viewing options.

Thus, NBC.com invites viewers to "watch full episodes" of some of its televisual properties through an interface that foregrounds a transhistorical network identity that cannot incorporate television history. For instance, NBC.com does not distract viewers by explaining the corporate deals that brought an ABC show to their archive, even though it might enrich viewers' understanding of the television industry or the show's production.[76] On NBC.com, Larson's series simply joins other

NBCUniversal properties, including *The Bionic Woman* (ABC, 1976–1977, NBC 1977–1978), *Charles in Charge* (CBS, 1984–1985), and *30 Rock* (NBC, 2006–2013), to comprise a nostalgic, brand-based version of television history. This brand does not reflect actual broadcast history, of course, but rather a manufactured media smorgasbord designed to appeal to certain consumers. The shows available on NBC.com suggest that the site targets Generation X viewers eager to relive childhood television memories. Hence historical context about any given series is highly limited on the site, as it is on all streaming platforms. The main series page includes original airdates in an unobtrusive gray typeface, but there is no other background information about the series or its stars. A teal banner above the viewing window offers viewers the opportunity to view photos or shop for the show on DVD and reminds them that they can "watch full episodes" of a variety of NBC-Universal properties. However, the website does not offer visitors any relationship to television history except as consumer-viewers. As befits a broadcast network website, NBC.com uses its series to deliver viewers to advertisers, including NBC itself, thereby adapting the commercial broadcast business model for internet viewers who grew up with it.

Like NBC.com, Hulu encourages transient viewing of its content for pleasure rather than historical or cultural insight. Although *Battlestar Galactica Classic*—as Hulu calls the 1978 series—is "currently unavailable," its series page remains and contains a single sentence of description (although one may click through for more information). While it was live, the site's only links, other than to the episodes themselves, were to Facebook and Twitter, giving viewers the opportunity to comment on and otherwise advertise their Hulu spectatorship. Hulu's viewing interface similarly isolates the show from all historical, cultural, and televisual context, setting the viewing window within a gray field with only a few white menu options—"watch commercial-free" (via Hulu's premium plan) being prominent among them. Hulu thus encourages a recursive viewing practice in which one can watch Hulu or write about watching Hulu with as little intervention from other cultural sources as possible. Hulu does not offer ratings, in keeping with its advertised indifference to content quality.

Netflix, on the other hand, emphasizes curatorship, although its logic of collection likewise obviates history in favor of taste.[77] It can be difficult to access a series page on the Netflix platform. Clicking on the series icon from a menu screen will start the series, rather than delivering the viewer more information about it. Once located, however, Netflix series pages offer troves of information about how to understand a given series among other series available on Netflix. Netflix still only provides a brief synopsis of any given series—such as "A caravan of 220 space vehicles sets off in search of a new and peaceful frontier, a place where humankind can safely flourish and grow"—but it does employ unique keywords to locate the show in a network of entertainment options. In addition to lists of stars and genres, the Netflix series page for *Battlestar Galactica* also informs viewers that "This show is: imaginative, exciting," using *imaginative* and *exciting* as hyperlinks to lists of other movies and series so described. Netflix series pages also prompt viewers toward "more like this," whatever *this* happens to be.[78] In this case, an algorithm predicts that viewers of *Battlestar Galactica* will find appreciable similarities in the original *Star Trek* (NBC, 1966–1969), *Galactica 1980*, and *The Twilight Zone* (CBS, 1959–1964). Viewers may add these titles to "my list," a personal collection within the Netflix collection that theoretically narrows their transience amid content it marks as analogous.

Few scholars credit Netflix for encouraging transient viewing. Instead, most comment on its viewers' interactivity, their tendency to engage deeply with high-quality series, and the practice of binge-watching, or watching multiple episodes back to back for long periods of time. Hyper-focus is not the same as deep engagement, however, and not all online spectatorship is necessarily interactive. (For more on binge-watching and hyper-focused spectatorship, see chapter 5.) As Sheila C. Murphy confesses in *How Television Invented New Media*, sometimes even the most tech-savvy viewers *"just want to sit back and watch."*[79] Countering Henry Jenkins's model of the ever more involved media user, Murphy characterizes online television spectatorship as "a kind of passivity that is shot through with interactivity."[80] These options for interactivity are not equal from one video-on-demand platform to the next, and they are not always the default option. For instance, Netflix and Hulu encourage passive binge-watching through their post-play features; if viewers do not actively intervene in the last fifteen seconds of an episode, the next one will begin playing automatically. Rather like the human refugees in *Battlestar Galactica*, their viewers are carried along from one episode to the next in a stream that lasts as long as the industry allows. In this manner, the platform encourages physically and mentally passive consumption. The easiest way to keep watching a streaming service is to just do nothing and let the platform plan your viewing for you. This may lead to binging, but it also suggests a certain spectatorial transience via indifference. Locked in an eternal present, the viewer moves through their entertainments without interruption or the opportunity for reflection. Their viewing keeps pace with narrative time, passing through episodes as a way of passing time. Of course, the viewer may pause their programming—as they might on any video format—to think, converse, or find out more about what they are watching. But doing so interrupts the platforms and typically takes the viewer away from it. It stops the stream, literally and figuratively.

Transient viewing is not limited to streaming media, however, as TVOD services likewise offer massive quantities of televisual content to their users devoid of historical or cultural context. Of such services, iTunes is the oldest and remains the most successful. On a computer or other digital device, a user opens the iTunes Store and is immediately faced with a menu of possible entertainments. Its interface allows users to rent or purchase many but not any television show, film, album, song, audiobook, podcast, or app they want. With iTunes, every work of art is reduced to a comparable product. The difference between *Battlestar Galactica*, *Star Wars*, and *Star Trek* becomes purely textual—limited to characters, gadgets, and other genre conventions—rather than cultural, industrial, or ideological. This system of equivalence encourages the same casual viewing habits as SVOD and AVOD platforms. TVOD is based on a unit-purchase rather than a subscription model, but the information it offers would-be viewers is remarkably similar. Since iTunes must convince users to purchase the property, it makes sense that they provide slightly longer descriptions of series and episodes. But neither type of platform supports or encourages anything more than a transient engagement with a series. Even the auteurist supplements offered on season box sets are no longer available; instead, other, barely related series become the supplement. TVOD also obviates the logic of collection, reducing episodes to files one does not in fact own but rather purchases access to, especially in the case of over-the-top devices like AppleTV. In sum, iTunes allows one to consume *Battlestar Galactica* at will but no more. Apple's celestial jukebox is always on, but it is not equipped to provide perspective on its hits.

Battlestar Galactica may come and go from one or another video-on-demand provider, but its role in 1970s US television culture or its commentary on 1970s political culture is not part of this new television culture. SVOD, AVOD, and TVOD platforms entice viewers by promising access to televisual abundance, but their interfaces strictly delimit that access. It's easy to share your log-in information for one of these services; it's much harder to use one of their video scrollbars to find and scrutinize a specific scene in a particular television episode. Transient viewing offers the fleeting pleasures of convenience in lieu of the rewards of critical engagement. It teaches viewers to expect and prize access over information, to assume that high-speed internet access is all they really need to understand television. Sometimes transient viewing is all a viewer wants, but without the option of a sustained relationship with a recorded series, viewers are in no position to question or critique television. While I was writing this chapter, *Battlestar Galactica* disappeared from every SVOD and AVOD platform except NBC.com, which interjects ads into the program every time one pauses it. This made textual analysis quite frustrating, to say the least. How will future *Battlestar Galactica* fans negotiate such assertions of corporate ownership? How will future scholars study legacy television when they cannot predict their access to it? What critical gains will come with the loss of physically stable research materials? I have no answer to these questions.

CONCLUSION

Video's various commodity forms all orchestrate viewers' experience of their contents, the context in which they understand them. Specifically, off-the-air recording, prerecorded videocassettes, season box sets, and video-on-demand platforms all coordinate specific relations between their episodes or series and television history, which never include broadcast, political, or cultural history, although they do proffer other logics of entertainment and appreciation. None of these formats offers a better or worse relation to television history than any other; the point is that they all engender different fantasies about history for different reasons. Remediation is not the same thing as loss, after all, but it can feel like it, especially in relation to a series, like *Battlestar Galactica*, that is all about loss. *Battlestar Galactica* follows a community that can never go home again, who have lost not just access to their history but the very planet on which it occurred. The refugees of *Battlestar Galactica* must rely on their mythic past to imagine a future on Earth. Commander Adama's reparative reading of the Earth legend gives him the faith to lead the humans. The series emphasizes—as this chapter emphasizes—that historiography is always political. How we choose to tell stories, and remember them, shapes who we understand ourselves, and our society, to be. Reparative readings of the series might encourage similar fortitude, while other historiographies could interrogate its place in cultural history, including its cynical attitude toward diplomacy. Research and criticism could generate those historiographies, but none of the platforms analyzed here encourage them. All video platforms inform the spectator's relation to televisuality, but they diverge radically in their representation of television history and its value for the future. In shaping viewers' access to and attitudes toward television history, they become political actors, intervening in the mechanisms of cultural memory.

No video format can ever have an entirely determinate effect on its users' relationship to television history, yet each of video's various technologies of memory encourages certain spectatorial commitments. For decades, television history was preserved only haphazardly, with entire series disappearing into the ether after broadcast. Today, some television history is maintained and distributed across multiple video formats at once. Such plenitude can seem redundant, pointless even, and it can make all formats feel equivalent by seeming to reduce access to a mere matter of convenience. But memories—and technologies of memory— are always partial, contingent, and biased. Memory is a simulacrum, and how we choose to remember, to access, television history shapes the process of historicization. To put it bluntly: *how* shapes our understanding of *what*. Whether they acknowledge it or not, how a critic watches informs their perception of what criticism does and can do.

CHAPTER 2

The Commercial Economy of Film History

Or, Looking for *Looking for Mr. Goodbar*

In chapter one, I argue that different video formats encourage different forms of remembering and that prerecorded video reinterprets television history and televisuality to serve the perceived interests of distributors. In sum, video distribution is not a neutral means of preserving media history but a way of writing it—and not writing it. When films and television shows are never distributed on video or fall out of circulation, they recede from popular memory and scholarly discourse. Such evanescence has nothing to do with artistic or historical merit. When a title becomes less popular or when the market shifts from one platform to another, distributors make pragmatic decisions in the interest of corporate profits. Thousands of film titles fell out of distribution in the shift from VHS to DVD, including cult classics like *Play It As It Lays* (Frank Perry, 1972) and Oscar-nominated dramas such as Richard Brooks's *Looking for Mr. Goodbar* (1977). To be sure, many movies do return to distribution via DVD or video-on-demand platforms after years languishing in studio libraries, but each format shift brings a shake-up.

As prints of no-longer-distributed films fade and their VHS copies deteriorate, these objects force viewers to encounter the material basis of film history, which is also the commercial basis of film history. In practical and profound ways, the film history we watch, teach, and write has been shaped by studio distributors and by profit margins that necessarily supersede archival logic or culture considerations.[1] There may be no alternative—given the larger capitalist structures framing the US film industry—and yet the loss of socially, politically, and artistically valuable titles leads critics and fans toward both paranoia ("why won't they rerelease this movie?") and recuperative praise of the lost title's underappreciated merits. Neither gesture addresses the actual experience or consequences of loss, however, of sitting with the deteriorating media object and learning from its passing rather than protesting it. As film scholars and fans, we can learn much from acknowledging and analyzing the disappearance—both material and cultural—of beloved films. Learning from loss is difficult and scary—a lesson coincidentally and passionately conveyed in the final, fading frames of Looking for Mr. Goodbar. However, it is the film historian's responsibility to recognize how the raw material of their work is manufactured, by whom, and why, and to consider how commercial economies of video distribution underwrite their critical practice.

This chapter investigates film history's dependence on commercial video economies through Brooks's Looking for Mr. Goodbar and its metacinematic depiction of loss, but this consonance is merely a critical convenience. Any film that has fallen out of circulation might anchor a similar analysis of the ways that the home video industry structures scholars' and casual viewers' relationships to film history. Indeed, there are many other films that this chapter could have been about, including Michael Lindsay Hogg's Beatles documentary Let It Be (1970), Martin Bell's documentary Streetwise (1984), and Michael Lehmann's Meet the Applegates (1990).[2] Looking for Mr. Goodbar ends with a powerful, self-referential image of extreme horror, a sickening blend of cinema and nightmare. It is New Year's morning, 1977, and Theresa Dunn (Diane Keaton) has brought home a stranger (Tom Berenger) for casual sex. But when her would-be lover is unable to achieve an erection, he becomes violent, first punching and strangling Theresa, then raping and stabbing her simultaneously. A strobe light renders this terrible conflation of penetrations as brief tableaux of obscene violence. When the assault ends, the camera slowly zooms out from Theresa's face. The light blinks ever more slowly; with each flash, her countenance recedes until it finally fades out entirely (figure 8).

A serious drama about the fatal consequences of sexism within the sexual revolution, Looking for Mr. Goodbar happens to include meaningful, self-referential analyses of its medium and its place in history that make it a particularly apt case study; I also personally love it, yet find myself only able to teach it as an illicit text and a forgotten landmark of 1970s US cinema. The film's withdrawal from video circulation

FIGURE 8. The final shot of *Looking for Mr. Goodbar* (Richard Brooks, 1977).

has imbued it with the elusiveness and ephemerality that were the dominant conditions of cinema *before* home video—which is ironic, given that it was released on multiple home video formats. As various distribution scholars have observed, however, the processes through which films reach their audiences (or fail to) include all kinds of industrial pressures.[3] As I will argue, some films must occupy what Nathan Carroll calls the "abject archive" to confer value on the very concept of reissuing others.[4]

Looking for Mr. Goodbar has been out of circulation since 1997, and one by one, surviving videotapes, LaserDiscs, and 16 mm prints of the film are succumbing to the ravages of time. Although illicit versions of Brooks's film continue to circulate on YouTube and other unlicensed video-on-demand sites—affirming fans' desire to share the movie and forestall its total disappearance—these versions are still marked by imminent loss: visual and aural traces of the source format's deterioration. So *Looking for Mr. Goodbar* now threatens its spectator's ego by forcing figural and emotional encounters with loss (the death of its heroine) and the imminent loss of the movie itself. Paramount Pictures holds the rights to *Looking for Mr. Goodbar* but has no plans to reissue the film. All licensed home video editions of the film will probably be unwatchable around 2027, after which Brooks's intervention into US cinematic representations of women's sexuality and the sexual revolution will be the stuff of legend rather than canon.[5] As a film historian and a fan of the film, that future fills me with dread, not to mention a professional quandary: What can a critic do when confronted with the disappearance of a beloved text?

The urge to *do something* often arises from a wish to save the film, to somehow prevent its disappearance. This fear of loss engenders a critical response that I call *the savior complex*. The savior complex motivates both of the strategies for textual analysis that Eve Kosofsky Sedgwick finds to be dominating contemporary humanities criticism: paranoid and reparative reading. In this chapter, I will show how both the paranoid, interrogative quest to uncover the truth about a film and the reparative, hopeful celebration of the movie itself are a fight to save the critic and their text from a hostile culture.[6] But in its degenerated video editions, *Looking for Mr. Goodbar* produces a figural encounter with loss that pushes its viewer to sit with loss as such. In so doing, it creates an occasion to examine the savior complex via an alternative reading practice I call *sitting with*. Sitting is the most common posture for motion picture spectatorship, and posture can—and should—provoke attentive analysis of the material conditions of film criticism. *Sitting with* also designates a spiritual posture and practice, a grieving ritual and a way of being present in contemplation. Sitting with a movie on a deteriorating platform and disappearing from cultural memory focuses the viewer's attention on the movie as object, and in this case on how attributions of film-historical value can depend on commercial distribution, specifically on digital reissues of back-catalog films. Digital video platforms and economies too often determine the subject and approach of film scholarship, but by sitting with degraded videos, scholars can become attendant to our mutual materiality and mortality, our mutual worldly transience. When a movie shows artifacts of its substrate's material deterioration, that transience provides an opportunity for me to face my fear of loss, of death.[7] It leaves me vulnerable and open to learning from a film rather than learning about it.

Scholars often do sit with deteriorating films and videos in archives and museums. Feminist film critics have demonstrated a particular drive to interrogate and interrupt and to recuperate and restore given the unjust loss of women's films and women's role in film history. But this chapter is not about archival research or nonprofit institutions' preservation practices. It is about personal and scholarly encounters with film history via commercial video distribution and about scholars' tendency to treat commercial video distribution like an archival practice. It is a polemic for film scholars to become more self-aware as historians about the political ramifications of our participation in economies of film-historical value. We need to address the role that loss—or, rather, the fear of loss—plays in historicist scholarship and consider the way that material history affects our critical politics, otherwise we run the risk of following commercial imperatives that have little to do with our own values as historians (feminist or otherwise).

To illustrate the value of this proposition—and ultimately of the reading strategy I call *sitting with*—this chapter begins by revisiting Brooks's *Looking for Mr. Goodbar*: its narrative, the cultural movements it depicts, and its initial reception. I then pursue paranoid and reparative readings of the film to see what each strategy can reveal about its imminent disappearance. First, I investigate why Paramount hasn't reissued *Looking for Mr. Goodbar*, which was nominated for three Academy Awards and a Golden Globe award and featured Diane Keaton in the same year as her Oscar-winning turn in *Annie Hall* (Woody Allen, 1977). Culling through government files, industry reports, and legal scholarship—like a good paranoiac—I reveal what the reader probably already suspects: that Hollywood distributors rely on licensing agreements and profit projections to decide which films to reissue. US film culture colludes in this commercial revisionism via review cycles that privilege commercial reissues and consign "abject archive" films to cultural obscurity.[8] Then, as a reparative reader, I return to the pleasures of the text and explore how *Looking for Mr. Goodbar*'s formal play harnesses narrative incoherence to launch a feminist critique of the sexual revolution. Using an old VHS copy of the film, I observe how Brooks introduces formal ruptures into otherwise classical Hollywood narration and continuity editing to expose their shortcomings and those of the ideologies they support. Sly fantasy sequences within the notoriously dour film also encourage hope for greater gender equality in the future.

Such hope does not remove static from a videotape, fix scratches on a LaserDisc, or persuade Paramount to reissue Brooks's movie, however. A reparative reader can love her movie to death, but she cannot love it back to life. Fortunately, sitting with my decaying VHS cassette provides an alternative to paranoid and reparative readings. By focusing my attention on its material format and acknowledging the tape's inevitable dissolution, I learn to accept my own savior complex and acknowledge the corporate structures and physical realities that govern my relationship to this film. Neither movies not their critics can escape the destructive power of time or the vicissitudes of corporate media cultures. Shedding that illusion is crucial to developing honest relationships with ourselves and our scholarly objects. The material realities of distribution change how we do criticism, and we need to recognize and interrogate those realities in order to evaluate how we choose the critical objects we analyze and the conclusions we are able to reach about them. As much as I love *Looking for Mr. Goodbar*, as important as I think it is, all I can do in the end is accept that I am watching the movie for me rather than for it, then learn from it and let it go. It is in this manner, by sitting with the film's searing final image and focusing on its presence in the world, that I do justice to the disappearing film.

LOOKING FOR MR. GOODBAR IN 1977

Before it even premiered, *Looking for Mr. Goodbar* was already subject to paranoid readings and controversy. One of a number of mid-1970s films made in response to the women's movement, the film was based on a 1975 *New York Times* best-selling novel by Judith Rossner, which was itself based on the sensational murder of a New York City schoolteacher. Producer Freddie Fields and distributor Paramount Pictures kept careful files on Rossner's novel, its public reception, and its financial success. Paramount regarded *Looking for Mr. Goodbar* as a potential gold mine: its lurid vision of promiscuous singles and swingers offered "excitement aplenty" by reflecting some of the culture's worst fears about singles bars, then a recent urban phenomenon.[9]

Between the mid-1960s and early 1970s, US lounge culture changed dramatically. As late as 1965, women were unwelcome in many US bars and taverns without a male escort.[10] Bars did not become places for women and men to meet and maybe go home together until singles bars developed toward the end of the decade. TGI Fridays in New York and Mother's in Chicago both lay claim to being the country's first singles bar, and both succeeded as a result of the same two powerful social forces: the women's movement and the sexual revolution.[11] The women's movement brought an influx of financially independent young women to major metropolitan areas, some of whom pressed for equal access to men's social spaces as well as their power and privilege. In August 1970, New York Mayor John Lindsay "signed a bill prohibiting discrimination against women by public establishments" in response to women's groups who picketed for entry into the famous McSorley's Old Ale House.[12] That same year, Chicago overturned its law prohibiting women from tending bar, a feminist victory that directly benefited singles bars, as female bartenders made these taverns more comfortable for female patrons.[13] Finally, singles bars answered a need for social spaces where people of different genders and backgrounds could mingle comfortably while searching for casual sex.

Such encounters could end well or poorly, and *Looking for Mr. Goodbar* depicts both outcomes in the life of Theresa Dunn, a schoolteacher who cruises downtown singles bars at night. These bars are critical to Brooks's interpretation of Theresa as a woman caught up in a great yet problematic sociological shift. His film begins with a montage of black and white photographs of bar patrons flirting and dancing (figures 9 and 10). Some of these carousers turn out to be characters in the movie, but most remain anonymous—protagonists in other dramas, perhaps. Male and female, straight and gay, Black and white, these heterogeneous bar patrons represent the social experiment of the singles bar and the sexual revolution. Crucially, their images historicize rather than localize Theresa's story. Every major metropolis had singles bars, and *Looking for Mr. Goodbar* could have unfolded in any of them.[14]

Brooks's film begins approximately one year before Theresa starts frequenting singles bars, on the day she loses her virginity to her married college professor, Martin (Alan Feinstein). Martin treats Theresa terribly—subjecting her to aspersions such as "I just can't stand a woman's company right after I've fucked her"—but she is deeply enamored of him. Theresa fantasizes that he will leave his wife for her; instead he leaves Theresa for another student. Although upset, Theresa is galvanized by their breakup and uses income from a new teaching job to move out of her father's house and rent her own apartment. Leaving behind the repressive Catholic ideology she grew up with, Theresa embraces her sudden autonomy; a montage shows her exploring her neighborhood, furnishing her studio, and discovering her sexual appetite (i.e., masturbating). She starts frequenting neighborhood bars and spots a young hustler, Tony (Richard Gere), who becomes her first conquest. About this time, she also meets James (William Atherton), a social worker assigned to one of her students, who pursues her relentlessly. Theresa resents James but dates him casually (and chastely) while continuing to sleep with Tony and pick up other men. Come Christmas, James gives Theresa a strobe light, which he says reminds him of her: "Light and dark. On and off. Now I see you, now I don't."[15] But when he tries to give her a ring, Theresa balks. Marriage promises all the stability and entrapment she so recently escaped. She dumps James, but he cannot accept her rejection and becomes violent, just as Tony does after Theresa refuses to let him stay the night.[16] She insists on having a room

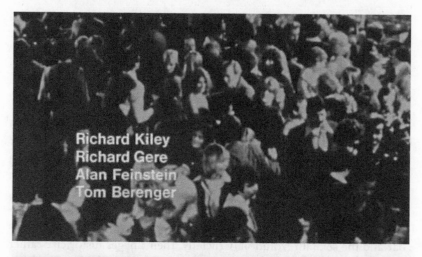

FIGURES 9 and 10. Singles-bar patrons from the opening credits of *Looking for Mr. Goodbar* (Richard Brooks, 1977).

of her own, physically and ideologically, which is ultimately what gets her killed.

As mentioned, Theresa's story ends on New Year's Eve 1976. She goes to a neighborhood bar to get away from James, who won't stop following her, and meets Gary (the aforementioned stranger played by Tom Berenger). Although they do not know it, Theresa and Gary were at the same drag parade earlier that evening, where Gary was celebrating the New Year with his male lover. Bigots attacked the parade, triggering Gary's internalized homophobia. Now he responds to Theresa's come-on as an opportunity to prove his heterosexuality, but drugs and alcohol render him impotent. Theresa is understanding but politely asks him to leave, whereupon Gary explodes, knocking her into a wall and knocking over the strobe light James gave her. Its intermittent flashes provide the only illumination as Gary rapes and murders Theresa. She resists his assault physically, but her final line, "Do it," confused viewers, some of whom heard it as a plea for death, others as a victim embracing rape. Either way, the film ends with Theresa's face, its features evacuated of the energy and charisma that made Keaton's performance—and the film—so compelling and disturbing (figure 8).

Like the film in which it appears, this image generated polarized reactions. If disposed against the film, viewers may find that its last fractured shot confronts them with the impotence of their look, which is powerless to save Theresa. The shot then epitomizes a feminist pessimism running through the entire film, one that many critics misread as cynical misogyny. According to such defensive logic, the movie's concluding image of total destruction reflects the film's inherent stillness and predetermined narratives, not to mention tragic confirmation that young women seeking sexual pleasure and independence always arrive at violent ends. It is both metacinematically and philosophically fatalist, suggesting that there is only one way for this story to end because it was prerecorded by a culture incapable of imagining or sustaining lives for sexually independent women. However, such exposition does not account for the devastating beauty of this stunning image. With each flash, the shrinking, overexposed shot becomes more powerfully iconic, as loss of detail stands in for loss of life. It is fascinating and haunting, as befits its subject matter. The elegiac rhythm with which the film alternates between image and blackness gives the spectator time to experience the loss of this young woman. It invites a less defensive, more open-minded viewer to reconsider Theresa's narrative and imagine other ways it might have ended. They might then fill in the darkness by envisioning other futures for Brooks's heroine—or simply refuse to revile the film that tells this tragic story. Through its beauty, Brooks's final shot can provoke the viewer to see more than violence in Theresa's death, to dream of change rather than accepting the status quo.

Despite or perhaps because of its shocking conclusion, audiences flocked to Brooks's *Looking for Mr. Goodbar*, which made over $14 million in its first eight weeks and over $22 million before it left theaters.[17] Its popularity defied a swath of negative reviews; in tones ranging from dismissive to outraged, critics rejected the film as dour and moralizing.

Several excoriated Brooks for being too old-fashioned, too Old Hollywood to handle such timely subject matter. In a late review for *New West*, Stephen Farber writes that "Brooks's blatant, literal-minded view of human motivation is sadly inappropriate to a contemporary story like *Looking for Mr. Goodbar*."[18] Vincent Canby disliked the movie so much that he organized his *New York Times* review around enumerating each "major mistake" Brooks made with the source material.[19] He criticizes Brooks's casting of Keaton even while praising her performance, as does Pauline Kael.[20] Kael also rejects Brooks's "moralizing psychology" as expressed in editing that, she contends, reduces the film to "an illustrated lecture on how nice girls go wrong."[21] Even Robin Wood, one of its few champions, regarded it as inconsistent and uncertain of its political commitments.[22]

Feminist critics were divided in their responses to *Looking for Mr. Goodbar*. Many considered it symptomatic of a growing backlash against the women's movement, while others saw it as an indictment of sexual double standards—suggesting that the film was important to contemporary feminists even though its meaning was ambiguous. Reviewers for *Off Our Backs* argue that Brooks's "unforgiveable" adaptation lacks the distinctly feminine sensibility that they appreciate in Rossner's novel.[23] *Cineaste*'s Betsy Erkkila reads it as "just another sexploitation film that masquerades (rather dangerously) as a women's film."[24] Erkkila sets out to expose the film's misogyny and remind readers that "just because a movie is about a woman, it is not necessarily either a 'woman's picture' or a feminist tract."[25] Molly Haskell counters such polemical critiques by lauding Brooks's movie as "the best possible film such depressing material could yield."[26] She argues that "it would be a mistake to read the movie as a simple anti-feminist parable of woman as perpetual victim, engaged in a drama of retribution for her sexual transgression."[27] Rather, Theresa knowingly makes "a pact with the devil"—that is, puts her own safety at risk—"in the name of sexual freedom."[28] Depicting Theresa's double bind makes *Looking for Mr. Goodbar* "an important film" to Haskell, although not an enjoyable one per se.[29]

Looking for Mr. Goodbar also fed ongoing popular debate about the late-century "women's picture" and the status of women in New Hollywood. As *Washington Post* critic Gary Arnold observed in August 1977, "Over the past decade leading roles for movie actresses have diminished to such an extent that women stars have come to be regarded as an endangered species."[30] Since the late 1960s, he argues, women have had fewer opportunities to carry a film, narratively or commercially. That pattern changed somewhat in the 1970s with filmic responses to the women's movement, including *Alice Doesn't Live Here Anymore* (Martin Scorsese, 1974), *The Turning Point* (Herbert Ross, 1977), and *An Unmarried Woman* (Paul Mazursky, 1978). This cycle inspired *New York Times* film writers to publish a series of think pieces on women in New Hollywood, all of which cite *Looking for Mr. Goodbar* as an example of "credible female life" returning to mainstream US cinema.[31] Viewers responded to *Looking for Mr. Goodbar*'s startling representation of 1970s women in a different way. Letters to the editors of *Ms.* magazine, the *Los Angeles Times*, and other magazines and newspapers suggest that audiences felt deeply disturbed, even "violated" by the movie.[32] Their missives suggest that Theresa's story had quickly become a benchmark against which real women measured their sexual risks and behavior. In the years to come, feminist scholars would also turn to *Looking for Mr. Goodbar* for evidence of a culture of violence against women.[33] In sum, critics and viewers took *Looking for Mr. Goodbar* as emblematic of all the contradictory ways that American sexual mores and US film culture were failing women. It would remain a lightning rod for such debates throughout the 1980s.

WHATEVER HAPPENED TO THERESA DUNN?

Part of the reason that *Looking for Mr. Goodbar* stayed in the public eye was its ancillary distribution—that is, its success on video and television. It was among the thirty top-grossing films for 1977, a financial success that, together with the film's cultural notoriety, made *Looking for Mr. Goodbar* an ideal candidate for home video distribution.[34] Home video was still a new technology in the late 1970s, with multiple corporate video systems competing to dominate the market. Paramount released *Looking for Mr. Goodbar* on at least five home-video formats between 1978 and 1980, demonstrating stronger faith in its product than in any particular video platform.[35] In 1978, the movie appeared on MCA/ Philips's DiscoVision and Magnavox's experimental Magnavision system, and within a year, it was also available on RCA's SelectaVision and MCA's revamped LaserVision.[36] It came out on VHS soon thereafter, and on May 16, 1980, ABC even screened it as a Sunday Night Movie of the Week.[37] It seems likely that many viewers would have taken advantage of that opportunity to record the notorious feature on Betamax and VHS, although no known off-the-air recordings remain.[38]

Paramount kept reissuing *Looking for Mr. Goodbar* on VHS until 1997; the last authorized video edition of the "Controversial Classic" came out on June 5 of that year. Its cover promises that "nothing can prepare you for this film's shocking ending"—an odd formulation, given the heroine's notorious death. Yet it is a fitting epigraph for a paranoid reading of the film and its distribution, especially if one interprets it as a warning that the film's notoriety would outlast cultural memory. In fact, the 1997 VHS release became *Looking for Mr. Goodbar*'s "shocking ending," at least in as much as the movie has not been reissued since. Brooks's film has never been distributed on DVD, Blu-ray, or any digital video platform. It has never been licensed to a subscription video on demand (SVOD) service, nor can one legally download it from any transactional video-on-demand (TVOD) service. Used VHS and LaserDisc copies are still for sale on resale sites such as eBay, but they are all at least seventeen years old and deteriorating rapidly. Even under the best storage conditions, magnetic videocassettes rarely last more than thirty years, and most become unwatchable long before then.[39] LaserDiscs can remain functional for twenty-five to fifty years, but again, improper storage (such as laying the discs flat on a shelf) dramatically decreases their lifespan. All remaining video copies of *Looking for Mr. Goodbar* will probably become unwatchable between 2027 and 2033 (if one even has the technology to watch them).[40] Archival prints of the film are all but unwatchable. The Academy of Motion Picture Arts and Sciences Film Archive and the UCLA Film and Television Archive own 35 mm and 16 mm prints of *Looking for Mr. Goodbar* respectively, but they are "almost entirely faded." In August 2014, a UCLA archivist warned me that it "might not be worth [my] effort" to try to see this film on film.[41] I would eventually, as Paramount still rents out one 35 mm print of the film to repertory theaters. Nevertheless, *Looking for Mr. Goodbar* remains legally inaccessible for most viewers.

To be sure, *Looking for Mr. Goodbar* continues to circulate illegally online. As of December 2019, one could stream a compressed and degraded version of the film on YouTube and download copies from various torrent boards. There are also illicit DVD editions of the movie available through various auction and resale sites. All such copies of Brooks's film are recorded from television or ripped from VHS or Laser-Disc editions. They bear the artifacts of multiple platforms and compression algorithms, artifacts that either come between the viewer and the movie, providing fodder for a paranoid argument about industry suppression, or change the text itself, creating new objects for reparative reading. But in as much as these illicit files are posted illicitly and vulnerable to industry censure at any moment—and in as much as they are all ripped from deteriorating media—they do not provide reliable access to this film or the history it represents. Thus, in a very real and material sense, *Looking for Mr. Goodbar* is not long for this world.

So please forgive my paranoia when I conclude that *Looking for Mr. Goodbar*'s distribution history rather resembles the plot of a 1970s conspiracy thriller: dark forces are erasing all traces of Theresa Dunn for reasons unknown. Trying to figure out why *Looking for Mr. Goodbar* has fallen out of legitimate video circulation is a classic exercise in Sedgwick's paranoid criticism. Writing in the wake of the AIDS crisis and her own cancer diagnosis, Sedgwick suggested that poststructural literary and cultural critics employ a "hermeneutics of suspicion" toward textual objects that places faith in exposure and affirms what critics already suspect about the work or the world.[42] Such critics seek to reveal the structures of repression and oppression just below the surface of a piece of literature (or film or cultural text). At its most generous, this position maintains that *if people just knew the truth*, they would resist. At its worst, it posits pessimistic genealogies of oppression and inequality wherein tomorrow can only be worse than today. Its appeal lies in the fantasy of answering *why*—in this case, why is this controversial, historically significant film not being reissued by its distributor?

The film's star and director offer no leads. Diane Keaton barely mentions *Looking for Mr. Goodbar* in her memoir *Then Again*. Brooks's film led to her first Best Actress nomination and secured her reputation as a serious dramatic actress, yet she avoids commenting on its production or reception, noting only: "[After *Annie Hall*] I was suddenly getting more opportunities. I met with Warren Beatty for his movie *Heaven Can Wait* and turned him down to hit the bars as Theresa Dunn in *Looking for Mr. Goodbar*. After *Goodbar* finished shooting, I went back to New York. When Warren called me on Christmas Eve, it wasn't about a job."[43] Richard Brooks died in 1992, and his papers at the Margaret Herrick Library offer no information on why Paramount has forsaken the film. A trip to the US Copyright Office or a search through its *Catalog of Copyright Entries* confirms that Paramount still holds the copyright it registered for the film on October 11, 1977.[44] However, its corporate communications office refuses to address the issue of reissue; when I enquired about a possible future reissue, Senior Vice President of Business and Legal Affairs Richard Redlich would only state, "It is our policy not to comment on business decisions of the nature of your inquiry."[45] Redlich refuses to explain why Paramount hasn't reissued *Looking for Mr. Goodbar*, but at least he confirms that reissuing is a "business decision" and thus financially motivated.

Most likely, Paramount Home Media has decided not to reissue *Looking for Mr. Goodbar* on DVD, Blu-ray, or video on demand because of a dispute over music rights. Many cult films, including Penelope Spheeris's *Dudes* (1987) and John Sayles's *City of Hope* (1991), were not reissued on DVD or digital video for decades because their distributors were unable to license the music on their soundtracks for such a release. MGM Vice President of Legal Affairs Greg Julian handles licensing rights for video reissues and observes that if "a big film [like *Looking for Mr. Goodbar*] is not available now, I would almost assure you that there is a reason in the rights structure."[46] In Julian's experience, studios never fail to exploit their famous back catalog titles; when they do not, it is because they cannot, usually due to music rights. Filmmakers must secure—or "clear"—a complicated, multitiered scaffolding of rights to incorporate copyrighted music in a motion picture. Such clearances become even more complicated when the films in question will be distributed on home video. Indeed, the intricacies of music licensing for feature films are enough to make anyone paranoid; one missing phrase, and a beloved movie can disappear forever.

In order to include a copyrighted song in a film and distribute that film in theaters and on home video, a filmmaker needs to secure permission for both the musical composition and a specific performance of it, which requires at least three different kinds of licenses. The synchronization or "synch" license covers the musical composition (the song as written) and gives the grantee the right to synchronize images to the song as written—that is, to integrate the song itself into the film's sound mix. Depending on when the contract was written—before or after the home video revolution—the media it specifies might or might not include any home video technologies via a special videogram sublicense. Once the sync license is in place, a filmmaker must secure permission to use a specific performance of the musical composition through a contract known as a "master use" license.

A synch license and a master use license were typically sufficient for a film that would only appear in theaters and on television, but home video distribution—and the revenue thereof—complicated the situation. After the rise of home video, film and television producers (or rather, their representatives) began amending specific "videogram" licenses to the standard synch license, but during the 1980s and 1990s, many musical composition copyright holders initiated legal disputes with film and television producers contesting the use of their songs in video editions of various films and television shows.[47] Courts sided with both the licensors—as in *Cohen v. Paramount* (1988)—and the licensees—as in *Platinum Record Co. v. Lucasfilm* (1983) and *Bourne v. Walt Disney Co.* (1995). This led studio contract lawyers to rely increasingly on sublicenses within the synch license that specifically grant video rights. The videogram language in a synch license will closely resemble the following: "Licensee may distribute copies of the musical composition, as reproduced in the program, in all forms of home video exploitation, now known or hereafter devised, for private home use."[48] The all-important phrase "now known or hereafter devised" assures producers that they need not fear future legal disputes, payouts, or—worst of all—court-ordered injunctions against video distribution, no matter how home video technology develops.

Before the 1980s, many synch licenses did not include adequate—or any—videogram sublicenses, which left some filmmakers vulnerable to legal action from song licensors when they distributed their movies on home video. In that case, a studio might decide not to distribute the film on any media platforms invented after the contract terminated. That could be what happened to *Looking for Mr. Goodbar*; if Paramount's lawyers only secured video distribution rights for a limited period of time, then they might face legal action for continuing to distribute *Looking for Mr. Goodbar* on any home video format. Brooks's film was available on VHS for almost exactly twenty years, so it is possible that Paramount only secured videogram rights to one (or more) of the songs on its soundtrack for twenty years. It may be that Paramount tried to relicense the song(s) for further video distribution in the late 1990s and the rights holder(s) wanted more money than Paramount was willing to pay. If so, then the studio may have decided that *Looking for Mr. Goodbar* was no longer a profitable video property for them. It is also possible that Paramount was unable to locate one of the rights holders and did not want to undertake the expense of remastering the 1977 film without being certain they would be able to exploit it. The public may never know the exact reason, but all possible scenarios suggest that the film is not being deliberately suppressed: distribution decisions are governed by profit, not politics, although politics often influence which films are perceived as potentially profitable. Viewers' access to film history is determined by nuances in decades-old copyright contracts written by lawyers who never imagined what it might mean to watch Theresa Dunn fade away— nor was it their job to do so.

Yet, as long as Paramount keeps *Looking for Mr. Goodbar* out of legitimate circulation, its presence in US film culture will continue to fade and its chances for future reissue to diminish. University libraries cannot buy pirated DVDs, so faculty rarely teach the film. Paramount is renting a 35 mm print of the film to repertory houses, but without a Blu-ray or Digital Cinema Package release, many theaters cannot program it, having been forced to relinquish their 35 mm projectors in the transition to digital projection. Decreased exposure leads to a decrease in demand, which makes Paramount's business decision even easier. As Bradley Schauer has discovered, back-catalog films need "projected sales of fifteen to twenty thousand copies" to justify a traditional DVD release.[49] Distributors have also sold DVDs and Blu-rays through manufacture-on-demand (MOD) systems since 2006 and 2013, respectively, but a MOD release is not enough to restore the film's reputation—nor is it legal if videogram rights have not been secured. That being said, MOD has saved many back-catalog titles from total obscurity, as do certain boutique video-on-demand platforms, albeit to a lesser degree.[50] MOD programs lower the break-even point for DVD printing to a mere seventy discs by charging more per disc and changing what consumers expect from a DVD. Part of the way that distributors distinguished DVD from VHS and LaserDisc was through bonus features, or what Paul Benzon calls a "paratextual aesthetics of surplus."[51] Paratextual surplus continues to distinguish DVDs and Blu-rays from MOD discs and their SVOD equivalents, which obey "an aesthetics of less . . . marked by distortion, deletion, and faulty reproduction."[52]

MOD discs—and the boutique SVOD services that are replacing them—typically employ older, lower-resolution transfers and almost never include bonus features. Yet MOD programs remain the last, best hope for films trapped in Carroll's "abject archive." These films, excluded from the business of film history, provide the "shadow support structure enabling the visible everyday operation of archival power."[53] Through their exclusion, they bestow value on the included, those movies that are reissued by mainstream archival distributors, such as the Criterion Collection.

MOD programs use a logic of scarcity to charge more for their relatively low-quality discs. As Schauer demonstrates in his industrial analysis of the Warner Archive MOD program, fans and collectors are willing to pay higher prices to have any access to abject archive titles.[54] Consequently, MOD programs were "the primary method of retail for older (pre-1990) films that have not seen a previous home video release" until 2013, when several MOD programs made the jump to SVOD.[55] Paramount and Warner Brothers were the first studios to back MOD distribution, signing with MOD Systems in 2006. Warner Home Entertainment has since established an extremely successful in-house MOD program, the aforementioned Warner Archive, which led to the SVOD service Warner Archive Instant in 2013 (closed in 2018 to make room for WarnerMedia's next proprietary SVOD platform, HBO Max). For $9.99 a month (slightly more than Netflix or Hulu), subscribers could stream approximately five hundred back-catalog films, about half of which were available in high definition. Warner Archive Instant's "aesthetics of less" distinguished it from Time Warner's other boutique SVOD service, Film-Struck, which extended the curatorial renown of Turner Classic Movies and the Criterion Collection with critical and historical bonus material unavailable on any other VOD service. (FilmStruck was also discontinued in 2018 in advance of HBO Max.) Paramount has licensed titles to Warner Archive Instant and FilmStruck as well as MOD distributors, including Olive Films.[56] *Looking for Mr. Goodbar* is not currently part of either deal, but given that many MOD movies are not remastered, Paramount could reissue its old transfer of *Looking for Mr. Goodbar* via MOD any time it wanted to.

But even if *Looking for Mr. Goodbar* had come out on MOD, only traditional DVD and Blu-ray releases occasion the critical reevaluations that generate public and academic interest. Within two years of the format's launch, DVD reissues of classic titles inspired a reparative review genre dedicated to celebrating new access to old favorites.[57] When Peter J. Nichols reviewed Artisan Entertainment's DVD release of Fred Zinnemann's *High Noon* (1952) for the *New York Times* in 1999, for instance, he discovered that DVD enabled viewing pleasures unavailable on prior formats. For instance, DVD's high(er)-resolution image and freeze-frame capabilities helped him to appreciate Gary Cooper's economy of expression in relation to Zinnemann's spare editing and production design.[58] Nichols's extended reconsideration appeared in the *Times*'s "Home Video" column, which also featured capsule reviews of "New Video Releases" to promote reissues. In 2003, "Home Video" became "New DVDs" so that Nichols could comment on both contemporary titles and recently rereleased classics.[59] In 2017, J. Hoberman took over the championing of new Blu-ray reissues in the *Times*'s "On Video" column. (The column is currently called "Rewind" and covers revivals across all platforms.) Hoberman's column persuades readers to reinvest in old chestnuts such as *The Picture of Dorian Gray* (Albert Lewin, 1945) and Disney's *The Jungle Book* (Wolfgang Reitherman, 1967) but cannot push them toward discs that do not exist.[60] Reissue reviews reignite public interest in newly available classics, so they don't occur without a commercial rerelease.

Consequently, only those films chosen by their studios for reissue receive such cultural approbation.

Film scholars likewise perpetuate distributors' economies of film-historical value. For instance, some DVD reissues occasion reparative analyses that draw on the discs' bonus material to endorse the previously undervalued titles. D. A. Miller began his reissue column for *Film Quarterly*, "Second Time Around," with a queer recovery of William Friedkin's *Cruising* (1980).[61] *Cruising* stars Al Pacino as an undercover cop searching for a serial killer in New York City's gay leather scene. Gay rights activists famously objected to the film's imbrication of homosexuality, sadomasochism, and murder, arguing that its homophobia would inspire more homophobic violence. Critics scorned the film for different reasons, calling it "exceptionally unpleasant" and dismissing its "plot structure [as] basically a mess."[62] Miller's article sparked a surge of critical interest in the film.[63] It was equipped to do so by Warner Home Video's decision to reissue the film, yet Miller does not interrogate how the studio's financial interests enable his recuperative project.

Miller begins his now famous rereading of *Cruising* with its poor reviews in order to refute them. Through close readings of *Cruising*'s 2007 DVD reissue, he finds in Friedkin's incoherence a thesis about incoherence: *Cruising* depicts a culture so paranoid in its homophobia that any defense of queer desire "can no longer be imagined with a successful outcome."[64] Using information from the short documentaries included on the "Deluxe Edition" DVD, Miller explains how the film takes up the homophobic logic of contagion—namely, that exposure to gay sex unleashes queer desire in otherwise straight viewers—and takes it seriously. There is no one killer of gay men in *Cruising*, Miller argues, but rather a "symbolic circuit whereby every gay man, at varying degrees of separation, becomes his own assassin. But—here's the rub—the circuit is never quite closed; the overwhelmingly visible spectacle of gay male sex may simply be irresistible to any man who beholds it, and remain so even after its violent recloseting."[65] Homosexuality is both contagious and irresistible, but its very irresistibility makes it dangerous given a straight world bent on destroying queer communities. *Looking for Mr. Goodbar* makes a similar point about the sexual revolution, as both its heroine and her queer killer are destroyed by the effects of internalized homophobia. However, *Looking for Mr. Goodbar* wasn't available for reparative review in 2007, nor is it now. Its contagion has been contained.

Thus it is that through video culture film-historical value is reassigned and film history rewritten. Such reassessments still depend on the abject archive, however. Value is relative, so some films must be forgotten for others to be remembered, some disregarded so others can be venerated. It is not that these excluded films are bad, unworthy, or commercially unviable; rather, exclusion is necessary to sustain the system. This is not to say that celebrations of *Cruising* and *Looking for Mr. Goodbar* are mutually exclusive—let's not get *that* paranoid—but commercial conditions of availability and unavailability structure scholars', critics', and fans' relation to film history. Some films return to cultural prominence through video reissue while others are consigned to exist only in discourse and memory.

FEMINIST INCOHERENCE AND VIDEO-ASSISTED REPARATIVE READING

But what if we—critics, fans, theorists, historians—did not respond to loss as a defeat and accepted it instead? Such an approach would constitute an alternative to paranoid readings of abject archive films, which can amass plenty of evidence for their claims without generating much utility. At the beginning of her essay on paranoid and reparative reading, Sedgwick asks, "What does knowledge *do?*"[66] Knowing why *Looking for Mr. Goodbar* is headed for obscurity may open up new ways to think about the film or film historiography, but it will neither lead to a reissue nor make the film's loss less painful. As Miller demonstrates, reparative readings try to ameliorate pain with pleasure. Pleasure provides energy to imagine new futures, alternative trajectories, and different perspectives on the past. Rather than seeking to expose hidden truths, a reparative critic opens up new frameworks of visibility to explore her object's potential to create and support better futures. Loving a film, embracing it as a part-object in the psychoanalytic sense (i.e., as an object defined by its function for the subject), allows the critic to ask what else it can offer, what insights and information it can give the viewer. Ultimately the goal of reparative reading is to discover how subjects can draw energy and inspiration from cultural productions. Whereas paranoid reading shores up the critic's ego—her sense of importance and self-worth—through negative affects and narratives of inevitability, reparative reading cultivates new ways of loving to inspire new visions for the future.[67] It requires a methodology akin to close reading—new historicism's favorite technique for exorcising hidden truths from recalcitrant texts—but without close reading's investment in exposure and revelation. It is just one of a number of so-called postcritical methodologies espoused as an alternative to "suspicious hermeneutics," including compassionate redescription, surface reading, thin description, and an erotics of art.[68] Reparative reading emerges from the same savior complex as paranoid reading, however, at least inasmuch as it involves the same ego investment. As reparation, its main concern is still "What can this film do for me?," not "What can I learn from this film?"

Reparative readers and their postcritical brethren do have the benefit of requiring a methodology specific—and sympathetic—to their object. Just as not all films qualify for reparative review, not all films can be redescribed in the same way. Since *Looking for Mr. Goodbar* has not been rereleased since 1997, any contemporary recuperation of the movie will require a different methodology than Miller's and will generate a different relation to the film. Without the kind of DVD bonus materials that ground Miller's review, for instance, one must rely on subjective textual analysis and embrace the affordances of outmoded video formats, such as VHS. Watching, rewinding, and rewatching *Looking for Mr. Goodbar* on my office VCR, I discovered a unique feminist pessimism in its formal experimentation and a vitalizing political energy beneath its dour tone. Through small scenes and gestures, *Looking for Mr. Goodbar* acknowledges that the world is set against its heroine's pleasure, even against her survival. This acknowledgment can be empowering for feminist viewers looking for critique of the sexual revolution. The film's formal play generates a transformative narrative incoherence—transformative because it disrupts the conventions of classical thrillers and melodramas to suggest that Theresa's story requires a departure from classical Hollywood storytelling.

These departures occur at the levels of performance, editing, and composition; despite having previously watched the film on a bootleg DVD, I found them easier to appreciate when engaging the "'wind' time" required to rewind a VHS.[69] Take, for instance, the short scene in which Theresa watches a New Year's Eve broadcast called "The Decade of the Dames." Theresa previously conflated sex and romance in the traditional manner, even though doing so brings her nothing but disappointment. She starts to separate these terms after watching this television report. Critics have scoffed at Brooks's so-called passing reference to the women's movement, suggesting that Theresa shows little interest in the program. Rewatching the short scene on video reveals otherwise. Keaton's physical performance in this short scene encapsulates Theresa's feminist awakening and even models media-inspired feminist awakening for the viewer. Through framing and editing, the scene marks a turning point after which Theresa starts to claim sexual autonomy and the film launches its critique of "sexual liberation" under heteropatriarchy.

The scene takes place on New Year's Eve 1975, while Theresa is at her family home babysitting. After turning on the living room television set, she moves to the living room mirror to watch herself working out with a bust developer, a midcentury spring-action contraption that (falsely) promised to help women enlarge their breasts (figure 11). Although initially preoccupied with this futile exercise, Theresa turns her attention to the TV when an announcer proclaims, "It was only five years ago that ten thousand women marched for liberation." It seems implausible that any television network would program a retrospective on the women's movement just before midnight on New Year's Eve, but one need not necessarily read such incongruity as bad screenwriting. It does important work for the movie, as it symbolically marries the arbitrary promise of New Year's Eve to the uncertain present and future of the women's movement. In any event, Theresa's eyeline match shows hundreds of women protesting for abortion rights, equal access to education, "and sexual freedom." With this shot, the women's movement eclipses Theresa's lonely capitulation to Western beauty standards both figuratively and ideologically. As the broadcast continues, Theresa keeps her eyes on the screen and relocates the bust developer to her hip. She continues to pump away absentmindedly, but her movements now emphasize how absurd the device is. Misusing the bust developer is a small gesture, one easy to overlook and not likely to be celebrated in a DVD bonus documentary. Yet the comedy of Keaton's physical performance comes through during self-directed rewatching and bespeaks the film's feminist principles. Her actions wordlessly capture Theresa's changing relationship to female sexuality, from trying to please to realizing she can demand to be pleased (figure 12).

Following this quiet revelation, Theresa starts to claim sex when she wants it. In the next scene, she shuts down one of Martin's tirades by standing over him and wordlessly lifting her skirt. Unfortunately, though, a person cannot simply will herself free in a society bent on her subjugation—or so *Looking for Mr. Goodbar* suggests. The film's pessimism is inchoate in its New Year's Eve documentary, which concludes that "this *was to be* the decade of the dames." The past-tense, deontic construction implies that the 1970s have already turned out not to be the decade of the dames, and as Theresa will soon discover, sexual freedom may include the freedom to have sex out of wedlock but not freedom from the virgin/whore dichotomy. She has the means and the

FIGURES 11 and 12. Theresa's feminist awakening in *Looking for Mr. Goodbar* (Richard Brooks, 1977).

autonomy to have sex with multiple men, yet she is still vulnerable to recrimination and violence. Tony, James, and her father all verbally and physically assault Theresa for her sexual choices; at various points, each implies that he might kill her. Like *Cruising*, *Looking for Mr. Goodbar* presents their violence as a symptom of heteropatriarchal ideology rather than a personal failing. The film traps Theresa and the women of her generation between the Charybdis of sublimating their desire into futile attempts to elicit desire in men and the Scylla of accepting punishment from men for recognizing and acting on their desire. In other words, it captures the incoherence of an era wherein female sexuality is a game that there's no way to win, with the New Year's Eve scene encapsulating this paradox in all its terrible power.

That's a grim message, but it intervenes significantly in Hollywood representations of the sexual revolution, which otherwise veer between humorous affirmations of and dark apologies for the status quo—for example, *Bob & Carol & Ted & Alice* (Paul Mazursky, 1969), *Carnal Knowledge* (Mike Nichols, 1971), and *Klute* (Alan J. Pakula, 1971). Brooks offers an alternative by embracing the narrative incoherence characteristic of 1970s US cinema to explore the gulf between Theresa's world and her desires. Editing is key to Brooks's technique here, as it allows him to move the spectator between reality and fantasy within the same scene. These shifts, which are sometimes almost imperceptible, bothered many contemporaneous reviewers, but they open up alternative worlds for Theresa where she can exert control. They enable the spectator—especially the video spectator, who can respond to confusion by rewinding and rewatching—to appreciate how Theresa questions and resists patriarchal culture, and so they have the power to encourage a viewer's own resistance.[70]

For instance, on the night that Theresa first spots Tony, the young hustler who will become her second lover, the film depicts her fantasy of him coming on to her, but it does this so subtly that a first-time viewer may mistake Theresa's inner world for external reality. Fantasy, the viewer later realizes, is the only form of cruising that Theresa feels capable of at this point. Still, fantasy is a powerful force. The scene begins with Theresa sitting at a neighborhood bar, enjoying a glass of wine as The Undisputed Truth's "Smiling Faces Sometimes" plays in the background. She sees Tony dancing and watches as he rifles through a lady's handbag. When he catches Theresa looking at him and smiles, the film cuts to her reaction, and the music suddenly changes to Boz Skaggs's "Low Down." Tony then appears at Theresa's elbow and offers her "the best fuck of [her] life." "Well, in that case . . .," she laughs, and reaches for her purse. But when she looks up, Tony is gone, and the soundtrack reverts to "Smiling Faces Sometimes." Theresa glances across the bar and then lifts her eyebrows in wry amusement. An eyeline match reveals Tony in the arms of another woman. Their whole exchange only happened in Theresa's head.

This scene represents one of the more understated fantasy sequences in the film, but Brooks takes the viewer into many such excursions from reality in order to dramatize desires Theresa cannot express or does not fully understand. Fantasy allows Brooks to explore the incoherence of desire, including Theresa's ambivalent attraction to Tony. For after each fantasy sequence, the spectator must revise their impression of what was real and what was merely imagined, a cognitive process that pushes them to understand Theresa rather than just focalize through her. More to the point, these fantasies invite critique of Theresa's reality as they force the spectator to distinguish between what Theresa wants and what she gets. This technique can confuse viewers, but it also teaches them that Theresa's world is incoherent.

Many reviewers failed to recognize Brooks's subtler fantasy sequences as fantasies, though, which led them to reject the film's narrative as confusing and Theresa's character as inconsistent.[71] Neither of these claims is correct, but it can take multiple viewings to understand that the film constructs its fantasy sequences around the incoherence and turbulence of desire. Nowhere is Brooks's strategic use of incoherence more effective than the scene in which Theresa appears to jump in front of an oncoming car after Martin dumps her. Walking home from their break-up, Theresa pauses at a street corner, looks behind herself, and then deliberately steps forward into oncoming traffic. A rapid succession of shots depicts Martin behind the wheel of his car, Theresa's exultant expression, a woman screaming, and then an ambulance rushing to a hospital. Next Theresa is being wheeled down a hospital corridor as her parents and doctors worry over her. If a skeptical viewer scoffs at the coincidence of Martin being the driver to hit Theresa, their credulity will be strained further when Martin shows up at the hospital to declare, "I love her. . . . It's my fault." It may break entirely when the doctor lifts Theresa's blanket and tells her father, "Congratulations, your daughter has a beautiful body" before kissing her left breast. Yet the scene is not revealed as fantasy until the doctor announces that Theresa is two months pregnant, whereupon she sits up and screams, "No!" The film then immediately cuts back to Theresa standing on the sidewalk, smiling to herself.

The viewer's skepticism is now resolved; what felt like an implausible narrative was in fact a fantasy. Its incompatible elements expressed Theresa's desires to be glorified as a martyr and reunited with her lover as well as her fear of pregnancy and her frustration with being an object of male exchange. In sequences such as this one, *Looking for Mr. Goodbar*'s critically denigrated incoherence reflects the "generalized crisis in ideological confidence" that Robin Wood finds disturbing many 1970s films. During this decade, Wood argues, "society appeared to be in a state of advanced disintegration, yet there was no serious possibility of the emergence of a coherent and comprehensive alternative," so films such as

Looking for Mr. Goodbar thematized anxiety and nihilism through the breakdown of narrative order.[72] To that end, the hospital fantasy sequence departs dramatically from continuity-editing conventions that the film employs elsewhere; it violates the 180-degree rule and uses no matches on action and few sound bridges. Those that do exist employ unnatural and distorted sound perspectives to undermine the illusion of mimesis. In sum, Brooks presents Theresa's fantasy chaotically, and that chaos reflects the incompatible ideological structures that created it. Theresa's married lover has left her, but the very masochistic self-sacrifice that she hopes might return him to her also reinscribes her in the patriarchal logic that she escaped through their affair. She cannot imagine an erotic life outside the system, and the film represents that problem through the breakdown of its narrative idiom. Incoherence becomes not just a narrative device but a political tactic—a tactic that may have failed for some viewers but possesses new potential on video (at least for now).

To be more specific, narrative incoherence creates opportunity for reparative reading by creating gaps and fissures where hope can grow. It is difficult—but not impossible—to perform reparative readings of classic Hollywood narratives, as Alexander Doty has so ably demonstrated.[73] But the unique forms of narrative incoherence, perversity, and ambiguity that flourished during the Hollywood Renaissance—in films such as *Chinatown* (Roman Polanski, 1974), *The Conversation* (Francis Ford Coppola, 1974), and, yes, *Looking for Mr. Goodbar*—all but demand reparative reading by destabilizing the very notion of a dominant interpretation. None of these films adheres to traditional notions of psychological motivation (or they withhold key elements of their characters' backgrounds in order to complicate it). None adheres to established notions of narrative closure; indeed, explanations often only complicate the inquiries that initiated them. While *Looking for Mr. Goodbar* is not a mystery like *Chinatown* or *The Conversation*, it similarly invokes and inverts the conventions of the thriller and the family melodrama to flummox its viewer. When spectatorial confusion is an organizing structure of a movie, it invites reparation on the viewer's part. We take what we can and make our own meaning from Theresa's story. Video facilitates this process as it allows viewers to repeat or return to particularly pleasing or troubling moments. It encourages them to approach incoherence as a puzzle rather than a problem; hence the proliferation of modular narratives and puzzle films in the home video era.[74] Working through the "'wind' time" of VCR navigation foregrounds the durational labor of textual analysis; it forces the viewer to spend time seeking answers and generating hope through reparative readings. But even reparations have their limits.

Seeing the text differently allows us to imagine the future differently; this is the promise, the hope, of reparative textual analysis. It seeks "to assemble and confer plenitude on an object that will then have the resources to offer an inchoate self."[75] Thus reparative readings do not deny horror or bad news—such as, the sexual revolution was unfair to women—but create more sustaining ways to live with them. In this case, reparative reading shows us that by embracing narrative incoherence, we can recognize and manage the incoherence of the sexual revolution for women. Yet as Robyn Wiegman discovers by delving deeper into the psychoanalytic theory on which Sedgwick's reparative reading is based, this affirmative approach to criticism still comes from a desire for mastery: "'Love' is never innocently given but instead part of a defensive maneuver against the infant's own murderous impulses towards the projections and part-objects that make up its world."[76] In other words, the reparative critic's love resembles an attempt to save the object but is at root an attempt to save themselves. Both the paranoid and the reparative reader are sustained through their critical acts, including narratives of loss that allow them to redeem a disappearing object. They both fight loss, which is a losing battle. By writing about the films of the abject archive and allowing them to remain abject, however, by acknowledging their abjectness without seeking to resolve it, critics can address loss without denying it. This is the material and psychic practice I call *sitting with*. Sitting with allows me to learn from a movie without using it to prove anything, rescue anyone, or shore up my own ego. It is an experience of durational copresence with an object that requires new forms of viewerly attention and care work for the text and the self.

WATCHING, GRIEVING, SITTING WITH

Sitting with is a mode of viewing that involves not just investigating or describing the film text itself but attending to its material presence in your life. In the case of deteriorating media, this includes recognizing, rather than looking past, damage and distortion and acknowledging them as part of the film and its history—or, as David Church puts it, "gently caress[ing] the decayed analog image with one's anxious vision."[77] Sitting with decaying videotapes and fading films is an act of observance that marks film as a durational art form whose duration in this world is bound by material reality. Importantly, it forgoes reparation for either the text

or the critic and accepts historical contingency. When I sit with a deteriorating video, I accept it as a partially present object rather than a partial
object. I adopt a parallax view in which I glimpse both the ideal text—
what Paolo Cherchi Usai calls the "Model Image," the untarnished, perfect print that never really exists—and the flawed edition actually in front
of me.[78] Acceding to rather than denying or bemoaning their difference, I
then consider the industrial machinations and material exchanges that
brought this object and me together. In so doing, I finally stop looking to
make the text—and myself—whole, stop insisting on explicating the past
or fabricating a future. Instead I focus on becoming open to the ambiguity of the present. In the case of *Looking for Mr. Goodbar*, this embrace
of ambiguity includes asking what the blurred and faded images and
compressed soundtrack of its remaining editions can tell me about film
history on video. Sitting with my battered 1997 VHS version of the
movie, I don't try to pretend it's something it's not (such as a remastered
digital reissue). I look carefully at what it really is, in all its flawed material specificity, and try to be receptive to the insights it can reveal as it
deteriorates further.[79]

In this regard, sitting with a film resembles the spiritual practices of
sitting with the sick, the dead, and the bereft. I say this not to belittle
these cultural traditions but to acknowledge the complex ways in which
different cultures process loss. In Judaism, sitting shiva allows those who
have lost close family members seven days to withdraw from the demands
of daily life, remember their relative, and inhabit their grief. Other
mourners visit the family, in a practice known as paying a shiva call.
They do so in order to sit alongside the mourners, not to celebrate the
life of the deceased or to distract the mourners from their pain. Indeed,
sitting shiva marks mourning as an act committed over time, as a means
of learning how to live with loss. Sitting with departing media likewise
requires a temporal commitment, requires being attentive to the evolution of deterioration and decay. In the United States, African American
women began a caregiving practice known as "sitting with the sick"—
visiting, nursing, cleaning for, bringing food to, and otherwise supporting the families of ill and elderly community members—to compensate
for nonexistent or inadequate state support.[80] Precisely because sitting
with the sick is rarely remunerated, it is marked as feminine, as care
work, and thus as a form of emotional labor and community service.
Sitting with media might also be thought of as care work, as it requires
close attention to—and sometimes repair of—disintegrating objects.
Community care work can be a form of self-care, and media care work

can be as well. Importantly, though, both prioritize care of an other; self-care is a side benefit, not the primary goal it is in reparative reading. In the American South, other traditions of sitting up with the dead and sitting up the dead reinforce the sociality of *sitting with*. Sitting (or "setting") up with the dead involved community vigils for a bereaved family on the night before burial. Especially in poor or isolated rural communities, burial preparations required assistance from neighbors and friends, who would then sit with the family after building the coffin, cleaning and dressing the corpse, and digging a grave.[81] Like sitting shiva, sitting up with the dead emphasizes death as a shared process of transition and an opportunity to reflect on life's transience as well as the life of the deceased. The same can—and should—be true of sitting with deteriorating media.

Sitting with my disintegrating tape of *Looking for Mr. Goodbar*, attending to and respecting its material decay, I notice how the color and brightness of Brooks's film have been severely compromised by VHS and must be encountered as they are, as probable departures from a Model Image I'll never see. Analog video has only a fraction of film's luminance ratio (40:1 versus 130:1). The early analog video transfer of *Looking for Mr. Goodbar* changed the movie's visual composition and thus the viewer's experience. The lowered luminance ratio feels especially relevant during its conclusion, which represents death almost entirely in terms of luma. Videotape is not a domesticated film format; it is its own technology with its own affordances and limitations. Consequently, the filmic and video conclusions of *Looking for Mr. Goodbar* are not the same even though they include the same content. The film's conclusion uses its medium to capture the winking of Theresa's inner light. The video conclusion also reminds us that film is light, but it reminds us of that via the absence of film itself. Hence Brooks's video teaches us that light is an impermanent medium, and that all lights go out. To ignore that is the critic's folly, the hubris of the savior.

To recap: *Looking for Mr. Goodbar* ends with a strobe lamp intermittently illuminating Theresa's face as Gary kills her. Overexposure from the lamp all but eliminates color from this attack, reducing it to black or white, life or death. When death comes, it comes as a twenty-second reverse zoom from Theresa's face, which ends when the strobe finally stutters out. Overexposure, attached shadows, and lateral framing render Keaton's features abstract, transforming her image into an idea of light as life rather than an expression of character. Analog video muddies this final shot so that Theresa's death mask appears to be sinking into a viscous void (figure 13). Regardless of what the image looks like on film, on

FIGURE 13. The final passing of Theresa Dunn in *Looking for Mr. Goodbar* (Richard Brooks, 1977).

video there is no sharp demarcation between the blue-white of Keaton's skin and the inky blackness that envelops it. The limited resolution of VHS and LaserDisc blurs her features, while the brightest parts of Keaton's overlit face flare out into the shadows that surround them.[82] The shot dramatizes the technical struggles between Brooks's film and the material constraints of its video transfer. Lost information becomes visible on screen in the ambiguous borders between light and dark. This lost information is not recoverable; loss is now the information the video conveys. Restoration and remastering would only obscure the truth of loss—the loss at the heart of the abject archive, the centrality of the abject archive to film history—although of course their appeal is hard to deny.

For while sitting with a corrupted image, one sometimes rediscovers fantasy as a hermeneutical gesture. Fantasy can be an important element of sitting with when acknowledged as such, when *thinking otherwise* gives the critic fresh perspective for *thinking what is*. In attending closely to *Looking for Mr. Goodbar*'s analog video transfer, for instance, one might wonder how the film would look with a fresh digital transfer, since digital video samples luminance differently than film or analog video do. Digital video privileges modulations of brightness and shade over modulations of hue, unlike analog video, which samples both simultaneously. It records luminance at every pixel and color only on every other pixel. Software filters then create averages between adjacent pixels to form the gradations of light and color according to the specified resolution for the final image.[83] For that reason, a film-to-digital video transfer of *Looking for Mr. Goodbar* might improve image resolution in Keaton's face during the final seconds of the film. The shadows of her eye sockets and cleft of her lips might not be reduced to dark smears—assuming they were not dark smears to begin with. Her features might retain their distinctness and thereby grant her death its specificity—if indeed specificity was Brooks's goal. It might turn out that *Looking for Mr. Goodbar* ends by emphasizing the tragic death of one woman killed by one man, who was also battling the incoherence of a heteropatriarchal sexual revolution that told him to embrace different strokes for different folks but also to be ashamed of his homosexual desires. In other words, sharper resolution and individuation in Theresa's death mask might connote accusation rather than oblivion, reminding the viewer that people die because of the conflicting messages our culture gives them about sex.[84] It might inspire the viewer to imagine other ways that Theresa's story could have ended or to defend and affirm lives like hers.

It *might*—but then again it might not. As long as *Looking for Mr. Goodbar* remains in the abject archive, some of its information remains inaccessible; inaccessibility is part of our relation to this film. Its elusiveness makes other information available, however, through fantasy, conjecture, and copresence. A deteriorating VHS cassette cannot recreate the filmic experience, but it can exert what Jane Bennett calls "*Thing-Power*: the curious ability of inanimate things to animate, to act, to produce effects dramatic and subtle."[85] Not that film cannot exert its own *Thing-Power*, but the decaying VHS makes its user physically (as opposed to just visually) aware that—in the words of feminist philosopher Karen Barad—"matter and meaning are not separate elements. They are inextricably fused together."[86] I live with my VHS cassettes, whereas I see films at a theater. My VHS and I share space in my home and office. We are affected, albeit differently, by the same heat, humidity, and gravitational forces. This copresence defines our relationship and makes me aware of the contingent physical processes that undergird human understanding.

Sitting with can also encourage its viewer to think differently about textual analysis and historical recuperation. These have been the primary methodologies of film historiography, especially feminist film historiography, but they both rely on commercial economies of film-historical value that determine what and how we do historical research. I will probably never get to see the final shot of *Looking for Mr. Goodbar* as a Model Image, but I can put aside my fear of not knowing, my fear of surprise and humiliation, and even my need for hope. By accepting and acknowledging the loss of visual information in Looking for Mr. Goodbar, I recover a pleasure in ambiguity that comes in the wake of the desire to save and is also an acceptance of materiality and mortality.[87] In its degraded video form, the movie challenges me to admit that I need it more than it needs me. It is, after all, an inanimate object, innocent of its decay and imminent obsolescence.

Moreover, my desire to know exceeds the film itself and makes the film symptomatic of a critical impulse. Narratives of loss sustain historians even when our scholarly practices deny or disavow them. The paranoid critic needs loss to illustrate their powers of revelation and explication. The reparative critic needs loss of esteem and the threat of obscurity for rediscovery and recuperation. Yet neither admits how much they need loss—need negative reviews, indifferent distributors, and hostile peer reviewers—to validate their visions, their versions of the universe. Such neurotic relationships to our objects inhibit our learning from them. After years of research, there is still a lot I don't and can't know about Looking for Mr. Goodbar. But as I watch Keaton's face, and try to capture it with my pause button to study its blurred contours, I start to experience her loss not as a wrong that has been done to me but as a chance to see differently. I now see that the image is not there for me, that it exists materially independent from me, and that it is whole to itself and without me.

Looking for Mr. Goodbar is beautiful and brilliant. It was underappreciated in its day and today. Exploring its devaluation, I might shore up my own value as a critic. Arguing for its feminist politics, I might affirm a future for feminist criticism. I might generate a kind of queer feminist hope for a more equitable, sex-positive future. But neither gesture is innocent; neither is free from my savior complex or the physical evanescence of motion pictures that it seeks to deny. By letting this movie go, I acknowledge our shared materiality and mortality. We are neither of us immortal; we will both be forgotten soon enough. Obsolescence, disintegration, and obscurity await the critic, too. The critic cannot save Theresa Dunn, but at least she can learn to stop trying.

CODA: BACK FROM THE DEAD

When I first published on Looking for Mr. Goodbar in summer 2015, I predicted that I would probably never get to see the final image of Looking for Mr. Goodbar as Brooks intended, meaning on a 35 mm exhibition print in relatively good condition.[88] I was wrong. On August 10,

2017, I took a train from Washington, D.C., to New York City to see *Looking for Mr. Goodbar* at Lincoln Center's Walter Reade Theater, where it was playing for one night only as part of the Film Society's '77 series. As the train rolled along, I thought about how strange it would be to watch this film on film after seeing it so many times on LaserDisc and VHS. Would the colors be brighter? How would that breathtaking final sequence feel when presented on a platform that actually does flicker like a strobe light? What would this cinematic screening do to—or for—my experience of sitting with *Looking for Mr. Goodbar* on deteriorating video formats? Having never before experienced a beloved film on film after getting to know it on video, I was worried that I would feel as alone in the theater as I did in my living room as I once again bore witness to the passing on of an artwork that history had already passed over.

What I found instead was an entirely new encounter with this old movie, a heartwarming—and heart-wrenching—revitalization of Brooks's project. New sensory information became available through the larger screen and more powerful loudspeakers, even while Theresa's story and Brooks's composition remained the same. The revelation was seeing them come alive for an audience. This is not to say that the audience brought *Looking for Mr. Goodbar* back to life. That would require more than a one-night revival. But watching *Looking for Mr. Goodbar* at Lincoln Center reminded me that even though we sit with their worldly incarnations, films do not actually die as we do. Their prints, tapes, and discs are perishable, and they can be lost or forgotten, but their relationship to time is different from ours and perhaps more difficult to predict. As Anne Friedberg put it, film occupies "an eternal present"; it is always happening as it happens.[89] This is why, as J. D. Connor writes in his essay on the '77 series, "seeing these films in the social intimacy of the theater today is more than antiquarianism, more than nostalgia. It is the chance to reactivate their fundamental question: how is society to be reconstituted?"[90] *Reactivation* is indeed the best metaphor for what happened to *Looking for Mr. Goodbar* in Lincoln Center in August 2017. It acted upon an audience and was acted upon by an audience again, and the particular apparatus of that time and that place gave a new meaning to the film that it did not have on any video platform or in its initial theatrical run.

The Film Society's '77 series brought together an international coterie of movies from a single year but a wild medley of genres: science fiction and the musical, blockbuster comedy and the international art film, documentary and queer punk dystopia. Such juxtapositions approximate the grab bag experience of the multiplex, where timing and not theme dictate programming choices and enable unexpected proximities. Series organizer Florence Almozini emphasized both *Looking for Mr. Goodbar*'s expressionist tendencies and its roots in classical Hollywood narration by scheduling it between *Eraserhead* (David Lynch, 1977) and *Sorcerer* (William Friedkin, 1977). Connor contrasts *Looking for Mr. Goodbar* and *Sorcerer*, noting that the former's neoclassicism was more popular in its day than the latter's oneirism.[91] Probably few viewers watched all three films in a row; I certainly did not. Regardless, Almozini's lineup forced one to consider what was happening in film history at that moment, which changes the viewing context for each individual film individually too. Whether or not they give into antiquarianism or nostalgia, the viewer still experiences the film as a historical cultural artifact, as an object from a prior era. Lincoln Center is not a museum, yet festival programming still marks Brooks's film as a preserved specimen. Indeed, making the effort to see a film on film amounts to sitting with a dying platform these days. I bought a ticket to an experience of loss—to a fleeting encounter with an obsolete technology for exhibiting a nearly forgotten film.

After buying said ticket (and popcorn, of course), I sat down with about a hundred other people who had come to see one of the most infamous titles of the abject archive returned to them on screen. The audience for *Looking for Mr. Goodbar* (at least as it manifested itself on a Thursday evening in New York in August 2017) appeared to be in its mid-thirties through mid-sixties and predominately although not exclusively white, with slightly more men than women in attendance. I mention this demographic impression in order to identify the collectivity of which I soon found myself to be a member. Looking at *Looking for Mr. Goodbar* with other people dramatically changed my experience of Theresa's isolation, which I had previously observed in isolation myself. I was surprised, and charmed, when the audience laughed at Martin's antiquated, cliché-ridden seduction of Theresa. Their bemusement uncovered a new pleasure in the text, although that pleasure required a certain spectatorial withdrawal from the film. That is, a viewer must compromise their immersion in order to regard a text as dated. In the immediate aftermath of our laughter, the film also felt tawdry, more like an exploitation movie than a social drama. When Diane Keaton's bare breast appeared on screen, enormous in its size and sexual connotation, it forced an affective change in the auditorium. A collective haze of embarrassment circulated among the crowd, inspiring nervous laughter. This collective discomfort enabled and required me to open myself up to my identity as an audience member, rather than hiding behind the mask of the scholar.

As anticipated, the film's conclusion was most affected by its presentation on film. The room for fantasy opened up by video's limitations was closed down by a grim resonance between the cinematic apparatus and the broken strobe light illuminating Theresa's death. When Gary starts attacking Theresa and inadvertently activates the lamp, the entire auditorium was alternately bathed in light or submerged in blackness. The clicking of the light also resembled the clink of a film projector advancing its reel, reminding us of the machinery enabling our experience of their scene. As viewers, we were physically and psychically overwhelmed by the flicker of the strobe light and by the multiply resonant soundtrack. Soon after, our theatrical experience was dominated by the disappearance and reappearance of Theresa's death mask. There was then no sound in the theater except for the click of the strobe light-cum-projector and the crackle of dust on the soundtrack. The sound of dust is not, of course, the sound of film itself but rather of the world beyond the film. As Michael Marder observes, "dust is a ledger of past existence," traces "of what has been and is about to pass away."[92] Its noise thus strikingly conveys the mixed temporality of film itself. In this case, it makes audible the particular experience of sitting with strangers in 2017 to watch a simulation of death recorded forty years earlier on a film print of unknown age.[93] While the sound of the strobe that was also a projector conflated two distinct moments in time—the *then* of the cinematic apparatus and the *now* of our spectatorship—the noise of the dust was all the time that had passed in between, the distance between the viewer and *Looking for Mr. Goodbar*.

When the film ended, I could not help but eavesdrop on the couple sitting in front of me, who were deeply moved by the film. When we were among the last patrons left in the theater, the man turned to his viewing companion and sighed, "Whoa, that was powerful," then added "It's kind of a shame. People saw it forty years ago, now we only remember the name. . . . It was a great movie, a great movie." She nodded, observing, "I saw it then too. I remember thinking it was a 'gets what she deserves' thing. But now. . ." Both agreed that the film's critique of the sexual revolution was easier to recognize in hindsight. They contrasted it to *Saturday Night Fever* (John Badham, 1977) as a film whose power has diminished thanks to its retrograde representations of women and rape. Their reactions affirmed my impression that film history needs *Looking for Mr. Goodbar*, but they also speak to the unique power of sitting with films of the abject archive. The power of *Looking for Mr. Goodbar* now emerges in part from its abjection, from the very economy of scarcity that limits viewers' access to it. Thus, we are still looking for *Looking for Mr. Goodbar* even when we have it temporarily in front of us. Its fleeting presence does not counter its enduring absence.

A film does not leave the abject archive for having played once at Lincoln Center—or at the American Film Institute's Silver Theater, where *Looking for Mr. Goodbar* also appeared as part of a program honoring Diane Keaton's 2017 Lifetime Achievement Award. Indeed, *Looking for Mr. Goodbar* also played at New York City's City Cinemas in July 2017 as part of an interactive drag performance starring Hedda Lettuce. Like all lost objects, *Looking for Mr. Goodbar* continues to pop up occasionally, even if it is never around when one goes searching for it. That search is the focus of this chapter, more so even than the movie itself. As scholars and viewers, we often assume Hollywood history, as part of US cultural history, to be publicly available. It may not be easily accessible—some movies will always be easier to get than others—but, we believe, those titles are all out there somewhere, in some archive, library, or thrift store. That impression is inaccurate and misleading. Films are private intellectual properties, for the most part anyway. They belong to their copyright holders, not the people who see them or the societies they reflect and inform. *Looking for Mr. Goodbar* belongs to Paramount Pictures, not to you, me, or film history.

It is crucial that we remember the legal principles behind the commercial economy of film history—the dominant economy of film history in the United States—as we consider the uncertain future of physical media objects in film culture. Without VHS and LaserDisc, there would be no pirate copies of *Looking for Mr. Goodbar* floating around torrent boards or YouTube. Even if *Looking for Mr. Goodbar* does eventually make it to iTunes, Amazon Prime Video, or some other video-on-demand platform, those files will be even less durable than a 1997 VHS cassette. Computer container codes, compression codecs, and interface technologies (such as USB or Thunderbolt) become outmoded quickly and with alarming thoroughness. Indeed, a movie stored on an external hard drive on a shelf may become unplayable long before the drive itself degrades (anywhere from a few years to a few decades, depending on use, dust, humidity, and other factors). Whether we recognize it or not, we are all always sitting with impermanent media objects. Their loss is inevitable. How we stop fighting loss and start learning from it, even welcoming it into the process of film appreciation, only becomes more crucial as technological change accelerates.

CHAPTER 3

"Let's Movie"

How TCM Made a Lifestyle of Classic Film

No one knows exactly what Turner Classic Movies (TCM) means by their tagline "Let's Movie," which is precisely what the network intended. Introduced in 2015, TCM's peculiar imperative turns a common noun, *movie*, into a verb, a rhetorical device known as anthimeria. Everyone knows what a movie is, but how does one movie? Is movie-ing simply watching movies, or does the displacement of *watching* by anthimeria suggest some other as yet unnamed engagement with motion pictures? In its first "Let's Movie" promo, TCM offers a number of elaborations on what to movie means. Over a montage of iconic shots from Golden Era Hollywood films, a man's voice intones, "Let's go to a place where stars never dim and dreams never die. . . . Let's get lost in light and shadow and dare to dream in living color."[1] Title cards in the video further urge the viewer to dance, fly, play, and swing—but noticeably not to watch, view, sit through, screen, or consume. Nevertheless, consumption is at the heart of the "Let's Movie" campaign. The ambiguity of "Let's Movie" furthers TCM's mission of expanding beyond linear television programming to become a post-network lifestyle brand.

The story of this transformation unfolds across twenty-five years—from the network's founding in 1994 to 2019—and offers an important lesson in the way that material culture both writes the history of film and opens up new futures for television networks in the post-network era.[2] In actively pursuing the transition to lifestyle brand, TCM began licensing a wide assortment of branded objects and experiential brand activations. A marketing term that describes "any campaign, event, or experience that enables your brand to engage directly with consumers and build a loyal brand community around your product or service," *brand activation* refers to both virtual and live participation opportunities.[3] It is a form of *experiential marketing*, to borrow another industry term. TCM is not the first media company to expand its market through branded merchandise and experiential marketing—Disney has been playing that game for nearly a century—but it is the first to do so by reframing properties created by others. In so doing, the network not only redefines itself but reframes film history for consumers.

Each of the products and events it sells reflects TCM's brand values— Hollywood glamour, bourgeois good taste, and belief in the importance of film historical knowledge—and is itself a capsule reading of film history. This chapter proceeds, through capsule readings of TCM-branded objects and brand activations, to investigate how TCM transforms viewers' interest in older films into an identity asserted through the purchase of consumer goods and services. That is what is meant by *lifestyle brand*: the production of a values-based, consumable identity through the circulation of popular commodities.[4] In the case of TCM, the transition from classic film network to lifestyle brand not only allowed the network to promote their brand story, it also revealed two important operative tensions within the brand values: between an egalitarian sense of community based on shared cinephilia and a glamorous individualism rooted in class aspiration and between an earnest reverence for film history and kitschy merchandise that cashes in on classic Hollywood's mystique. The TCM lifestyle brand manages these conflicts—and teaches viewers how to love classic film—through its curatorial emphasis on taste making. TCM's branded merchandise and travel instruct consumers how to read—and participate in—film history and film appreciation. Their objects are thus a branding of cinephilia that has important ramifications for how classic film will be remembered by convergence-era audiences.

When it was launched in 1994, TCM's defining promise to its viewers was classic films "uncut and commercial-free"—a reverential approach to programming that soon created real fiscal constraints for the fledgling network.[5] Without ad sales, TCM relied on cable carriage fees for revenue; marketing network-branded merchandise and experiences was one of their few options to increase profits. Such a brand-forward approach to product diversification is unusual among television networks. As TCM's integrated marketing manager Kristen Welch explained to me during a visit to the company's Atlanta offices in June 2018, "When you think of television as a whole, people will be fans of a specific property within television. So you might be a fan of *Game of Thrones*, but you may not call yourself an HBO fan." By contrast, she asserts, "people don't say, well, I watch TCM, but I'm really a fan of the movie or the director; they say they're a fan of TCM."[6] TCM does not technically own any of the titles they screen; its former library now belongs to a different division of WarnerMedia. Consequently, the network cannot create product lines around specific movie titles; only Warner Bros. can do that. However, this seeming weakness—the network's lack of proprietary films or series—led directly to its greatest strength: brand recognition. As a lifestyle brand, TCM monetizes its reputation through goods and experiences that transcend particular classic film titles to realize *classic film* as an idea and brand value.

To that end, TCM-branded products invite viewers to embrace a broader definition of the film experience. For the brand managers at TCM, "product is that natural progression of that feeling" movies give viewers; products extend the immersion that classical Hollywood films create formally and narratively through continuity editing, double plotlines, and similar techniques.[7] To support this model of loving film as living film, the network now bills itself "the ultimate destination for classic film."[8] TCM takes that geographic metaphor quite literally in organizing tours, festivals, cruises, and other travel experiences and also explores its virtual possibilities through fan clubs and online education. In so doing, it reinvents classic film cinephilia for the post-network era, wherein *network* now means something closer to *brand* than *television channel*. TCM's post-network cinephilia-as-lifestyle comprises a proprietary approach to loving film that balances sincere appreciation for industry and art history with a company imperative to "truly own that category of classic film."[9] This goal amounts to an exercise in taste making as understood by Pierre Bourdieu—who defines *taste making* as a kind of "symbolic violence," or the imposition of norms on one group by another—for it determines what loving film should mean to twenty-first century audiences.[10]

Bourdieu's work on taste provides a critical touchstone for this chapter, supporting my larger theorization of the lifestyle brand and the role it plays in twenty-first-century media cultures. Bourdieu observes that taste "function[s] as a marker of 'class,'" and specifically of class difference.[11] "Taste," he goes on to explain, "is the practical operator of the transmutation of things into distinct and distinctive signs. . . . It raises the differences inscribed in the physical order of bodies to the symbolic order of significant distinctions."[12] Taste is no mere matter of personal preference, in other words, but a way of distinguishing oneself within hierarchies of cultural capital. For Bourdieu, writing in France in the late 1970s, the major force shaping taste and social class was education; forty years later, one must add brands and marketing to that mix. Lifestyle brands in particular promise to shape one's taste and incorporate one into a desired group or social echelon. Notably, they offer consumers entrée into a brand community: "a specialized, non-geographically bound . . . form of human association situated within a consumption context."[13] As Albert Muniz and Thomas O'Guinn have shown, brand communities offer members "a shared consciousness, rituals and traditions, and a sense of moral responsibility." Unlike fan communities, brand communities are not organized around specific intellectual properties, performers, or creators; instead, the brand is "the tie that binds."[14] Indeed, creating a taste culture and turning it into a public is the mission of the lifestyle brand; today, it is the mission of Turner Classic Movies.

In order to explore TCM's transition into a lifestyle brand, the values that brand represents, and the operative tensions within the brand, this chapter begins by historicizing the network's genesis within Ted Turner's media empire and the proliferation of cable networks during the 1990s, the first decade of the post-network era. Here I analyze the tautology behind TCM's use of *classic*—it's a classic because it's on TCM and it's on TCM because it's a classic—and how TCM originally defined cable-era cinephilia as around-the-clock access to a curated selection of titles. I then consider how its corporate branding strategies changed in the twenty-first century when TCM reinvented itself as a lifestyle brand and inverted the traditional relationship of network to program. Next, I examine TCM's twentieth-century forays into consumer goods via home video distribution, soundtrack albums, books, and printed ephemera— all of which are now available at TCM's online store. I turn then to TCM's twenty-first century experiential marketing initiatives, which began with consumer experiences, namely the TCM Classic Film Festival in 2010, and include subscription services, such as a wine club and Massive Open Online Courses, and travel enterprises, such as the ever-popular TCM Classic Cruise. These are just some of ways that TCM monetizes its brand; the network engages in many other enterprises that this chapter will not address—such as the Turner Classic Movie Database (modeled on IMDb: Internet Movie Database); its subscription fan club, Backlot; its theatrical screening series; and its short-lived but much-loved subscription video on demand service, FilmStruck.[15] Through all of these initiatives, TCM crafts a consumerist, brand-oriented identity that it invites viewers to occupy. Actual spectatorship has become one way to "movie" among many, one gateway to the TCM lifestyle: a branded way of being in the world wherein cinephilia broadens to the point that films themselves becomes peripheral to it.

TURNER'S FOLLY

To understand why TCM became a lifestyle brand, one must understand how Ted Turner positioned the network in advance of its 1994 launch and how it subsequently became the paradigm for cable-era cinephilia. Turner Classic Movies began as the by-product of Ted Turner's personal ambition to own a Hollywood movie studio—which he did, briefly, in 1985–1986. Turner's rise as media mogul began when he inherited his father's Atlanta-based billboard company. In 1968, Turner started buying other media platforms, first a radio station and then a series of floundering television stations. In the mid-1970s, Turner started licensing his television stations to local cable providers and dreaming of national distribution. A series of cable-friendly rulings from the Federal Communications Commission made it possible for Turner to begin broadcasting via satellite in December 1976. In 1979, Turner changed his company and station name to Turner Broadcasting Systems and (W)TBS, introducing the latter as the first nationwide cable "superstation."[16]

TBS's identity and success were organized around product familiarity—well-known sitcoms, movies, and prime-time dramas—but the expense of licensing content from rights holders quickly began to threaten the network's business model. As biographers Robert and Gerald Jay Goldberg explain, Turner "didn't like TBS's strategic position. To be a long-term factor in this business, he said, you either had to grow in viewership . . . or in the programs you owned."[17] So the young mogul decided to buy a movie studio to expand his library and avoid licensing fees. Early on, Turner identified MGM/UA as his preferred studio, largely because it had been one of his father's favorites. By 1985, MGM/UA had not produced a major hit in quite a while, but it did possess one of the best film libraries in the world, with over thirty-five hundred MGM titles plus another fourteen hundred from Warner Brothers and RKO, not to mention scores of television series. Such a library could provide programming for TBS and any other entertainment channels Turner wanted to open for years to come.

Despite the depth and breadth of MGM's library, buying the studio was still a risky move for Turner's communications group. To meet owner Kirk Kerkorian's $1.5 billion selling price, Turner had to take on massive debt, and some thought he overpaid, especially since many of the best titles in its catalog had already been licensed to other television stations.[18] Turner, it seemed, had not done his homework. He had to sell the production and distribution arms of MGM back to Kerkorian in August 1986, leaving him with nothing but the MGM library, at a cost of over $1 billion. Fortunately, that was all Turner needed to expand his growing television empire. In October 1988, Turner launched another cable superstation, TNT, using classic film and television properties from the MGM (now Turner) library. Its first telecast, after "The Star-Spangled Banner," was Gone with the Wind (Victor Fleming, 1939), one of Turner's personal favorites. In 1991, Turner bought Hanna-Barbera Productions, snapping up its Yogi Bear and Huckleberry Hound cartoons as the basis for yet another cable channel, the Cartoon Network, which launched in October 1992.[19] Suddenly Turner's MGM deal seemed inspired rather than foolish. Owning libraries was key for avoiding exorbitant licensing fees. In the 1990s, new cable networks were succeeding by offering "familiar, often overused, program material" that appealed to both ironic and nostalgic sensibilities.[20] Indeed, "a 1991 study found that more than 95 percent of 'dramatic' (i.e., fiction) programming on basic cable and 91 percent on premium cable consisted of material that already had appeared either on broadcast television or in movie theaters in the United States."[21] So powerful was this trend that MGM/UA shareholders even brought a class-action lawsuit against Kerkorian in 1990 for selling the studio to Turner at too low a price.[22]

To more fully exploit his prize, Turner launched yet another cable network dedicated to showcasing the MGM film library. That network, Turner Classic Movies, premiered at 6:00 p.m. Eastern Daylight Time on April 14, 1994, one hundred years to the day, Turner claimed, from the first film screening in the United States.[23] For TCM's first film, Turner once again selected Gone with the Wind. Before Scarlett O'Hara sashayed on screen, however, viewers met the network's genteel host for the evening and for decades to come: Robert Osborne. A former actor and popular historian, Osborne was tasked with delivering short introductions and concluding reflections on all TCM's prime-time films, as well as some of its daytime selections. With these comments, Osborne set the tone for Turner's fledgling classic movie channel—adoring yet cultured—and distinguished it from its closest competitor, American Movie Classic (AMC), which had also tried to hire Osborne as host.[24]

On TCM, Osborne would promote his debonair enthusiasm for classic Hollywood as the template for cable-era cinephilia. In his introduction to *Gone with the Wind*, Osborne walks down the staircase of a living room set, greets viewers, and defines the new network's mission:

> Hi, welcome to Turner Classic Movies. I'm Robert Osborne, I'm going to be your host right here as we present some of the best, the finest films ever made, twenty-four hours a day. . . . And along the way I'm going to be sharing some of my own memories of Hollywood, things I've seen and heard as a columnist with *The Hollywood Reporter*, things I've also discovered through personal friendships with some of the people who made the movies we all love. I think you're going to love Turner Classic Movies, and we're all going to be doing our best to keep you with us.[25]

With this speech, Osborne performs two important functions. He predicts the transfer of affection by which TCM will interpellate viewers' devotion through the films they play (i.e., love the movie, love the station). He also concisely explains TCM's mission: to screen films, and only films, twenty-four hours a day and to contextualize them with historical analysis, trivia, and behind-the-scenes anecdotes not available on other stations. Notably, Osborne does not attempt to define what TCM means by *classic*; indeed, TCM's promotional materials and staff resolutely refuse to define *classic*. One might assume classic films comprise "the best, the finest films" ever made—but TCM has also programmed plenty of clunkers over the years. Classic films thus appear to be films played on Turner Classic Movies, a tautology that supports the network's curatorial aspirations. *Classic* serves TCM as a branding device, which is to say as an empty signifier, as viewers can embrace the value best when it is least encumbered by potentially objectionable definitions.

Oddly, Osborne does not mention TCM's most cinephilic promise to its fans, namely that it would broadcast all its films "uncut and commercial-free," which required TCM to forgo advertising income, essentially limiting its revenue to carriage fees, the money that cable providers pay a network to provide programming for subscribers.[26] This was not a unique promise among cable stations; AMC had been screening classic movies without editing or interruptions since 1984. Nevertheless, TCM needed to convey respect for film history and overcome Turner's recent, highly publicized attempt to market colorized video versions of classic black and white films, including *Casablanca* (Michael Curtiz, 1942) and *The Maltese Falcon* (John Huston, 1941). Turner claimed, "All I'm trying to do is protect my investment in MGM," but his temerity still drew protest from Jimmy Stewart, Billy Wilder, Martin Scorsese, and the Director's Guild of

America, not to mention a lawsuit from RKO Pictures.[27] TCM never played any of Turner's colorized classics, instead advocating the values of historic preservation and respect for artistic vision. No surprise, then, that Scorsese later became one of TCM's most famous advocates, even writing a column for its magazine, *Now Playing*.[28]

In sum, TCM was conceived, marketed, and programmed as a cine-reverential cable channel. TCM's imagined audience has always been domestic viewers who craved twenty-four-hour access to classic film—in short, cinephiles, at least as defined by contemporary film theorists. Antoine de Baecque and Thierry Frémaux understand *cinephilia* as an identity—one might say a lifestyle—"organized around films."[29] Thomas Elsaesser observes that cinephilia is "more than a passion for going to the movies, and only a little less than an entire attitude toward life."[30] Love of film guides the cinephile's self-perception and existence, making it more than just connoisseurship; so Christian Keathley points out.[31] Keathley does note that cinephilia began as a historically bounded movement within postwar French film reception, but he also emphasizes the significant influence of television on that movement. In France, the cinephile's embrace of film was part of "a rebellious response" to television's allegedly inferior programming.[32] In the United States, meanwhile, early televisual exhibition of classic films fed the nascent cinephilia of future filmmakers and scholars. The home video era changed cinephilia again, rendering some—but not all—of film history easily accessible to the casual viewer. Like AMC before it, TCM made access—and thus cinephilia—even easier. In exchange for choice, viewers gained immediacy: film history was transmitted straight into their living rooms along with informative commentary. TCM represented such accessibility as connoisseurship. Just as a film became classic by virtue of appearing on Turner Classic Movies, a viewer could identify as a cultural savant and cinephile by virtue of watching TCM. With help from Osborne's introductions, TCM appeared to occupy the curatorial role that repertory theaters and their programmers once filled. Linear programming narrowed the overabundance of film history, a new problem of the home video era. In a video store, one suffered from too many options: what was actually worth watching? On TCM, Osborne explained why films the network chose were important. During TCM's post-network paradigm shift—when it stopped identifying as a cable channel and focused on becoming a lifestyle brand—it would abandon its own model of cable-era cinephilia in favor of cinephilia-as-lifestyle, a consumption-driven enthusiasm for film that could facilitate new revenue streams for the company.

For while the TCM audience is not available for advertisers (per the network's commercial-free credo), it is still available to the network itself. Within a year of its launch, TCM began monetizing its reputation as a curator of classic film through soundtrack albums, followed by videocassettes, DVDs, film books, and print ephemera. What started out as a convenient means to exploit the MGM-cum-Turner Communications's film library became a branded empire. In the twenty-first century, TCM further expanded its brand through licensed home goods and apparel, consumer experiences, subscription brand activations, and travel enterprises. In this manner, the network went from paratext to urtext, redefining classic film and classic film spectatorship.

WHAT IS A BRAND, ANYWAY?

Before exploring the specific consumer goods and events that comprise the Turner Classic Movies lifestyle brand, it is necessary to consider what a brand is, how television's historically vexed relationship to branding changed in the post-network era, and how the relationship of text to paratext shifts for movies exhibited on a network-cum-lifestyle-brand. Becoming a *brand* was and remains crucial to TCM's post-network identity. TCM's research on their "brand health" indicates that one of the top three reasons viewers give for watching the channel is that it is a "trusted brand."[33] Correspondingly, the former general manager of TCM, Jennifer Dorian defined Turner Classic Movies as "the brand for movie lovers" and notably not as a television network.[34] This distinction is important. A cable network is a television station with rights to deliver programming via certain radio frequencies on providers' coaxial cables or fiber-optic cable grids. *Brand*, meanwhile, connotes a stronger sense of identity and consumer affinity. The American Marketing Association defines *brand* as "a name, term, sign, design, or a unifying combination of them intended to identify and distinguish a product or service from its competitors."[35] Brand historians argue that this definition is outdated, however. Commodity individuation did motivate the development of brand marketing from the 1880s through the 1920s, but during the 1990s, brand strategists turned toward values-based marketing to distinguish their products within an ever-more crowded marketplace. As marketing historian Paul Grainge notes, this change meant that "branding was no longer a matter of transmitting the meaning of goods. Instead, it meant identifying the 'core values' of a product or service and managing these as an issue of communicable vision."[36]

Hence contemporary branding is a social and a market phenomenon, in that brands associate material goods with specific principles to attract consumers. Take the Dove Beauty Bar, for instance. Introduced in 1955, the Dove Beauty Bar supposedly differed from regular bar soap by containing moisturizers. For the next thirty-odd years, Unilever advertised Dove around that distinction—for example, "Dove doesn't dry your skin the way soap can."[37] Then in 2004, Unilever launched the Dove "Campaign for Real Beauty," which featured models older, heavier, grayer, or otherwise divergent from mainstream beauty ideals. The campaign claimed to be "widening the definition of beauty"—while also selling Dove-brand hygiene products.[38] The chemistry and functionality of Dove products had become less important to its brand identity than a feminist spirit. Such values-based marketing is by no means limited to personal care products; all kinds of brands align their products with particular ideals to build customer loyalty. As digital cable offerings expanded in the United States—from seventy-nine channels in 1989 to roughly eight hundred in 2018—television networks also began to differentiate themselves from the increasing competition through brand values.[39] When FX declares itself "Fearless," AMC promises "Something More," or TCM commands "Let's Movie," they establish a network ethos (of grittiness, originality, or cinephilia) that transcends any individual program. The goal is to attract viewers based on characteristics they either possess or aspire to possess.

Values-based marketing works in tandem with increased consumer involvement in brand development, another important strategy of contemporary marketing that TCM embraces. During the twentieth century, brands exercised relative sovereignty in telling the public what made their products worth buying. Consumers did occasionally reappropriate brands, as when British skinheads adopted Doc Martens in the late 1960s or punks embraced Converse in the 1970s, but brand managers treated these trends as anomalies at the time. In the new millennium, corporations started to cultivate and celebrate consumers' role in crafting brand identity. Branding became a conversation; as Cynthia Lury explains, a "brand is a frame that organizes the two-way exchange of information."[40] Lury further defines *brand* as "a platform for the patterning of activity, a mode of organizing activities in time and space" that extends far beyond any given product.[41] To harness consumers' willingness to identify with their brand values, companies work to become "brand-led," to no longer see themselves as producing goods but rather as "marketing company[ies], and the product is our most important marketing tool."[42] For such corporations, including TCM, "the brand is a social currency, a way in which people bring meaning to various exchanges."[43] So while brand-led companies must now negotiate the meaning of their brand with consumers, the brand can grow more meaningful than any product or service attached to it. Such relationships greatly expand a brand's potential markets and revenue channels—it's how Eddie Bauer logos end up on Jeeps and Porsche starts hawking watches—and it is exactly why TCM decided to transition from leading with one product (linear television programming) to leading with its brand, "the ultimate movie lover destination."[44]

When TCM became a brand-led platform in the early 2000s, it had to change its marketing strategy dramatically. Instead of differentiating itself from other linear cable channels, it began espousing a values-based identity that transcends television. TCM's discourse around its new identity is critical. Phrases like "Let's Movie" and "the ultimate movie lover destination" establish an ethos rather than promoting a specific product. *Destination* in particular establishes a capacious geographical metaphor that allows the brand to organize a potentially infinite array of products and services around the idea of loving movies. *Movie lover* offers TCM consumers an identity to adopt and express through their affiliation with the brand. Crucially, TCM represents its transition to lifestyle brand as being consumer, not company, driven. Hence Dorian claims, "Our fans took us there. They eat, sleep, and drink and breathe and dream movies. . . . We were meeting consumer demand when we decided to expand into more than being a network presenter."[45] Whether or not this is historically accurate, it reflects TCM's goal of becoming a lifestyle brand "that inspires, guides, and motivates beyond product benefits alone but is also capable of contributing to the definition of lifestyle of those who adopt it."[46]

Consequent to this transition, the movies programmed on TCM now contribute to viewers' understanding and experience of TCM rather than vice versa. In literary terms, this means that the paratext has not just eclipsed but become the text for TCM consumers. As originally conceived by Gerard Genette, paratexts are the "'threshold' between the inside and the outside of the text"; they shape our reading practices and the way we make meaning from texts.[47] Genette's examples of paratexts include the cover of a book and its front matter as well as reviews, author interviews, and other support materials that accompany the publication of a book. In updating the concept of the paratext for film and television, Jonathan Gray includes "hype, synergy, promos, narrative extensions, and various forms of related textuality" like websites, merchandise tie-ins, and fan art.[48] These supplements play a "constitutive role in creating textuality," or the meaning consumers create from content.[49] Historically, television networks have been paratexts to their programs, but TCM now overshadows its movies as the primary object for audience investment.[50] This is a stunning reversal, given that the movies on TCM are some of Hollywood's most celebrated and iconic, including (in July 2018 alone) *Rebel Without a Cause* (Nicholas Ray, 1955), *King Kong* (Merian C. Cooper, 1933), *Meet Me in St. Louis* (Vincente Minnelli, 1944), and *Gone with the Wind*. How does a twenty-five-year-old cable channel become a "brand that inspires, guides and motivates beyond product benefits alone" when the products in question are so famous?[51] Gray acknowledges that "paratexts sometimes take over their texts," but in this case, TCM carefully crafts the impression that there is more to loving classic films than merely watching them, that loving classic films is a way of being in the world.[52]

FROM CABLE CHANNEL TO COMMODITY CURATOR

Fittingly for a network trying to associate its brand with curation and a cinephilic lifestyle and expand its audience's practices of filmic consumption, Turner Classic Movies' first forays into branded merchandise were in audio and video distribution and print products. These pilot projects all promote the channel by attaching its name to beloved films; they present the network as a benevolent middleman but not (yet) as a loveable entity in its own right. TCM began merchandizing in 1995, less than one year after its premiere, with motion picture soundtracks on audio cassette and compact disc. One of its first was for *The Wizard of Oz* (Victor Fleming, 1939), which was then owned by Turner Broadcasting.[53] The TCM logo appears only as a small black and white image on the back of the cassette's packaging; nevertheless, branded soundtracks marked an important step in tie-in merchandising for the network. They demonstrated that the TCM brand might have value beyond just programming. Turner quickly released TCM-branded soundtracks to *Show Boat* (George Sidney, 1951) and *Gigi* (Vincente Minnelli, 1958).[54] In 1997, the company produced a *Sounds of TCM* anthology album that includes "Lara's Theme" from *Doctor Zhivago* (David Lean, 1965), the overture from *Ben-Hur* (William Wyler, 1959), and "Anything You Can Do (I Can Do Better)" from *Annie Get Your Gun* (George Sidney, 1950)—all properties (then) owned by Turner Broadcasting.[55] Soundtrack albums constituted a relatively straightforward approach to monetizing the Turner library;

nevertheless, they helped promote the new network and supplement its revenue from carriage fees.

In 1996, TCM started distributing VHS editions of classic films from the Turner library. They began harnessing the promotional power of home video two years before that, however, with the VHS release of MGM/UA's seventieth anniversary documentary, *That's Entertainment III* (Bud Friedgen and Michael J. Sheridan, 1994). Before the encomium begins, video viewers are treated to two advertisements for TCM: a montage of the great MGM films soon to appear on TCM and a personal address from Robert Osborne. The montage renews MGM's famous promise of "more stars than there are in the heavens" to herald Turner's "thrilling new channel" and features clips from *North by Northwest* (Alfred Hitchcock, 1959), *Citizen Kane* (Orson Welles, 1941), *King Kong*, and—of course—*Gone with the Wind*. By citing MGM's old slogan, the new channel affiliates itself with the fabled studio without explicitly mentioning the latter's acquisition by Turner. Instead, TCM seems merely to share the spectator's love of classic Hollywood. Then Osborne appears, introducing himself as TCM's host and promising to take the viewer "behind the dressing room doors" if only they will "give [their] cable company a call and ask them to carry Turner Classic Movies."

In these ads, TCM promotes itself as providing "the greatest movies of all time, all the time." This logline—so reminiscent of Sony's "Watch Whatever Whenever" for Betamax—builds on the on-demand ethos of the home video era to rebrand the linear television channel as a video distributor. When TCM launched its own video distribution imprint, its first set of releases amounted to a multi-genre smorgasbord of classical Hollywood filmmaking and included *Citizen Kane, Clash by Night* (Fritz Lang, 1952) *Fort Apache* (John Ford, 1948), *The Hunchback of Notre Dame* (William Dieterle, 1939), *The Magnificent Ambersons* (Orson Welles, 1942), *Mr. Blandings Builds His Dream House* (H.C. Potter, 1948), *Suspicion* (Alfred Hitchcock, 1941), and *Swing Time* (George Stevens, 1936) (figure 14). The cassettes were all branded "Turner Classic Movies" and all began with introductions by Osborne. Some included post-feature bonus content, such as theatrical trailers, star retrospectives, and short documentaries. Later the network moved into omnibus video productions that foregrounded its curatorial prowess. In 1999, TCM partnered with the British magazine *Total Film* to release *Totally Classic: A Bluffer's Guide to Classic Movies*.[56] Released in part to promote the network's UK premiere, the *Bluffer's Guide* anticipates the pedagogical strategy that would inform TCM's subsequent publishing ventures—that

FIGURE 14. RKO's *Citizen Kane* becomes a Turner Classic Movie on VHS.

is, educating people on the fun side of film history and providing the tools for them to make it part of their identity.

In 2004, TCM entered book publishing by partnering with British publishing house I. B. Tauris on their British Film Guides series. The series—which provides historical, artistic, and cultural insight into celebrated British movies—had already been running for six years before TCM got involved. Joining an established imprint served an important marketing function for TCM. Tauris had a reputation for scholarly and commercial nonfiction, and the British Film Guide series already contained a number of popular titles, including *The Thirty-Nine Steps* (Alfred Hitchcock, 1935; British Film Guide by Mark Glacy, 2002) and Hammer Film's *Dracula* (Terence Fischer, 1958; British Film Guide by Peter Hutchings, 2003). Taurus thus helped TCM expand brand awareness shortly before Turner Classic Movies UK stopped broadcasting over the air for free and joined the Sky satellite network.[57] Working with Tauris allowed TCM to affirm its position as the UK's "premier movie channel dedicated to keeping the classic movies alive for fans old and new," while also marking itself as having expertise one paid for.[58]

British Film Guides notwithstanding, classic Hollywood was and remains the center of TCM print merchandise. The first US print products to bear the Turner Classic Movies imprint were two decks of movie flashcards on "Famous Pick-Up Lines" and "Gangster Speak" from classic Hollywood films. Introduced in 2003, the flashcards offer a witty saying on one side with a frame grab and limited production information for the source film on the other. Printed on thick, creamy card stock, the flashcards would make decent coasters, which may be what inspired TCM and Chronicle to start producing "Classic Cocktail" coasters in 2004. In 2005, they added a set of "Hollywood Kisses" notecards, which allow buyers to disseminate their filmic taste widely to correspondents (who then become potential TCM customers). The notecards marked the beginning of TCM's long-term collaboration with Chronicle Books, a deal that would include TCM *Classic Movie Crossword Puzzles* (2009) and TCM *Classic Movie Trivia* (2011). Both books provide means for extending one's engagement with film, of incorporating it into one's other pursuits. They suggest ways of loving classic film in the world and as an identity that TCM can support.

Over the years, TCM has expanded its line of books and printed ephemera to include more historical and more frivolous options. In 2016, the network turned its annual must-see series, "The Essentials," into a book on the artistic and cultural significance of fifty-two classic films. It is worth noting, however, that Turner released an Essentials wall calendar ten years before the Essentials book, suggesting that décor precedes scholarship in the network's publishing priorities.[59] Bringing those impulses together, however, TCM has produced a number of glossy coffee table guides, including *Into the Dark: The Hidden World of Film Noir* (2016), *Must-See Musicals: 50 Show-Stopping Movies We Can't Forget* (2017), and *Must-See Sci-Fi: Fifty Movies That Are Out of This World* (2018). Although mostly comprised of illustrations and panegyrics, these books are not without justifications for their selections and contain solid historical (if not original) research. As coffee table books, though, they are designed for display as much as (if not more than) for reading. Specifically, they display the good taste and cultural sophistication of their owners to the owners' guests.

The notecards, wall calendars, and coffee table books all reveal TCM's goal of migrating their audience's engagement with classic film from spectatorship to "the stylization of life," to borrow Max Weber's phrase.[60] To that end, they also now publish a classic film cookbook, *Turner Classic Movies: Movie Night Menus—Dinner and Drink Recipes Inspired by Films We Love* (2016). The titular "We" includes the reader with sibling authors Tenaya and André Darlington in culinary cinephilia. Organized chronologically from *The Divorcée* (Robert Z. Leonard, 1930) through *Moonstruck* (Norman Jewison, 1987), the Darlingtons' cookbook offers thirty menus paired with movies that feature "rousing food and drink scenes," such as the many parties that make up *The Divorcée*.[61] For that film, the Darlingtons recommend Clover Club Cocktails and Beet Red Devil Cake with Chocolate Frosting.[62] The combination isn't bad, actually, but the concept behind it—

using a television network to curate one's meals around classic film—reveals how far TCM has deviated from its original network mission. The company's new agenda is articulated on the cookbook's back cover, next to a prominent TCM logo: "Turner Classic Movies is the definitive resource for the greatest movies of all time. We engage, entertain, and enlighten to show how the entire spectrum of classic movies, movie history, and movie-making touches us all and influences how we think and live today."[63] The company *engages*, *entertains*, and *enlightens*, actions which might include but are in no way limited to *presenting*, *broadcasting*, and *historicizing*. Cinephilia, it seems, is no longer merely a way of appreciating film but a way of living it.

All of the products described in this section are currently available for sale in TCM's annual catalog or online at the official TCM Shop. Launched in 2012, the Shop sells both TCM-branded goods and a wide array of additional merchandise to help consumers "Make It a Movie Night with TCM."[64] Conspicuous among the many goods sold under this imperative are "TCM Exclusive" apparel and home goods. These include T-shirts, sweatshirts, and baseball caps, all sporting a TCM logo, as well as a TCM blanket, TCM Scene Notes candles, TCM coffee mugs of various styles, stemless wineglasses etched with the TCM logo, a TCM wine charm set, and a TCM cocktail shaker set. The blanket, which allegedly retails for $219.95 but seems to be perpetually on sale, is made of 100 percent wool and bears only a discreet corner logo to associate it with TCM. The rest of the TCM Exclusive products are, shall we say, less restrained. Even the TCM Cinema Salt features the network's name and logo prominently—far more prominently than those of its actual producer, Beautiful Briny Sea. To be sure, the TCM Shop also sells unbranded merchandise, such as the hats, jewelry, and other accessories chosen to extend its popular "Noir Alley" and "Mad About Musicals!" screening series. The site also helps shoppers celebrate the holiday season with a variety of TCM Christmas tree ornaments and other yuletide gifts (figure 15).

All the myriad branded and unbranded products for sale in the TCM Shop emphasize class refinement through film(-related) consumption. Buying TCM goods, one buys into a taste culture, which means into a specific set of social fantasies and aspirations. TCM's lifestyle products promise consumers social distinction so that others will recognize the TCM logo and understand its bearer to be culturally refined and affluent.

The degree to which TCM monetizes its network reputation to sell this dream is in itself noteworthy. Most television stations merchandize their intellectual properties, rather than the network brand. Hence

FIGURE 15. Turner Classic Movie's 2017 Holiday Gift Suggestions. Photo courtesy of TCM. TM & ©2017 Turner Classic Movies. A Warner Media Company. All Rights Reserved.

AMC, TCM's original rival, sells merchandise connected to its proprietary series, including *Breaking Bad* (AMC, 2008–2013) and *The Walking Dead* (AMC, 2010–), but no AMC merchandise.[65] The same is true of HBO. Among TCM's perceived merchandising peers—which Dorian identifies as HGTV and the Food Network—the former has no merchandise enterprises and merely offers a list of "our editors' shopping tips and product recommendations" while the latter partners with Kohl's on cookware, dinnerware, and kitchen accessories sold only at Kohl's.[66] The only network monetizing its reputation in a manner similar to TCM is the Public Broadcasting Service (PBS), which extends its bookish cultural capital to compensate for ever-decreasing government support. Unlike TCM, however, PBS sells both PBS-branded merchandise and programming tie-ins (when it owns a show's merchandizing rights).[67] TCM does not have merchandizing rights to any of the films it exhibits, not since Turner Broadcasting was purchased by Time Warner in 1996. Therefore, the only brand it has to market is its own. Remarkably, that brand has become the umbrella for a wealth of even stronger, more recognizable properties: all of the films that play on TCM. Selling books, soundtracks, and DVDs helped TCM establish itself as a knowledgeable curator of film history, as more than just a channel delivering content. Its forays into branded merchandise encouraged viewers to identify as fans of the network's curatorship, to affirm the values that curatorship conveyed—indeed that it conveyed any values at all.

Thus, it is partially through its branded merchandise that TCM managed to produce the autonomous brand identity that it now further monetizes through consumer experiences, subscription services, and travel enterprises.

CLASSIC FILM AS CONSUMER EXPERIENCE

Marketing experts define *consumer experiences* as lived encounters with a particular brand, which helps explain how TCM's live events build on its earlier merchandizing initiatives. Consumer experiences also strengthen brand reputation and customer loyalty while opening up new revenue streams. However, TCM's consumer experiences reveal tensions within the brand's values, specifically between its emphasis on community and its investment in social distinction and private property. These conflicts are particularly noticeable at the TCM Classic Film Festival and the biannual TCM-Bonhams memorabilia auction. TCM bills its Classic Film Festival as "a place where a community of movie fans of all ages can share their love of classic movies with each other," but it is also an extended commercial for TCM.[68] Launched in 2010 at the Los Angeles Roosevelt Hotel, where it still resides, the festival celebrates both "the history of Hollywood and its movies" and TCM's "loyal and passionate fan community."[69] As festival programmer Genevieve McGillicuddy explained, TCM envisioned the festival as a benevolent gesture: "let's build a place where our fans [can] come together and continue to foster that community."[70] To determine whether and how TCM fans understand themselves as a community would require an ethnography beyond the purview of this chapter. More germane to this industry study is understanding how TCM's consumer experiences craft a glamorous idea of *brand* community that serves the company's financial interests. Community is not intrinsically a commercial value, and yet the idea of community is very valuable to TCM, even if it is ultimately at odds with the individualism of private property sales.

Held every April, the TCM Classic Film Festival screens between fifty (in 2010) to eighty-seven (in 2018) feature films over a four-day period and includes lectures, historical presentations, team trivia games, and staged conversations with famous actors, critics, filmmakers, and their children. Access to "talent" was key to the festival's initial appeal and its subsequent success. Attended by celebrities Esther Williams, Angelica Huston, Jean-Paul Belmondo, Jon Voigt, and Alec Baldwin (the cohost of TCM's series *The Essentials*), the 2010 festival offered attendees a novel chance to glimpse and, to a lesser extent, mingle with Hollywood stars. Such opportunities included celebrity appearances at the opening night gala, a book signing by Tony Curtis, and of course the screenings themselves; *Vanity Fair* called it "Comic-Con for the Martini Set."[71] Social mixers like the trivia contest also encouraged attendees to treat the festival as a chance to see and be seen by others who share their passion. And what a lot of seeing it was; TCM sold over two thousand festival passes in 2010, for $500 to $1,200 apiece.

Who can afford to see and be seen at TCM consumer experiences has been an issue since the first festival was announced on November 4, 2009. That same day, Miss Goddess posted to a TCM-sponsored discussion forum, "I hope I can go! I'll have to save my pennies."[72] She was not alone. Over the next few days, many forum members expressed hope that the festival would be affordable and fear that it would not be. When the pass prices were announced later that week, Kyle in Hollywood commiserated with other dismayed fans: "They're stuck in my throat now too."[73] Fans compared TCM's festival prices unfavorably to similar media events, particularly Disney's D23 Expo (an annual fan convention launched the year before). One lzcutter quipped, "I keep hoping those prices quoted in the press release are a typo."[74] When some discussants referenced the ongoing recession, others chastised them for being ungrateful; "I think TCM is generous enough as it is showing COMMERCIAL FREE movies 24 hours a day," michaelb4 insisted. "So now TCM has an opportunity to generate some revenue they should charge whatever they want."[75] This debate signaled a confusion among viewers and arguably among TCM staff about the goal of the network's consumer experiences: were they to be inclusive fan gatherings or for-profit enterprises? They could be both, of course, but which did the company value more?[76]

The considerable cost of attending a TCM Classic Film Festival reaffirms brand values around taste and class that were already manifest in other products. Through its marketing, print guides, and high-end housewares, TCM associates its brand with Hollywood glamour and a cultivated appreciation for film history. These are not democratic principles; to paraphrase Bourdieu, they are fundamentally tied to class hierarchy and distinction. Were the festival less expensive—and thus less exclusive—TCM could not maintain the same aura of glamour around the event and by extension the network. For as Erin Hanna reminds us, "Exclusivity is not actually defined by presences at all, but by the power to produce absences."[77] By 2013, festival reporters were beginning to notice physical manifestations of exclusivity and class distinction at the event. These included barricades set up between the bustle of Hollywood Boulevard and the red carpet of TCM's opening night gala, "dividing Hollywood as it chooses to present itself from Hollywood as it actually is."[78] That distinction (in the Bourdieuian sense) is central to TCM's curatorship and the consumer experiences it creates. In 2017, the *New Yorker* ran an eight-page graphic article commenting on the festival as fantasy space, more Hollywood than Hollywood itself. Written and illustrated by Mimi Pond, the report begins by placing the festival within the "tawdry carnival of souls" populating Hollywood Boulevard.[79] It is because Hollywood Boulevard is crammed with souvenir shops, Spider-man impersonators, and wax museums that that the TCM festival feels like an oasis of real film appreciation. It feels cultured and elite in contrast to the crass commercialism outside, and it must maintain this distinction to affirm the value of the network and by extension the value of TCM-branded goods.

When I went to the festival in 2019, its tenth consecutive year in operation, I found the event imperatives for distinction and community to be in tension with each other and with the films themselves, which were also in tension with the branding imperative of the conference. When I arrived at the Roosevelt at noon on Thursday, the community was already in full swing, even though the festival ostensibly did not begin until 1 p.m. and the first screenings would not begin until 6:30 that evening. TCM Backlot, the network's subscription fan club, was hosting a trivia contest wherein attendees could win company swag for knowing things like which Hollywood movie was the first to be released on VHS.[80] At the trivia contest, I picked up an official Backlot ribbon to attach to my festival lanyard. Ribbons would turn out to be a major festival theme; alongside TCM-sponsored lapel pins and homemade buttons, they served as badges of attendance and participation—which is not exactly the same thing as community. The community ostensibly convened at Club TCM, a bar and function room accessible only to pass holders.[81] At Club TCM, one could buy refreshments; peruse posters from past TCM festivals; admire costumes from classic film productions, including Darth Vader's uniform from *Star Wars* (George Lucas, 1977); and participate in scheduled panels like "Meet TCM," "The Descendants: Growing Up in Hollywood," and "The Complicated Legacy of *Gone with the Wind*." At all of these events, focus was on the guests of honor; *community* meant the chance to be in the same room with people who'd known or written about people you'd admired on screen. Sharing space is not the same thing as forging bonds, however, either with other festivalgoers or with guests of honor. While festival-goers often struck up conversations with each other and TCM staff while in line for various events, the guests of honor were mostly there to be seen, not engaged. Distinction came from having been near those who had been near the stars: a kind of cultural capital by proximity.

With all the emphasis on queuing, communing, and celebrity sighting, however, the movies themselves came to feel relatively marginal to the festival itself. One of the best parts of any film festival is discovering movies one might not otherwise seek out, but at the TCM Classic Film Festival, discovery took a backseat to familiarity and nostalgia. On Friday afternoon, for example, I found myself choosing between *Raiders of the Lost Ark* (Steven Spielberg, 1981), the Cary Grant–Irene Dunne comedy *My Favorite Wife* (Garson Kanin, 1940), F. W. Murnau's *Sunrise: A Song of Two Humans* (1927), the Sidney Poitier melodrama *A Patch of Blue* (Guy Green, 1965), and *Broadway Danny Rose* (Woody Allen, 1984). Given the target market for this festival—regular TCM viewers and other classic film fans—I think it's fair to say that no one was unfamiliar with these titles; if they hadn't seen the movie itself, they were at least acquainted with its director or stars. The festival's selections were almost all American and almost all commercially produced; with the exception of one Cinerama screening and two nitrate prints, they were exhibited via conventional digital platforms and film formats. TCM's was not a celebration of hard-to-find or rare classics, then; instead, the programming seemed designed to reward festival-goers for their extant knowledge of film history, to make them feel good about what they already knew and loved. Boundaries were not pushed; all of the films screened affirmed TCM's inclusive, feel-good approach to Hollywood history.

Needless to say, that feel-good approach was also for sale at the festival Boutique, a pop-up shop within a nearby candy store. In addition to festival T-shirts, tote bags, shopping bags, backpacks, keychains, and water bottles, there was a slew of discreetly branded TCM gear—such as suitcases, dopp kits, makeup bags, and shot glasses—as well as overtly branded TCM gear: travel mugs, wine stoppers, film journals, refrigerator magnets, even a children's book, Jennifer Churchill's *Movies Are Magic* (2018). The Boutique also carried merchandise from previous festivals, still at full price. Every time I stopped by the Boutique, it was doing brisk business, although it took me a while to find it; there was only one ad for the shop, on a four-page fold-out in the print program guide. The TCM wines, on the other hand, were very well marketed, particularly the 2019 TCM Classic Film Festival Cabernet Sauvignon and a 2017 Marx Brothers White Blend. Tabletop signs for both were littered around the Roosevelt's various bars. So were TCM Wine Club coasters that promised to help you "find a delicious co-star for your favorite film." That costar was always TCM; whether you came to the festival to meet fellow fans or catch glimpses of the stars, see movies or buy books about seeing movies, TCM was the ubiquitous paratext overshadowing every text.

In contrast, TCM-Bonhams' biannual auctions focus participants' attention on consumption as experience, so much so that community becomes a function of consumption. In 2012, Bonhams began offering free memorabilia appraisal sessions for pass holders at the TCM film festival.[82] In 2013, the companies held their first joint auction. Like appraisal sessions, auctions establish unique social relationships between consumers and the goods or services involved. As opposed to posted price sales (i.e., normal shopping), auctions are inherently competitive. If a mango is for sale for $1, whoever reaches it first will get to buy it at the advertised price, regardless of the number of other people who want to buy it. But at an auction, everyone interested in the mango will have the opportunity to bid on it, with the mango going to the highest bidder.[83] Some auction theorists hold that auctions adhere to a private value model, wherein each bidder operates according to their personal assessment of the object's worth. Others suggest that bidders follow a correlated values model, wherein a bidder's assessment of an object's worth is influenced by other bids. As René Girard observes, desire is contagious, and auctions rely on the social transmission of desire to earn more for their sellers.[84] Thus auctions are intrinsically social even as they affirm the principles of private property.

This tension—between social exchange and private property—defines TCM auctions and the role they play in realizing TCM as a lifestyle brand. The competition of auction creates a sense of community around valuing film memorabilia while also fostering a sense of exclusivity, as there are only so many items for sale and not everyone can leave a winner. In his introduction to the catalog for TCM's first auction, "What Dreams Are Made Of," Robert Osborne explains its mission as equally rooted in individualism and egalitarianism: to "make pieces of classic movie history available to one and all."[85] Osborne's introduction emphasizes sales to private individuals, as it evokes tangible traces of bygone productions simply passing from one caretaker to another. Individuals are not the only parties interested in movie memorabilia, however; libraries, museums, and archives are also frequent buyers. Their presence affirms that the logic of the TCM-Bonhams auction is collecting, with all its aristocratic associations. Yet in a television promo for the 2013 auction, Bonhams' director of entertainment memorabilia, Dr. Catherine Williamson, explains that "collecting memorabilia is different from other collecting disciplines in the sense that it's a really democratic collecting field."[86] Here Williamson uses "democratic" as a euphemism for affordable and to belie the elitism inherent to high-end auctions like "What Dreams Are Made Of." Williamson points to costume sketches as a relatively affordable memorabilia category for the budget-minded collector. The 2013 auction catalog estimated most costume sketches would sell for between $300 and $1,000, but all went well above that. Meanwhile a lead statuette that was used in the production of Huston's *The Maltese Falcon* went for $4,085,000.[87] To be fair, Williamson did warn promo viewers that the statuette would be "an incredibly expensive piece."[88] Yet its prominent position in the catalog and subsequent press coverage affirmed the glamorous and exclusive aura around Bonhams, TCM, classic Hollywood, and the TCM brand community.

As Vivian Sobchack points out in her essay on Huston's *Maltese Falcon* and its various material manifestations, aura is central to the value accorded film memorabilia—and thus to the allure of memorabilia in TCM's consumer experiences.[89] As defined by Walter Benjamin, aura refers to a work of art's unique fixity in time and space. Movie memorabilia is not necessarily unique—there are many Maltese Falcons, as Sobchack details—yet memorabilia's appeal is deeply tied to the premise and promise of aura.[90] Memorabilia—especially props and other production-related ephemera—promise to capture film's evanescence in a tangible, fungible form. As Sobchack explains, production ephemera "may serve some as a substitute for touching the *film* and inhabiting its dream."[91] Like all objects of desire, memorabilia obtain value from the ideas people project onto them. Like all commodity fetishes, they obscure social relations to serve the fantasies of capital. Nowhere is that clearer than in TCM's auction of what would become the most expensive prop in the history of movie memorabilia. As mentioned, there are many Falcon statuettes in existence, only some of which allegedly appeared in Huston's film. The particular statuette in TCM's inaugural auction happened to be the only one confirmed by Warner Bros. as appearing on screen.[92] Prior to the TCM auction, the bird belonged to a private individual, Dr. Gary Milan, who loaned it to the Warner Bros. studio museum on occasion.[93] At the TCM auction on November 25,

2013, it was purchased by another private individual, Steve Wynn. It has not appeared publicly since.[94]

As social as the process of auction might be, its goal is typically the transfer of private property. When the property in question is film memorabilia, such transfers endorse fantasies of public art becoming private collectibles. Own the bird and you own the film; so the logic goes, except that no amount of money will ever make the movie private again.[95] There are countless video copies of *The Maltese Falcon* circulating all over the globe, so even Warner Bros. cannot cage the *Falcon* anymore. Nevertheless, Steve Wynn purchased the right to put *his* bird in a cage, to keep it from the community whose desire affirmed its value. Osborne is correct that the TCM auctions bring fans together to "make pieces of classic movie history available to one and all," but the bidders so assembled are neither all for one nor one for all. They are temporarily united for a limited public exchange of private property then re-atomized as they rush home with their treasures or their disappointments. Thus, the famed "winner's curse" of the ascending-bid auction (which holds that bidders only triumph by paying a price everyone else thought exceeded the object's value) is in fact a shared curse. Often, public observance of the object's value exists only as a hinge between two phases of private ownership. In that brief appearance, however, the object shores up the value of other concepts to which it is attached—e.g., *The Maltese Falcon*, classic film, and Turner Classic Movies as "the destination" for classic film and classic film memorabilia. Via such projections, TCM makes its consumer experiences meaningful for the brand; they attach the brand to deeply held desires and beliefs about social distinction that exceed the event itself.

DRINK IT UP!

As consumer experiences, the TCM Classic Film Festival and the TCM-Bonhams biannual auction are both instances of event-based brand activation, but brand activations do not have to unfold as live, in-person events. They can transpire in a consumer's very own home, as in the case of TCM's online and delivery subscription services. These experiential marketing initiatives also make TCM a part of its consumers' lifestyle by expanding their connections with the brand beyond advertising, sales, and programming. TCM has developed a range of subscription-based brand activations, including but not limited to free Massive Open Online Courses (MOOCs) and the TCM Wine Club.

Individually and in aggregate, these services make TCM a part of their subscribers' way of life; they constitute TCM-sponsored cinephilia as a way of being in the world.

The MOOCs and the Wine Club extend TCM's brand values and identity in ways its merchandizing and consumer experiences cannot. The MOOCs, for instance, affirm TCM's as a free service for movie fans—a misguided impression, but one the network works hard to bolster. As mentioned, crucial to TCM's initial branding was the promise to broadcast movies "uncut and commercial-free" twenty-four hours a day. "Uncut and commercial-free" was never the same thing as free— cable viewers always paid for their subscriptions, after all—but TCM still positions its expertise as *freely given* to fans alongside the movies it programs. *Free* is in tension with *exclusive* and *glamorous*, of course, but not entirely so, as TCM demonstrates through its MOOCs. After online education began to attract mainstream media attention around 2014, TCM became interested in offering complimentary courses to its fans.[96] On June 1, 2015, TCM launched its first MOOC, TCM Presents Into the Darkness: Investigating Film Noir, taught by Ball State professor Richard Edwards via the Canvas Network's learning management platform. Timed to coincide with the network's Summer of Darkness film noir screening series, the course was a massive success, leading to three subsequent online courses. Through such experiential marketing, TCM was able to move into a new field—education—and increase viewership while affirming their service as free and selling more TCM goods.

The TCM MOOCs developed out of a serendipitous combination of personal friendships and corporate partnerships, all of which were served by extending the TCM brand and its reputation for classic film curation. The process began when TCM's director of business development, Shannon Clute, reached out to Edwards, a former colleague.[97] Clute and Edwards met as assistant professors at St. Mary's College in Los Angeles; they worked together on the film criticism website and podcast *Noircast* between 2005 and 2012 and coauthored a book, *The Maltese Touch of Evil: Film Noir and Potential Criticism* (2011). Edwards then joined the Division of Online and Distance Education at Ball State University while Clute transitioned to TCM. The Canvas Network was already one of Ball State's institutional partners when Clute reached out to Edwards, and the triumvirate partnership offered beneficial synergy to all three brands: new audiences and brand extensions for TCM and Ball State and a high-profile promotional opportunity for Canvas.[98]

Clute and Edwards codesigned Into the Darkness as a nine-week survey of film noir with a careful balance of information and entertainment, rigor and concision. As Edwards explained to me, he and Clute always understood TCM's MOOCs as being general education for adult learners. They are not part of any degree-granting program, and yet Edwards tries to ensure that each course has "just enough meat for those who have a background in film," without becoming pedantic.[99] Edwards organizes the MOOCs' content into what he calls "snackable" segments, although "the question becomes . . . how do you make something snackable that has any sort of heft to it? How does it not just become a sugary confection that you almost instantly forget?"[100] The answer, Edwards found, is to replace video lectures with recorded conversations, exams with games and quizzes, and graded writing assignments with discussion forums that emphasize peer learning. In this fashion, Edwards ensures that "any single day is only fifteen to twenty minutes of mental exercise," or "the time it takes to drink a cup of coffee."[101] TCM students are thus able to integrate film education into their lifestyles, to experience it as complementary to their daily rhythms rather than placing stress on them.

Into the Darkness was a hit with students and for TCM. 20,603 people enrolled in the course, although only 14.1 percent passed (in a year when most MOOCs averaged a 15 percent completion rate).[102] TCM was delighted to have an "immersive class that's driving people to the programming."[103] So they repeated the initiative with courses on slapstick comedy, the films of Alfred Hitchcock, and the musical genre. The 2018 Mad About Musicals! MOOC was TCM's most successful yet, with 26,107 students enrolling and 5,103 completing the curriculum. As Steven Denker, TCM's senior director of marketing, informed me, "Course engagement . . . increased week over week ending at 69.8 percent."[104] But coordinating course content and network programming schedules was a challenge, as TCM's corporate needs must sometimes trump instructors' pedagogical preferences.

When choosing what media to teach, a professor is always limited by physical and financial access, but TCM's MOOC instructors are further limited by broadcasting rights, because ultimately the network—not the student—is the MOOC's true client. To plan Mad About Musicals!, Professor Vanessa Theme Ament (a colleague of Edwards's at Ball State) provided the network with a list of American musicals that she considered important, after which TCM investigated the broadcasting and streaming rights for various films.[105] About three months before the course was set to begin, Ament received an inventory of "films that are almost guaranteed to be a part" of the course because they are "perennial favorites of the network" (titles TCM knew it could license affordably and its viewers would tune in for).[106] But like all TCM MOOC instructors, Ament did not learn exactly which films TCM would broadcast during her course—the films from which she could take clips and frame grabs—until six weeks before the course started. This arrangement might seem to put the cart before the horse, but in fact it reveals programming to be the horse and the course the cart. For the goal of every brand extension is to strengthen the brand and increase revenue— and organizing a course around TCM programming helpfully pushes students to watch more TCM. (Indeed, Ament and her students repeatedly live-tweeted course-related broadcasts to encourage viewing.)

As it did for Edwards's original film noir MOOC, TCM found many additional ways to monetize the Mad About Musicals! theme: with the accessories, hats, coffee table books, and other consumer goods collected in the Mad About Musicals! Boutique.[107] None of these items explicitly cited a film from the syllabus, as TCM had not licensed merchandizing rights. Instead, they visually evoked iconic musicals from the course, such as *The Music Man* (Morton DaCosta, 1962) and *Cabaret* (Bob Fosse, 1972). Thus, its MOOCs contribute directly to TCM's sales revenue and further enhance viewers' engagement with the brand. The synergy among films chosen for Mad About Musicals!, the structure of the course, and its product tie-ins all encourage consumers to engage holistically with the course theme, to extend their experience of it across all aspects of their lives. Take the TCM Melody: Chainmail Statement Necklace, for instance, a bib-style bronze-colored piece available at the TCM shop for $78 (figure 16).[108] TCM claims that its "bold statement . . . channels the iconic musicals of the 1970's"—but not any musical in particular. Specifying a film might violate its copyright and challenge the TCM brand. In theory, wearing the necklace might broaden my experience of being a TCM MOOC student, TCM shopper, and classic film fan. It should express my participation in those taste cultures, regardless of whether anyone else associates it with those groups. In practice, it's just a necklace; nothing about its design particularly recalls 1970s musicals (although it does really jazz up a T-shirt and jeans). Like all souvenirs, it demonstrates how the "personal operates within contemporary consumer society"—that is, as a reason to shop.[109] My souvenir accessory expresses my personal taste and places it in conversation with the wider world, in this case, a world organized by TCM.

FIGURE 16. My TCM Melody: Chainmail Statement Necklace commemorates but does not visually invoke TCM's Mad About Musicals! MOOC. Photo by author.

TCM's Wine Club also activates the brand's values beyond their original purview, bringing subscribers into regular contact with an intoxicating reinterpretation of classic film as class distinction. In an October 2015 press release announcing the formation of the franchise, Dorian argued that because "TCM at its core is a curator of movies," the new brand extension was a natural expression of the network's taste making powers and its mission "to bring our fans additional classic film lifestyle experiences." TCM, she claimed, was "an authentic source for wine and movie parings."[110] What *authentic* might mean in such a context is a mystery; why TCM might want the licensing fees from Laithwaithe's Wine and Wines That Rock, LLC is easier to understand. Following an initial shipment of fifteen bottles for $79.99 (plus tax and $19.99 shipping and handling), club members agree to buy another twelve bottles every three months for $149.99 (plus taxes and fees). A few of these bottles—three in the initial shipment—will be "collectible movie-themed wines."[111] When I joined the club in summer 2019, my collectibles were the *Sunset Boulevard* 2015 Old Vine Zinfandel, a Marx Brothers Red Blend, and a Dean Martin Signature Selection red blend.

The other twelve bottles came from vineyards unknown to me but included many popular red and white varietals.

When I interviewed Dorian in June 2018, she admitted that, "It's not the greatest wine . . . the wine is fine. The wine is absolutely fine."[112] At roughly $15 a bottle—$7 for the starter shipment—it certainly isn't expensive. But it's also mediocre at best. A relative who works in the wine industry informed me that wine clubs, like airlines, make money by buying up lesser-quality vintages and rebranding them as exclusives. This works because the real appeal of the TCM Wine Club is not the wine but the sense of belonging to a refined and exclusive taste culture. The wines themselves are almost beside the point, which may be why it's difficult for subscribers to learn what they'll be receiving in advance.

Denker insists that the wine club is not simply a tie-in opportunity for the network but a way of "meeting fans where they're at."[113] The geographic metaphor extends the destination trope in TCM's marketing discourse and, crucially, places responsibility for TCM's cross-marketing with the fans, who are allegedly looking for ways to unite their tastes in wine and film. To that end, almost all of the vintages in a TCM wine club shipment come with a tasting note that recommends a film to consume along with the wine. As one might expect, the connections are tenuous; the notes offer lighthearted readings of the films and wines but do not cultivate synesthesia or consider the benefits of inebriated spectatorship. One TCM tasting note matches the Silver Puffs Sauvignon Blanc with Ernst Lubitsch's *The Shop Around the Corner* (1940), noting that a key plot twist in the film hinges on a red carnation in "a nice parallel" to the art on the bottle. Another note pairs *North by Northwest* with Ridgerider Cellars' 2016 Chardonnay because the former "has it all . . . action, comedy, and romance" and the latter possesses "something for everyone—apple, pear, warm vanilla, and a hint of oak."[114] The democratic spirit behind this pairing recalls the broader tension between populism ("meeting fans where they're at") and class aspiration in TCM's brand values. It resolves the conflict, however, by leaving open the possibility that while everyone might enjoy these things, only some do. By pairing wine with film, TCM proffers a correct—or at least superior—approach to consuming both of these commodities, thereby reaffirming cultural distinction through drink.

TCM's collectable movie-themed wines are a slightly different story, in as much as they more explicitly read film through vino-culture. To explore this pairing process, I took my bottle of *Sunset Boulevard* zinfandel to a screening of *Sunset Boulevard* (Billy Wilder, 1950) at Cornell Cinema in Ithaca,

FIGURE 17. Bottled aspiration, also known as the TCM Wine Club's *Sunset Boulevard* 2015 Old Vine Zinfandel. Photo by author.

New York, in July 2018 (figure 17). The bottle advised that I "prepare to be seduced by its subtle violet scents and dark, black-and-blue-fruited heart." It did possess a bright, briary aroma reminiscent of raspberries, but its overall effect was rather tart. While juicy, the wine was also quite acidic; after a few glasses, my companion observed, "it tastes like aspiration." In that regard, it does have something in common with the protagonist of *Sunset Boulevard*, Joe Gillis (William Holden). A failed screenwriter, Gillis takes advantage of a demented former movie star (Norma Desmond, played by Gloria Swanson) to hide from his creditors. Gillis aspires to write a script someone will produce, Desmond to reclaim her former glory on the silver screen. They both want to attain or regain cultural capital—ambitions not dissimilar from those invoked by the TCM Wine Club.

To be fair, I would have been drinking a glass of wine at that screening whether TCM had chosen it for me or not. So what's the harm in TCM amusing its fans—and making some extra money—by promoting particular vintages to accompany its programming? The club members are happy (or their money back), TCM is happy (or at least prosperous), and if the whole deal reeks of exploitative brand extension, well, so what? Theater owners have been profiting off of concessions sales for decades, although moving the candy and popcorn trade into theater lobbies was critiqued as vulgar initially.[115] Several scholars have addressed the importance of food consumption to cinema viewing. Historian James Lyons notes that food occupies "a crucial role in organizing the experiential meanings of the cinema."[116] Amelie Hastie argues that food "can function to ground us between the material and immaterial conditions of film-viewing . . . and it also materializes (or perhaps mechanizes) our affective investment in what we see."[117] Hastie shows that such connections vary in strength depending upon the unique qualities of films, foodstuffs, and other contingencies of exhibition. TCM's Wine Pairings intervene on such contingencies, for better and worse. By telling viewers how to read a wine through a film and vice versa, they (attempt to) shape the viewer's material experience of movie spectatorship. The TCM Wine Club not only mechanizes but *monetizes* this component of the spectator's epistemological process. Promotional materials for the wine club suggest, quite explicitly, that these conjunctions cannot be left up to chance but should be curated, professionally even. If, as Hastie suggests, "food functions as a locating agent . . . locating our bodies in the social space of the cinema," then the TCM wines and their pairings extend our bodies into the network's branded universe.[118]

CLASSIC (MOVIE) TOURISM

Many scholars have argued that the physical arrangement of the viewer's body before a viewing device is part of the material and psychic apparatus of motion picture exhibition. So too is the movement of that body, including bodily movements away from screens and into worlds organized in reference to the screen. This principle clearly underwrites TCM's travel enterprises, which include movie-themed bus tours of New York City and Los Angeles, putatively movie-themed European vacations, and the TCM Classic Cruise. These tourism initiatives are extremely successful for TCM as they both make money and affirm the brand's power to activate "the movie experience" as a tourism heuristic. Whether encountering New York as a set(ting) for classic Hollywood or playing "Bingo with Ben" Mankiewicz (a TCM host) aboard a Disney cruise ship, TCM tourists move through the world as an expression of their identification with the network and its brand community. These travel enterprises are thus deeply material; they reappropriate the viewer's body *and the world around them* as media through which consumers can experience TCM's post-network interpretation of cinephilia as lifestyle.

Most TCM travel enterprises emphasize brand community over film spectatorship, but the bus tours at least teach viewers to see their cities as playgrounds of film history. The network began organizing these three-hour tours in 2013–2014 in partnership with On Location Tours (in Manhattan) and Starline Tours (in Los Angeles) to celebrate its twentieth anniversary.[119] The New York tour includes the Empire State Building ("featured in *King Kong*") and Grand Central Terminal ("seen in *North by Northwest* and *Superman*" [Richard Donner, 1978]) as well as a ride through Central Park and past the Plaza Hotel, FAO Schwarz, and Tiffany's.[120] The Los Angeles tour takes place aboard a custom-built bus with a sixty-five-inch television screen; guests watch clips from dozens of movies shot around town as they pass relevant filming locations, some of which are no longer recognizable as such. For instance, a school now stands where the Ambassador Hotel once hosted Benjamin and Mrs. Robinson's secret rendezvous in *The Graduate* (Mike Nichols, 1967). Other locations are still recognizable—such as the house where Dom Toretto (Vin Diesel) lives in *The Fast and the Furious* (Rob Cohen, 2001)—but less evocative of TCM's nostalgic vision of Hollywood history. When I went on the Los Angeles tour in 2019, I noticed how our guide rendered *classic film* a lens for interpreting the environment, a way of experiencing—and implicitly critiquing—contemporary LA. I used to live in the city, but personal referents faded as TCM taught me to regard familiar landmarks as film sets.

As tourism enterprises, the TCM bus tours expand the pedagogical mission of TCM's other brand activations by teaching their guests a localized approach to living as movie fans. TCM staff describe the New York tour as "another way to articulate the brand on a local level."[121] Even more than the film festival, the tours situate TCM in a regional film culture, giving it the sense of place it lacks as an internationally syndicated cable network. When asked, Robert Osborne held that the tours made the channel "more accessible" to viewers: "We're not just on the air. . . . We make the movie experience available to people."[122] Like "Let's Movie," however, what counts as "the movie experience" seems open for expansive interpretation—and the more expansion, the more profits. Thus, buying cookies at Zabar's serves as the tour's "accessible" extension of *Manhattan* (Woody Allen, 1979). Does eating sweets from a market featured in a movie count as part of that "movie experience," though? Or, put another way, what does "movie experience" mean if it *does* include shopping at a store featured in a movie?

TCM's international tours push this question even further. In April 2017, during a gap in its cruise service (about which more later), TCM announced that it would begin offering tours of Italy in partnership with Adventures by Disney. These six-day, seven-night TCM Destinations trips, which occurred in August 2017 and October 2018, included stops in Rome, Florence, and Venice and featured a range of Italianate activities, from private tours of the Sistine Chapel to pasta making at a Tuscan farm to mask making in a traditional Venetian workshop. If these pursuits do not sound particularly film-oriented, well, the trips also incorporate bus and pedestrian tours of the great cities, including some locations where films were shot—such as the Spanish Steps and the Ponte Vecchio, featured in *Roman Holiday* (William Wyler, 1953) and *A Room with a View* (James Ivory, 1986), respectively. In Rome, TCM guests also visit Cinecittà Studios for a tour and screening; the last event on the 2018 itinerary was dinner aboard the Jolly Roger, a reproduction Venetian galleon. As this Jolly Roger does not advertise any association with Captain Hook or Peter Pan, its connection to participants' "movie experience" is beyond me— although, to be fair, I was not able to take the tour.[123] Both the 2017 and 2018 tours nearly sold out, however, suggesting that TCM has convinced some consumers that "movie experience" refers to a way of life, a lifestyle, rather than an explicitly film-related occurrence or event.

That lifestyle isn't for everyone though. All of TCM's travel-based "movie experiences" are expensive and their marketing redolent of various forms of class exclusivity. *Exclusive, private*, and *luxury* recur regularly in marketing copy for its travel enterprises.[124] Thus it would seem that "movie experience" contains a specific class fantasy for TCM and its brand community. These trips reinterpret movie culture as highbrow and upscale, the terrain of cultural elites. But marking the movie experience as elite is ironic, given the medium's age-old, often derogatory association with mass culture. That being said, even as TCM's travel enterprises disavow the movies' historically democratic ethos, they reintroduce the historic sociality of cinema culture, albeit as a sociality based on luxury and taste hierarchies.

TCM's "movie experience" tourism thus mitigates the alienation of modern life in the same manner that Stanley Cavell attributes to cinema in *The World Viewed*. There he argues that movies present the world to us without allowing the world to see us watching; for Cavell, the "movie experience" is "not a wish for power over creation (as Pygmalion's was), but a wish not to need power, not to have to bear its burdens."[125] He expresses our desire to watch the world from the outside in a way that "makes our displacement appear as our natural condition" and masks from us our modern alienation.[126] Tourism can serve the same need. As Jonathan Culler notes, "tourism reveals difficulties of appreciating otherness except through signifying structures that mark and reduce it."[127] Package tours in particular recreate the collectivity of the audience, affirm the deserving specialness of that audience, and present the world for their edification and amusement. Hence a TCM tour need not strictly devote itself to a filmic theme to recreate for participants "the movie experience." Movies and tourism rely on a similar set of sign relations to affirm their viewer's relationship to the object(s) viewed. This includes affirming the viewer's right to look by marking the object looked upon as a spectacle, be it a spectacle of authenticity, local film culture, or both.

Given the importance of spectacle to TCM's version of the "movie experience," it should come as no surprise that TCM's most popular travel enterprise remains the TCM Classic Cruise. Introduced in 2011 only to be suspended in 2017 and reintroduced in 2019, the TCM Classic Cruise is a five- to seven-day oceanic excursion featuring all the onboard activities, ports of call, and shore activities one might expect of such a venture, plus an additional array of classic film screenings, talks, games, and other movie-themed diversions. TCM cruises were initially hosted by Celebrity Cruise Lines and departed from Miami, stopping at Key West, Grand Cayman, and Cozumel, among other islands. The first cruise (in December 2011) welcomed over eighteen hundred paying customers; special guests included Ernest Borgnine, Eva Marie Saint, Tippie Hedron, and of course Robert Osborne and Ben Mankiewicz.[128] The Alloy Orchestra was also onboard to accompany the Harold Lloyd feature *Speedy* (Ted Wilde, 1928). Tickets for the cruise ranged from just under $800 to nearly $2,500. In 2013, TCM began partnering with Disney Cruise Line, using a slightly smaller ship (the *Disney Magic*, which holds 1,754 passengers) for a slightly longer voyage (six days) at a slightly higher price point ($1,095 or more).[129] By 2016, the TCM Classic Cruise was taking place aboard the *Disney Fantasy* (which accommodates up to 4,000 passengers) over the course of seven days for $1,910 to $3,660 per person.[130]

Shortly before the 2016 cruise, TCM announced that they were retiring the event. No reason was given. The cruises had sold out every year, but the company may have been looking for greater profit margins on their travel enterprises. In our interview, Dorian acknowledged that the cruise was "very labor-intensive and expensive."[131] TCM's special guests also struggled with the demands of cruise life. As Dorian explained, "It's very hard for older talent to commit to being at sea for four or five days.

Or seven days." For all of these reasons, TCM found that they "couldn't really grow the business," which led them to abandon the venture in favor of lower-impact travel enterprises, such as the TCM Destinations tours.[132] But the mystique of the cruise endured, and in 2019, TCM revived their maritime venture. This time, I joined them.

On October 22, I set sail on TCM's eighth Classic Cruise: a six-day, five-night jaunt from New York to Bermuda and back. As one might expect, cruise programming included up to four movies playing simultaneously, plus daily events with TCM's hosts and special guests: Cicily Tyson, Mitzi Gaynor, Diane Ladd, and Leonard Maltin. There were also singles mixers, karaoke and trivia contests, author talks, and a wide variety of liquor tastings. The tastings boasted no overt connection to classic cinema, but they did contribute to the material culture of movie-themed cruising that TCM and Disney produce for their guests, one in which movies provide a theme for leisure and socialization but are not, in fact, an object of much focus. For it is difficult to concentrate on a film while simultaneously sipping Pinot Grigio in a hot tub, as I discovered during one midday screening of *Abbott and Costello Meet Frankenstein* (Charles Barton, 1948). Not that there was anything wrong with the outdoor screening system involved. But when the bubble jets are gurgling, the waitstaff circulating, and bathers shooting down a two-story waterslide just offscreen, one cannot immerse oneself in performance, narrative, or mise-en-scène. The longer I participated in cruise life, however, the more I understood that watching movies was not the point of a Turner Classic Movies cruise.[133] If a cruise can be said to have a point, then the point of the 2019 TCM Classic Cruise was brand community. Through its messaging, programming, and merchandising, TCM gave its cruisers the experience of being part of a cinematic elite: the true fans, the ones who *lived* their love of classic film completely, at least for five nights and six days.

Life as a TCM community member began the moment I stepped into my stateroom and encountered TCM's "exclusive gifts" to its "friends": an uncannily soft TCM Cruise–branded throw blanket and a TCM Cruise whiteboard. Guests were supposed to affix the latter to their stateroom door to identify their favorite classic movie, favorite "actor/actress," and the number of prior TCM cruises they'd attended—thereby positioning themselves within the community, I suppose. Many cruisers embellished their doors with magnets and photographs to further individuate their film tastes and enthusiasm for TCM. Additional TCM

Cruise merchandise—such as tote bags, beach towels, and baseball caps—was for sale at the various Disney boutiques onboard. I bought a cap the second morning of the cruise and was warmly saluted for it by total strangers. We had all been encouraged by Disney and TCM to pack costumes for the cruise's All Hallow's Eve party, and many cruisers eagerly complied. Group participation was, in sum, an important way of signaling one's enthusiasm for TCM, the cruise, and, tertiarily, classic film. Even when I attended screenings alone, as I often did, live commentary from the TCM hosts affirmed the value of collective viewing. Hence, host Alicia Malone introduced *Gentlemen Prefer Blondes* (Howard Hawkes, 1953) by recalling what it meant to her growing up in Australia, how she understood Dorothy and Lorelei's bond then and as a TCM employee now. Watching Malone's live introductions, I viscerally felt how important identity affirmation is to the experience TCM offers its customers; through consuming TCM goods, they claim membership in an exclusive (because marginal) community where they hope to feel less alone.

David Foster Wallace attributes the forced festivity of mass-market cruises to despair—or "the unbearable feeling of becoming aware that I'm small and weak and selfish and going without any doubt at all to die"—but I detected no fear of mortality aboard the TCM Classic Cruise, where it might have been quite prominent, given the network's preoccupation with Hollywood history and aging stars.[134] Wallace argues that cruises offer "various fantasies of triumph over . . . death and decay," a thesis uncannily similar to André Bazin's argument that cinema "embalms time, rescuing it simply from its proper corruption."[135] It would be easy to claim that a classic film cruise unites these two industries of death denial in a deluded frenzy of consumer empowerment. But as it happens, I simply didn't sense any such despair mitigation aboard the TCM Classic Cruise. I searched behind the tchotchkes, drinks, buffets, and dance parties for evidence that either TCM or its customers were disavowing their mortality. I never found any. Invoking mortality would certainly lend a desirable gravitas to this cruise report; it sure worked for Wallace and Bazin. But not all fantasies derive from denying death. The fantasy underwriting the TCM Classic Cruise was one of living and socializing around a stable, coherent, commodified identity. The cruise promised community recognition, which is not the same as immortality but is far easier to deliver, especially aboard a hermetically sealed resort floating in the middle of the Atlantic.

CONCLUSION

Reviewing the many merchandise and consumer experiences that TCM developed in their quest to become a lifestyle brand, it's easy to forget how much consumers love the brand, how much they value the services TCM provides. Scoff at the cheap wine, coffee table books, and scented candles—I certainly have—but remember that a lot of people buy them and love them. Fan enjoyment is unique from—although not incompatible with—corporate strategy, but this chapter has focused on the latter at the expense of the former in order to argue that TCM has become a lifestyle brand, rather than "just" a television network, and that the taste culture it creates through its commodities meaningfully impacts classic movie spectatorship in the twenty-first century. Over sixty million unique viewers accept TCM's invitation to "movie" every month, and many more expand that movie experience through branded merchandise, live consumer experiences, subscription services, and travel. This suggests that the TCM lifestyle brand does meaningfully enrich at least some viewers' lives. As Bourdieu observes, taste "transforms necessities into strategies, constraints into preferences"; it is part of "what [Max] Weber calls the 'stylization of life'" and as such is crucial to making sense of the world and one's place in it.[136]

Needless to say, TCM is not the first media company to try to commodify viewers' enthusiasm for motion pictures. Disney started licensing Steamboat Willy to children's writing tablets in 1929; the Ideal Novelty and Toy Company began selling Shirley Temple dolls in 1934; and then of course there is the ongoing merchandizing juggernaut of *Star Wars*. Notably, however, these franchises all revolved around specific film properties and stars.[137] By contrast, TCM has created a material reception practice around the *exhibition* of classic film. It is a small but incredibly important distinction. Whereas Steamboat Willie and Shirley Temple fans were purchasing notepads and dolls to express their affection for that character and actress, TCM fans are buying T-shirts, taking tours, and going on cruises to express their enthusiasm for a network, for classic film as delivered by TCM. The medium is the message, as McLuhan tells us, and in this case the object of affection.[138]

TCM's conversion to lifestyle brand has important and problematic implications for the future of classic film spectatorship. During the 1990s and early 2000s, when cable networks enjoyed their greatest market penetration in the United States, TCM competed with AMC, VHS, and later DVD to bring classic film fans the movies they wanted to see. During the late 2000s and 2010s, as cable subscriptions waned and physical media sales plummeted, TCM became one of the only networks devoted to classic film. It took advantage of this market position to consolidate its identity as the destination for classic film and strengthened that position by associating itself with related social values, such as exclusivity and glamour. When TCM introduced its own subscription video-on-demand service, FilmStruck, in 2016, it both responded to the lack of classic films on other popular services (particularly Netflix, Hulu, and Amazon Prime) and extended its version of cable era cinephilia into a new market. FilmStruck closed in November 2018, after AT&T bought WarnerMedia. Viewers, critics, and filmmakers all mourned its passing. Martin Scorsese, Steven Spielberg, Alfonso Cuarón, and Berry Jenkins were among the many auteurs to publicly entreat Warner Bros. Chairman Tony Emmerich to save FilmStruck, claiming that "without it, the landscape for film fans and students of cinema is especially bleak."[139] The *Washington Post*'s Ann Hornaday described the loss of FilmStruck as nothing less than "erasing cinema's history"—which it patently is not.[140] As I discuss in chapters 1 and 2, commercial video platforms construct distinct historiographies for their media that are always partial, contingent, and self-serving. Nevertheless, TCM has become the gatekeeper to Golden-Era Hollywood for many twenty-first-century media viewers. These viewers may not buy TCM merchandise, enroll in TCM MOOCs, or even watch movies on TCM, but TCM has nonetheless achieved ownership of the concept of classic film. It does so by framing classic film spectatorship as a branded material practice, rather than a personal encounter with cultural history.

It would be unfair to say that Turner Classic Movies is ruining classic film spectatorship when so many of their fans love the brand and its presentation of film history. If sales numbers are anything to go by, many viewers want their "movie experience" to include wines, bistro mugs, and bus tours. Their enthusiasm suggests that how film theorists frame motion picture spectatorship needs to change. In "Ideological Effects of the Basic Cinematographic Apparatus," Jean-Louis Baudry distinguishes between *l'appareil de base*, all of the material technology that goes into producing, distributing, and exhibiting a motion picture, and *le dispositif*, the viewing situation for a motion picture, which includes the material scene of viewing and the subject position that that scene and the film itself impose on the viewer.[141] TCM's various brand extensions have become part of *l'appareil de base* that allow the network to remain in business. They also form part of *le dispositif* for twenty-first-century classic film fans. Branded merchandise and experiential marketing now contribute to the "interrelationship between a technology, a specific film form with its mode of address, and a specific positioning of the spectator"—namely, post-network-era cinephilia.[142] By making itself a lifestyle—a lifestyle epitomized by the tagline "Let's Movie"—TCM organized a new psychic relationship of viewer to screen, a new mode of cinematic interpellation. With every cookbook and festival pass they sell, TCM teaches viewers how to be classic film fans in the world. They are not just manufacturing Christmas tree ornaments; they are manufacturing the future of Hollywood history.

CHAPTER 4

Spirits of Cinema

Alcohol Service and the Future
of Theatrical Exhibition

In June 2014, the president of the National Organization of Theater Owners (NATO) hailed alcohol sales as "the future" of film exhibition.[1] For many contemporary theater owners, beer, wine, and cocktails provide the added revenue necessary to keep the lights on—or off, as the case may be. Alcohol is currently featured on concessions menus at all kinds of exhibition spaces, from megaplexes to art houses, single-screen community theaters to rowdy neo-rep houses like the Alamo Drafthouse. This is surprising, because alcohol has a deleterious effect on human vision and cognition; the more you drink, the worse you are, physiologically, at watching movies.[2] However, concessions sales are a vital part of every exhibitor's business plan, and alcohol sales have proved incremental to (i.e., do not detract from) other concessions sales. Bringing alcohol into movie theaters changes how viewers understand cinema culture; it is part of a larger industrial trend toward framing moviegoing as an experience. Historically, theater owners have repeatedly used alcohol sales to court audiences and brand their distinctive approach to showing motion pictures. In recent decades, alcohol has helped exhibitors distinguish and cultivate taste communities and elevate their business—not artistically but economically. Who goes to the movies, why, and what it means to them is changing because of the material presence of alcohol in cinemas. Some twenty-first century theaters are rebranding moviegoing as a luxury while others rely on alcohol to invoke an underground or regionalist atmosphere or to attract particular viewer demographics.

Stage historians Christine Woodworth and Amy E. Hughes have documented the "thinly-veiled class-based anxieties that emerge when certain critics and audience members confront food in the auditorium."[3] Today, exhibitors continue to use alcohol to invoke and profit on social divisions in ways unprecedented by popcorn or candy.

Concessions are a relatively understudied component of cinema history, and focusing on adult concessions is more esoteric still.[4] But as Richard Maltby, Daniel Biltereyst, Philippe Meers, and other advocates of new cinema history have argued, film reception is about much more than movies and their makers. New cinema historians challenge the dominance of film- or production-based chronicles of cinema, implicitly following Douglas Gomery's precedent in *Shared Pleasures: A History of Movie Presentation in the United States*. There Gomery investigates the impact of industrial monopolies, labor practices, technological innovations, and, briefly, concessions sales on the business of film exhibition. Gomery reports that popcorn stands and candy machines were integrated into lobbies and auditoria to increase exhibitor revenue during the Great Depression, when financial necessity overcame class prejudices around eating at the movies.[5] His research and Maltby et al.'s disciplinary intervention provide the groundwork for this study of alcohol's effects on movie exhibition. Whereas the next chapter focuses on historical intersections of cannabis culture and televisual poetics, the way that some television series cultivate inebriated spectatorship to entice post-network viewers, this chapter focuses on how adult concessions are changing the material culture of film exhibition and the meaning of moviegoing. This project is overtly political, in that all histories of American drinking are mired in class and ethnic anxiety. How theater owners integrate alcohol into their businesses reflects important preconceptions about what they believe cinema to be, what role it plays in their audiences' lives, and who they want their audiences to be. Sometimes these suppositions clearly reflect class hierarchies and white privilege—as in the case of the contemporary cine-bistros—and sometimes they are more reflective of subcultural capital or ethnic stereotypes, as in the case of twenty-first-century neo-rep houses and the Big Three theater chains (AMC, Regal, and Cinemark). But collectively, the trend toward adult concessions is exacerbating cultural and socioeconomic divisions within US cinema culture. Few journalists or film scholars have attended to this shift, but the alcohol is nevertheless changing the spirit of cinema.

To illuminate how social suppositions have shaped both alcohol and concessions sales, this chapter begins by exploring alcohol's history in

US cinemas up to 1975, paying particular attention to the underappreciated role of saloons and taverns in early film culture and to drive-ins and repertory houses' reputation for illicit drinking in midcentury America. It was in 1975 that John and James Duffy opened their first Cinema 'N' Drafthouse outside of Orlando, Florida, inspiring a spate of imitators selling beer and wine at second-run theaters. Then, in 1989, Fred Schoenfeld opened the Commodore, the first first-run cinema in the United States to sell beer and wine. It took time, but Schoenfeld's precedent forever changed the culture around adult concessions in US cinema. Indeed, the Commodore inspired three distinct alcohol-driven exhibition trends. First, the boutique cine-bistro sells alcohol to offer viewers class distinction and an elite viewing experience. (For more on Pierre Bourdieu's theory of class distinction, see chapter 3.) Boutique cine-bistros use normatively white class markers to distinguish themselves from nearby multiplexes, even when their programming is exactly the same. Second, the neo-rep house creates a uniquely playful (if sometimes problematically masculinist) spectatorial atmosphere by pairing offbeat programming with easy access to alcohol. Such establishments invoke the principled curatorship of mid-century repertory cinemas but encourage intoxicated engagement with low-brow genres rather than sober reverence for classic Hollywood and international art films. Third, the corporate megaplex integrates alcohol as part of a standardization of luxury and the pursuit of specific audience demographics, particularly Latinx viewers. Together with reserved stadium seating and leather recliners, dine-in theaters and lobby bars have helped big theater chains rebrand their cinemas as deluxe entertainment destinations and court underexploited markets. Identity categories routinely direct commercial interests in contemporary marketing, but AMC's focus on Latinx audiences is particularly noteworthy here, because it associates ethnic identity with heavy drinking (or at least disproportionate spending on alcohol).

All three of these approaches to adult concessions reflect a significant change in the business of cinema. Once alcohol is on the menu, it effectively turns movie theaters into restaurants that happen to show movies. Every theater owner or programmer I spoke with affirmed that they had to prioritize food and beverage sales. Film was the lure that got customers in the door, but exhibition was not lucrative enough to be their sole priority. Most first-run theaters must return 60 to 90 percent of their ticket revenue to distributors.[6] But there's always money in the concession stand, so to speak—up to 85 percent of a cinema's revenues, in fact.[7] Consequently, cinema owners and managers pursue the audiences and the films that will help them sell as much food and drink as possible. They need viewers to approach films as accompaniments to their meals rather than treating concessions as optional enhancements to their movies. As Amelie Hastie contends (following Patricia Mellencamp), one can discern exhibitors' "expectations of and beliefs about various film-going practices" from the kinds of food they serve.[8] Like the meal service it is often paired with, alcohol both elevates and demystifies theatrical spectatorship by making it part of a larger, multisensory experience. Importantly, the food and booze that most cinemas serve—be it burgers and beer or flatbreads and wine—come with other strong cultural associations. In diverse but significant ways, they cultivate multisensory entertainment experiences that push viewers to understand moviegoing along a recreational spectrum.

Thus, I agree with NATO's president: alcohol is shaping the future of moviegoing in the United States. Whether or not you have ever snuck a beer into a drive-in or purchased a glass of wine at a cine-bistro, drinking has become a central component of American cinema culture. To believe otherwise is to perpetuate a fantasy about the solvency of US cinema that neither exhibitors nor viewers can afford. The material culture of adult concessions reflects and shapes the economics of that industry and the social politics of contemporary cinema.

LEARNING TO IMBIBE (AT THE) MOVIES

The US history of movie theater concessions begins with stage theater concessions, which begins with alcohol.[9] As theater historian George Overcash Seilhamer observed, American theater started "in taverns and taprooms."[10] Woodworth and Hughes further explain that these unsavory origins haunted theatrical concessions for centuries. From the 1840s on, temperance reformers sought to cleave theater from its inebriate past. They were particularly concerned about "consumption of food and drink . . . at venues that openly and proudly catered to immigrants and working-class audiences."[11] At times, their initiatives generated legislation, as when New York State passed an Anti-Concert Saloon Law in 1862 that forbade the sale of alcohol in any theaters.[12] Before that, both cheaper and more elite theaters regularly sold drinks "during shows and at intermission, and liquor was an integral facet of the urban entertainment scene."[13] Indeed, theatrical tipplers came from all walks of life, although reformers saw drinking as an ethnic and class assimilation issue.

When immigrant and working-class communities later produced ardent filmgoers, the same biases that plagued stage theater concessions also bludgeoned movie exhibitors. This may explain why concessions remain an unpopular topic among film scholars, for few have explored how tavern culture facilitated film's rapid popular rise. Some historians allege that early film was exhibited in saloons and taverns, but primary evidence to that effect is scant.[14] However, pre-cinema entertainments did thrive on proximity to public houses. Woodworth and Hughes note that "during the 1860s and 1870s, [vaudeville] impresario Tony Pastor . . . maintained a saloon next door to his theatre on the Bowery, which patrons could visit before or after performances and during intervals."[15] The addition of film to vaudeville programs did nothing to alienate such theaters from neighboring tap houses; as Cynthia Baron reports, "early on, nickelodeons were often located in close proximity to saloons."[16] Indeed, one of the most famous movie exhibitors in cinema history got his start in the back of a tavern, specifically the Freedman House in Forest City, Pennsylvania. Samuel "Roxy" Rothafel began tending bar at the Freedman House in 1907, in order to court the owner's daughter. When an event room in the rear of the tavern became available in 1908, Roxy developed a plan to turn it into "a mixed-use vaudeville theater and roller-skating rink."[17] On December 24, 1908, the Family Theatre began showing a combination of live vaudeville acts and motion pictures, with the Freedman House serving as "the de facto lobby of the theater."[18] In the years to come, Roxy would become the most important theater manager in the country, the visionary behind the movie palace phenomenon. In that important sense, then, the bright lights of US cinema were first lit in the back of a bar.

Despite Roxy's success at the Family Theatre, tavern culture and film culture would not mingle for long. Prohibition reframed cinemagoing as an abstemious, family-friendly pastime, an ideology to which many viewers still adhere. During the first decades of the twentieth century, temperance reformers continued to gain social and legal influence, culminating in the ratification of the Eighteenth Amendment to the Constitution in January 1919.[19] Filmmakers cashed in on the temperance movement with moralizing melodramas meant to educate immigrant and working-class viewers on bourgeois Anglo-American social expectations. Whereas once alcoholics were represented as harmless clowns, movies like *A Drunkard's Reformation* (D.W. Griffith, 1909), *Ten Nights in a Bar Room* (Oscar Apfel, 1921; Roy Calnek, 1926), and *The Curse of Drink* (Harry O. Hoyt, 1922) courted sober audiences.[20] As propaganda, they were highly effective; Robin Room of the Alcohol Research Group notes that "In 1915, the mayor of Seattle claimed that 'the films were directly responsible for influencing the people of the State of Washington to vote that State dry.'"[21] Historian Michael Aronson observes that "filmmakers hoped to appear ideologically aligned with reformers and thus gain the status and stature necessary to help separate their entertainment from other, less wholesome sites of leisure—particularly the neighborhood saloon."[22] Many temperance supporters expected that Prohibition would lead drinkers to spend more time engaging with their families in wholesome recreation—going to edifying films, for instance. Producers and exhibitors shared their dream; as industry reporter Bill Higgins explains, after the Eighteenth Amendment passed, "Hollywood thought that cinemas would be flooded with former bar patrons."[23] They weren't alone. Many merchants expected that after Prohibition Americans would spend the money they saved not drinking on food, clothes, and entertainment. None of that came to pass.[24] Instead, many people lost their jobs. Film exhibitors thus failed to see much if any boost in attendance, and the temperance film cycle quickly collapsed.[25] Audiences in the 1920s were more interested in fantasies of the drinking life: flapper and gangster movies in which the girls danced, the liquor flowed, and the bullets flew. Then came the Great Depression.

As Douglas Gomery and Andrew F. Smith explain, the Great Depression of 1929 altered exhibitors' attitudes toward in-house concessions because they needed to open new revenue streams to keep their businesses afloat.[26] Whereas theater owners previously shunned food and drink for lowering the class connotations of cinema—for being more reminiscent of the fairway than the opera hall—economic precarity robbed them of such pretensions. First came candy machines and then permanent lobby concession stands with popcorn, which would become Americans' quintessential movie snack.[27] Smith notes that "independent movie theaters"—those without the financial support of a parent studio—"were the first to capitulate to popcorn's financial allure."[28] Such arrangements saved many theaters from going under. In 1936, concessions sales totaled $10 million.[29] By 1949, Smith reports, exhibitors were reliant on concessions income, so much so that, as he puts it, "theaters were really in the popcorn business." Exhibitors were also beginning to notice that some films facilitated popcorn sales better than others. "Movies aimed at children" always increased concessions profits, particularly "Abbott and Costello comedies, while the worst were generated with horror films."[30] As audiences started spending more money on concessions, exhibitors could and did think about more than just star power in choosing films. Most never seriously considered adult concessions, but the rise in concessions culture still facilitated some early experiments in drinking at the movies—particularly at drive-in theaters.

During the mid-twentieth century, only a few US drive-in theaters ever sold beer, but that does not mean that drinking rarely happened at such venues. Rather, "ozoners," as they were known in the industry, provided opportunities for audiences to explore the pleasures of smuggling their own booze to accompany a picture. As alternatives to conventional hardtop first-run cinemas, drive-in theaters have been understudied, no doubt because their records are comparatively decentralized and fragmentary. However, anecdotal evidence suggests that viewers smuggled alcohol into these venues more often than their competition. Sodden reception at drive-ins—and repertory houses—inverts another illicit midcentury exhibition trend: unlicensed screenings in bars and taverns, where the drinks might (or might not) have been legal but the movies weren't. All of these venues were relatively peripheral to mainstream cinema culture at midcentury. However, they are crucial to any chronicle of cinema as experience, which is how exhibitors typically frame alcohol's integration into contemporary moviegoing.

Almost as soon as beer sales were legalized by Congress (on December 21, 1932), beer was on the menu at America's first drive-in theater. Richard Hollingshead Jr. opened the first Automobile Movie Theater, as it was known, in Pennsauken Township, New Jersey, on June 6, 1933.[31] One week later, its concession stand began offering "beer and lunches"—odd phrasing, since the drive-in was only open at night. Historian Kerry Segrave reports that Hollingshead sold alcohol "to reinforce the idea that a drive-in was a place to go and watch a movie, have a meal and a beer, things you couldn't do in an indoor theater."[32] Nevertheless, beer created considerable cultural challenges for the theater. Drunk driving had been illegal in New Jersey since 1906, so selling beer to people watching movies in their cars might not have gone over well with local police. No other drive-ins sold beer until 1950, when the Meands Drive-In outside Albany, New York gave it a shot "as part of an experiment to assess exhibitors' attitudes."[33] Meands sold 60,000 beers during this trial run, yet the initiative allegedly failed because "the family image of drive-ins worked against any widespread or easy access to alcohol at these theaters."[34] Prohibition may have ended, but popular opinion still rejected adult concessions at all-ages shows.

While drive-ins rarely sold alcohol, that does not mean that no one drank there. Both scholarly histories and popular reminiscences are rife with anecdotes of customers bringing their own drinks (usually beer) to the ozoner. Segrave quotes a 1950 *Saturday Evening Post* story about a husband and wife who nearly divorced because she wanted to go to the movies and he wanted to stay home and drink beer; sneaking beer into a local drive-in evidently saved their marriage.[35] Segrave also cites a few examples of budget-minded fathers bringing their own beer along for the family night out, suggesting that not everyone had a problem with adult drinks at an all-ages show.[36] In a 1976 reflection on drive-in culture, Andrew Horton celebrates "the crisp clink of beer cans hitting gravel" as a quintessential element of outdoor exhibition.[37] A similarly nostalgic "Flashback to the Drive-In's Heyday" in the *Chicago Tribune* includes multiple Windy City viewers who brought coolers of beer to the show— or cleaned up after those who did.[38] Films such as *Drive-In* (Rod Amateau, 1976), *Drive-In Massacre* (Stu Segall, 1976), and *American Drive-In* (Krishna Shah, 1985) also commemorate carousing and canoodling at outdoor theaters. Illicit histories are difficult to chronicle, however; the real teenagers whose exploits these films parody weren't exactly filling out audience surveys before they drove home. Nevertheless, the frequency with which historians and filmmakers allude to drunken drive-in antics verifies their significance in the US cultural imaginary.[39] Drive-ins faced immeasurable industrial and economic challenges in the twenty-first century (at least until the COVID-19 pandemic), but many of those that survive now sell alcohol, harnessing their old reputation for sodden spectatorship to entice contemporary viewers. Indeed, new drive-ins are actually opening with liquor licenses. The Coyote Drive-In of Fort Worth, Texas, and Doc's Drive-In in Buda, Texas, both launched in the 2010s with beer and wine available on site. These twenty-first-century ozoners have not solved the problems of exhaust fumes and obstructed views, but they have managed to repackage nostalgia for drinking at the drive-in as a solvent exhibition model.

Repertory theaters were also common sites for illicit inebriation at midcentury and became among the first theatrical models to embrace adult concessions. The first generation of US repertory houses opened in the mid- to late 1960s. Often but not exclusively located in urban centers, rep houses were where one went to see "films that rarely, if ever, appeared on the screens of the mainstream and art theaters," such as revivals of Hollywood's back catalog.[40] As cinema historian Ben Davis notes, such revivals had previously been "associated with the nonprofit film societies [and] membership clubs. . . . The repertory theaters, on the other hand, ventured into the commercial arena as for-profit versions of the nonprofit film societies. They were a rare undertaking that mixed art with commerce," including concessions.[41] Some sold only "dubious popcorn." Others, like the Charles Theater in New York City, gave free coffee to ticket holders.[42] None sold alcohol, but plenty were known for the drinking and drugging that went on inside. New York's Bleecker Street Cinema, for instance, was a notorious hangout for hippies, artists, and downtown scenesters who "were loud and boisterous and indifferent to rules."[43] The Charles was known for a "pungent aroma of marijuana that frequently wafted through the theater."[44] Midnight screenings were particularly notorious for being "perfumed" with cannabis, particularly at the Elgin, the New York rep house that invented the concept of midnight movies.[45] That said, illicit drinkers and pot smokers are about the only category of misbehaving patrons that Toby Talbot does *not* complain about in her memoir about running the New Yorker Theater. Whether this is because patrons never drank at the New Yorker or because Talbot happened to be more annoyed by "picknickers" [*sic*] with smelly food is anybody's guess.[46]

Rep houses were hit hard by the rise of home video in the 1980s, but profit margins were slim even before that. The New Yorker went out of business in 1973, the Bleecker in 1991. Most of the midcentury rep houses still in operation now sell alcohol to offset their operating costs. Hence one can now drink legally at the Quad Cinema in New York, the New Beverly in Los Angeles, and the Castro Theater in San Francisco (which became a rep house in 1976 when Mel Novikoff took over operations). The Brattle Theatre in Cambridge, Massachusetts, became a nonprofit and added adult concessions to keep its doors open in 2009. Many have also shifted their programming from the classic Hollywood and international art films that characterized their early years to a more eclectic range of titles, effectively transitioning to the neo-rep model explored later on in this chapter.

Rep houses also faced competition from underground screenings, which served as sites for not only illicit drinking but also illicit viewing. Their renegade spectatorial environments provided important precedents for certain adult concessions trends today. As opposed to underground films—meaning intentionally low-budget or rough-hewn avant-garde productions—underground screenings are unlicensed public or word-of-mouth exhibition series held in multiuse spaces, from artists' lofts to living rooms to neighborhood bars. As Jack Stevenson chronicles in *Land of a Thousand Balconies*, underground exhibitors often find synchronicity with bar owners looking to bring in extra clientele. As an independent programmer in Boston, San Francisco, and Europe, Stevenson gleefully embraced the tenet that "environment can actually change a film." His various series occupied "dive bars, a back room at a food co-op, a ceramics workshop, church basements, bookshop hallways and even, God forbid, real theatres."[47] For a couple of years in the mid-1980s, Stevenson ran the Straight to Hell Film Festival at a particularly disreputable Boston bar called Chet's: "There was no sign outside, you just had to know where the place was, up that long dark staircase. . . . The tacky, intimate feel of the joint was perfect for the kind of sleazy film spectaculars I wanted to pull off, with an accent on trash, gore, and porn. . . . Chet, a short, pudgy man with a mass of curly hair, didn't care what I did. As long as I attracted a beer-drinking crowd, I could have staged live executions for all it mattered to him."[48]

The Straight to Hell Film Festival did not draw the same enraptured cineastes and historians who frequented repertory theaters. Instead, Stevenson fondly recalls, "dopers and boozers lined up in a row at the bar staring at the screen with glassy-eyed absorption."[49] Stevenson's description invokes a movie culture organized around inebriation as the right and proper state in which to encounter certain kinds of films. Drinking did not just fund underground screenings, then; it fueled the ironic viewing position that programmers like Stevenson cultivated. The Straight to Hell Film Festival achieved such aims until New Year's Eve 1987, when both Stevenson and Chet were locked out by the building's owner. Evidently Chet never had a license for his bar; the bar itself had been an underground affair, nothing but a quasi-abandoned loft that Chet stocked by "buying cases of Bud at the liquor store around the corner and carrying them upstairs."[50]

Finally, adult cinemas were frequent sites of taboo tippling in the 1960s and 1970s (and later, for those that survived) while, inversely, some gay and straight bars featured (and continue to feature) questionably licensed adult film screenings. In *Times Square Red, Times Square Blue*, his lyrical autoethnographic history of New York City's adults-only and grindhouse scene, Samuel R. Delany makes repeat reference to illicit drinking and drugging. Delaney fondly recalls falling asleep in various 42nd Street porn houses after smuggling in "a sixpack of beer, a hip flask of wine, or a bottle of vodka."[51] He reminisces about how "the drug activity" at the Venus Theater on Eighth Avenue "was often so high as to obliterate the sex activity" while telling a story about Gary, "a lanky, affable guy" who attended the Venus with "his two forty-two-ounce bottles of beer . . . to sit in the last three or four rows of the orchestra . . . [and] wait for one of three older guys to service him, me among them."[52] Alkyl nitrite "poppers" were also popular filmic accompaniments for midcentury men cruising the gay porn theaters, so much so that they feature prominently in *The Back Row* (Jerry Douglas, 1973), a hardcore feature about hooking up in hardcore theaters. Just as booze and drugs ended up in adult theaters, though, adult films ended up in bars. Writing in 1975, Paul Siebenand notes that in early 1970s Los Angeles, gay "entertainment bars were opening right and left. Many showed porn loops."[53] The contemporary LA fetish bar Leather today extends its aesthetic through background screenings. As Ryan Bowles Eagle reports, "the pornography they screen 'just kinda fits'" with the house culture.[54] Similarly, Twisted Spoke, a biker bar in Chicago, features a Saturday-night "smut and eggs" event whose pleasures included hardcore films and a full brunch menu from midnight until closing.[55] Such bars do not always license the films they screen, but they nonetheless perpetuate a culture of intoxicated spectatorship that began at Delaney's dearly departed porn houses.

Between the tavern-adjacent nickelodeons of the 1900s and bar-based underground screening series of the 1980s, US cinema culture manifested a wide range of attitudes toward alcohol. Drinking culture was critical to the early success of many movie exhibitors, including Samuel "Roxy" Rothafel, and while Prohibition-era temperance reformers sought to reclaim film as a family-friendly (meaning dry) entertainment genre, audiences continued to drink at drive-ins, repertory houses, porn houses, and mainstream theaters. Many underground screening series also relied on alcohol sales to support their cinematic subcultures, which resisted the idea that all public film exhibitions needed to be safe for children. American ideologies and economies of alcohol have shaped US cinema culture since its inception, often by importing class and ethnic prejudices into the theater to underwrite ideas about who should go to the movies and what it should mean to them. In the 1970s, the second-run US exhibitors started selling beer and wine in theaters again. When they did, they had to respond to and address the history of cinematic tippling and audiences' prejudices around it. As I will show, they did so by embracing a tavern or pub model that hailed the history of working-class drinking culture in the United States, even as it also reframed that history to support their own business models.

SECOND-RUN FUN IN THE THEATER-PUB

Given that all the midcentury experiments in selling alcohol at drive-in theaters failed, how did adult concessions become "the future of movie-going in this country"?[56] The answer is illicit cinematic drinking, for it was "sneaking in . . . a couple of six-packs" at the drive-in that inspired James and John Duffy to try selling adult concessions again.[57] Originally from Ohio, the Duffy brothers were real estate managers in Florida when they "first thought of the idea while doing a feasibility study for a shopping center near Disney World. They noticed that the area offered few nighttime diversions for the many young workers at the theme park."[58] John Duffy observed that "You had such a large number of employees working at the attractions and there was a lot of down time at night," leading to a kind of ready-made market of young adults with disposable time and income.[59] Young women, the Duffys noticed, had nowhere to socialize after work if they "didn't want to be hassled."[60] Hence the brothers opened their first Cinema 'N' Drafthouse outside Orlando, Florida in September 1975. The business succeeded quickly, with a little help from the bad economy.

Specifically, the high price of gas in 1975 pushed the Duffys toward conventional rather than drive-in exhibition and second- rather than first-run features—that is, movies that had already been in circulation for six to ten weeks.[61] With second-run movies the Duffys could charge less per ticket—$1.50, 25 percent less than the national average of $2.03.[62] This was important to would-be viewers wounded by high gas prices and stagflation. Second-run status also meant that the Duffys paid less to distributors: only "a couple of hundred dollars down" plus about 35 percent of their box office gross versus up to $50,000 down plus 80 percent of the box office gross for first-run features at the time.[63] Cheaper tickets also left customers with more money to spend on concessions, profits the Duffys weren't obligated to share with distributors. Although teens still comprised 70 percent of cinema regulars in the 1970s and 1980s, the Duffys targeted Disney World employees ages eighteen to thirty-four: "the high spendable-income market," as John Duffy put it.[64] In fact, the Duffys set minimum age requirements at their theaters in order to avoid the possibility of selling alcohol to minors.[65] As James Duffy explained to me, "We weren't afraid of turning some people away because we had so much business."[66] Since servers didn't have to check identification inside the auditorium, the Cinema 'N' Drafthouses could sell alcohol in the theater as well as the lobby. Customers simply hailed their server or, later, flipped on a small red light at their table to place their order.[67]

Focusing their business on alcohol and other concessions sales (rather than ticket sales) proved quite successful for the Duffys. In 1985, the *Fort Lauderdale Sun Sentinel* reported that "While the typical patron spends $1 inside a traditional theater, Drafthouse customers average about $6 each on items such as beer, wine, pizza, and sandwiches."[68] James Duffy later estimated that concessions sales sometimes reached twenty dollars per person. Concessions prices were reasonable. In 1987, the two Fort Lauderdale-area Cinema 'N' Drafthouses were charging $3.50 for chicken wings or nachos ($7.87 adjusting for inflation today), $3.25 to $3.75 for most sandwiches ($7.31–$8.44 today), and as little as $4.00 for a pizza ($9.00 today). A pitcher of beer started at just $5.50 ($12.37 today), with options ranging from Budweiser to Killian's Red and Heineken. Consequently, two-thirds of the Drafthouse's gross profits came from concessions.[69]

To promote their innovation in US film culture, the Duffys spent approximately $500,000 annually on advertising, mostly on radio and newspaper spots.[70] An October 1975 ad in the *Orlando Sentinel* reveals that their marketing strategy was organized around alcohol sales and targeted the same clientele as other adult-oriented cinemas. The company logo incorporates a beer stein into the D of Drafthouse (figure 18), while below it ad copy enjoins the reader to "enjoy a pitcher of beer or wine at your table during feature (18 yrs. & over)."[71] To the left of this entreaty is a small announcement for the theater's current feature: *The Drowning Pool* (Stuart Rosenberg, 1975), which had then been in circulation for over seventeen weeks. Patrons who attended the late show were invited to stay until 2:00 a.m. for "Old-Time Comedy Classics," suggesting that the Cinema 'N' Drafthouse anticipated that its customers were coming to drink at the movies, not at any specific movie. The ad ran just below the fold in the back pages of the *Sentinel*, beneath a list of "Weekend Movies at Area Theaters" and among many other theater promotions. Its location is important. Above the fold were advertisements for local hardtop and drive-in theaters showing current studio fare. Below the fold were ads for adult theaters, Turkish bathhouses, off-track betting, ticket scalpers, and roller-skating rinks for some reason. Thus, the Cinema 'N' Drafthouse was graphically and socially situated right on the border between mainstream and taboo entertainments. There was something seamy about a movie theater that sold beer, but it wasn't too outré to advertise on the same page as *The Apple Dumpling Gang* (Norman Tokar, 1975).

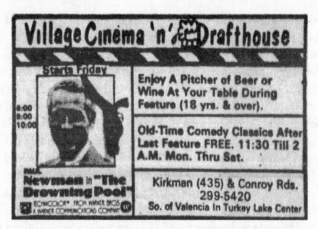

FIGURE 18. An October 1975 ad for the Village Cinema 'N' Drafthouse from the *Orlando Sentinel*.

The Duffys' concept took off quickly and decisively. Although the brothers initially "got a lot of resistance from the movie distributors," it only "took about five years to end up getting all the distributors to accept us," because their receipts were so good.[72] By 1985, the Duffys had set up corporate headquarters in Atlanta and franchised nineteen Cinema 'N' Drafthouse theaters, in addition to two they owned themselves. Their projected sales for that year were $12 million, up from $4 million the year before.[73] They increased sales to $15 million in 1986 by adding another four theaters.[74] By February 1992, there would be twenty Cinema 'N' Drafthouses franchised across the United States—from Texas to Minnesota—all targeting young adults who liked beer with their movies. Most of these were franchise operations, but the Duffys were selling franchise licenses for $15,000 to $20,000 and retaining 3 percent of the gross profits from each theater. In addition to the name, franchisees got the benefit of the Duffys' unique perspective on theater operations. "We're a restaurant rather than a theater," John Duffy explained to reporter Philip Shaikun. The Duffys taught franchisees that they were "in the food business," not the movie business, because that's where the majority of their revenue came from.[75] To lose sight of that simple truth was to lose sight of what made the Drafthouse "a shot to stimulate the movie business," as *Time* magazine hailed it in 1981.[76]

Despite the success of this business model, however, the Cinema 'N' Drafthouse empire ultimately collapsed. The Duffy brothers both retired around 2000, but in 2011 a reporter from *Naples Daily News* spent six months investigating their trail of broken deals and unpaid debts, which started in December 1982. As Clark discovered, the Duffys had opened various other theater-pub businesses over the years, including Cinema Grill, Entertainment Film Works, and American Screen Works. The Duffy corporations were defendants in almost seventy lawsuits and "ordered to pay at least $24.6 million in judgements . . . for refusing to pay all kinds of bills."[77] Of the eighty-eight theaters that the Duffys' businesses contracted for, fifty-eight "either never opened or were open less than three years."[78] This was not because the theaters weren't popular; rather, the Duffy corporations failed to pay employees, landlords, builders, "investors, lenders, distributors, and even the lawyers" who represented them.[79] Neither Duffy ever faced criminal charges, although one reporter did compare James Duffy to Bernie Madoff.[80] To be fair, the theater business was in serious trouble during the 1990s and early 2000s, the years when Duffy theaters experienced the most closures and attendant lawsuits. The Duffys certainty took advantage of this downturn to expand their empire, but they may have been victims of it as well.

Although some of the Duffys' adventures in exhibition ended badly, their idea did not. Many local entrepreneurs imitated the Duffys' combination of second-run movies and adult concessions. In 1979, a Cinema Pub opened just twenty minutes away from the original Cinema 'N' Drafthouse; in 1980, two other nearby establishments, the Apopka Lounge and the Empty Pitcher Cinema, also copied the Duffys' idea.[81] Three more cinema-restaurants emerged in the Orlando area over the course of the 1980s, for a total of seven. One of these, the Enzian Theater, is still in business today, possibly because it took pains to differentiate itself from the Drafthouse model. The Enzian promotes itself as a not-for-profit repertory house "specializing in foreign and offbeat films."[82] Such product differentiation was important for single-screen theaters in the glutted cinema market of the 1980s. As John Duffy explained to the *Wall Street Journal*, "There's no way the small, independent operator can compete against the large screen owners these days," unless they "find a niche."[83] Across the country, another restaurant-cum-cinema chain was already proving him right: the McMenamins Brewery of Portland, Oregon, which opened the first theater-pub in June 1987.

It's unclear whether McMenamins is the first modern brewery to expand into film exhibition, but it was an early innovator in what has become a thriving revenue channel for many contemporary beer labels.[84] McMenamins' dining empire began in 1974 with Mike McMenamin's

Produce Row Café, a restaurant with a robust craft beer list. In 1984, Mike and his brother Brian opened another bar, the Hillsdale Brewery and Public House, with the intention of selling their own brand there once they successfully lobbied the Oregon legislature to allow the production and sale of beer at the same facility. The so-called "brewpub law" passed in 1985, greatly expanding the McMenamins' profits and ambitions.[85] In 1987, the brothers opened a third Portland pub, this one built around cinematic exhibition. The Mission Theater & Pub was built as a church and later served as a union hall and a stage theater before the brewers reinvented it as "an establishment that preached the merits of watching movies and drinking beer."[86] At first, the Mission Theater specialized in repertory festivals, but when those failed to solicit sufficient clientele, management turned to the second-run model that was working so well for east coast cine-restauranteurs.[87]

Uniting the single-screen theater with the regionalism of the craft microbrewery, McMenanins inaugurated a highly successful business model; indeed, the chain now has nine different theater-pub locations across Oregon and Washington.[88] But film scholars have struggled with how to make sense of the exhibition model innovated by the Duffy and McMenamin brothers. In his *History of Movie Presentation in the United States*, Douglas Gomery allots one sentence to the entire movement, noting that "the various Cinema 'N' Drafthouses, Cinema Plus, and Cinema and Pizza function as restaurants with movies as an added attraction," and pays no attention to how they integrate those attractions or what that integration means to patrons.[89] Cynthia Baron suggests that drafthouses and theater-pubs were "returning to a configuration that perhaps resembles early nickelodeons with their adjoining saloons"; she also hypothesizes that such exhibitors were expanding "the sports bar idea" for moviegoers.[90] As Anna McCarthy has shown, television has a long and robust history in American watering holes, augmenting the community life of taverns and saloons since well before the development of the modern multiscreen sports bar.[91] That history is certainly salient for understanding the Duffys' model of community recreation, but it does not account for the peculiar experience of the theater pub for viewers who were raised on mainstream, prohibitionist cinema culture. The second-run theater pubs must also be understood as alternatives to the corporate multiplex and neighborhood twin theaters where viewers also saw films during the 1970s and 1980s. As alternatives, they inspired three distinct twenty-first-century exhibition trends explored below, beginning with the boutique cine-bistro.

CLASS DISTINCTION AND THE BOUTIQUE CINE-BISTRO

Second-run theater-pubs helped demystify the ordinary pleasures of moviegoing and reintegrate alcohol into US cinema culture, so it is ironic that they inspired some twenty-first-century exhibitors to reify elitist fantasies of luxury entertainment through alcohol. I refer here to the high-end or boutique cine-bistro exemplified by restored movie palaces like the Commodore in Portsmouth, Virginia; luxury twin and triplet theaters like the Metrograph and the Nighthawk in New York City; and regional chain multiplexes like the Warren (now Regal) Theater in Moore, Oklahoma. These exhibitors use adult concessions to suggest elite cultural status, that they take movies (and movie goers) more seriously than the competition. Describing their services with buzzwords like *gourmet, premier, prestigious,* and *curated,* such theaters rewrite age-old associations of cinema with proletarian entertainment. They borrow the class distinction of wine and cocktail culture to sell expensive alternatives to megaplex film culture. Such difference is often temporally marked, via either overt nostalgia for bygone glamour—as in the cases of the Commodore and the Metrograph—or futurist reinterpretations of classic Americana, as in the case of the Warren. In what follows, I demonstrate that the high-end cine-bistro was the first of the three paradigms governing the integration of alcohol into US cinema culture in the twenty-first century. More conspicuously class-oriented than either the neo-rep houses (which court rebellious audiences interested in celebrating niche film fandoms) or the big chains (which use market research to court ethnic audiences they believe spend more on concessions), high-end cine-bistros encourage fantasies of cultural superiority. In their marketing materials, they use alcohol and food service to separate themselves from the competition. Through the material presence of alcohol in their swankily appointed lobbies and auditoria, they encourage customers to feel like they are making a distinguished choice.

The first "first-run movie theater with full-service dining," the Commodore takes pride in its history; indeed, it asserts that history with two plaques heralding its inclusion in the National Register of Historic Places.[92] Originally built as a late-era movie palace in 1945, the Commodore was designed by architect John J. Zink as the crown jewel of William "Bunkie" Wilder's regional cinema chain. It was named after US Commodore James Barron, buried nearby, and its many hand-painted murals celebrate Virginia history and the nearby Norfolk Naval Shipyard. From 1945 until the early 1970s, the Commodore was a single-screen first-run theater. Then competition from a new multiplex pushed it to play hard-core pornography. The Commodore operated as an adult theater until 1975, when it closed down entirely. It remained empty until its current owner-manager, Fred Schoenfeld, bought the theater in 1987, with dreams of restoring it to its former glory—dreams, he realized, that could only be financed through dinner service and alcohol sales.

On January 19, 2019, I drove down to Portsmouth to interview Schoenfeld and experience the Commodore's historic luxury in person. Born in 1945, Schoenfeld began working as a projectionist when he was only twelve years old and attended the Commodore himself as a child.[93] After graduating college with a degree in electrical engineering, Schoenfeld moved to Kansas City and began working for Durwood Theaters, which later became AMC. In 1968, he moved back to the Virginia Tidewater area, looking to build his own theater. Instead he rented a former supermarket in western Portsmouth's Churchland neighborhood and converted it into a three-screen multiplex—the very same multiplex that later put the Commodore out of business. Schoenfeld subsequently bought two other area theaters, so he was already a seasoned exhibitor when the opportunity to renovate the Commodore presented itself. One of those theaters, a drive-in, provided crucial information for Schoenfeld as he developed his business plan for the Commodore.

Schoenfeld bought the Cinema City Theaters hardtop and drive-in in 1978. The drive-in could accommodate over five hundred cars, and "most cars had two or three people," Schoenfeld recalled, "so at intermission we would have a thousand people coming to concession," for hotdogs, hamburgers, and other meals that had to be cooked. Meal service elevated food and labor costs, but Schoenfeld nevertheless found that concessions provided the vast majority of his profits. He figured that by adding "real food" to the Commodore, he could make much more than the "three or four dollars" in per capita concessions sales that he saw at his other hardtops.[94] Indeed, by January 2019, the Commodore was averaging eighteen dollars per guest in refreshment sales. Schoenfeld acknowledges that ingredients for the Commodore's menu cost more than those needed for the drive-in's; consequently, he averages a 66 rather than an 80 percent net profit on food sales. But that still amounts to almost twelve dollars per guest for a 190-person theater (not counting the balcony seats, where one can only buy snacks, not full meals). "That's what keeps [theaters] alive," Schoenfeld explains; "the money you need to survive is in the food."[95]

FIGURE 19. The old-fashioned glamour of the Commodore. Photo by Seth Perlow.

Hence Schoenfeld designed the Commodore to support both pleasurable dining and top-tier film exhibition. First, he rebuilt the manager's office as a kitchen and tore out the main floor's auditorium seating to replace it with tiers of low-backed armchairs grouped around two- to four-top tables, each equipped with its own phone so patrons can call in their orders (figure 19). The tables have small dome lamps to illuminate menus and meals; they give the theater the air of a 1940s nightclub. Its retro aesthetic belies the Commodore's advanced digital projection and sound systems, however. A THX-certified theater, its speakers are embedded in the walls behind canvas murals by artist Jim Johnson, who spent eighteen months meticulously recreating and augmenting the original artwork.[96] Schoenfeld boasts that during "a movie that's got a lot of sound effects, the tables start to vibrate and the glasses start to walk around on the table."[97] Served by two Barco 4K projectors, the forty-one-foot screen features both house and screen curtains, and Schoenfeld is meticulous about maintaining the tradition that the audience never see a blank screen. (The show starts when the house curtain parts and the first images appear over the screen curtain before it rises). The Commodore has a 600-pound backup battery for the Barcos plus a generator in case the power goes out. In sum, the show always goes on, and it is always technically superior, while the theater around it evokes an outmoded elegance.

Schoenfeld's restoration of the Commodore helps code its food and alcohol service as luxury cinemagoing. In addition to Johnson's hand-painted murals, the Commodore boasts restored terrazzo marble floors in the bathrooms, a refurbished marquee with nine hundred lights, and a 1940s-era gas-powered popcorn popper in the lobby. Fresh popcorn is one of the "previews" (i.e., appetizers) on the Commodore's menu. The rest of the menu includes classic drafthouse fare—nachos, burgers, pizza, and the like—and more gourmet options, such as cheese plates and crab and shrimp soup. I went with the veggie burger after watching Schoenfeld bake the rolls himself; I was also nervous about attempting to eat soup while watching a movie. I needn't have been though. During negotiations with the Virginia Alcoholic Beverage Control (ABC) for his liquor license, Schoenfeld agreed to dim but not extinguish house and table-top lights. Soft lighting allows ABC agents to walk in and look for under-age drinkers, just as they would at any other Virginia restaurant. It also bespeaks the Commodore's equal emphasis of food and film consumption. Food is a *visible* part of watching a movie at the Commodore, as is the theater itself. Here it is important to note that Schoenfeld could have turned the lights off completely if he'd made the Commodore an over-twenty-one establishment. However, Schoenfeld both needed and wanted to cater to family groups, and he wanted customers to recognize the care that went into his cuisine. The crab and shrimp soup isn't just a revenue stream, in other words; it is intrinsic to making the Commodore the Commodore. As industry reporter Alissa Wilkinson observes, food and beverage "offerings aren't just a way of bringing in revenue; they're a way of branding a theater, bolstering its aesthetic, and signaling to customers what kind of movie going experience they're about to have."[98] While the Commodore does emphasize food over beverage, the latter remains crucial to its business model and its influence on cinema history and the boutique cine-bistro movement.

Working at the Commodore taught Matthew Viragh how to introduce alcohol to New York City movie theaters. A native of Fort Worth, Texas, Viragh enjoyed drinking at the Alamo Drafthouse while studying at the University of Texas at Austin. When he moved to New York in 2002, Viragh was surprised to learn that that state did not allow alcohol in cinemas, thanks to a post-Prohibition law that prohibited alcohol sales at movie theaters while sanctioning them for stage theaters. "Being from Texas, I was like, I want a fucking beer when I watch a movie," he later recalled to one hometown paper.[99] Viragh set about to learn the cine-bistro business (not, notably, the neo-rep house business). In 2008, he spent six months interning with Schoenfeld, and in summer 2011, he opened the first Nighthawk Cinema in Brooklyn's Williamsburg neighborhood. The Nighthawk only served from its lobby bar initially, while Viragh's lobbyists and lawyers challenged the ban on alcohol in cinema auditoria. "It was really annoying," Viragh observed, but customers "would just slam [their drinks] and go in," a practice that led to "a lot of people falling asleep during the films."[100] Then on August 17, 2011, Governor Andrew Cuomo signed bill 4772-2011, allowing New York cinemas with "a licensed restaurant on premise" to serve alcohol in their theaters.[101]

The Nighthawk not only has a restaurant, it has a menu by Michelin-starred chef Saul Bolton. That menu changes weekly to reflect and enhance current programming, a practice known as menu engineering. Today a variety of companies exist to help theater owners with menu engineering; some, such as Rick Fogel's Bar Starz, focus specifically "on providing and perfecting alcohol strategy." Fogel argues that "merely offering alcohol isn't enough" to encourage the kinds of bar revenue exhibitors hope for; he counsels clients that "the secret is in promoting it as part of the experience."[102] Although the Nighthawk does not work with Fogel, it pursues a similar strategy. The chef supplements Bolton's regular offerings—which include burrata plates, tuna niçoise, and beet falafel—with film-specific promotional menus. Thus, in May 2019, the Nighthawk offered a range of drink and food options in conjunction with *Long Shot* (Jonathan Levine), *John Wick 3: Parabellum* (Chad Stahelski), and *Booksmart* (Olivia Wilde). For *Booksmart*, they concocted a "Wilde and Free" cocktail with white rum and "California citrus" and "Prepare to Get Bashed" pizza rolls with "CBD infused marinara."[103] While such menu engineering perpetuates the Anglocentrism of mainstream theatrical releasing, it has nevertheless served the Nighthawk well.[104] With drink sales comprising 30 percent of its profits by 2017, Viragh was able to open a second location in Brooklyn's Park Slope in December 2018.[105]

The only thing more prestigious for a boutique cine-bistro than a menu by a Michelin-starred chef is having a Michelin review of your own. Such is the case for the Commissary restaurant at Alexander Och's Metrograph theater, which opened on the Lower East Side of Manhattan in April 2016.[106] Promoted as "a world of hospitality harkening back to the great New York movie theaters of the 1920s," the Metrograph is also and explicitly a gentrification of that experience.[107] Tickets are only slightly above the borough average, but the food is fancier and more expensive than at other New York cine-bistros.[108] The Commissary menu evokes a distinctly European notion of fine dining and includes halibut amandine creole and lamb chops à la Greque. Customers cannot bring their drinks into the theater with them at the Metrograph, and yet its restaurant is so prominent in the design and marketing of the theater that to visit the Metrograph without grabbing a drink or a meal at the Commissary is to miss the point of the theater. Nevertheless, the concessions bar features an international assortment of candies and gourmet popcorn, with an optional exotic turmeric seasoning blend. These high-end touches contrast with the minimalist auditoria, which evoke some Lower East Side character with their painted brick walls and red-velvet theater chairs. Thus, the Metrograph seeks to combine Hollywood glamour, European refinement, and downtown New York cool, for a price. The cultural touchpoints it references are all distinctly white, however, even if the audiences it draws are more diverse. Indeed, I was never able to locate a nostalgically themed ciné-bistro in the United States that explicitly incorporated nonwhite cultural referents.

Skeptics might wonder whether this high-end cine-bistro trend is limited to coastal cities. Not only does such cynicism overlook the southern military culture of Portsmouth, Virginia, where the movement was born, but it also underestimates the appeal of the ciné-bistro trend. Exhibitors across the country are using food and alcohol service to distinguish their theaters and, by extension, their guests. Take the CinéBistro chain itself, which features twelve locations in Ohio, Georgia, North Carolina, Florida, Colorado, Virginia, and Maryland. Offering "movies with taste," CinéBistros use the language of hospitality and indulgence to elevate their exhibition practice. They refer to their ticket counters as concierge desks, their stadium seating as "the lap of luxury." They note that their "pampering . . . [is] geared for an adult audience who appreciate the dinner and movie experience free from the distractions common in traditional movie theatres."[109] The food and drink are likewise presented as improvements on typical bistro fare. At the CinéBistro Brookhaven outside Atlanta, my partner and I enjoyed "truffled" fries and Wagyu beef sliders, but we might well have ordered the lobster salad sliders, sesame-seared tuna salad, or sixteen-ounce bone-in ribeye steak served with crispy brussels sprouts. All embellish classic American cuisine with a high-end twist. I ordered from among the "interesting whites" available by the glass, but bottles of Perrier Jouët were also on offer (for $230).[110] Brookhaven is a mostly white middle-class suburb of Atlanta, the CinéBistro one of the anchor businesses in a mixed-use development. In other words, CinéBistro Brookhaven was not built to service an economically privileged community but to foster a sense of economic privilege for neighborhood viewers. It creates an oasis of class fantasy through overcharging for flavored french fries and mainstream Hollywood features.

The Warren, in contrast, creates class distinction by physically raising its cine-bistro patrons above other moviegoers. At the Warren, alcohol is only served upstairs in a private lounge and "Director's Suite" screening rooms. Tickets for these venues are comparatively expensive: $14 for the balconies (where one can carry in lounge drinks) and $22 for Director's

Suites versus $10 for dry seats downstairs. The upstairs venues can only be accessed through the aforementioned lounge, which is guarded by a bouncer who turns away any customers under twenty-one or with downstairs tickets. The Warren is decorated with neon art-deco-inspired glasswork that resembles a futurist reinterpretation of Golden-Era Hollywood glamour. When this megaplex-cum-movie-palace opened, it was part of a small regional chain owned by Bill Warren of Wichita, Kansas. Like many other provincial cine-bistros, the Warren theaters used food and alcohol to distinguish themselves from the Big Three chains. Mike and Bill Barstow's Main Street Theatres, for instance, operates eight locations across Nebraska and Iowa, all of which sell alcohol in their lobby bars and restaurants. As committed as the Barstows are to "elevating" the theatrical experience, however, they do not allow servers in the auditoria, because "we want to make sure that our church is inside those four walls."[111] The Emagine theaters of Michigan, Minnesota, Illinois, and Wisconsin emphasize magic over Christianity in their publicity materials and offer even more luxury features than the Warren or Main Street chains. The Emagine 18 in Novi, Michigan provides "wait service in [its] luxury seating area" as part of owner Paul Glantz's plan to brand class distinction for the chain: "product differentiation will play a significant factor in shaping our success and setting us apart from the competition. Our theatres are located in upscale suburban areas where consumers wish to be treated to a superior experience, and they have the means to pay for that quality service."[112] So whereas CinéBistro understands its theaters as projections of fantasy, Emagine sees cinemas as reflections of class status. At all these regional theaters, then, material signals of exclusivity and luxury distinguish the cine-bistro from local competitors. Bars in the lobby and drinks in the auditoria facilitate fantasies of culturally elite moviegoing, which helps exhibitors charge more for their services. Importantly, though, most cine-bistros still target a middle-class clientele; they traffic in illusion of social superiority, not actual class distinction.

SODDEN SUBCULTURES IN NEO-REP HOUSES AND MICROCINEMAS

Superiority is not always tied to economic class in US cinema culture, and neo-repertory houses such as the Alamo Drafthouse and Pittsburgh's Row House use alcohol to foster local taste communities instead. Unlike high-end cine-bistros, neo-rep houses emphasize a subcultural cool assembled around the appreciation of cult and genre cinema. While they may also play first-run features, neo-rep theaters organize their brand identity around idiosyncratic approaches to film history. They embrace concessions of all kinds, but especially beer.[113] How they integrate alcohol into film culture differs from house to house, however. In some, alcohol is an indispensable part of their approach to film appreciation while in others it truly feels like a concession, a thing granted, a means of doing business. That position describes many contemporary microcinemas, particularly those dependent on alcohol sales to meet their operating costs. As in cine-bistros, though, viewers face a conflation of cinema and drinking culture, although neo-rep houses are more likely to orient their programming toward encouraging drink sales. In certain cases, however, this sensibility creates a masculinist bias that alienates female cinema workers (and presumably patrons).

Of all the neo-rep houses screening films and tapping kegs today, by far the most prominent is the Alamo Drafthouse. Now a franchise with thirty-nine locations, plus another six in the works (as of September 2020), the Alamo Drafthouse began in 1997 in Austin, Texas, as a second-run theater located on the second floor of a converted parking garage. Cofounders Tim and Karrie League had previously tried operating an art house in an abandoned neighborhood cinema in Bakersfield, California. Without a liquor license, though, they could not keep the business afloat.[114] So in 1996, they moved to Austin with the idea of launching a "full-service dine-in cinema." After raising $240,000 from family and friends, they spent a year creating "something between a movie theater, an attic, and a living room."[115] Using hay bales for sound insulation, the Alamo opened with a double-feature of *This Is Spinal Tap* (Rob Reiner, 1984) and *Raising Arizona* (Joel Coen, 1987). That selection speaks to the ethos of Alamo culture. Neither film is at all obscure—both were released in the recent past, well regarded at the time, and widely available on home video—but as offbeat comedies, both are enhanced by collective viewing conditions and a party-like atmosphere. That is exactly what the Leagues intended to construct at the Alamo.

Today, Alamo Drafthouses complement "a fresh mix of Hollywood product and indie fare" with wings, pizzas, chili cheese dogs, adult milkshakes, and a wide array of cocktails, wines, and beers.[116] (There are no dry Drafthouses.) They maintain their neo-rep credibility with idiosyncratic revival series (such as Video Vortex, Terror Tuesdays, and "Champagne Cinema"); film clubs and "kids camp" (featuring classic family films at choose-your-own prices); and participatory sing-a-long, quote-a-long, and dance party screenings. Such programming helps Alamo management evade charges of opportunism; as fan Richard Linklater avers, "They're not just people using movies as a draw to get people in to buy beer."[117] Or if they are, they are also passionate proponents of cinema. Alamo's regional programmers organize their screening series as compromises between their personal tastes, those of their community, and the bottom line, which is always adult concessions. Since founding their first Alamo, "the Leagues have had to rely on food and drink sales" to supplement ticket revenue on both new releases and niche programming.[118]

However, the Alamo's heavy drinking culture sometimes creates a hostile viewing and working environment, especially for women. At one early repertory show—a 1997 screening of *Blue Velvet* (David Lynch, 1986)—Tim League offered a special on Pabst Blue Ribbon, the favorite drink of the film's psychotic antagonist. The result, he recalls, was "mayhem. People were yelling and shouting and telling jokes," disrupting the film so much that League began making his own notoriously harsh no-talking pre-rolls to play before Alamo shows.[119] Combined with the machismo of Texas film nerd culture, alcohol also created unsafe working conditions for some of the Leagues' staff. Multiple female employees have accused both Tim and Karrie League of ignoring sexual harassment and disregarding histories of sexual assault among favorite customers and coworkers—"the untouchables," as one article dubs them.[120] News of the Leagues' mismanagement started to emerge in 2017, in conjunction with the #MeToo movement, and while the Alamo has since drafted and publicized a code of conduct for all its theaters, creating a theater culture around inebriation and bravado is probably intrinsically dangerous.[121] Certainly it points to the unequal dangers of sodden spectatorship. Neo-rep house culture is particularly male-dominated even within the male-dominated exhibition industry.

Not all Alamo employees support this masculinist culture, yet all must promote the company's rambunctious approach to commercial exhibition. This includes programmers, who must make concessions to, well, concessions, as well as local tastes. Justin LaLiberty, the former creative manager at the Alamo Drafthouse Yonkers, described balancing first-run and revival programming as "the hardest part of my job."[122] Of the Yonkers theater's six screens, five must be dedicated to new releases, leaving one with which to maintain the Alamo's reputation as an offbeat revival theater. Given this limitation, LaLiberty favored genre programming— "our bread and butter," as he puts it—which tends to be popular with local viewers and sell a lot of drinks, beer in particular.[123] Beer is indeed one of the Alamo's selling points; in Yonkers, LaLiberty notes, the Alamo has the best tap list around, so people come just to sit at the lobby bar and try different local craft brews. The beer also helps make film history enjoyable, something very important to LaLiberty's understanding of his programming and the role of neo-rep houses in contemporary cinema culture. Describing the film club he ran on Wednesday nights, LaLiberty observes, "it's academia with beer, and with movies that are fun. And movies that aren't fun. But they can coexist. And I think that's really important." This isn't just a matter of using a spoonful of liquor to make the medicine go down. LaLiberty repeatedly affirms that programming a neo-rep house requires "a lot of research," research on the community, film history, and which films meet which community needs when.[124] In this manner, neo-rep houses provide a service similar to that of their predecessors—making film history accessible—but the terms of that accessibility have changed in the wake of home video. Curatorship of the films and the experience is crucial to the neo-rep house business, and alcohol is a crucial component of that plan both ideologically and practically.

The Alamo Drafthouse is only the most famous of many neo-rep house chains and theaters whose business model relies on adult concessions. Some smaller operations, like the Row House in Pittsburgh, were also conceived with alcohol as a central element of their business plans. While the Row House does book some first-run fare in their weekly screening series, their emphasis is on film history and festivals. Opened in June 2014 by Brian Mendelson, the Row House not only serves beer but is attached to Mendelson's craft beer store. As Tim Jones has argued, the Row House's approach to curatorship is inextricable from its investment in regional microbrews; both "place emphasis on creative production and consumption embedded in neo-local values."[125] Like Turner Classic Movies, then, the Row House understands itself as a values-based business, that value being regionalism. While the Row House may attract viewers from outside its Lawrenceville neighborhood, its aim—as both a cinema and a bar—is to offer an enhanced and enhancing experience of community. Hence Mendelson argues, "we don't compete with Netflix. We don't compete with AMC [the television channel]. We compete with: [you] are going out for the night. Where are you gonna go?"[126] The Row House brings together film history and beer appreciation in order to get neighborhood residents in contact with one another, a commercial form of community development similar to that of first-generation rep houses like the Brattle.

The legendary Brattle Theatre of Cambridge, Massachusetts, is one of many historic rep houses that have begun selling alcohol to diversify their revenue streams. Opened in 1953 by Cyrus Harvey and Bryant Halliday, "the Brattle Theatre began [as] an alternative film exhibition program with the expressed intention of countering mass tendencies in the market" and courting nearby Harvard students.[127] Establishing a relationship with Harvard's film community was exceedingly important for the Brattle's survival; as historian Jim Lane points out, the fledgling theater "needed to secure a loyal audience as quickly as possible."[128] Following Janet Staiger, Lane observes that ads for the Brattle and reviews of its films reflected Harvard's extant taste cultures and hierarchies. While Lane does not explicitly state that all of the Brattle's revenues in those early years came from ticket sales, *Harvard Crimson* reporter Rebecca Mazur notes that it was not until the early 1980s that anyone added a concession stand.[129] As noted, repertory houses faced financial upheaval during this era. Adding concessions enabled new owners Susan and J.D. Pollack to keep the Brattle open when so many of its brethren were closing.

Unfortunately, popcorn alone could not solve the Brattle's financial woes. When a new multiplex opened nearby in 1995, the Brattle lost the limited second-run market it had begun to exploit. Viewers who couldn't wait for it on video now went to the Kendall Square Cinema instead.[130] In 2000, the Brattle became a nonprofit, but video-on-demand services further diminished its market share in the mid-2000s.[131] Despite a massively successful fundraising campaign between 2005 and 2007, the Brattle Film Foundation secured a liquor license in 2009 to begin selling beer and wine at their concession stand. This move helped the theater weather the Great Recession but was not without controversy.[132] Technically, businesses needed to "have a kitchen and provide food for patrons" to secure a liquor license in Cambridge at that time.[133] The Brattle served food—assuming popcorn counts as food—but it didn't have a kitchen, which angered some other business owners. The Foundation held onto their liquor license, though, and today derives 27 percent of its annual income from "other earned revenue."[134] It's unclear from their annual reports what that category comprises, whether the Brattle could survive without beer and wine, but losing them would clearly strain the theater's finances.

The Alamo, Row House, and Brattle are all conventionally designed theaters, built to seat hundreds of patrons in a traditional exhibition atmosphere. But the neo-rep house movement also includes smaller, improvised theaters known as microcinemas that use alcohol to sustain niche film communities. Coined by renegade exhibitors Rebecca Barten and David Sherman in 1993, the term *microcinema* denotes an amateur, unsanctioned, communal viewing space.[135] Like underground screenings, microcinemas are often closely associated with local experimental and avant-garde filmmaking scenes, but some incline toward documentary, classic, cult, or paracinema genres. When set up in bars, microcinema theaters muddle film and booze like mint and lime in a mojito, creating a deliciously unique viewing experience. At certain microcinemas, it can be unclear whether patrons are there for the movie and also the booze or the booze and also the movie; in the end, each facilitates the consumption of the other. Take Nicholas Nicolaou's Bijou Film Forum, which operated in Greenwich Village from the early 1990s until 2019. As Nicolaou himself explains, "Basically, what you had there was a bar on the ground floor and there was a three-foot wall and you pushed it and went down into the club" and its basement screening room.[136] In a 2014 article about the Bijou, Lance Richardson describes it as

a long empty bar, opening out over a dark room where a handful of men wandered around looking lost. . . . The theater's lounge area resembled something from a David Lynch movie: tables and chairs out of a jazz club, an old TV flickering telenovelas, a solitaire arcade machine, large drawings of Elvis and Ray Charles, posters for *The Rugrats Movie* and, of all things, *The Bachelor*. The modest screening room contained about 100 seats. The screen, where one would expect to see hardcore flicks of rough trade and borderline-illegal sex acts, was instead showing *Last Holiday*, the 2006 feel-good comedy in which Queen Latifah is misdiagnosed with a terminal illness.[137]

As Richardson intimates, the Bijou was known as a cruising spot as well as a microcinema. Like many underground cinemas, it was a multiuse space wherein motion pictures provided a screen for other things humans like to do in the dark. As a microcinema, the Bijou captured the particular alchemy of liquor, film, and communal exchange that differentiates such exhibition from other repertory practices.

Not all microcinemas sell alcohol to cover their costs (or facilitate cruising), but many do, especially those operating legally and licensing the films they screen. Chronicling the microcinema movements in Montréal, Toronto, New York, and Austin, Donna de Ville observes that many rely on adult concessions to lure viewers and pay the bills. The (in)famous Blue Sunshine Psychotronic Film Centre (2010–2012) in Montréal showed an eclectic range of experimental and paracinema titles; its founders "used their personal savings to fund the project," then began charging admission, which "included one alcoholic or nonalcoholic beverage."[138] In Toronto, Stacey Case's Trash Palace also sold alcohol to offset its overhead costs. Begun in 2007 Trash Palace moved four times during its roughly ten-year run, spending the last couple of years at the Doors Pub in nearby Hamilton, Ontario.[139] It ceased operations sometime in the late 2010s, but its closure should not be regarded as failure. "For a number of reasons," de Ville explains, "a microcinema typically exists less than five years," after which another one (hopefully) springs up in its place.[140] As informal spaces that nonetheless take film seriously, microcinemas respond to, challenge, and even change mainstream exhibition practice—including concessions.

Microcinemas insist that venue matters; they reject the antiseptic, anesthetizing neutrality of contemporary mainstream film exhibition in favor of character and community. Suns Cinema in Washington, D.C. is an excellent example of this phenomenon. Suns opened in May 2016 as a storefront saloon with a drop-down screen in its picture window. Decorated like a bohemian cinephile's salon with mismatched chairs, movie posters over zebra wallpaper, and a mirror emblazoned "REDЯUM," Suns started as a one-room operation with space for approximately thirty patrons. In May 2019, its owners took over the residential apartment upstairs to physically disaggregate the theater and bar, which allows them to keep selling drinks to patrons without tickets. Co-owner David Cabrera emphasizes that the scale of Suns' operation creates a communal experience that is key to their understanding of cinema and their role in D.C. film culture. He points out that both floors of Suns could fit in one multiplex auditorium and that no multiplex can create the same intimacy between viewers.[141] That intimacy can cut both ways; sometimes it leads to serendipitous group viewing experiences, as when everyone joined in on catcalling a sold-out screening of *Slumber Party Massacre* (Amy Holden Jones, 1982), and sometimes it just means that a few sarcastic hecklers ruin the show for everyone else. Every time I go to Suns, I find that the unconventional space—and the convivial energy of my fellow patrons—makes me wonder what brought them out to that movie on that night. Suns projects from Blu-ray discs, so all of its titles are necessarily available on home video. Viewers come not for rarity, then, but for the pleasure of communal spectatorship—and the drinks.

Concessions are very much a part of Suns' culture, for its owners as well as viewers. At Suns, ticket sales typically only cover the cost of licensing a film; all of the cinema's other expenses must be offset through food and beverage sales. As Cabrera explains, the entire operation is thus "contingent upon selling alcohol."[142] He and his partner, Ryan Hunter Mitchell, therefore privilege "drink-friendly" movies when making their programming decisions. They tend to reserve Friday and Saturday nights for ironic choices that customers enjoy more when tipsy, although sometimes the Sunday night classics also end up being big hits at the bar; *Andrei Rublev* (Andrei Tarkovsky, 1969) was one such surprise. To promote beverage sales, Cabrera does his own menu engineering, developing drinks with titles that pun on the evening's film selections, such as "Averna Herzog Eats His Shoe," an herbaceous cocktail with cherry notes that Suns offered in conjunction with Les Blank's short documentary *Werner Herzog Eats His Shoe* (1980).[143] Cabrera and Mitchell also add an intermission to every program over seventy minutes; this allows viewers to go to the bathroom—alcohol is a diuretic after all—and, most importantly, to buy more drinks. Cabrera is very sagacious about the role alcohol plays in his theater. While he does not identify as a bar-owner—as many independent exhibitors now do—he accepts that alcohol underwrites the film culture he wants to create. That culture was never intended to be "stuffy," yet Cabrera also sees the theater as having "a moral responsibility" to the community it entered.[144] A historically Latinx neighborhood in northwest Washington, Mount Pleasant has gentrified rapidly in the last ten years, becoming whiter and more affluent. Despite attracting a mostly white clientele (at all the shows I've attended), Cabrera and Mitchell try to ensure that Suns serves Mount Pleasant's local culture, rather than eclipsing it, by programming screening series with local activist and artist groups, including Black Youth DC 100, the DC Punk Archives, and Multiflora Productions. Without alcohol, Cabrera and Mitchell could never afford to make community values a central component of their business plan, nor could any of the other neo-rep houses cited in this section.

THEATER CHAINS' DEMOGRAPHIC APPROACH TO ADULT CONCESSIONS

While boutique cine-bistros, neo-rep houses, and microcinemas have embraced adult concessions for decades, the Big Three theater chains—AMC, Regal, and Cinemark—were slower to adopt alcohol service. This may reflect their commitment to the ideal of family-friendly moviegoing, as teenagers and early twenty-somethings comprised the largest demographic of frequent moviegoers from the late 1960s through 2010.[145] Hence in 2005, NATO's president, John Fithian, could claim, "We've experimented and experimented, and people basically want popcorn and soda and candy."[146] Alcohol sales in other movie venues reveal that this is not always the case, but NATO and its members were not then targeting audiences they associated with adult concessions. By 2014, that had changed, leading Fithian to boast, "We're lobbying almost every jurisdiction in the United States to allow alcohol in cinemas. This is the future of our business, and thank God."[147]

Regional multiplex chains were the first of their kind to begin exploring adult concessions. In the 2000s, Muvico Theaters, Rave Motion Pictures, National Amusements, and Movie Tavern all tried renovating old multiplexes and building new ones to serve alcohol. As industry scholar Juan Llamas-Rodriguez argues, these theaters were part of an industrial turn toward full-service dine-in exhibition. Their executives were participating in the growing "'luxury branding economy,' a sector premised on selling exclusivity and sumptuousness" that ironically depends upon standardization.[148] For many US cinemas, this standardization includes assigned seating, leather recliners, and on-site bars and restaurants, if not in-seat service. Through such material changes, executives are trying "to distinguish the movie-going experience at their establishment" from those offered by competing multiplexes.[149] For if everyone is showing the same blockbusters, then exhibitors must differentiate themselves through services and amenities rather than content. As Llamas-Rodriguez helpfully notes, this interpretation of the moviegoing experience "points not only to the activity of watching a film but also to that of going to see a film— that is, to the events and places that precede the film watching, as well as the embodied spectator who undertakes such an activity."[150] By emphasizing experience over spectatorship, the chains make the movies themselves less important. Then it scarcely matters that alcohol disrupts the senses and compromises cognition. When moviegoing is an "experience" rather than an encounter with an art-object, then the exhibitor's goal is simply to maximize customer pleasure, not to present the art-object under the best possible conditions.

Of course, many would argue that chain cinemas rarely offered quality screening conditions, that their megaplexes have historically been poorly designed and poorly staffed, with barely edible concessions. The chains' turn toward standardized sumptuousness is not (just) a response to these shortcomings, however. It also reflects a particular demographics-based approach to market growth. That is, the introduction of alcohol to large multiplex chains happened concomitantly with a fresh pursuit of minority audiences, particularly Latinx Americans. AMC provides an ideal case study for exploring this marketing initiative because it is the largest theater chain in the United States, with the highest per capita concessions sales ($4.66 per guest, as opposed to $3.92 at Regal). The first of the Big Three chains to adopt adult concessions, it is also a publicly traded company, which means that its investor reports are available online.[151] These reports suggest that AMC regards US Latinx families as an under-exploited market and that they see full-service concessions as a way to both attract and capitalize on that demographic. To be sure, demographic profiling is a standard component of corporate marketing, but at AMC theaters, this strategy has the effect of racializing particular components of its service. Specifically, the chain's adult concessions contribute to an exploitation of ethnicity wherein heritage is harnessed as a marketing tool.

Founded by Maurice, Edward, and Barney Dubinsky in Kansas City, Missouri, in 1920, AMC became the largest theater chain in the United States when it acquired Carmike Cinemas in December 2016. An early leader in the multiplex and megaplex movement, AMC has long focused on concessions-friendly design, being the first theater chain to add cupholders to their armrests in 1981.[152] In 2008, AMC piloted a new "Dine-In" concessions service, making it possible for "guests to order restaurant-style food [and alcohol] with the push of a button, from the comfort of their own luxurious movie seat."[153] As Jennifer Douglas, vice president of AMC's Dine-In Theater Operations, explained in 2017, AMC was initially conflicted about whether the Dine-In initiative should support the corporation's long-standing emphasis on "family friendly all ages" exhibition or to offer "a more adult . . . more premium experience," for which they could charge higher prices.[154] In the end, AMC created two kinds of Dine-In venues: Fork & Screen and Cinema Suites. Viewers of all ages can attend Fork & Screen shows, while no one under twenty-one is allowed in Cinema Suites. As the descriptor "Dine-In" suggests, the concept behind both Fork & Screen and Cinema Suites was to blend dinner and a movie into one cohesive experience that offers all the comforts of staying in and all the amenities of dining out. They mostly feature the same pub fare one finds at cine-bistros and neo-rep houses, but the menu is glossier, featuring high-resolution pictures of salty fries and loaded nachos. AMC's Dine-In theaters also emphasize their superiority to traditional megaplex exhibition through enhanced material amenities. AMC used Dine-In theaters to launch their reserved-seating system, AMC Signature Recliners, and Coca-Cola Freestyle soft drink dispensers. These innovations allowed AMC to raise ticket prices even in dry auditoria. (Both Fork & Screen and Cinema Suite theaters impose ticket surcharges, which are really deposits meant to guarantee that viewers will also be diners.) Today, some AMC Dine-In cinemas offer loyalty club members free Wi-Fi in the lobby bar, a subtle inducement to spend time at the bar rather than just stop by it on the way to the show.

FIGURE 20. The MacGuffins bar at the AMC Georgetown in Washington, D.C.
Photo by author.

In sum, AMC's Dine-In initiative aimed to transforms cinemas into full-service venues for patrons' entire evening out. It was successful enough for the company to extend adult concessions and spread the "experience" ethos to its other locations. For not all AMC theaters are Dine-In; as of June 2019, only 42 of AMC's 380 locations had Dine-In auditoria. Most AMC theaters now feature a MacGuffins lobby bar, however (figure 20). MacGuffins was introduced in 2008 to enhance the lobbies of Dine-In theaters but subsequently spun off to become an independent feature. Physically separate from the regular concession stand, MacGuffins bars have their own seating areas, where patrons can enjoy drinks before or after the movie, though they are also invited to take their drinks into the theater with them. MacGuffins has proved far more popular—and profitable—than Dine-In theaters for AMC. As the corporation revealed in its 2013 Initial Public Offering (IPO) filing, a MacGuffins bar costs approximately $150,000 to install but generates a 100 percent cash-on-cash return within one year.[155] (By contrast, cash-on-cash returns for Dine-In theaters ranges from 11 to 34 percent—not bad, but not as good as MacGuffins.) As of June 2017, AMC had 250 MacGuffins "adult beverage concept locations" in the United States; by December 2018, that number had risen to 300.[156] The vast majority of AMC locations serve alcohol now, indicating that alcohol sales are not a novelty but rather a new business norm and serious revenue channel for the biggest theater chain in North America.[157]

AMC uses their Dine-In and "adult beverage concept locations" to target one of US cinema's fastest growing audience demographics: Latinx Americans. According to the Motion Picture Association of America's 2017 annual report, 24 percent of frequent moviegoers (people who go to the theater once a month or more) were "Hispanic/Latino."[158] Whites still make up 54 percent of frequent movie goers, but they comprise 61 percent of the overall population. Latinx Americans constitute only 18 percent of the US population, so the Association considers them "overrepresented" among frequent movie-goers.

AMC has also been pursuing Latinx audiences because it operates more downtown locations than its major competitors. In its IPO filing, AMC claims that "65% of Latinos live within 20 miles of an AMC theatre." As of November 2011, 51 percent of AMC customers were either Lantinx or African American.[159] CEO Gerry Lopez also observes that "Hispanic families come to the movies often, come in larger groups, spend more on food and beverage and spend more to see films in premium formats."[160] He points to the past and future growth of Latinx audiences in the United States, marking them as a potential market for AMC to corner. Referring to Latinx Americans as "our best customers," the IPO filing outlines AMC's focus on minority markets and MacGuffins bars as its two strategies for further growth.[161]

AMC has exploited its turn toward "adult beverage concept locations" as marketing hooks for Latinx and other audiences whose moviegoing is on the rise, such as adults ages twenty-five to thirty-nine. In the early 2010s, AMC began planning how to use alcohol to lure these viewers. As their senior vice president of food and beverage, George Patterson, reported in 2014, "We did a little research a couple of years ago and found that adult consumers might consider coming back to the movie business if alcohol was offered. Guests love it. A glass of wine really improves a bad movie."[162] Also in 2014, Fithian announced that "Hispanics are far and away the most important consumers at our cinemas" because they spend 30 percent more than other ethnic groups on concessions and because they "want higher end concessions and alcohol as part of the cinema going experience."[163] As a result, Fithian declared, NATO would begin lobbying state legislatures to allow adult beverage sales in megaplex theaters. Fithian's logic reveals how US exhibitors understand ethnicity: as market segments to be exploited.

AMC has not been as candid as Fithian in linking adult concessions initiatives to its pursuit of Latinx audiences, but it has consistently intertwined these schemes. In summer 2014, industry bloggers started noticing that AMC's Dine-In menus featured "two dishes with chipotle peppers, three types of tacos, five kinds of quesadillas, a fiesta trio, a fajita chicken wrap," and "five types of margaritas."[164] Indeed, AMC spokesperson Ryan Noonan confirmed that these dishes were created for a "seasonal menu that would line-up closer to a Hispanic moviegoing population."[165] AMC also acknowledged that it was pitching its Dine-In—and later its MacGuffins—offerings to Latinx Americans because "concessions, including alcohol, overindex among Hispanics."[166] Around 2014, AMC also hired a vice president of specialty and alternative content (now content strategy and inclusive programming), Nikkole Denson-Randolph, to find Latinx and other minority films for limited-run releases in AMC theaters. As Denson-Randolph explains, these films can be loss-leaders for AMC because their purpose is to demonstrate that AMC cares about supporting these cultures. Currently, Denson-Randolph's programs include Pantallas AMC ("bringing you the best films that appeal to the Latino culture"), Asian-Pacific Cinema, and Indian Cinema—because Indo-Americans buy 50 percent more movie tickets per capita than the national average.[167] As regards Latinx viewers specifically, AMC believes that "Hispanics are more likely to see blockbusters than your average moviegoer," and that they represent a growing market.[168] Therefore AMC is willing to lose money programming Latinx films on their smaller screens if doing so encourages Latinx moviegoers to favor AMC for big releases. Indeed, just as Hollywood executives now contend that "you don't have a major hit without Hispanic audiences," exhibitors now understand Latinx viewers as crucial to making their theater a hit.[169]

In sum, AMC has targeted adult concessions and Latinx viewers simultaneously since the early 2010s because they believe that Latinx audiences are a growing demographic of frequent moviegoers who spend more money on food and drink than other ethnic groups. AMC executives aren't putting margaritas on the menu because they want to combat anti-Latinx prejudice in the United States, in other words; they're there to make Latinx customers feel comfortable spending money at AMC. Of course, many AMC patrons may not notice such targeted marketing, especially when drunk on the "Marvelously Mixed" cocktails AMC introduces to promote each new Marvel movie. Whether or not tipsy viewers recognized the demographic profiling behind their margaritas and churros, however, these concessions reinforce stereotypes about Latinx Americans even while courting them. The "future" of American cinema thus perpetuates prejudices about ethnicity and drinking similar to those that dogged its early days, albeit to very different ends.

CONCLUSION

When I started researching this chapter, I assumed that alcohol was a new addition to cinema concessions. I was shocked to learn that exhibitors had been pairing films and adult beverages for as long as the former had been commercially exhibited in the United States. But if scholars understand little about drinking at the movies, that may be because we haven't thought for very long about how we go to the movies, focusing instead on what we see.

This is a problem, because it prevents reception historians from acknowledging the full history of how viewers watched movies. Even when no theaters in the United States served alcohol, moviegoers still drank. For obvious reasons, it is impossible to say when viewers first began smuggling inebriants into the cinema, although many of the settings covered in this chapter were particularly notorious for clandestine drinking. Today, the practice is even more widespread. As of 2015, all of the major US theater chains prohibited customers from bringing their own drinks or snacks into the theater—which isn't to say that it doesn't happen anyway. People smuggle in candy, pastry, seafood salad—and of course liquor.[170] Supplying one's own refreshment reclaims the autonomy of bodily experience in moviegoing; no one tells me what goes best with a movie, what gustatory sensations I want to combine with any given film. And sometimes what I want to import—what will really *make* the movie for me—happens to be a little bit of the hard stuff.

The internet is rife with advice on how to sneak alcohol into movie theaters: hide vodka in a water bottle, carry a flask somewhere on your person, or pack a whole minibar in your backpack (also known as the "massive purse method").[171] Thrillist suggests soaking gummy candies in alcohol before smuggling them into a theater, as if Haribos that smell like rum will somehow attract less attention than a "pocket shot" or miniature bottle.[172] One mother in Georgia tried using her child's sippy cup as a smuggling vessel and ended up charged with reckless conduct and public intoxication—although not child endangerment, oddly enough.[173] In most states, drinking in a movie theater can qualify as public intoxication and even trespassing, if theater management asks you to leave and you refuse. Legal liabilities aside, though, clandestine drinking enhances some films in ways that critics have yet to acknowledge.

While many films try to invoke the excitement of illicit drinking, most movie theaters are highly sanitized shrines to orderly amusement. The juxtaposition between on-screen rebellion and off-screen decorum can ruin the show, unless one takes matters into one's own hands—or miniatures of Captain Morgan's rum into a matinée of *Superbad* (Greg Mottola, 2007). A friend and I tried this while in graduate school in Ithaca, New York, where none of the movie theaters serve alcohol. We wanted to take a break from grading and recall what it felt like to resent school from the other side of the lectern. After a stop by the concession stand for popcorn and Cokes, we were ready to regress. The lights went down, I tipped the liquor into our massive sodas, and the movie did what it was supposed to do. *Superbad* follows the travails of three middle-class white suburban boys as they try to obtain alcohol for a high school graduation party. One of the original "frat pack" comedies of the 2000s, *Superbad* isn't super bad, but it isn't super good either. Its blinkered vision of privileged teen angst excludes any nuances that might encourage viewers to question why they are romanticizing high school. Not that we realized that at the time. Drunk on cheap liquor and petty malfeasance, we laughed heartily at every joke and gag. Like the affluent, white protagonists of *Superbad*, our race and social class protected us from any meaningful repercussions from our minor rebellion. I don't recall the slightest sense that I was doing anything really wrong; regression felt like our prerogative, which is precisely what films like *Superbad* teach their viewers. But drinking in the theater did make moviegoing feel like an event again, which is also how distributors want viewers to interpret their would-be blockbusters. The event may have overshadowed the movie, but I still fondly recall seeing *Superbad* over a dozen years later. Illicit drinking brought me into the ethos of the film and realized Columbia Pictures' intention from their product.

It is only recently that film theorists began considering how viewers' bodies shape their experience of motion pictures and spectatorship. This may be because motion picture projection has, since its introduction in the 1890s, seemed like a quintessentially ethereal entertainment. Made of light and later sound, the film experience cannot be touched, but that does not mean it is immaterial. Theater architecture and design have been shown to have an enormous effect on how viewers make sense of film as a cultural event and an art form. Objects we consume while watching film likewise shape what we understand the cinema to be and how we interpret the films we see there.

This chapter has outlined the evolution of adult concessions and explored three different ways alcohol influences exhibition practice in the twenty-first century. Its point is that adult concessions are now inextricable from the industry and experience of cinematic exhibition. Concessions culture is cinema culture; to ignore that is to ignore how cinemagoing is understood by exhibitors and practiced by consumers. Whether any given viewer imbibes or not, spirits have become the lifeblood of cinema in the twenty-first century. Indeed, many exhibitors need alcohol sales to survive. The material presence of alcohol in cinemas is not a fluke, fad, or accident. It now makes theatrical reception possible. Yet alcohol remains among the most powerful and least studied forces shaping US cinema culture and US history more broadly.[174] We would do well to understand cinemas as bars that happen to show movies rather than theaters that happen to sell drinks. Indeed, this distinction may be critical to their economic recovery in the wake of the COVID-19 pandemic. Only by reckoning with the ethereal's dependence on the material can we appreciate how culture actually transpires.

CHAPTER 5

Blunt Spectatorship

Inebriated Poetics in Contemporary
US Television

While the previous chapter examined inebriated spectatorship as a business strategy among contemporary film exhibitors, this chapter addresses how television creators are embracing inebriation among TV viewers and coopting popular media reception practices, such as watching TV stoned, for commercial and aesthetic ends. After years of kowtowing to the War on Drugs, many mainstream television producers are now recreating the varied cerebral effects of America's favorite narcotic: cannabis.[1] These shows do not merely depict stoner lifestyles, though. Rather they employ poetics of inebriation that construct intoxicating spectatorial positions. (By poetics, I mean the principles and inner logic guiding a work of art—in this case, a television series.) Intoxication is not an often-discussed element of film or television reception, and yet intoxicants are some of the most influential material forces in contemporary television culture. What we smoke, eat, and drink while consuming media has a profound impact on how we make meaning from that media, how we receive its messages about our culture, and how we incorporate those messages into our world view, including our views of one another. Television series imitate and otherwise recreate inebriation effects to entertain and entice viewers (thereby increasing their market share). In so doing, they reflect changing attitudes toward drug use, but they also mold viewers' impressions of television culture and drug culture. Fostering inebriated affects for sober viewers and structurally rewarding the inebriation of stoned viewers, they affirm racialized and gendered suppositions about getting stoned. Indeed, most affirm a white worldview that may challenge sexist social mores but does not contest the white gaze of mainstream US television.[2]

Cannabis cultivation, possession, and consumption have been illegal in the United States since 1937, but in the 1990s many states began decriminalizing the drug for medical and even recreational use.[3] As smoking pot has become more legally and socially acceptable in the United States, pot's relationship to US cultural production likewise changed. Cannabis has a long history of representation in music and film, and its impact on television is no less important. It is, however, more heterogeneous and less widely known. During the 1970s–1990s—as part of its infamous War on Drugs—the US government paid for antidrug public service announcements on TV and encouraged American television producers to create "very special episodes" of popular shows to deter drug abuse. In the twenty-first century, though, television has openly embraced drug cultures—particularly white drug cultures whose representation belies the racist design and effects of the War on Drugs.

These cultures may be medicinal, illicit, or both. In 1997, the Federal Communications Commission (FCC) reversed a long-standing ban on direct-to-consumer prescription drug advertisements on television; now "some programs—the nightly news and sitcoms aimed at older Americans—get most of their advertising from drug makers."[4] Not all of these advertisements are for drugs that get you high, of course, but television creators were simultaneously incorporating drug references into their narratives and inebriated affects into their poetics. Whereas once television was disparaged as a "plug-in drug," now it plugs into contemporary social attitudes toward drugs, both legal and illegal.[5] One can watch television advertisements to see what medications Americans are taking and watch television programs—such as *Weeds* (Showtime, 2005–2012), *Snowfall* (FX, 2017–), and *Martha and Snoop's Pot Luck Dinner Party* (VH1, 2016–)—to find out how drugs influence American culture.

As I will show over the course of this chapter, many contemporary television series operate as virtual inebriants by cultivating affects associated with cannabis intoxication—namely distraction, enhanced or hyper-focus, and paranoia—via specific formal and narrative strategies. In so doing, they both interpellate sober viewers into inebriated subject positions and structurally reward viewers who happen to be high. By increasing segmentation and replays, already common features of fiction television narration, TV creators interpellate and oblige distractible stoner-subjects. By increasing seriality and narrative world-building, they solicit intense spectatorial concentration, similar to the hyper-focus of some cannabis highs, and the extended viewing sessions known as binge-watching. Finally, by exaggerating narrative enigmas, introducing surreal aesthetics, and encouraging active interpretation, certain series guide viewers toward paranoid spectatorship—paranoia being another affect often associated with cannabis. The paranoid spectator is not mentally ill, of course; rather it is a subject position created by the show to enrich its viewer's enjoyment of its narrative.[6] By emulating cannabis inebriation, the series I analyze seek to increase viewers' pleasure to increase viewership and thereby increase profits (either through advertising revenue or subscription sales). Not all television programs interpellate an inebriated spectator, of course, but many do, *regardless of whether or not individual viewers happen to be stoned*.

To properly investigate inebriated spectatorship, one must begin by defining inebriation. From the Latin *ébriáre*, meaning to intoxicate, *inebriate* means "to stupefy, render unconscious, or madden or deprive of the ordinary uses of the senses or reason, with a drug or alcoholic beverage."[7] From caffeine to nicotine, antidepressants to high-fructose corn syrup, many of the substances Americans consume alter their senses or reason. So, if we define inebriation as the modification of consciousness by drugs, alcohol, or other psychoactive agents, many of us are intoxicated much of the time. Sobriety then becomes a vanishing horizon of unmediated perception. The *Oxford English Dictionary* defines sobriety as "moderation in the use of strong drink" and "moderation in any respect; avoidance of excess or extravagance."[8] In practice, however, sobriety tends to be negatively defined as being unaffected by psychoactive substances. Narcotics phenomenologist David Lenson points out that "sobriety is supposed to be the primary or 'natural' condition, the thesis, and intoxication is assumed to be secondary, unnatural, and antithetical," but in fact intoxication may be more common than sobriety in most people's daily experience.[9] Television is not technically an intoxicant, but its critics often decry it as poison, and it has reflected US attitudes toward inebriation for its entire commercial history. The first American television sponsor was a drug company, Bristol-Meyers, which began subsidizing NBC's *Geographically Speaking* in late 1946. The first evening newscast was sponsored by cigarette manufacturer R.J. Reynolds; the program was even renamed *Camel News Caravan* in 1949.[10] Aspirin and cigarettes are not traditionally considered intoxicants, but that distinction may be cultural rather than medical. Sobriety and intoxication are socially constructed concepts that enforce cultural norms. Today, televisual poetics of inebriation are sanctioning racialized worldviews through the edgy allure of cannabis-related affects.

Here it is worth noting that cannabis inebriation affects individuals in complex, even contradictory ways. Since the late 1960s, researchers have known that cannabis' effects on its consumers are "highly variable, even in small doses."[11] There are substantial differences in the highs produced by different strains of the herb and from different methods of consuming it.[12] Cannabis is also biphasic, which means that the same strain can have opposite effects on the same person depending on the amount consumed. As Michael Pollan points out, pot's effects are "notoriously susceptible to the power of suggestion."[13] Doctors Andrew Weil and Norman Zinberg concur, observing that what users expect cannabis highs to feel like and the conditions under which they get high shape how users perceive their highs.[14] All inebriants are affected by what Zinberg and Weil call "[mind]set and setting," but weed more than most, making its representation in media particularly subjective.[15]

Many talented writers have tried to explain what it feels like to be stoned. Allen Ginsberg regarded it as a more mindful alternative to hegemonic structures of attention: "Marijuana consciousness is one that, ever so gently, shifts the center of attention from habitual shallow, purely verbal guidelines and repetitive secondhand ideological interpretations of experience to more direct, slower, more absorbing, occasionally microscopically minute engagement with sensing phenomena."[16] Similarly, Pollan argues that the "cognitive dysfunction" of a cannabis high enables a form of "extremist noticing" that "admit[s] a whole lot more information about a much smaller increment of experience." He calls it *wonder*.[17] What does it feel like? Well, "if you imagine consciousness as a kind of lens through which we perceive the world, the drastic constricting of its field of vision seems to heighten the vividness of whatever remains."[18] Lenson acknowledges the emotional impact of cannabis inebriation, describing it as "an alienation from perception followed in most cases by an affective reconciliation."[19] In other words, pot changes how its user feels about objects perceived as well as perception itself. It is this affective processing of perception that accounts for pot's famed association with giddiness, euphoria, beatitude, anxiety, and paranoia. Noticing yourself noticing can be a lot of fun, even profound, but it can also be highly distressing, depending—as Weil and Zinberg argue—on "set and setting."

This chapter analyzes the construction of distracted, hyper-focused, and paranoid spectators through poetics of inebriation in late twentieth- and early twenty-first-century US television genres, including sitcoms, reality TV, and prime-time serial dramas. During the period in question, viewers could access these shows via over-the-air broadcasting, cable subscriptions, DVD and Blu-ray season box sets, and licensed and unlicensed video on demand platforms (e.g., Netflix, iTunes, and Daily Motion). Twenty-first-century television producers know that television is no longer platform specific; thus, my analysis of inebriated spectatorship focuses on the spectatorial subject position constructed by shows themselves—divorced, as much as is ever possible, from their delivery platforms. Nevertheless, industry history certainly informs my reading of contemporary television's poetics of inebriation. Industry studies can illuminate producers' relationships to inebriant manufacturers and antidrug lobby groups, but only attention to the poetics of television programs reveals how such relationships inform the spectatorial subject. Therefore, this chapter relies on textual analysis to show how US television creators began thematizing and capitalizing on inebriated reception around the turn of the twenty-first century.

The chapter begins by briefly outlining the discursive history of inebriated and distracted spectatorship and the industrial history of US television's relationship to the War on Drugs. Together, these archives provide the historical context necessary to understand television creators' sudden and surprising shift to poetics of inebriation in the twenty-first century. The inebriated spectator played an important role in early film theory, one dialectically linked to disparagements of television's distracted spectator decades later. That history is crucial to understanding why it is so important to reclaim distracted (and other forms of inebriated) spectatorship now, but so is television's eager participation in the War on Drugs, which ended in a federal payola scandal in 2000. Understanding how television creators helped condemn drugs in the twentieth century reveals how novel their embrace of drugs was for viewers in the twenty-first century and provides an important industrial explanation for why the poetics of inebriation did not appear earlier in the history of the medium. In that context, I turn to the development of the poetics of distracted, hyper-focused, and paranoid spectatorship, showing how they normalize inebriated affects for US television audiences and how many reify a white, privileged relationship to cannabis that obscures the detrimental effects of US drug laws on communities of color. Along the way, I acknowledge that the poetics of inebriation are not the only forces inducing distraction, enhanced focus, and paranoia among television viewers. (They are also distracted by secondary screens, for instance, and urged toward binge-watching by many subscription video-on-demand [SVOD] platforms' post-play features.) However, these poetics reflect an important incorporation of inebriated viewing practices into contemporary television style, demonstrating that material media cultures affect not just media viewers but producers too.

First, though, I need to note the social and professional privilege that enabled this research. Were I not a cisgendered upper-middle-class American white woman in a tenured faculty position at a private US research university, I probably would not have been able to write about cannabis at all, let alone in a manner that acknowledges my own consumption and the normalization of inebriation in contemporary television. My race, gender, and class background provide me with the de facto cultural authority to pursue controversial—some might even say silly—research agendas. Every time I toked up to watch *Broad City* (Comedy Central, 2014–2019) or *Atlanta* (FX, 2016–), I benefitted from social inequalities and professional hierarchies that enable me to do this work by denying that opportunity to others. I only got stoned in regions where recreational cannabis had been decriminalized, but I bore less risk doing so because I am white. I received a generous research fellowship from Georgetown University to pursue the research contained in this chapter because I am a tenure-line faculty member—and I can admit in print that I smoke pot because I am a *tenured* faculty member. It is not enough for me to use that privilege for what I consider worthy research endeavors, however. I am also responsible for doing everything I can to resolve social and economic inequalities and expand intellectual freedom for all scholars—which includes drawing attention to contemporary poetics of inebriation as mired in white privilege and the War on Drugs as a system of racist oppression.

Relatedly, I choose not to use the terms *marijuana* or *marihuana* except to denote the racist ideology behind cannabis prohibition in the United States. As cannabis historian Martin Lee notes, "*Marijuana* is a Spanish-language colloquialism . . . popularized in the United States during the 1930s by advocates of prohibition who sought to exploit prejudice against despised minority groups, especially Mexican immigrants."[20] When California moved to outlaw pot in 1915, it did so primarily as a pretext for persecuting Mexican Americans. Later on, Federal Bureau of Narcotics Commissioner Harry Aslinger would use fear of miscegenation as a way to stir up anti-marijuana sentiment on the East Coast. During the 1990s, arrests for cannabis possession drove "the most dramatic expansion of the drug war" to date and the mass incarceration of Black men.[21] The American history of *marijuana* is a history of racism, the same racism fuels my white privilege and allows me to add this chapter to that history. The War on Drugs emerges from and feeds racial prejudice, as does the language we use to talk about drugs. Both must be questioned and contested.

HISTORICIZING IRRESPONSIBLE SPECTATORSHIP

Once upon a time, writers embraced a wealth of metaphors to explain how moving images could intoxicate and otherwise enchant viewers. Both film and television were occasionally disparaged as narcotics, and both were recognized for their relationships to dreams and daydreaming—even as the film spectator was assumed to be wholly immersed in their medium and the television viewer easily diverted from theirs. This history informs television's current poetics of inebriation and the social values they convey to viewers.

Between the 1890s and 1930s, early film theorists routinely compared movies to drugs and other inebriants when exploring viewers' fascination with and immersion in motion pictures. Famously, Dziga Vertov referred to audience-pleasing fiction films as "cine-vodka" and "cine-nicotine," noting that "the spectator sucks from the screen the substance which soothes his nerves."[22] But Siegfried Kracauer observed a trend "from the 'twenties to the present day" (meaning 1960) of comparing film "to a sort of drug" that "lulls the mind" with "stupefying effects."[23] Citing Jean Epstein, Kracauer argues that just as "doping creates dope addicts . . . the cinema has its habitués who frequent it out of an all but physiological urge."[24]

The inebriated spectator was integral to early spectatorship theory, but it eventually lost pride of place to the dreaming spectator. René Clair was among the first to describe cinema's spectator as succumbing to a "dream-like state" at the cinema.[25] For many mid-century film theorists—including Henri Angel, Edgar Morin, André Breton, and Roland Barthes—dreaming offered a particularly pertinent metaphor for commercial moviegoing.[26] Hence Kracauer invokes dreaming to describe the "lowered consciousness" that Hollywood and other commercial film industries induce to captivate his "apprehensions and hopes."[27] The analogy maintained its critical popularity into the 1970s, when the apparatus theorists turned to Lacanian theories of the unconscious to reinterpret film's effect on its viewer.

Dreaming is, of course, an expression of the unconscious mind (at least according to Sigmund Freud), suggesting a thematic if not methodological lineage between midcentury film phenomenologists and modern spectatorship theorists. Indeed, this connection undergirds the first groundbreaking essay of apparatus theory, Jean-Louis Baudry's "Ideological Effects of the Basic Cinematic Apparatus," which builds on Plato's allegory of the cave to explain how the cinematic spectator regresses to a state akin to dreaming.[28]

Baudry was one of the last florid fantasists of spectatorship theory. In his wake, film scholars largely spurned fanciful metaphors in favor of quasi-scientific theories of subject formation, from psychoanalysis to cognitive psychology. They also stopped thinking about altered states of media reception. Cognitivist film theorists, for instance, certainly could consider the effect of inebriants on neurological functions and viewers' epistemological processes, but none have. Ethnographic and historical scholars of film reception likewise assume sober viewers. I can count on one hand the reception studies of inebriated film viewers. Intoxication was once a vital metaphor for understanding film's effect on its viewers. Now, scholars mostly take it as given that the "cinema proposes a curious and expectant spectator," that movie theaters (attempt to) provide riveting, immersive experiences, and that viewers engage these experiences with all of their faculties intact.[29]

Television studies emerged contemporaneously with film studies' turn away from apparatus theory and toward ethnography and historicism.[30] This genealogy might explain why the field rarely engages in the fantastical allegories that characterized early film theory. Describing television spectatorship for an inceptive anthology in the field, Robert Stam noted, "it's not Plato's cave for an hour and a half, but a privatized electronic grotto, a miniature sound and light show to distract our attention."[31] Indeed, *sober* distraction emerged early as a key concept for articulating the uniqueness of television's spectatorial subject. As Lynn Spigel reveals, midcentury magazine and newspaper articles and advertisements addressed the threat of televisual distraction head on—by gendering it. Building on the work of Tania Modleski—who finds that soap operas formally anticipate and accommodate female viewers distracted by household duties—Spigel argues early television executives honed a "model of female spectatorship . . . based on previous notions about radio listeners . . . whose attention wasn't focused primarily on the medium (as in the cinema), but instead moved constantly between radio entertainment and a host of daily chores."[32] As a writer for *Variety* explained in October 1951, television producers embraced a "catch as catch can" approach to soliciting the female spectator's attention, using sound cues; short, discontinuous segments; and narrative recapping and repetition to create a "take it awhile, leave it awhile" framework for spectatorship.[33] Distracted and distractible, women were both an ideal audience for mid-century television and a problem for it to solve as it conquered American households.

Distraction also overdetermined scholars' explorations of television spectatorship. In *Visible Fictions: Cinema, Television, Video*, John Ellis universalizes the midcentury housewife's alleged distractibility with his theory of the televisual glance. He argues that whereas "gazing is the constitutive activity of cinema"—because its architecture and culture eliminate most distractions from the viewing experience—"broadcast television demands rather a different kind of looking: that of the glance."[34] Ellis takes the idea of the gaze from Laura Mulvey's essay "Visual Pleasure and Narrative Cinema," although he removes gender from the terms of his analysis to focus on material viewing conditions. Whereas "cinema offers a large-scale, highly detailed and photographic image," Ellis claims, "TV does not encourage the same degree of spectator concentration. There is no surrounding darkness, no anonymity of fellow viewers, no large image, no lack of movement amongst the spectators, no rapt attention."[35] "TV is a diversion," he contends, that neither requires nor can require any "extraordinary effort . . . invested in the activity of looking."[36]

Many scholars dispute Ellis's glance theory, but it remained a defining trope of television studies throughout the 1990s. They contest its intrinsic positioning of television as an aesthetically impoverished, implicitly feminized domestication of cinema, but in so doing they maintain Ellis's negative suppositions about distraction. Thus, when John Thornton Caldwell asserts that television became self-reflexive during an era of "extreme stylization . . . in the 1980s," he begins by dismissing glance theory's "cherished assumption" that "television viewers are, by nature distracted and inattentive."[37] He believes "the myth of distraction" prevents television studies from acknowledging artistically ambitious programming: "Why extrapolate that this preoccupation with something else is symptomatic of the way that television is *always* watched? Why not use an engaged and entranced viewer as the example upon which to build a theory of viewership?"[38] Why not avoid universalizing altogether, instead of simply reversing the terms of Ellis's theory? Caldwell does acknowledge the historic—and problematically gendered—origins of distracted television spectatorship.[39] But rather than critique the damage done by associating distraction with femininity, he argues for the masculine rigor of modern television—a trend that many have followed.

Consequently, distraction continues to bedevil twenty-first-century television scholarship like a demon that must be exorcised lest it reduce the status of the entire medium. The most popular weapon against such charges has been critical appreciation for so-called "quality television," with its serialized dramas, complex comedies, and well-rounded anti-heros. Whereas "most television storytelling for its first few decades was designed to be viewed in any order by a presumably distracted and undiscriminating viewer," the rise of home recording devices and DVD season box sets, as well as the fracturing of TV audiences by digital cable networks and video-on-demand platforms, enabled television producers to tell more complex stories that appeal to smaller audiences that advertisers considered desirable because of their affluence.[40] Some trace quality TV's narrative conventions back to *Hill Street Blues* (NBC, 1981–1987), but most credit *The Sopranos* (HBO, 1999–2007) with inciting a new "golden age" in television that includes *Arrested Development* (Fox, 2003–2006; Netflix, 2013, 2018–2019), *Breaking Bad* (AMC, 2008–2013), *Game of Thrones* (HBO, 2011–2019), *House of Cards* (Netflix, 2013–2018), *Lost* (ABC, 2004–2010), and *The Wire* (HBO, 2002–2008). While these shows may be popular across genders, they are mostly driven by white male protagonists and draw on male-centered genre traditions; some include explicit scenes of sexualized violence against women. Feminist and antiracist television critics have pushed back against such patriarchal canon formation by championing quality television by, for, and about women and minorities. However, they have not challenged the presumption that distracted viewing is inferior, wrong, even reprehensible. Rather, they continue to assume that good TV is TV that rivets its spectators. Bad TV is TV that allows for inattentive or intermittent viewing. But these beliefs have a history, a misogynist history. So rather than reserving praise for quality television series aimed at attentive viewers, one might ask what's wrong with the distracted spectator? Can there be a reparative history of distracted viewing and the television shows that enable it? How do certain television poetics encourage distracted spectatorship and other, allegedly deviant spectatorial practices, such as binge-watching and paranoid interpretation? And why weren't these practices encouraged earlier?

Preoccupied housewives aside, most US television producers did not solicit distracted or inebriated spectators prior to the 1990s and 2000s because until then they were active participants in their government's War on Drugs. One year before President Richard Nixon declared illegal narcotics "public enemy number one" in June 1971, the National Clearinghouse for Drug Abuse Information—a branch of the US Department of Health, Education, and Welfare—released its first televised public service announcement (PSA), "Why Do You Think They Call It Dope?"[41] In it, a precocious boy responds to a pushy dealer with a briefcase full of drugs by itemizing the dangerous side effects of each, from airplane glue to acid. Within a few years, television producers joined the War on Drugs by offering "very special episodes" in which popular characters denounce illegal narcotics. The trend arguably began with *Fat Albert and the Cosby Kids* (CBS, 1972–1984; first-run syndication 1984–1985), which in September 1973 ran an episode called "Mr. Big Timer" wherein Albert helps the police arrest a local drug dealer. *Diff'rent Strokes* (NBC 1978–1985, ABC 1985–1986) soon emerged as a leader in the very special episode phenomenon, addressing a wide range of social issues. In March 1983, for instance, "The Reporter" saw series lead Arnold Jackson (Gary Coleman) trying to warn various adults about children buying and selling drugs at his middle school. No one believes him until special guest star Nancy Reagan shows up. The first lady never gets to employ her catchphrase, "Just Say No," but the moral of the story is still clear: "All drugs are dumb," and television networks have much to gain from spreading the word.[42]

In the wake of Ms. Reagan's guest appearance, very special episodes took off among television producers keen to generate publicity while also contributing to the public interest standard under which their networks operated.[43] This eagerness led to some pretty ham-fisted writing, as one can see in the "Just Say No" episode of the children's sitcom *Punky Brewster* (NBC, 1984–1986; first-run syndication, 1987–1988) wherein nine-year-old Punky (Soleil Moon Frye) and her best friend Cherie (Cherie Johnson) fall in with a quartet of hard-partying sixth graders. The episode concludes by bleeding Punky's fictional morality play into documentary agitprop with footage of Frye leading an antidrug rally in Atlanta, Georgia. This peculiar shift reflects the slippery epistemology of very special episodes, wherein a popular actor's seeming investment in a social issue adds urgency to a fictional character's moral choice and vice versa. It is also worth noting that the vast majority of antidrug very special episodes (including "Just Say No" and "The Reporter") featured white drug dealers, casting decisions that may have helped audiences ignore how the War on Drugs was targeting African and Latinx Americans.

Very special episodes also blurred the line between messaging and merchandizing, especially in the case of the syndicated television movie

Cartoon All-Stars to the Rescue (Milton Gray et al., 1990). Produced by Roy Disney with financing from McDonald's and the Ronald McDonald Children's Charities, *Cartoon All-Stars to the Rescue* unites dozens of popular cartoon franchises to combat Smoke, an anthropomorphized puff of pot voiced by George C. Scott. When a teenage miscreant named Michael steals his little sister Corey's piggy bank to buy weed, the cartoon-character merchandise around her room comes to life to right the wrong. Corey's heroes include the Smurfs, ALF, Garfield, Winnie the Pooh, Alvin and his chipmunks, even Bugs Bunny and Daffy Duck. Cheesy though it is, *Cartoon All-Stars to the Rescue* did one thing very well: generating publicity and profits for its participants. All four broadcast networks and several independent stations and cable networks aired the special simultaneously at 10:30 a.m. on Saturday, April 21, 1990—Saturday morning being the prime time of cartoon programming.[44] Following this roadblock launch, Disney subsidiary Buena Vista Home Video released a VHS version of the telemovie—introduced by President George H. W. Bush and First Lady Barbara Bush—for sale at McDonald's restaurants. While the cartoon rights holders did license their characters to *Cartoon All-Stars to the Rescue* for free, the product placement for their tie-in merchandise was priceless. When else has a sitting president endorsed a movie about a Garfield lamp and a Winne-the-Pooh doll saving a young boy's life?

Very special episodes continued apace throughout the 1990s but took an alarming turn toward the end of the decade when the federal government began covertly paying television networks to produce antidrug content. Over the course of the 1990s, private donations for PSAs declined; in response, Congress allocated $1 billion to the White House Office of National Drug Control Policy (ONDCP) for a new five-year television ad campaign.[45] The catch was that the networks had to agree to donate an additional thirty-second spot for each one the government bought—a deal many were willing to accept in 1997 when the advertising market was languishing. By 1998, however, dot-com dollars had revived ad sales, and the networks resented the deeply discounted PSA time they'd agreed to. And so, without congressional approval, the ONDCP offered the networks a deal: the government would "forego its contractual right to a portion of matching advertising time in exchange for inclusion of antidrug themes in the plots of specific shows."[46] These included prime-time dramas *ER* (NBC, 1994–2009), *Beverly Hills, 90210* (Fox, 1990–2000), and *Seventh Heaven* (WB, 1996–2006; CW, 2006–2007) and sitcoms *Home Improvement* (ABC, 1991–1999) and *The Wayans Brothers* (WB, 1995–1999), as well as an almost random assortment of other popular series, including *General Hospital* (ABC, 1962–) and *America's Most Wanted* (Fox, 1982–2011; Lifetime 2011–2012).[47] In these deals, the ONDCP negotiated script changes, often over multiple drafts, before evaluating finished episodes based on the strength of their message and the relative popularity of the show. The agency then deducted corresponding monetary value from the network's ad-time debt, leaving the network free to resell that time to new buyers.[48] However, the White House did not acknowledge that they were sponsoring the content of these shows, which amounts to payola, according to legal scholar Ariel Berschadsky.[49] *Slate* exposed the illegal scheme in 2000, without consequence. Evidently viewers already associated network television with the War on Drugs so closely that few cared when the War broke the law.

Even before the ONDCP scandal, though, television's relationship to drugs was changing dramatically. In 1997, the Food and Drug Administration (FDA) loosened its restrictions on pharmaceuticals advertisements on television. For most of the twentieth century, drug ads either could not disclose which condition the drug was approved to treat (leading to maddeningly vague slogans like Claritin's "At last, a clear day is here") or had to include lengthy disclosures about complications and possible side effects. The new FDA regulations allowed drug makers advertising on TV to say what their drug was for and then refer viewers to a website, 800 number, or print advertisement for further information.[50] Spending for pharmaceuticals commercials skyrocketed, from $360 million in 1995 to $1.3 billion in 1998.[51] That new market no doubt contributed to networks' eagerness to buy back their advertising time from the ONDCP. Television's War on Drugs was ending; together with an industrial turn toward niche- rather than broadcasting, this change enabled creators to rethink their relationship to (mostly white) cannabis cultures and their various affects. As I will now demonstrate, revamped formal techniques would evoke highness and accommodate inebriated viewers while narrative content shifted toward normalizing rather than maligning illicit inebriants. Through textual analysis it becomes clear that the inebriated spectator is no longer a footnote of film theory nor distraction a televisual faux pas; they are now an organizing conceit of contemporary televisual poetics.

TUNING IN, TUNING OUT

Incorporating inebriated spectatorship into television culture did not require a major shift in televisual poetics. Rather producers intensified certain formal techniques conducive to distraction, enhanced focus, and paranoia. Distraction, for instance, both requires and permits television producers to accommodate short attention spans, for which certain viewers were already notorious. Producers were already adept at accommodating—and thereby creating—distractible spectators by segmenting television narratives into short, discontinuous units. Narrative fragmentation trains viewers to attend to the medium in sporadic bursts and enables programmers to string unrelated series and interstitials together into a longer flow of contiguous but not necessarily coherent entertainment. These techniques, segmentation and flow, emphasize disjunction, juxtaposition, and contrast. Under their influence, the rhythms of television can resemble the heterodox temporality of a cannabis high, wherein time may seem to pass both more slowly and more quickly than usual. In scientific studies, cannabis users often report that their attention becomes hyper-focused on minutiae and that they are also easily distracted by new stimuli—precisely the sort of intense but fleeting attention solicited by televisual segmentation. Poetics of distraction reclaim such inattentiveness and reorganize viewer identification around it, sometimes as progressive critique, as in *Broad City*, and sometimes as reactionary entertainments, as in *Jersey Shore* (MTV, 2009–2012).

Since its premiere on Comedy Central in 2014, *Broad City* has embraced a hyper-segmented, even disjointed approach to narration—and feminist politics—built on the momentary amusements of its pot-smoking heroines. Writer-creators Ilana Glazer and Abbi Jacobson play Ilana and Abbi, two white, Jewish, middle-class New York millennials who struggle with uninspiring jobs and the peculiarities of other New Yorkers, including their various lovers. They also consume a lot of cannabis, which is central to the comedy of their situation. Abbi and Ilana's screw-ups could easily become monotonous were it not for the punctuation provided by inebriation. Getting high gives the women fresh perspective on their world and affirms the transcendental power of their friendship. Journalists have described the show's politics as "sneak-attack feminism," but it would be more accurate to say that *Broad City* fuses feminism with stoner humor by manipulating the disjunction intrinsic to segmentation and flow.[52]

Segmentation and flow are not intrinsically feminist, of course, but Jacobson and Glazer exploit these televisual principles to reclaim distracted spectatorship and inebriated liberation. John Ellis defines segmentation as the division of TV programming into "small sequential unities of images and sounds whose maximum duration seems to be about five minutes." Ellis observes that "broadcast TV narration takes place across these segments," whether they comprise scenes in serialized narratives, stories in news shows, or commercial breaks.[53] Segmentation manages inattentive viewers by continually soliciting their notice with "vivid segments where the principle of logic and cause and effect is subordinated to that of association."[54] Thus it works in concert with the programming principle that Raymond Williams calls flow. Williams observes that linear television is not actually organized around discrete programs, as it claims, but rather glides through "series of differently related units in which the timing, though real, is undeclared, and in which the real internal organization is something other than the declared organization."[55] He characterizes such programming as "irresponsible" because it requires no discipline of its spectator, who may dip in and out of multiple flows on multiple channels without consequence.[56] Flow suggests that interruption is actually antithetical to television poetics, because television presents itself in such a moment-to-moment fashion that it cannot be interrupted. Plenty of television scholars have disputed the implied universality of Williams's concept of flow, but like the distracted spectator, it continues to haunt television criticism. Not all television programming relies on segmentation and flow—cf. CSPAN and Norwegian *Sakte-tv* (slow TV)—but when present they have "extraordinary effects on television as a sequential experience."[57] Indeed, by emphasizing segmentation, some contemporary television series hail a viewing subject whose flow of consciousness is equally irresponsible, more baked than businesslike.

Broad City employs a poetics of hyper-segmentation to draw the spectator into collusion with its heroines' stoner feminism. It uses pot and its oft-noted effects of temporal distortion to create funny disjunctions from Abbi and Ilana's inappropriate reactions to normal situations and their normalized reactions to outlandish situations. These distortions embellish the fantasy sequences, cutaways, and digital effects that Mittell associates with "complex comedy" in the twenty-first century.[58] Within a single beat, the show moves from one joke to another with minimal causal connection; this device can make a sober viewer feel stoned and a stoned viewer feel at home. Coincidence is one of Glazer and Jacobson's favorite comic devices, as evidenced by the cold open for "Apartment Hunters" (season one, episode nine), a music video spoof that turns out to be a fantasy sequence. Dressed in homage to Nicki Minaj and Missy Elliott, Ilana and Abbi dance into a bank to the Drake song "Started from the Bottom" (2013), mugging for the camera like Elliott does in the video for her song "The Rain (Supa Dupa Fly)" (Hype Williams, 1997).[59] After a minute, a female voice starts repeating "ma'am" to the beat of the song; this voice becomes more and more insistent until it interrupts the song . . . and Abbi's reverie. Evidently Abbi forgot to sign the check she is trying to deposit. Ilana tries to defend Abbi to the disgruntled teller, but a "low funds" alert on her phone interrupts their conversation, annoying the teller even further. Finally, the scene ends with Ilana handing the teller several rolls of nickels she would like "to cash" for quarters.

Each of these jokes bears some narrative connection to the one before it, but their effects are not cumulative, which is to say that none requires the viewer to have paid attention to the previous joke to understand it. Cashing nickels in for quarters is funny even if it does not proceed from Ilana's cell phone alert; mocking a snobby bank teller can be humorous whether or not it is preceded by a music video parody. (This is especially true given Abbi's reaction to the teller, which is to insist that she did not sign the check because "I wasn't sure if there was a special teller I should go to for checks that are this large.") Each joke becomes, in effect, its own microsegment, lasting between ten and twenty-five seconds. Given such hyper-segmentation, it scarcely matters whether a viewer has just come in on the episode or got distracted and lost track of the plot. Within a few seconds, another joke will arrive that may reward but does not require any prior knowledge of the series or situation. By soliciting moment-to-moment engagement, the show achieves a poetics of segmentation akin to and accommodating of distracted, inebriated spectatorship.[60]

As the episode goes on, a plot does emerge, but *Broad City* peppers its heroines' travails with incongruous statements and actions that create humorous microsegments within longer narrative beats. Abbi tries (and fails) to use her new windfall to find a better apartment while Ilana tries (and fails) to stop the overdrafts on her bank account by locating and returning a missing cable remote. Because there is no laugh track, verbal jokes and physical gags whiz by without notice, which makes them ideally suited for stoned viewers. As intoxication phenomenologist David Lenson observes, drugs "dramatize the anomalies and dilemmas of consciousness," as does Glazer and Jacobson's unpredictable, rapid-fire approach to humor.[61] Their comedy recreates weed's disruptions of human cognition, the way that its high slightly alienates users from their surroundings, making them focus on and find amusement in small anomalies. *Broad City* accentuates moment-to-moment micro-

FIGURE 21. Ilana expands her mind in *Broad City* (Comedy Central, 2014–2019).

ecologies of humor, each of which generates its own small punch line or gag before dispersing as a new microecology coheres.

These humorous disjunctions often contain violations and overt critiques of restrictive gender norms, which is how *Broad City* marries its poetics of inebriation to feminist politics and reclaims distractibility as resistance.[62] Later in "Apartment Hunters," Ilana decides that the best way to find her lost cable remote is to get as high as she was the last time she used it. The camera executes a string of successive zooms as Ilana works her way through a large joint and recalls, "last year . . . Brooklyn . . . my old apartment on Flatbush . . . bad sex. Really bad sex. The worst sex . . . Dale!" (figure 21). Dale is her ex-roommate and an obsessive, unattractive weirdo. Ilana betrays no shame for having slept with him, however, as she never shows shame for her sexual appetite, drug use, poor work ethic, or inappropriate behavior. Case in point: the episode ends with Ilana earnestly advising a seven-year-old not to do drugs because of the impact they have had on her short-term memory. "I'm missing hundreds of pairs of underwear," she warns the girl, in what amounts to a send-up of Reagan's "Just Say No" injunction. Ilana's hedonism positions her as id to Abbi's superego in their odd-couple comedy, but Abbi also refuses to adhere to sexist and antidrug cultural norms; she's just quieter in her noncompliance. Pot helps both characters reject social expectations and pursue the things that make them happy, including casual sex, more drugs, and—most of all—their friendship.

Cannabis also loosens Abbi and Ilana's causal reasoning in ways that enable them to critique and resist normative femininity, and the show encourages its inebriated spectator to do likewise. "Two Chainz," for example (season 3, episode 1), revolves around Abbi's anxiety about what to wear to a friend's gallery show—until she realizes that such concerns are trivial and antifeminist. The episode begins with Abbi worrying that her shirt is not cool enough for the event, so she buys a new one at a pop-up boutique, but the sales attendant forgets to remove a prominent security tag. Abbi is about to give up and skip the show when Ilana observes, "Dude, who cares about a stupid little tag? Artists aren't judged by what they wear. Look at Joss Stone. She's a genius, and she's never even worn shoes." Ilana's claim is patently hyperbolic, but after ten seconds' silent consideration, it convinces Abbi. Weed lowers the women's inhibitions enough to allow them to do what they want— go to a cool gallery show—without being held back by societal expectations. It is also worth noting that Abbi does not smoke pot onscreen in "Two Chainz"; she does not decide to wear a seemingly stolen shirt because she is stoned. Rather, weed has created a private counterculture between Abbi and Ilana that enables them to resist capitalist ideology— and inspires the spectator to do the same. To be sure, white privilege facilitates their rebellion, but *Broad City* generally overlooks racial inequality to pursue its stoner feminism.[63]

Within the limits of white feminism, *Broad City* uses a poetics of distraction for feminist critique, but not all shows do. Inebriated poetics can also enable reactionary storytelling, as in the case of *Jersey Shore*, where recaps, replays, and teasers create a poetics of repetition to titillate an inebriated spectator and assist inebriated viewers. Many reality shows intoxicate their cast members to exacerbate tensions on set, but *Jersey Shore* also extends inebriation into their narrative poetics, encouraging viewers to invest in characters by inviting them into their headspace.[64] When watching the series sober, I found its various repetitions unnecessary, even irksome. When I was high, though, those same devices became incredibly helpful as I struggled to keep track of the trivial rivalries, arguments, and brawls that compose each season. Repetition also kept me emotionally involved with the cast even as it reduced them to stereotypes.

Jersey Shore celebrates a culture of inebriation, as its cast—eight Italian-American-identified young adults—drink, have sex, and fight at a house share in Seaside Heights, New Jersey. Certain scenes imply that they also smoke pot and take other recreational drugs. In the pilot episode, viewers see cast member Vinny Guadagnino wearing sunglasses at night as he reclines in the hot tub. Many female reality television stars resort to wearing sunglasses when they have not had their makeup done, but Vinny's shades suggest another use for the fashion accessory: hiding red eyes and dilated pupils.[65] Off camera, friends of the cast were arrested leaving the house with illegal narcotics, and one cast member has admitted to being high during filming.[66] In sum, *Jersey Shore* and its paratexts give viewers plenty of reasons to assume that its cast members are intoxicated much of the time. Repetitions, replays, and teasers encourage viewers to identify with yet attend lightly to the drunken drama of the series; they suggest that the series' ideal spectator is one who shares the inebriated mindset of the cast.

As Derek Kompare notes, repetition is an intrinsic element of televisual poetics. Television, he suggests, may not be "the ideal conduit for 'live,' new events" but rather "a machine of repetition, geared toward the constant recirculation of recorded, already-seen events."[67] That machinery includes syndicated reruns of popular television series, instant replays during sports coverage, as well as the recap sequences that begin new episodes of ongoing series, reminding viewers of what happened in previous episodes. Reality television incorporates multiple strategies of repetition into its narrative techniques, all of which assist distracted viewers and encourage attentive viewers to relax their cognitive faculties. *Jersey Shore* is typical in offering recap sequences at the start of every episode. Each episode also ends with teasers that predict the physical and verbal confrontations yet to come, effectively rendering them repetitions when they arrive. There are also teasers before many commercial breaks: quick snippets of upcoming scenes designed to pique viewers' interest and keep them watching across the interruption. Then there's the so-called "ad-break double-take."[68] In an ad-break double-take, the same scene is repeated before and after a commercial sequence. Unlike teasers or cliffhangers, which leave a scene unresolved across a break, ad-break double-takes simply recycle the same footage with little to no editorial intervention. The recycling is the point; the ad-break double-takes "make repetition, interruption and distraction pleasurable" by emphasizing the significance of their content.[69] They accommodate distraction, but they also solicit it, marking a show—regardless of its narrative content—as appropriate for stoned or otherwise compromised viewers.

Ad-break double-takes proliferate throughout all six seasons of *Jersey Shore*, as they do through many reality television series. The first appears about two-thirds of the way through the series' second episode, "The

Tanned Triangle," when Mike "The Situation" Sorrentino sees a house-mate whom he recently kissed, Samantha "Sammi" Giancola, making out with fellow housemate Ronnie Ortiz-Magro. Actual chronology can be difficult to discern on *Jersey Shore*, but both kisses appear to happen on the same night at the same club. The drama begins when the camera captures Mike and Sammi kissing on the dance floor. After a brief aside for a subplot involving housemates Paul "Pauly D" DelVecchio and Jennifer "JWoww" Farley, the episode cuts to Sammi and Ronnie dancing and kissing as Mike asks in voiceover, "What is going on right now?" Pauly D announces, "That's a whole drama situation right there," before Mike confronts Sammi. Then an establishing shot and a "coming up" title teaser introduces a commercial break. After the break, a new segment begins with a previously seen shot of the Situation and Pauly D looking to their left, followed by an apparent eyeline match to earlier footage of Sammi and Ronnie kissing. The episode then expands the confrontation between Sammi and Mike, excerpted before the commercial break, with key lines of dialogue repeated for emphasis. In this manner, a few idle kisses become a dramatic event to titillate viewers and improve ratings. For stoned viewers who (like myself) may have become distracted in the flow from episode to break and back, the repetition fosters an undeserved sense of narrative mastery. Of course I know exactly what's going on—because *Jersey Shore* anticipated my inebriation and took the necessary steps to accommodate it.

Perhaps the more infamous and egregious of *Jersey Shore*'s many double-takes occurs when a belligerent bar patron punches Nicole "Snooki" Polizzi in the face ("Fade to Black" [season one, episode four]). *Jersey Shore* predicted the assault in the previous episode's final teaser, rendering the event itself a mere elaboration of prior knowledge. The teaser includes the actual moment when Snooki gets hit by a stranger (later identified as Brad Ferro), but producers chose to excise the punch from "Fade to Black," instead pairing its soundtrack with a black screen. The encounter happens at a boardwalk bar where the housemates run into three "typical college fraternity losers," as Vinny describes Ferro and his friends, who heckle the cast members and steal their drinks. Snooki orders Ferro to "get your fucking ugly ass out of our faces," then the screen goes dark and someone asks incredulously, "Are you gonna hit a girl?" The episode ends by crosscutting between Snooki crying on the floor and Ferro being arrested by local police; intermittent fades to black punctuate the drama, perhaps in homage to the episode's title.

Snooki's assault reappears at the start of the next episode, "Just Another Day at the Shore" (season one, episode five), beginning with the verbal exchange that preceded Ferro's punch. The scene repeats, shot for shot, after which Sammi and Jwoww help Snooki to the bathroom and Ronnie, Vinny, Pauly D, and the Situation follow Ferro outside. Eventually everyone heads home to discuss the assault. Snooki goes straight to bed, but various housemates visit her to sympathize and declare their loyalty. Finally, Ronnie and Sammi go out to the porch, where Ronnie hangs his head in his hands and declares "I'm like, I feel so mad because, like, Mike saw it happen." This confession invites yet another replay of the incident, specifically of Snooki lying on the floor of the bar holding her face, now slowed down and presented with a slight iris effect to convey subjective memory. Later on, Ronnie and Vinny recount the incident to Ronnie's parents. Shortly thereafter, Snooki calls the Seaside Heights police to receive an update on her assailant's arrest. As she listens to the recorded message, shots from the assault sequence appear again: Ferro being escorted from the bar, Ferro being arrested. There's a commercial break, and the scene repeats without the Ferro footage, a slight variation on the classic ad-break double-take.

Snooki's assault was a ratings boon for *Jersey Shore*; no doubt producers repeated it to exploit attendant publicity. However, its many repetitions also reveal complex vectors of identification among cast members and between cast members and viewers that reinforce both inebriated spectatorship and traditional gender roles. As Snooki explains in multiple interview segments, she did not feel much rapport with her housemates before the assault. Her drunk behavior on their first night together—only a few nights before the fight with Ferro—embarrassed her and repelled some of her housemates. Once victimized, though, Snooki finally feels accepted by the group, who embrace their role as protectors. As Ronnie explains to her, "Like, we love you. Like, we were all fucking heated tonight. Like, we all almost went to jail for you. We love you, Snooks. We love each other, you get that? We're like one big family." Amanda Ann Klein observes that abjection is intrinsic to gender and character roles on *Jersey Shore*; here it undergirds the cast's understanding of themselves as a collective.[70] Ronnie maintains that it was Snooki's assault and the rest of the cast's social abjection that prompts them to identify "like" a family. Revisiting the incident through replays and conversations stresses the impetus for their unification and shared identification as a televisual property.[71]

Repetition also facilitates the spectator's identification with the cast and with themselves as a *Jersey Shore* viewer. Abjection is critical to both of these dynamics, in an unsavory yet important example of the poetics of inebriation. *Not* seeing what happened to Snooki again and again increases the spectator's empathy for her, while the many diegetic rehearsals and double takes increase the spectator's identification with themself as a *frustrated* viewer of the show. In an article entitled "The Most Annoying Thing About Reality TV," *Gawker* critic Brian Moylan excoriates the ad-break double-take: "There's a commercial break and when we get back, we see the exact same clip. We don't need to see that because we *just fucking saw it*." Moylan's anger reveals a deeper self-loathing, expressed in his conviction that reality TV producers really believe the genre's fans (and critics) to be "a bunch of twitching, ADD-addled idiots who can't keep their fingers off the remote control long enough to watch an entire television program."[72] As much as Moylan—and others—may feel insulted by reality television's propensity for repetition, they are also interpellated by it. Not misinterpellated, either: "We're a culture that prides itself on having seen it all. When you show us all the good stuff over and over and over again, we actually have seen it all," Moylan concludes.[73] In sum, the repetitions induce in the viewer feelings of abjection similar to those the show organizes around its cast. The repeats make us aware of ourselves as reality TV viewers and as compromised subjects, perhaps as compromised as the subjects we're watching.

Crucially, though, repetition also limits the spectator's identification with the cast, distantiating them from cast members so that they can still look down on them. There's something surreal and dissociative about watching scenes of human wretchedness replayed again and again for entertainment. Such distantiation encourages the spectator to identify with themselves as spectator and to judge the cast members they are watching. In the case of *Jersey Shore*, this dynamic is fundamentally reactionary, organized around negative stereotypes about Italian Americans that reinforce Anglo-American gender roles.[74] Whiteness, then, is very much at issue in *Jersey Shore*'s poetics and performances of inebriation; the cast is depicted at the limits of a kind of racialized propriety, such that white self-policing becomes central to the show's entertainment value. Ad-break double-takes and other techniques of repetition encourage viewers, high and sober, to engage with the inebriated melodrama of the cast members; such techniques foster a powerful sense of involvement in the series, whether one happens to be fully attentive or not.

OF BINGES AND BONGS

Both *Broad City* and *Jersey Shore* exploit televisual poetics of distraction to construct an inebriated spectator position, be it progressive or conservative. But distractibility is not the only side effect of cannabis inebriation, nor the only mode of inebriated spectatorship in contemporary US television. As previously noted, pot is a biphasic drug, meaning that it can have opposite effects on different people or on the same person when consumed in different amounts. Cannabis can make its users absent minded or facilitate deeper engagement with a specific object or task. Certain cannabis strains—such as Sour Diesel and True OG—are renowned for reducing stress and distraction and increasing concentration.[75] Particularly indica-heavy strains can produce a physically—but not mentally—sedentary high known as *couch lock*. *Couch lock* might also describe a wide-spread development in twenty-first-century television consumption: watching three or more episodes of a given series in succession, a practice more commonly referred to as binge-watching. As I will show, some television shows pursue a binge-friendly poetics of enhanced focus to increase viewers' investment in their emotional dramas, which can either blind viewers to the social prejudices informing those dramas (as in *Breaking Bad*) or encourage a kind of viewerly compassion that feels progressive even when it isn't (as in *High Maintenance* [HBO, 2016–]).

Binge-watching comprises "a hybrid of technology and culture" unique to the 2010s.[76] It combines subscription video-on-demand media platforms and high production value, highly serialized television shows with a television culture that celebrates attentive connoisseur spectatorship. Viewers certainly watched television in large doses before the 2010s—telethons, TV marathons, and mini-series all have histories of keeping audiences on the couch for hours—but binge-watching is a new media phenomenon. It is a result of the "watch what you want, when you want" ethos of home video and the "on-demand culture" of VOD services combined with new television poetics that encourage longer viewing sessions.[77] As Jonathan Crary notes, both television and internet cultures "produce an unprecedented mixture of diffuse attentiveness and quasi-automatism, which can be maintained for remarkably long periods of time."[78] Crary was writing in 1999—before DVD season box sets enabled even an approximation of modern binge-watching (see chapter 1)—and notably he is *not* writing about actual viewers or viewing practices but about the ideologies of attention imposed by different media. Yet he accurately predicts how a conjunction of television and telematics would impact spectatorial norms. VOD services standardized the conditions for an even more sedentary reception culture, wherein attention could be both diffuse and highly focused, delivering the viewer into a fictional world they might occupy for hours on end.

Plenty of television viewers binge sober, yet descriptions of binge-watching often rely on metaphors of inebriation. In her critical review of television journalism, Ri Pierce-Grove shows that reporters frequently employ addiction and narcotic metaphors to explain the lure and pleasure of the binge.[79] They invoke an "aura of compulsion" around binge-watching wherein "the watcher enters something like a different state of consciousness."[80] James Poniewozik describes sinking into a binge as "The Suck: that narcotic, tidal feeling of getting drawn into a show and letting it wash over you for hours."[81] Binge-watching is an acculturated mode of spectatorship wherein television's serial storytelling becomes a lure to entrance viewers of the on-demand age. Tanya Horeck, Mareike Jenner, and Tina Kendall note that while binge-watching evokes concentration and connoisseurship, not to mention "longevity, duration, and endurance," it also points to on-demand viewers' "reduced attention spans," as they decline the "longer, ongoing commitment" of linear television releases for "watching hour after consecutive hour in short blocks of time that makes them *feel* longer and more intense."[82] This feeling reflects and reinforces poetics of enhanced focus and their emotional engagement of the spectator.

The culture of binge-watching and hyper-focused spectatorship has changed which television shows receive the most cultural approbation and why. As Pierce-Grove observes, discourse around binge-watching strongly associates it with prestige or quality television (even though data suggests that *Gilmore Girls* [WB, 2000–2006; CW, 2006–2007] may actually be the most frequently binged show on Netflix).[83] Among these series, *Breaking Bad* stands out for the impact that bingeing has had on both the show and its critical reception. *Breaking Bad* traces the moral devolution of a high school chemistry teacher, Walter White (Bryan Cranston), as cancer and financial necessity drive him to make and sell methamphetamine. Walt's character becomes darker, meaner, and more self-interested with each passing season, complicating his relationships with his family and business associates. During its first season on AMC, the series averaged less than a million viewers per episode. Five years later, an estimated ten million people tuned in for the finale.[84] Industry analysts attributed the series' late popularity to the Netflix effect: once seasons one and two were added to the SVOD service in September 2011, viewers binge-watched both and then became so-called "appointment viewers," catching new episodes live on AMC and driving ad prices up to $250,000 per spot.[85]

Breaking Bad's success, and the subsequent success of similar series, suggests a symbiosis among highly serialized, "quality" dramas; SVOD services; and binge-watching. As Jason Mittell notes, one of the hallmarks of serial storytelling, across all television genres, is "a sustained narrative world," the richer, the better.[86] *Breaking Bad*'s creator, Vince Gilligan, defines his show as "hyperserialized," because of its involved, interlocking episode, season, and series arcs.[87] These stories, plus the excitement of illegal drug trafficking, provided ample fodder for complex narration and caught the eye of Netflix executives. As Netflix's chief content officer, Ted Sarandos, explained in 2012, "the more serialized a show, the more interested we are in it."[88] Netflix bingers kept *Breaking Bad* in production at AMC—a fact Gilligan has gratefully acknowledged.[89] The series' symbiotic relationship to binge-watching thus provided popular and academic critics with a unique opportunity to explore how shows encourage hyper-focused spectatorship. However, their praise focused almost exclusively on the series' narrative complexity, intertextual references, and compelling performances. Consequently, critics often dismissed or outright ignored the show's appalling racial and sexual politics. This suggests that enhanced focus can blind viewers to the larger social systems shaping a series. For in its story and its storytelling, *Breaking Bad* suggests that women and Latinx Americans are less important than white men, that they can be regarded as objects that serve or impede white men's ambitions. Indeed, the show's sexism began attracting attention only as the series neared its finale and fans of the series set up "hate boards" to express their contempt for the series' lead female character.[90] And while some academics have addressed the series' stereotypical representations of Latinx men, the problem never got the popular attention it warrants.

Especially when combined with binge-watching, poetics of enhanced focus change the spectator's experience of character and amplify melodrama, making emotional stories that much more emotional and potentially obscuring their political implications. As Poniewozik explains, *Breaking Bad* "tells the story of a man's descent, or rise, from ordinary life to murderous criminality" over the course of about two narrative years.[91] AMC stretched that short interval over five and a half years of broadcast time; between when the show premiered in January 2008 and ended in September 2013, "live viewers saw Walter White's change distended . . . in a way that emphasized the gradual slope of moral compromise."[92] By contrast, Poniewozik observes, "the binger saw him change in time-lapse, in a way that suggested that the tendency to arrogance and evil was in him all along. Neither perception is wrong. In fact, both themes are thoroughly built into the show. But how you watch, in some way, affects the story you see."[93] As Gilligan explained to the *Wall Street Journal* in 2012, *Breaking Bad*'s creators "keep in mind fans who take the story 'in a giant inhalation'" as well those who watch each episode as broadcast.[94] Gilligan's metaphor acknowledges the inebriating quality of ingesting large quantities of a complex serial narrative, as well as the physiological rush of consuming elaborate dramas in large doses. It also affirms that *Breaking Bad*'s creators anticipate a hyper-focused spectator, whom they solicit using conventions of serial narration such as season-long story arcs, episode cliffhangers, and recurring visual motifs. These devices keep viewers watching, but watching for what?

The poetics of hyper-focused spectatorship have specific hermeneutical effects, namely discouraging contemplation in favor of riveted narrative engagement. Intoxicated with story, the spectator is encouraged to lose sight of the world outside the show, which may include the social and historical inequalities that organize its world. In the case of *Breaking Bad* specifically, critics only eventually noticed the misogynist treatment of female characters within the show's world. They failed to observe the vilification or exclusion of Latinx characters from its version of Albuquerque, New Mexico. Misogyny and racism are never addressed within the series; rather they structured the show's universe while its poetics direct viewers' attention elsewhere.[95]

Neither the mainstream media nor television scholars commented on the tenor of Walter's relationship with his wife, Skyler (Anna Gunn), until part two of *Breaking Bad*'s final season began in 2013. In August 2013, *A.V. Club* critic Stephen Bowie observed, "real sexism is built in to the show, which rarely evinces any curiosity about Skyler's inner life, apart from how it affects Walt," and Anne Gunn penned an op-ed for the *New York Times* condemning the long-standing social media forums where Walt's fans threatened her with violence.[96] Later that fall in the *Atlantic*, Silpa Kovvali bemoaned "the show's inability to create a single non-infuriating female character," a complaint then echoed by other magazines and newspapers.[97] Over the next five years, a handful of scholarly articles and book chapters would appear questioning the series' representation of Skyler and fans' animosity for Gunn.[98] Yet many leading television scholars continue to dismiss Walt's disregard for Skyler's intelligence, sovereignty, and mental health, arguing that they are symptoms of his larger devolution. They write as if narrative focus on his experience precludes analysis of hers. Jason Mittell does devote three pages of his book *Complex TV* to re-narrating *Breaking Bad* around Skyler's character arc, such that it becomes "the tale of a wronged wife destroyed by her husband's criminal ambitions and emotional abuse" and "offer[s] a vital critique of Walt's damaged masculinity."[99] The trouble is that *Breaking Bad* isn't Skyler's story; as Mittell's phrasing makes clear, the series structurally subordinates Skyler's experience in order to focus on Walt's. Indeed, it does that job so well that even politically progressive critics like Mittell miss the fact that Walt isn't just mean to his wife, he tries to rape her.

The attempted rape scene comes early on in the series and thus early on in Walter's moral devolution, suggesting that rape is *not that bad* in the ethical calculus of *Breaking Bad*. As television scholar Paul Elliott Johnson points out, the scene (in season two, episode one) was originally praised by critics as evidence of Walt's complexity and virility.[100] In it, Walt comes home from watching his distributor, Tuco Salamanca (Raymond Cruz), beat another man to death. A loud buzzing sonically conveys Walt's trauma, as he stands in front of the television, deaf to Skyler's entreaties. Eventually, he follows her into the kitchen, close to tears. He hugs her from behind and begins to cry, at which point his embrace becomes a forcible attempt at sex. Skyler asks him to slow down; when he doesn't, she commands "Enough! . . . Hold up! . . . Stop it. . . . STOP IT!" at which point he finally does. That the show continues to represent Walt as a sympathetic character, even a sympathetic antihero, after he assaults his wife is deeply troubling. That *Breaking Bad*'s critic-fans would make jokes about the scene is horrifying. Mittell, for instance, notes that Walt's "sex life with Skyler *perks up* when he discovers his dark side in the first season, culminating in an aggressive nonconsensual encounter in their kitchen."[101] Perhaps the series' poetics of hyper-focus is so immersive that even trained professionals get lost in it magic. But somehow, many scholars never mention the attempted rape while analyzing Walt's attitude of gendered and racialized entitlement.[102]

Walter's assault on Skyler was not the only troubling scene in this episode to escape censure, however; critics also overlooked its dehumanizing representation of Latinx men, which is part of a pattern throughout the series. The episode, and thus the whole second season, begins with Tuco brutally murdering his assistant No-Doze (Cesar Garcia). Tuco is one of many irrational, violent Latinx drug lords that *Breaking Bad* routinely depicts as violently emotional, even sociopathic, in contrast to Walt's white rationalism. In this particular incident, Tuco attacks No-Doze for telling Walter and his partner, Jesse Pinkman (Aaron Paul), to "Remember who you're working for." After No-Doze dies from blows to his head, Tuco starts kicking him in the ribs in frustration. Yet Tuco is by no means *Breaking Bad*'s most despicable narcotics kingpin; Gustavo Fring (Giancarlo Esposito) kills thirteen people over the course of the series. His calm demeanor and bourgeois lifestyle serve as ironic counterpoints to his viciousness—all the more ironic, on this show, because he is Latinx. Then there are Tortuga (Danny Trejo), the Salamanca twins, and various other members of the Juárez drug cartel, all of whom are less developed and indeed less human than their white counterparts. With two exceptions, Latinx characters only enter *Breaking Bad* as drug dealers. Those exceptions are Carmen Molina (Carmen Serano), the assistant principal at Walt's school who is also the subject of an unwanted sexual advance from Walt, and Steven Gomez (Steven Michael Quezada), a Drug Enforcement Administration (DEA) agent regularly referred to as "Gomie." As Emily VanDerWerff points out, "Albuquerque's population is nearly half Latino," making *Breaking Bad*'s near universal criminalization of Latino characters that much more offensive.[103] VanDerWerff is the only mainstream media journalist to comment on the show's racial politics. Malcom Harris wrote about its white supremacy for the *New Inquiry* (later reprinted in *Salon*) and Maitri Mehta discussed the accusations of racism for *Bustle*, although she ultimately recommends that readers "not write off *Breaking Bad* as racist. After all, it doesn't vilify people of color more than white people."[104] No, just more systematically and to the exclusion of almost any other depictions of people of color. But so carefully does the series keep its spectator focused on Walt's experience of gender and race—which is to say, on privileged obliviousness—that critics largely failed to recognize its chauvinism.[105]

What makes *Breaking Bad* so bingeable is the immersive, protagonist-driven narrative world it invites viewers to occupy; what makes *Breaking Bad* so problematic is that immersion in that world inhibits critique of it. This issue is directly related to the spectatorial position the show creates, because its enhanced focus is also premised on narrative enworlding. Viewers are encouraged to sink deeply into the characters' universe, not to question the assembly of that universe, the prejudices and genre traditions that organize it. Its intertextual allusions and in-jokes never draw attention to its racism. Enhanced focus isn't self-critical, it turns out. It directs its spectator toward issues, tropes, and patterns the series wants them to appreciate, not those it considers beneath notice.

To that end, poetics of enhanced focus often offer viewers exciting visual details to encourage hyperattentive viewing. Just as cannabinoid receptors in the cerebral cortex help pot users narrow their attention to specific stimuli, highly serialized television series solicit close analysis of small particulars to increase viewer loyalty. This controlled and controlling gesture shapes the spectator's experience, as it suggests that some details (such as costuming) are more important than others (such as white supremacy). While stonedly binge-watching the first season of *Breaking Bad*, I became fixated on the color symbolism in Kathleen Detoro and Malan Breton's costume design. Each character has a signature color that they almost always wear. Walter habitually dresses in green. The sole exception in the first season is when he and Skyler attend a former colleague's birthday party. Walt is deeply out of his element there—and wearing blue. Skyler, for her part, almost always has on blue; her sister Marie (Betsy Brandt) dresses in purple; Marie's husband Hank (Dean Norris), a DEA agent Walter routinely outsmarts, sports yellow; and Walt's partner Jesse consistently wears red. (He also drives a red car and put chili powder in the meth he cooked before teaming up with Walt.) These trends continue with little variation throughout the series' first four seasons. Does all this color symbolism actually symbolize anything? No, but it gives the spectator a pattern to follow. It creates the impression of a complex system that must be closely tracked. After three episodes of thematic costuming, I began obsessing over what each character was wearing, squawking in victory each time the pattern continued. The impression of complexity created by such pseudo-symbolism—and by the Bruce Banner I was smoking—made my perceptions feel important, which encouraged further concentration and even longer viewing sessions. Hyper-focus revealed itself to be a new way of watching TV—as Steiner and Xu put it, "a hybrid of technology and culture"—which is not to say that it was a better or richer way of watching TV. Rather it facilitated my investment in meaningless visual details and deepened my engagement with the show, if not with its politics. It rewarded my inebriated concentration and evoked similar concentration in the sober viewers I dragged into my obsession.

To be clear, this chapter is not advocating cannabis as a televisual aid nor "quality television" as the sole genre deploying poetics of enhanced focus. Other shows encourage an inebriated spectatorship of enhanced focus by toying with the serial narrative form. *High Maintenance*, for example, engages the viewer by disrupting their expectations of protagonist-driven storytelling and offering them a narrative universe that they can only glimpse, never master. As the universe in question happens to be twenty-first-century Brooklyn, such narration reflects the diverse spectrum of communities sharing space in the borough. The show's only regular character is its organizing conceit: the Guy (Ben Sinclair), a local pot dealer who delivers his wares by bike. Each episode features one or two vignettes about different people who cross paths with the Guy. Some are customers; some aren't. Some never exchange a single word with the Guy. Thus, the Guy and his product do not provide continuity between episodes so much as contiguity. Few characters besides the Guy appear in more than one episode, and there is no narrative development between most episodes. What emerges instead is a sense of a certain place (Brooklyn) at a certain time (the 2010s) and a spectatorship of compassion that celebrates difference as such without recognizing social inequality. This compassion arises from the show's structural approach to depicting community while also evoking the empathic pleasures of a good cannabis high. In its own way, however, it reveals the blinkered outlook of enhanced focus just as much as *Breaking Bad*'s chauvinism.

Through discontinuous episodes, *High Maintenance* encourages its spectator to wander its fictional Brooklyn—a dynamic that also makes it highly bingeable. Because each episode bears little to no relation to the previous episode, there's no telling whose stories it might contain.[106] By the same token, the vignettes within any given episode have at most a coincidental relation to one another. "Tick" (season one, episode four) begins as the Guy visits with a couple of tense new parents who vehemently decline his product. It's not clear how the Guy knows them; still, he takes their recycling out as he leaves. The camera follows him outside, then changes direction to accompany Wei (Clem Cheung) as he collects the couple's bottles and takes them to a sorting facility, where he meets his wife, Joon (Kristen Hung). Wei and the Guy never notice one another, yet Wei leads the spectator into the first of the episode's two vignettes, both of which address intergenerational strife (figure 22).

Wei and Joon's story focuses on their relationship with their son Liang (Stephen Lin), a musician visiting from Berlin. At lunch, Liang's girlfriend gives Joon an iPhone to help her stay in better touch with her son. Joon is excited, but Wei scoffs at the gift even though he is perceptibly troubled by the growing distance between him and Liang. Later, the camera accompanies Joon to a Brooklyn Public Library class on

FIGURE 22. The Guy and Wei cross paths in *High Maintenance* (HBO, 2016–).

iPhones, then leaves with another student, Jim (Peter Friedman), a retired captain of industry who recently moved to Brooklyn to reconnect with his adult daughter and her family. This is the same family whose recycling the Guy took out at the beginning of the episode. Evidently the Guy was at the house to deliver to Jim, who has embraced cannabis along with morning raves and adult daycare in his quest to become more open to the pleasures life can offer.

Jim's daughter, Quinn (Bridget Moloney), is having a hard time learning to live with this new version of her father, however. Wei is in the background when Quinn and her husband come home from a dinner party and find the brownstone they share with Jim full of smoke. (While babysitting, Jim accidentally put an electric kettle on the gas stove, scorching its plastic.) In the ensuing fight, it becomes clear that neither Jim nor Quinn understand how to address the injuries of their shared past. But the night ends with Jim reaching out to Quinn via text message, using GIFs and emojis he learned about in the aforementioned library class. Smartphones cannot resolve these families' problems, but like the thematic links created within the episode's vignette structure, they do offer hope for future communion.

Notably, "Tick" ends with a long shot of Wei playing the erhu alone in the Jay Street subway station, a place where he once performed with Liang. As the credits roll, Wei's solo concert suggests that he shares Liang's desire for greater connection even if he is unable to express his wish verbally. The long shot of Wei airing his sorrow exemplifies the series' deep compassion for its characters. Indeed, compassion emerged as *High*

Maintenance's defining characteristic for many critics, as distinctive as its conceit and far more important to its spectatorial address.[107] The series rarely presents its characters as jokes but rather frames their foibles as unique contributions to the city's vibrant tapestry. Hence the *New Yorker*'s Rachel Syme compares its stream of consciousness to "the surprise of noting the humanity of others," even animals, such as the canine protagonist of the shaggy dog episode "Grandpa" (season 1, episode 3).[108]

This compassion comes not from the Guy but from the show's poetics, the perspective it creates for its spectator on its world. While many critics describe the Guy as mellow, affable, even benevolent, he also exhibits an air of menace at times. During "Tick," an interstitial scene catches up with the Guy as he encounters a man passed out drunk in an abandoned chair on the sidewalk. Two hipsters are waiting for the man to awaken so that they can take the chair. As the Guy's focus shifts from the man to his observers, he becomes visibly upset. His brow furrows with first confusion, then rage. The Guy seems unable to abide the furniture vultures' indifference to human suffering, although he eventually walks away without helping the drunk man. In season two, the spectator learns a bit more about the Guy's past—that he has an ex-wife and a girlfriend with a substance abuse problem. His vexed relationships with both suggest narcissistic obliviousness and a certain willful immaturity. Such anecdotal insights add complexity to the Guy's character without turning him into yet another of twenty-first-century television's troubled white male protagonists (e.g., Walter White) because his drama never becomes central to the show.

Rather, the Guy provides a vehicle for the show's investigation of Brooklyn. Whether or not the viewer has "a weed guy," the Guy becomes their guy, which makes watching *High Maintenance* akin to participating in Brooklyn cannabis culture. As I have argued elsewhere, though, this conceit privileges the Guy's white perspective and leads the show to focus on "post-racial" hipster enclaves over communities of color.[109] Perhaps because Sinclair is one of the series' writer-creators (along with Katja Blichfeld), *High Maintenance* never questions its focalization, how the Guy's privileged detachment arises from the systemic social inequalities of his borough and his country. Instead the show shares his privilege, as seen in the easy thematic equation it draws between Wei's situation and Jim's. For all its shortcomings, though, the series does solicit enhanced focus (and by extension binge-watching) through a compassion for difference as such, which remains a radical move within American television. Indeed, the show's poetics of connection are difficult to resist: it's reassuring to focus on the things we have in common rather than the institutions and ideologies driving us apart.

It bears repeating that enhanced focus is one version of inebriated spectatorship, one that encourages a specific kind of viewer behavior called binge-watching. Binge-watching is a spectatorial practice; enhanced focus is one facet of a subject position created by a television series that any viewer may adopt or reject. Just because you do not binge *Breaking Bad* or prefer to wait a week between each episode of *High Maintenance* does not mean that these shows are not interpellating you as an inebriated spectator. The terrible (and wonderful) thing about spectator positioning is that it exists whether we submit to it or not. Turning one's focus to the formal composition of enhanced focus may undermine its effects in that instance, but it does not change the structure of address or the ideologies that address imposes on the spectator, be they racism or race-blind compassion.

DOOBIE-OUS INTERPRETATION

High Maintenance suggests that compassion is an important side effect of cannabis inebriation, but it is far from universal. In fact, the affect most commonly associated with pot is paranoia. Coined by Hippocrates from the Greek words for beside (*para*) and mind (*nous*), paranoia literally means being out of one's mind, although psychologists define it as "the unfounded or excessive fear that other people are trying to harm us."[110] Today it is considered a character flaw, even a personality disorder, and is often associated with conspiracy theorists and schizophrenics. Many pot smokers complain that the herb makes them paranoid, but it remains unclear whether cannabis induces paranoia or merely exacerbates underlying conditions like depression, anxiety, and low self-esteem.[111] In stoner cultures, paranoia typically denotes a spectrum of negative affects, from acute self-consciousness and suspicious thinking to hallucinations of malevolent conspiracies.

There's just one problem, for me, in writing about cannabis, paranoia, and television: smoking pot doesn't make me paranoid, and not for lack of trying. While attempting to induce paranoia, however, I did notice how certain television programs encourage paranoia by cultivating suspicious viewing subjects. Paranoia is a way of looking at the world, after all, one that television can certainly foster. The paranoid spectatorship stimulated by some contemporary television series strongly resembles the paranoid criticism that Eve Kosofsky Sedgwick describes dominating literary studies at the end of the twentieth century. Both read their objects "against the grain," looking for covert meanings and hidden ideological agendas. For Brian Carr, paranoid interpretation expresses a particularly strong readerly appetite for meaning: "In the framework of paranoid interpretation, desire and knowledge imaginarily coincide with an object such that everything, imagined to include nothing, becomes something."[112] Thus paranoid reading can be a deeply pleasurable—indeed, intoxicating—experience, even though paranoia also denotes an unpleasant mental condition. Oddly, the critics who claim to reject these pleasures are often the best at describing them. Rita Felski notes that paranoid interpretation offers "the satisfaction of detecting figures and designs below the text's surface, fashioning new plots out of old, [and] joining together the disparate and seemingly unconnected."[113] It provides "a sense of prowess in ingenious methods of interpretation, appreciation of the economy and elegance of particular explanatory patterns, [and] the intellectual satisfaction of a heightened or sharpened understanding."[114] So while it may seem hyperrational, paranoid spectatorship is not necessarily serious, sober, or political. Thus, poetics of paranoia often accompany shows about government intrigues or criminal conspiracies, but they invest their spectator in the continuation, rather than the resolution, of such machinations.

Call it interactivity or call it media manipulation; either way, there is much to be gained for television producers in hailing their spectators through poetics of paranoia. Especially as practiced by some fan communities—and scholars!—paranoid interpretation can deliver real joy. As Felski points out, paranoid readers "take pride in casting off their former naïveté, congratulate themselves on their perspicacity, feel sharper, shrewder, more knowing, less vulnerable."[115] Online fan forums also suggest strong viewer loyalty to shows that solicit paranoid reading. Witness the enthusiastic—and deeply paranoid—fandoms for the complex conspiracy dramas *The X-Files* (Fox, 1993–2002, 2016–2018), *Lost*, and even *Breaking Bad*.[116] All three shows engage their viewers by providing visual and aural subtleties that encourage the "perennial, never consummated project of interpretation" (to quote a woman quite against it).[117] These series suggest through dialogue and production design that the spectator must pay vigilant attention to every detail for covert references to past episodes and must retain such information for future episodes. As Jason Mittell explains, these series make demands of their spectator, offering the promise of narrative omniscience in exchange for suspicious thinking.[118] They encourage the stoned paranoiac's "desire to uncover fully the reality of the text" by strongly implying that there's more to the show than sober, casual viewers can appreciate.[119] Whether or not their added layers of complexity actually mean anything or enrich one's experience of the show is another issue. As poetics, they train spectators to constantly question their media (and other institutions of authority)—albeit for entertainment, not social critique.

Here I point again to the engaging but uninformative color symbolism of *Breaking Bad*. As previously discussed, Walter and Jesse wear complimentary colors (green and red) and are in conflict more often than they are in harmony. The existence of this pattern hints at a puzzle to be solved, but, to return to Eve Kosofsky Sedgwick, we must ask: "What does [such] knowledge *do*—the pursuit of it, the having and exposing of it?"[120] The answer is not much, except further engage the viewer with the show. I spent a fair amount of time (and weed) contemplating *what it all means* before sobering up and realizing that Walter and Jesse's colors don't reveal anything about the nature of their conflict; their dialogue and body language do that. The olive tinge of many of Walt's shirts gives his skin an unhealthy pallor (as does the greenish color correction routinely applied to the entire frame), but viewers already know that he has cancer, so such symbolism does not provide any new information. Green can also signify hope, envy, avarice, or bad luck. On Walter White, it suggests all of these things, but because of the larger narrative context in which it appears, not despite it. Indeed, color symbolism only affirms what the spectator already knows. Skyler starts wearing green in season four when she decides to help launder the money Walt earns manufacturing meth. Her new penchant for green reveals . . . that she's decided to help Walt launder money. Nevertheless, *Breaking Bad*'s color symbolism is structurally significant; it solicits inebriated spectatorship by creating an occasion for paranoid interpretation. In this context, paranoid spectatorship extends textual pleasure without necessarily adding meaning. It makes watching television more of an activity for viewers who may not mind fishing for red herrings, because the pleasure is in the process.[121]

While the series mentioned above exploit paranoid interpretation for entertainment value, others do engender paranoid spectatorship as a form of political critique. These include *Atlanta*, Donald Glover's Afrosurrealist meditation on social and professional malaise among southern Black millennials (who smoke a lot of pot). *Atlanta* uses improbable visual and narrative devices to dramatize its characters' experiences of structural inequality. These devices also foster paranoid spectatorship among non-Black viewers by marginalizing the white gaze. The show thus explores two forms of politicized paranoia. It depicts paranoia among African American characters living in a world where "they" (the agents and beneficiaries of white supremacism) really are out to get you. It also encourages paranoia in its white spectator by structurally reminding them that they are not privileged or important observers of this world. By decentering its white spectator, *Atlanta* offers viewers an example of what US television might feel like if it did not reflect and enforce white cultural hegemony. The series thus approximates a radical Black poetics of inebriation even as it acknowledges the ongoing cultural and industrial ubiquity of the white gaze.

Atlanta's pilot suggests that the series will follow Earn (Donald Glover) as he struggles to manage his cousin Al's burgeoning rap career and sort out his relationship with Van (Zazie Beetz), the mother of his young daughter. Unlike most complex comedy series, however, *Atlanta* is not particularly invested in advancing its narrative arc.[122] Al (Brian Tyree Henry) does achieve some professional success over the show's first two seasons, but *Atlanta* does not track his career. Similarly, Earn and Van never clarify their relationship but rather drift together and apart. As Bijan Stephen observes, "the characters glide through their days as if on perpetual sidequests—there's a main objective, but they're always distracted by what it takes to get through the day."[123] Such descriptions miss the urgency and anxiety that attends the series' narrative drift, however, as the situations in question always reflect racial inequality. Each episode finds the characters reacting to circumstances beyond their control, deeply exasperated, and "about to snap."[124] It's easy to forget that Earn is financially dependent on Al because he has no other job prospects, moreover, and that he is functionally homeless after dropping out of Princeton University for reasons unspecified. Real precarity attends the outlandish incidents these characters must navigate. It also connects the series' picaresque format to the fantastical imagery through which *Atlanta* expresses its characters' lack of control over their lives and encourages paranoid reflections on US racism.

Depicting its characters' travails with an Afrosurrealist aesthetic allows *Atlanta* to excite viewers' curiosity while also commenting on the social injustice that undergirds their struggles. Consequently, implausible characters, props, and plot twists complicate the series' verisimilitude and convey the characters' subjective experiences of Black life under white supremacy. In the series pilot, for instance, Earn's uncanny encounter with a mysterious stranger reflects his larger anxiety that he may be

FIGURE 23. Earn faces the surrealism of Black life in *Atlanta* (FX, 2016–).

doomed to fail, that there is indeed a system set up against him. Earn is listening to music on his headphones while riding a late-night bus back to Van's apartment when a tall man in a tan suit and bow tie sitting across from him quietly remarks, "Your mind is racing. Tell me, yo." Earn cannot have heard the stranger over his music, yet he removes his headphones and responds, wondering aloud whether he is one of the "people on Earth who are supposed to be here just to make it easier for the winners." As Earn speaks, the stranger removes a jar of Nutella from his jacket pocket and starts spreading it on a piece of white bread. As he completes this snack, the stranger observes, "Resistance is a symptom of the way things are, not the way things necessarily should be"; he then orders Earn, "Bite this sandwich!" When Earn declines, the stranger becomes unnervingly hostile. Suddenly a police car passes the bus, sirens blaring. Earn turns to look, and when he looks back, the stranger is gone; nothing but an open jar of Nutella remains where the man once sat (figure 23). Peering out the opposite window, Earn sees the stranger and a medium-sized dog (which was not previously part of the scene) walking off into a dark forest. He glances down at his daughter, asleep in his arms, and starts to text Van, then erases the message. Earn never mentions the stranger to anyone, and the character only reappears once, during a fake commercial within the fictional talk show *Montague* ("B.A.N.," season one, episode seven). There the stranger introduces himself as Ahmad White and offers "the answers you deserve" to anyone willing to call 1-260-33QUEST or stop by his "Liberty Center for a free juice and Nutella sandwich."[125] White's mysticism is never explained, nor does it need to be, because the character already performed his structural function. He captivated the spectator's imagination while providing an opportunity for Earn to express his paranoia about white supremacy without naming the latter as such.

Critics' reactions to *Atlanta*'s fantastical flourishes have, thus far, been highly racialized. White critics praise such moments for giving *Atlanta* "the hallucinatory quality of déjà rêvé," but critics of color note that "*Atlanta*'s genius is to show the surreality of black life in America, and without the typical network explanations."[126] The latter analysis gestures toward an Afrosurrealist interpretation of the series, for as Terri Francis observes, "While Afrosurrealist works may signify on magical or hallucinatory levels, their sense of heightened reality often arcs toward current or familiar political, cultural, and ethnic contexts and references."[127] Francis further notes that "it is the political that binds abstraction to society in the Afrosurreal as in surrealism generally speaking."[128] To that end, *Atlanta* invests its depictions of Black pain and violence with unexpected and uncanny details to remind viewers that such phenomena should be shocking, not mundane. Thus, when an episode set in "The Club" (season one, episode eight) ends in gunfire, a celebrity bystander makes his getaway in an invisible car. This scene unfolds very rapidly, so rapidly the viewer may not believe what they saw. As shots ring out in the parking lot, Earn and Al rush to their car in the foreground while a man seated in midair speeds past in the background. Screeching tires fill the soundtrack as pedestrians are knocked aside by the man's transparent vehicle. Earn heard rumors of the invisible car earlier that evening and dismissed them, as any reasonable person might. But in *Atlanta*, things that can't happen are mixed with things that shouldn't happen but do, creating a structure of paranoia wherein the spectator must keep questioning the show's reality and their own. This is the project of Afrosurrealist critique; as Amiri Baraka explains, Afrosurrealist arts tell "morality tales [through] magical, resonating dream emotions and images; shifting ambiguous terror, mystery, [and] implied revelation."[129] As *New York Times* columnist Wesley Morris notes, *Atlanta* performs this work by exploring connections between "fantasy and depression, weed and trauma."[130]

Indeed, weed is central to *Atlanta*'s Afrosurrealist aesthetic, the paranoid interpretation it encourages among viewers, and the coping mechanisms of the characters. Almost every episode features one or more characters smoking cannabis, including its resident stoner-sage, Al's friend Darius (Lakeith Stanfield). As Glover explains, pot is integral to the series' exploration of Black life under white supremacy. Acknowledging that many viewers "come to *Atlanta* for the strip clubs and the music and the cool talking," Glover insists that "the eat-your-vegetables part is that the characters aren't smoking weed all the time because it's cool but because they have P.T.S.D. [posttraumatic stress disorder]— every black person does."[131] In fact, researchers have shown that experiences of racial discrimination can make Black men up to three times as likely to use cannabis.[132] Earn, Van, and Al all smoke pot to deal with stress and anxiety. Their drug use never seems as carefree as Abby's, Ilana's, or the Guy's, however, and *Atlanta* is quick to affirm that African Americans suffer worse consequences for selling or consuming cannabis than whites. In the series' second episode, Earn spends a night in jail after the police catch him carrying half a blunt. Four episodes later, Van is fired from her job as a public-school teacher after confessing that she will fail a quarterly drug test. (Her school district cannot afford to process the tests it collects, so Van is fired because she admitted to using cannabis, not because she used cannabis.) Smoking pot isn't an escape from the problems of racial inequality for *Atlanta*'s characters, in other words. Rather, it represents a calculated risk taken despite and in response to systemic discrimination. The series' Afrosurrealist aesthetic ties the characters' inebriation to its critique of American racism, entrancing viewers with beauty and whimsy while also inviting them to reflect on the absurdity of racism's daily injustice.

As *Atlanta*'s inebriated poetics encourage viewers to contemplate the racialization of US cannabis cultures, they may induce—indeed, seem designed to induce—racial paranoia in the series' white spectator. Through its Afrosurrealist gestures and calculated depictions of minor white characters, *Atlanta* reminds white viewers that their hegemony is not as accepted (or acceptable) as most US media suggest. *Atlanta* has no recurring white characters, but white characters do appear when and as necessary to contextualize the lead characters' experiences of racism. This pattern emerges in the pilot, when a white acquaintance of Earn's uses a racial slur in his presence. It arguably culminates at a retreat for German culture enthusiasts who reject Earn for bristling at their ethnic pride ("Helen," season two, episode four). In Glover's words, these characters allow the series to "show white people, you don't know everything about black culture."[133] Their presence gives white viewers a mortifying locus for racial identification within the show. In so doing, the marginalized white characters help *Atlanta* disrupt television's universalizing white gaze and remind white viewers that there is nothing natural about their privilege or television's support of it.

Nowhere is this dynamic—and the paranoia it induces in the white spectator—clearer than in "Juneteenth" (season one, episode nine). The episode begins with Earn lighting a joint as he wakes up in bed next to an unidentified lover then leaping up suddenly upon recalling that Van is picking him up for a Juneteenth party thrown by her mentor, Monique (Cassandra Freeman). As Earn and Van enter Monique's extravagant McMansion, a barbershop quartet dressed in antebellum garb serenades the party with an African American spiritual. Monique then introduces Earn and Van to her white husband, Craig (Rich Holmes), who arrives shouting "Happy Freedom Day!" A steep low-angle shot warns the viewer that Craig will be an object of derision, that the show does not hold him—or his patronizing benevolence toward Black people—in the same high regard that he holds himself. Details of the mise-en-scène further demonstrate that there is a difference between celebrating Juneteenth, as Craig does, and respecting Black history. Hence the party's cocktail menu features "Emancipation Eggnog—made with free range chicken eggs" and "Forty Acres and a Moscow Mule." Such microaggressions accumulate until Earn erupts, declaring "this party is dumb" and ordering Craig to "stop stunting on me about my culture." Even when Earn confronts him, however, Craig cannot recognize his embrace of Black culture as appropriation. Holmes plays Craig as earnestly enthusiastic throughout Earn's tirade and indeed the entire episode; this relentless good cheer is yet another manifestation of racial privilege that protects Craig from Earn's righteous anger. Consequently, Craig's white paternalism feels both surreal and also deeply real. It reflects Glover's instructions to his white actors: "it's more painful if you think you're not the villain."[134]

Atlanta extends this pain to white viewers by inviting them to recognize themselves in characters like Craig and by making conspicuous references to Black popular culture that they probably won't understand.[135] Excluding white viewers from some of the show's humor is part of its antiracist critique; as Glover has explained, "If *Atlanta* were made just for black people, it would be a very different show. But I can't even begin to tell you how, because blackness is always seen through a lens of whiteness."[136] *Atlanta* reminds white viewers of that lens by exposing its myopia and showcasing Black artists without explaining their work. Hence every episode features a carefully curated soundtrack of southern trap as well as lesser known soul tracks, such as Billy Paul's "Am I Black Enough for You?"[137] Cameo appearances also connect the show with contemporary Black media cultures, including the appearance by YouTube comedian Retro Spectro (Nileseyy Niles) as a "trans-racial" white man.[138] Non-Black viewers may just see Spectro as a young Black man with dreadlocks claiming to be a middle-aged white guy and attribute the joke to the series' signature absurdity. Black viewers are more likely to recognize the social media performer, however, and appreciate how his character challenges post-racial fantasies by "subscrib[ing] directly to the racist system of a racial hierarchy as we know it, even as it assumes a possibility of racial choice."[139] As Joshua Adams observes, "The 'ambiguity' non-black viewers and critics ascribe to *Atlanta* is more reflective of their unawareness of the black linguistic and comedic traditions it taps into."[140] When white viewers start to suspect that there's more to *Atlanta* than meets *their* eyes, they may wonder, "What else am I missing?" In such moments, paranoid spectatorship does important political work by checking the white gaze and white viewers' expectation of having other cultures explained to them on their terms.

Such entitlement is symptomatic of the white supremacy endemic to US television; indeed, it is present in television's earliest metaphor, its claim to provide a "window on the world."[141] Traditionally, US television brings the world to the white American spectator in a way that they can understand and that affirms their cultural values. It doesn't suggest that such values are relative or that some groups might not care to translate their culture for white audiences. In its sly, stoner way, *Atlanta* reminds white viewers that their privilege makes them complicit in America's system of racial privilege; as Glover tells the *New York Times*, "I don't have to clean that up for you. You have to deal with the fact that that's out there. I can't change that, really. I can just show you."[142]

Marginalizing the white gaze can arouse paranoia in viewers who are used to adopting it. So too can Afrosurrealist imagery that combats "'miserabilism,' or as Franklin Rosemont defines it, 'the rationalization of the unlivable.'"[143] Watching *Atlanta* stoned brings both of these devices into sharper relief, encouraging the viewer to question their experiences of race and television. While high, I became increasingly paranoid that *Atlanta* was watching me too. I am not referring to that age-old fantasy that the television monitor contains a camera; rather, my inebriation helped the series hail me as not just a spectator but a white spectator. The show and the weed potentiated each other's paranoic effects to make me aware of my racialized viewing position. Feeling particularized as a racial subject is a rare experience for white Americans. Most US media affirm white spectatorship; it is shocking—and exhilarating—to encounter a show that decenters whiteness instead. For some, that shock is probably unpleasant. Personally, I loved it. I found that watching *Atlanta* stoned helped me appreciate the transgressive potential of television's inebriated poetics. *Atlanta* proves that inebriated poetics can do more than just move the industry away from its past complicity in the War on Drugs. It can also expose—maybe even outmode—television's white gaze, the racialized logic behind its window on the world.

CONCLUSION

Inebriated spectatorship is just one way that cannabis and television are realizing new levels of symbiosis. Pot is also invading television promotion. In 2017, Netflix celebrated the launch of its new series *Disjointed* (2017–2018) by partnering with a Los Angeles dispensary to sell ten strains of medicinal herb named after popular Netflix series.[144] As Netflix explained, "each strain was cultivated with the specific shows in mind, designed to complement each title based on their tone. For example, sillier shows may be more indica dominant, while dramedies will be more sativa dominant to help the more powerful scenes resonate."[145] Like all tie-in products, Netflix's "Banana-Stand Kush" helps the company promote and further capitalize on its intellectual property (in this case, *Arrested Development*) while also stage-managing the scene of its consumption. Inebriated spectatorship is not just a textual system, in other words. It's a marketing plan.

Cannabis and inebriated poetics do not, then, necessitate a break from business as usual. Just as weed can be biphasic (that is, have opposite effects depending on where, how, and in what amount it is consumed), inebriated poetics are deeply mutable, capable of either affirming or destabilizing US ideologies of race and gender. As this chapter has shown, they can either reinforce extant cultural values, including racial and gender biases, or challenge them. While television was assisting in the War on Drugs in the 1970s–1990s, it helped rationalize the persecution of people of color under a system of law enforcement known colloquially as the New Jim Crow.[146] In the twenty-first century, an explosion of cable networks and video-on-demand platforms divided the television market and created opportunities for new poetics to address niche demographics. Not all of these forms of address advance the cause of social justice, but inebriated poetics can, if it reminds viewers that sobriety and intoxication are not universal categories but social constructs that help enforce other ideologies. Acknowledging cannabis's role in television culture makes some of those ideologies visible and invites us to consider how television became (and remains) deeply implicated in systems of racial persecution. In the next chapter, I examine how material cultures of violence in movie theaters activate racist discourses, particularly the widespread supposition that cinema should be a white space. Taken together, then, these two chapters suggest that attending to the material cultures around television and film helps reveal previously unrecognized or underappreciated racist dynamics in and around these media.

CHAPTER 6

Shot in Black and White

The Racialized Reception of
US Cinema Violence

It's easy to see how video technologies and network tchotchkes comprise material media cultures; they're objects one can physically possess that reflect and intervene in audiences' relations to film and television. Alcohol and cannabis likewise exert a material, psychoactive presence in viewers' lives, one that has affected their reception practices and their interpellation as spectators. Violence is another important component of material media cultures, but it cannot be studied in the same ways as consumer goods or inebriants. Violence is both incontrovertibly material—when a punch lands or a bullet hits, there's no denying its physical force—and ephemeral. You can hold a fist but not a punch, and you can read about a shooting but should not recreate it. The material transience of physical violence belies its long-term significance, however. Cinema violence—shootings, stabbings, riots, and other physical assaults at movie theaters—is one of the most consequential material forces in twentieth- and twenty-first century US film culture. It changes how films so beset are received by viewers and how people romanticize cinema, usually to the detriment of communities of color. In this chapter, I analyze cinema violence as a material condition affecting film reception and show how its discursive representation feeds racist suppositions about who should and should not be going to the movies. These discourses often overshadow the movies themselves, such that it becomes nearly impossible to consider the film outside the frame created by the violence that accompanied its theatrical run.

In the twenty-first century, cinema violence is often associated with mass violence, particularly mass shootings, but this recent connection controverts its longer history and distracts from the effects that cinema violence discourse can have on film reception. Cinema violence is a particular subcategory of spectator violence, a term coined in 1951 by Albert D. Kirwan to describe riots, assaults, and murders at public events (e.g., political debates, sporting matches, concerts, and plays).[1] Cinema violence has existed since at least 1910, when Martha Blair shot at John Hutchinson at a Coney Island cinema for reasons unknown.[2] This incident did not garner much media attention, but the antiracist riots outside certain screenings of *The Birth of a Nation* (D. W. Griffith, 1915) certainly did. As these examples reveal, only some incidents of cinema violence capture national attention or change the way a given film is remembered. We don't know what movie was playing when Blair shot Hutchinson, but we remember *The Birth of a Nation* as a film that incited hatred and violence.

Cinema violence inspires panicked reception cultures when the film involved triggers racialized prejudices about violence in the United States, particularly the fantasy that affluent white Americans ought to be—even deserve to be—insulated from public violence. The fantasy that white Americans should be excluded from public violence emerges from US histories of slavery, institutionalized racism, and de facto segregation that include the cinema. Theoretically, cinemas have not been segregated in the United States since the Civil Rights Act of 1964, yet theater locations and the always increasing price of admission effectively exclude many people.[3] Panicked reception cultures help enforce such norms. For instance, after James Eagan Holmes fired on a mostly white audience in Aurora, Colorado, in 2012, he was accused of violating the "sanctuary" of movie theaters.[4] This naive, seemingly benign claim belies the long history of cinema violence in the United States to perpetuate a white fantasy about the multiplex as a safe space. No one bewailed the sanctity of the theater when Black teenagers were being shot and blamed for shootings at *Boyz N the Hood* (John Singleton, 1991) or *Juice* (Ernest R. Dickerson, 1992). Rather, the US media variably understand cinema violence as predictable or random, contemptible or tragic depending on (1) the racial identity of the shooter, (2) the racial identity of the victim(s), (3) the racial identity of the audience targeted by the film's distributor, (4) the racial identity of the film's protagonists, and (5) the racial discourse of prior moral panics about cinema violence. Historicizing the discursive panics around cinema violence as a reception practice exposes the cultural supposition that white

Americans ought to be exempt from public violence while other groups are plagued by it. Such bigotry enacts its own kind of violence, for it has compromised the careers of many promising filmmakers of color whose films were associated with cinema violence. That is why I argue that cinema violence is always ultimately white violence, for in the panicked reception cultures it engenders, white audiences and filmmakers are inevitably indemnified where their counterparts are blamed (though all are equally innocent).

Cinema violence has ruined the reputation of films and filmmakers, yet film critics and scholars have been averse to analyzing cinema violence in conjunction with the films associated with it. The fear seems to be that there is no way to talk about the films—their subjects, genres, and composition—without implying that they incited violence. The movies themselves play a crucial role in cinema violence discourse, not through any fault of their own but because their fictions inadvertently provide scripts for interpreting the assaults. During the moral panics that follow cinema violence, protestors and journalists frequently tacitly reference and borrow reasoning from the afflicted films. Scrutinizing the panicked reception cultures around cinema violence thus requires one to read these films alongside the discourse that condemned or exculpated them. Only by comparing news reports and reviews with the films and their advertisements and trailers can one unpack the misguided associations through which the films are called upon to explain why some people hurt other people at the movies.

This chapter offers a history of cinema violence and the panicked reception cultures it inspires to show how the representation of race in films linked to cinema violence has changed popular perceptions of those films and that violence. The rock and roll riots at *Blackboard Jungle* (Richard Brooks, 1955) and *Rock Around the Clock* (Fred F. Sears, 1956) established a paradigm for this dynamic. The music in these films triggered longstanding fears of juvenile delinquency and miscegenation, leading to an outsized media reaction. These fears resurfaced and shaped public responses to Walter Hill's *The Warriors* and Michael Pressman's *Boulevard Nights* after several young people died at or after associated screenings in 1979. Both films represent street gangs respectfully and compassionately, but both were excoriated in the press for inciting gang violence. Fears of gang violence continued to generate panicked reception cultures through the 1980s and 1990s, especially when cinema violence occurred at films by or about African American men. Cinema violence did occur in conjunction with other kinds of films during this period, but it never affected their reception. Only Black films were blamed for inciting violence (in the Black and white press), even though the films themselves condemn violence.

The association of cinema violence with gang violence had to loosen during the 2000s, however, when assailants began attacking moviegoers at white Hollywood blockbusters, including *King Kong* (Peter Jackson, 2005), *X-Men: The Last Stand* (Brett Ratner, 2006), *The Dark Knight Rises* (Christopher Nolan, 2012), and *Trainwreck* (Judd Apatow, 2015). The media condemned these shooters as madmen, but they also paid far more attention to their motives and means than they had for Black assailants. Moreover, the films themselves were never blamed for inciting violence, as they were when they were by, about, and marketed to African Americans. Instead, journalists both Black and white bemoaned these incidents as "random" and "tragic," a discourse that exculpated white film culture. Indeed, the press roundly regarded violence as plaguing these movies rather than the movies as the plague bringing violence, as was the case before. The disparity between these reactions suggests that the US media and its audiences still respond to cinema violence in Black and white, even when the movies themselves resist such racist logic.

THEY'RE ALL OUT TO GET *THE WARRIORS*

It's difficult to pinpoint the first time cinema violence triggered a panicked reception culture, the first time media discourses inextricably tied a film's meaning and legacy to the material mayhem that marred its theatrical run. However, the framework for panicked reception cultures was forged after the rock and roll riots that accompanied *Blackboard Jungle* and *Rock Around the Clock* in 1955–1956. In this paradigm, the press sensationalizes isolated assaults, distributors exploit the ensuing scandal, and audiences debate whether the film solicited violence (and should be censured) or was one of its victims. The problems at *Blackboard Jungle* began with young viewers dancing in the aisles and damaging theater property as Bill Haley and the Comets' "Rock Around the Clock" sounded over the movie's opening credits. "Rock Around the Clock" is vague to the point of obscurantism in its sexual innuendo, but it was the first rock song to be included in a motion picture soundtrack, which is likely what had teenagers boogying in the aisles. As Mark Kurlansky notes, the violence at screenings of *Blackboard Jungle* occurred because theater owners brought in police "to keep the young audience in line. This led to conflicts in which the police tried to force the youths to remain in their seats."[5] In London and Dublin, impromptu dance sessions devolved into mayhem, with audiences vandalizing the furniture.[6] No one was hurt, but the shenanigans led to widespread reports of "rock and roll rioting" in Boston, Massachusetts; Hartford, Connecticut; Atlanta, Georgia; and Princeton, New Jersey, as well as England, Norway, Australia, and Indonesia.[7] Kurlansky explains that *rioting* was a pejorative expression applied by authority figures who did not understand the music's energizing effect on young audiences.[8] Many were also threatened by rock and roll's roots in Black musical traditions. Haley and his Comets could not have been whiter, but their music grew out of rhythm and blues—then known as "race music"—and triggered white fears of interracial sexuality.

Reporters wildly exaggerated the violence at *Blackboard Jungle* and *Rock Around the Clock*, but the films' distributors promoted their stories to capitalize on fear of teenagers out of control.[9] Minor vandalism in Brooklyn, New York was thus reported as wanton destruction and lawlessness: "Youngsters virtually wrecked a subway car after coming out of the theater. They threw seats out the window, broke light bulbs, and terrorized adult passengers until police apprehended several kids."[10] Notably, the Brooklyn incident took place after a publicity screening of *Rock Around the Clock*, and Columbia Pictures exploited the controversy to publicize their quickly assembled B-movie. It was quite a boon for the studio when US Senator Estes Kefauver then launched "a one-man inquisition on the subject of movie violence and juvenile delinquency." During the first day of his hearings, Senator Kefauver alleged that *Blackboard Jungle* inspired a group of young girls in Tennessee to commit arson, but his claim was decisively repudiated by Dore Schary, an MGM executive who reminded the senator, "there's no fire in the picture."[11] Nor was there any threat of miscegenation, yet miscegenation was the specter inspiring moral panics over rock and roll, including the panicked reception culture around *Blackboard Jungle* and *Rock Around the Clock*.[12]

The public anxiety surrounding *Blackboard Jungle* and *Rock Around the Clock* created a blueprint for the panicked reception of *The Warriors* and *Boulevard Nights* in 1979, which was driven by fears of African American and Latino street gangs. These episodes exhibit the metonymic slippage common to moral panics and panicked reception cultures, as they ostensibly concern different incidents and films yet share a cumulative energy. Before *The Warriors* premiered on February 7, 1979, its marketing campaign tantalized potential viewers with surly teen gangs it dubbed "the armies of the night" (figure 24). Above an image of men

FIGURE 24. 1979 Poster for *The Warriors*. Courtesy Photofest/
Paramount.

and women in gang colors, some brandishing baseball bats, the poster
warns, "They are 100,000 strong. They outnumber the cops five to one.
They could run New York City. Tonight they're all out to get the Warriors." Paramount coupled this provocation—conjuring a future in
which law is threatened by a new order—with equally exploitative
television spot. Both promised that *The Warriors* would contain an
extravaganza of juvenile delinquency, much like *Blackboard Jungle*.

Ironically, *The Warriors* contains remarkably little violence for a film
ostensibly about violence. As it begins, nine members of the eponymous

crew—a multiracial street gang from Coney Island—are making their way to the Bronx, where Cyrus (Roger Hill)—the messianic leader of the biggest gang in the city—has called a meeting of all the major New York crews. Although Cyrus's Riffs are exclusively African American, Cyrus envisions an integrated future for all the gangs. "Can you count, suckers?" he asks his assembled audience:

> You're standing right now with nine delegates from a hundred gangs, and there's over a hundred more. That's 20,000 hard core members—40,000 counting affiliates—and 20,000 more not organized but ready to fight. . . .
> The problem in the past has been the man turning us against one another. We have been unable to see the truth because we have been fighting for ten square feet of ground: our turf, our little piece of turf. That's crap, brothers. The turf is ours by right, because it's our turn. All we have to do is keep up the general truce. We take over one borough at a time, secure our territory, secure our turf . . . because it's all our turf.

Cyrus's thesis—"the future is ours"—earns wild applause from his crowd, but as their cheers crescendo, a gun is passed hand to hand until it reaches Luther (David Patrick Kelly), the leader of the Rogues, an all-white biker gang. Luther shoots and kills Cyrus, ending the nascent insurgency and inciting panic. As the police descend and gang members flee in all directions, Luther deflects blame onto the Warriors. Most manage to escape the ensuing fracas, but they have become marked men.

All the Warriors want is to ride the subway home to Coney Island, but on their way to the station, they encounter the first of many gangs out for revenge: the Turnbull ACs, an integrated group of skinheads (yes, really) who maraud the Bronx from a desecrated school bus. The Turnbulls are introduced alongside the Baseball Furies (wannabe Yankees in glam rock make-up), the Punks (Manhattan miscreants in overalls and roller skates), and assorted other Gotham gangs in a warmongering montage set to a cover of the Martha and the Vandellas' hit "Nowhere to Run." This sequence reinforces the fantastic, even cartoonish flair with which Hill adapted Sol Yurick's book, itself an adaptation of Xenophon's *Anabasis*. The film's first shot (of the Coney Island Wonder Wheel lit up against a blackened sky) establishes its fluorescently bright color palette, the artificiality of which is amplified by a synthesized score and flashy wipes between scenes. Together with the gangs' elaborate costuming, these techniques emphasize the surreal qualities of Hill's epic.

The Warriors certainly stresses stylization, yet it is also a well-researched representation of 1970s New York City and its gang scene. During the 1960s and 1970s, the city suffered immensely from the emigration of

middle-class residents, a decreasing tax base, and national economic stagflation. These factors brought the five boroughs to the brink of bankruptcy
in 1975, leading officials to cut many of the social programs that reduced
gang operation during the 1960s. Gang activity immediately started rising,
especially in the Bronx and Brooklyn.[13] At that time, experts estimated
there to be 20,000 active gang members in New York City—the same
number Cyrus cites in his speech.[14] Additionally, the Warriors' embroi-
dered leather vests closely resemble those worn by contemporaneous New
York gangs, particularly the Savage Skulls.[15] In fact, one of the few ways
in which The Warriors misrepresents 1970s New York City gang culture
is its emphasis on integration. Most of the gangs in The Warriors are multiracial, with the notable exceptions of the all-white Rogues—who kill
Cyrus and blame the Warriors—and Cyrus's African American Riffs.[16]

Although most of New York's 1970s gang activity centered in the
South Bronx, Coney Island, where the Warriors are from, suffered
similarly—a fact that the film exploits to emphasize gang members' dis-
enfranchisement. By 1979, "the People's Playground" was falling apart
due to bad planning, mismanagement, and the city's ever-decreasing tax
base. The last of Coney's monumental amusement centers, Steeplechase
Park, had closed in 1964.[17] Over the course of the 1970s, New York
City attempted a number of urban renewal projects in Coney Island,
but inadequate job opportunities for new residents led to a sharp
increase in violent and property crimes.[18] By 1979, the neighborhood
was a known as a "desolate, rubble-strewn community," and filmmakers had "cast Coney Island as a symbol of urban decay."[19]

Hill certainly participates in this trend, but instead of simply exploiting Coney Island's downfall, he uses it to explain the Warriors' bond.
When the Warriors emerge at the Stillwell Avenue subway station after
their harrowing adventure, gang president Swan (Michael Beck) surveys
a dilapidated vista and demands, "This is what we fought all night to
get back to?" Gray skies echo gray concrete, and everything is dirty.
Swan's question goes unanswered diegetically, but Hill's mise-en-scène
suggests that it is and that it isn't worth it. Being a Warrior gives these
young people a way to survive in a city without a future. In sum, Hill's
movie demonstrates deep sympathy for its juvenile delinquents without
glorifying their lifestyle. Instead it explores—and asks its viewer to
consider—how a delinquent state and lack of social support lead to
individual malefaction.

The juxtaposition of The Warriors' fanciful aesthetic and its compassion for its subjects makes for a richer, more complex text, but that

complexity may have contributed to the panicked reception culture that developed once the film seemed to be inspiring gang violence. During its first week in theaters, three young men died, allegedly in conjunction with a *Warriors* screening. In each case, police and the press blamed local gangs for the murder, while the press further distorted and exploited the incident(s) to capitalize on bigoted fears of gangs and African Americans. *The Warriors* fed those fears through its nonjudgmental representation of street gangs, which attracted heterogeneous audiences. In so doing, the film challenged white fantasies of the cinema as a safe, because de facto segregated, space, leading to public censure.

The first victim, Marvin Eller, went to see *The Warriors* at a drive-in theater in Palm Springs, California on February 12, 1979, and was shot in the head just outside the snack bar restroom at around 6 p.m. Who shot him and why remains unclear. One report claims that Eller "argued with a youth who blocked the way to the bathroom."[20] Another suggests that Eller's death was part of a racially motivated face-off between two local gangs, the African American Blue Coats and the white Family.[21] Others would claim that Eller "was *fatally stabbed* . . . in a reenactment of the film's savage bathroom battle."[22] Here Eller's assault seems to have been confused with that of Timothy Gitchel, who died at another *Warriors* screening elsewhere in California. But the reporter's narrative reference to the film is also misguided and misleading. While the Warriors do fight the Punks in a subway men's room, the idea that two California gangs would decide to avail themselves of the closest lavatory to recreate their brawl is absurd. Local investigators agreed that the movie had nothing to do with Eller's death. "It was just a big coincidence," in the words of Palm Springs Sargent Bob Cooper. The press largely ignored such naysayery, however, especially when two other young men died under similar circumstances.[23]

The second young man, Timothy Gitchel, was fatally stabbed in the lobby of a theater showing *The Warriors* in Oxnard, California, also on February 12. Every report on Gitchel's death notes that he was white and his assailants were Black, although the number of alleged assailants varies. While *Time* attributes his death to one "black youth," the *Christian Science Monitor* reports that Gitchel and his friends were "jumped by a gang of fifteen," and the *Los Angeles Times* raises the number to twenty.[24] It remains unclear what led to the conflict between Gitchel, his friends (two of whom were also stabbed), and the other young men. Lieutenant Dan Hanline of the Oxnard Police Department said that "the dispute started when a black youth asked for a quarter from Timothy Gitchel and then bloodied Gitchel's nose when the money was not given."[25] Hanline never explained how that dispute escalated to murder, but journalists were quick to blame the movie. *People* magazine reported that "just as *The Warriors* came on, the four youths suddenly found themselves battling at least fifteen blacks who were suspected of drinking and smoking grass during the previous show." "They were caught up in battle fever," one of *People*'s sources claimed, with "the look of crazy in their eyes."[26] Eyewitnesses are often unreliable, however, and in this case, the police concluded that "there was no known connection between the movie and the fighting in the lobby," as "neither group may have seen the movie."[27] Nevertheless, Gitchel's family told reporters that they intended to file suit against Paramount and the theater for inciting violence.

No such suit was ever filed, but the family of the third victim, Martin Yakubowicz, did sue Paramount and the Saxon Theater Corporation of Boston, Massachusetts, after Yakubowicz was attacked and killed in a Boston subway station by a young man who had just come from the film. Yakubowicz was traveling home from an afterschool job on February 15 "when he got into an argument with six young men he knew; one of them had a knife strapped to his right leg. A few minutes later, a knife had been plunged in to Yacabowicz's [sic] stomach."[28] While Yakubowicz did not belong to a gang, the young man who killed him did.[29] Allegedly Michael Barrett also yelled "I want you" at Yakubowicz shortly before stabbing him. *The Boston Globe* and other newspapers cited this as a line from the film; it isn't. Barrett could not have quoted *The Warriors*, in fact, because he slept through the screening that evening, after getting drunk on beer, whiskey, and wine.[30] Nevertheless, Massachusetts politicians and journalists were quick to condemn Hill's film. State Senator Michael LoPresti called for censorship within days of Yakubowicz's death. *Boston Globe* film reviewer Bruce McCabe seconded his demand, but the district attorney's office declined to pursue such a ban after two of its officers viewed the movie and declared it "a bore."[31] Still, the judge at Barrett's trial took the time to censure "purveyors of violence for profit" while sentencing Barrett.[32] In 1981, Yakubowicz's father filed a wrongful death suit against Paramount and the Saxon Theatre Corporation contending that "Paramount produced, distributed and advertised *The Warriors* in such a way as to induce violence," which would preclude protection under the First Amendment.[33] Judge Justice O'Connor found in favor of the defendants, however, because the film "does not at any point exhort, urge, entreat, solicit, or overtly advocate or encourage unlawful or violent activity."[34]

In short, "it wasn't no movie," as a young friend of Martin Yakubo-wicz's told the *Globe*; rather "people don't understand how it is" even when they fear it—"it" being gang activity.[35] Notably, the *Warriors* kill-ings happened in places where gang violence was already a concern, where a movie about gang violence would seem not exotic but ominous. In 1979, "Boston rank[ed] third, behind Los Angeles and Philadelphia, as the most lethal gang city in America."[36] Palm Springs is only a little over one hundred miles from Los Angeles; Oxnard barely sixty. Other violence associated with screenings of *The Warriors*—a "subway ram-page" in New York City, a theater manager beaten in Pasadena, some rocks and bottles thrown at a drive-in theater in Oxnard—also hap-pened in areas where street gangs were considered a growing menace.[37] In cities with minority gangs, violence at screenings of *The Warriors* was routinely blamed on African Americans.[38] Only in Boston, "where gang violence is predominantly white," were whites blamed for the unrest.[39]

Boston was also the site of a second, even more outlandish *Warriors* scare in March 1979, when Charles Eltringham, a young hitchhiker from Wilmington, Delaware, was discovered hiding next to a dumpster, badly beaten by men he said called themselves "the Warriors."[40] Eltringham claimed that around 2:00 a.m. on March 4, three men picked him up in Lexington, Massachusetts, and drove him to South Boston. During the ninety-minute ride, his captors "joked about killing him, torturing him and forcing him to submit to sexual indignities, even while punching him and cutting him with a knife."[41] "We're the Warriors and you're taking your last ride," they reportedly yelled.[42] At a Massachusetts hearing of the Special Committee to Study Spectator Violence, Eltringham testified, "I believe if they hadn't seen the movie it wouldn't have happened."[43] Certainly Eltringham is entitled to his opinion, but given that the filmic Warriors do not drive cars or engage in random acts of violence and that Eltringham's Warriors also reportedly called themselves the "Sultans of Death," it seems unlikely these marauders really beat Eltringham because of a movie.[44] Residents of Boston were willing to believe otherwise, how-ever, due to Yakubowicz's murder and the recent, troubling rise in street gangs in their city. *The Warriors* furnished a target for a panicked recep-tion culture that itself provided an outlet for the public's fears.

As word of the alleged *Warriors* incidents spread, popular opinion turned against the film, despite Paramount's best efforts to the contrary. After the incidents of February 12, Paramount contacted all 670 exhibi-tors showing *The Warriors* and offered to release them from their con-tracts or pay for extra security at future screenings.[45] After Yakubowicz's

death, Paramount pulled all trailers, television spots, and newspaper ads
for *The Warriors*. As Gordon Weaver, a vice president of Advertising and
Publicity at Paramount, explained, "What we didn't want to have happen
on a radio or TV was a report of someone being stabbed to death followed
by an ad saying 'Go see *The Warriors* at a theater near you.'"[46] On February 23, Paramount introduced a new print ad for the *Warriors*. Entitled
"Pauline Kael Writes about *The Warriors*," it consists of nothing more
than the unabridged text of Kael's review for *The New Yorker*. Kael loved
the film, suggesting that "it has *in visual terms* the kind of impact that
'Rock Around the Clock' did behind the titles of *Blackboard Jungle*."[47]
Others must have shared her opinion, because they picketed ongoing exhibitions of the film, just as their predecessors had rallied against *Blackboard Jungle*. In New York City, "a volunteer group of youths who patrol
the subways staged brief protest against the movie's violence outside the
Loew's State 1 on Broadway."[48] In Los Angeles, pediatrician Ernest J.
Smith led a demonstration condemning *The Warriors* as "dangerous to all
Americans, regardless of race, color, or creed."[49] These protests were
covered in newspapers across the country, typically with references to violence at local *Warriors* screenings, no matter how minor.

Many writers explicitly called for the film's censure. As previously
noted, *Boston Globe* film reviewer Bruce McCabe recommended that it
be banned, arguing that "the sophisticated reaction to this film is that
the film mustn't be censored, that censorship is wrong. That reaction,
however, is not appropriate to this film and the violence it's so obviously
breeding. . . . The film must be taken out of circulation."[50] On March 4,
the *Globe* published an editorial under the title "A Call to Arms" echo-
ing McCabe's claim that "*The Warriors* is causing trouble" and arguing
that "it is escalating legitimate fear in urban neighborhoods, where
people feel threatened enough without a movie that glorifies gang warfare."[51] Over the next two and a half weeks, the *Globe* published one
op-ed condemning the "motion picture whose after-effects seem to be
civil disorder, mayhem and murder," as well as nine letters from readers
debating the relative merits of censorship.[52] Some papers, such as *Variety*, covered the other side of the controversy, praising Paramount for
standing up to calls for censorship and interviewing media effects
scholar George Gerbner to refute causal links between screen violence
and spectator violence.[53] On the whole, though, fear of *The Warriors*
outweighed fear of censorship, as it would for the next few years whenever a network or cable station proposed broadcasting Hill's movie on
television.[54]

The panicked reception culture around *The Warriors* also spread beyond Hill's film. After all, the purported threat is never the real subject of a moral panic; *The Warriors* agitators were not afraid of Hill's film but of street gangs, especially minority street gangs. Moral panics also have their own momentum and a great facility for replacing one object with the next. Thus, many articles about the *Warriors* killings fearfully anticipated other gang films on their way to theaters. In March 1979, *The Baltimore Sun* nervously declared that "this may be the Year of the Ram in China, but in Hollywood it's the year of the Gang." After summarizing the violence associated with *The Warriors*, the article warns that "five more gang films are ready for spring release," including *Boulevard Nights* and *The Wanderers* (Philip Kaufman, 1979).[55] The implicated filmmakers quickly disavowed any similarity between their movies and *The Warriors*. Kaufman promised the *Los Angeles Times* that *The Wanderers* was "very different from *The Warriors* . . . in nature, tone and temperament" (not to mention quality and coherence).[56] Similarly, *Boulevard Nights* producer Tony Bill stressed that his was "a movie about people and relationships (set in East Los Angeles). Those who have seen it say the horror show that seems to be following *The Warriors* will be countered by the humanity of *Boulevard Nights*."[57] Unfortunately for Bill, his viewers did not understand moral panics. *Boulevard Nights* got lots of free advance publicity because of its topical association with *The Warriors* but suffered when violence marred its opening weekend.

Boulevard Nights premiered on Friday, March 23 in 103 theaters, two of which became sites of cinema violence. That night, one teenager was shot and two were stabbed outside a restroom at the Mission Drive-In in Ontario, California. The next night, four people were stabbed and one shot outside the Alhambra Theater in San Francisco when a fight erupted between members of two rival gangs.[58] A *Los Angeles Times* story on the incidents first compares them to those that accompanied *The Warriors* and then notes that *Boulevard Nights* "opened . . . in cities with large Hispanic populations," implying that the gangs and victims involved in the *Boulevard Nights* incidents were Latinx.[59] Bill tried to defend his film by insisting that violence "is really the antithesis of the point of the film," yet protestors still picketed.[60] Jocelyn Vargas, the young woman shot outside the Alhambra Theater, sued Bill, alleging that he "knew, or should have known, that said movie was a violent movie and would attract certain members of the public to view said movie who were prone to violence and who carried weapons."[61] While Vargas's suit was dismissed by the California State Court of Appeals, public opinion had turned against the film, as it had against *The Warriors*.

Unlike *The Warriors*, *Boulevard Nights* actually is an anti-gang film, yet after it was condemned for inspiring gang violence in Los Angeles and San Francisco, Bill found Warner Bros. ambivalent about opening the movie in other cities. He responded with incendiary comments that alienated potential audiences, such as, "All I know is that if the Chicano community can't handle a movie that takes a dramatic look at the most vital aspect of their lives, then something is wrong."[62] Bill and Warner Bros. did not capitalize on their film's notoriety as Paramount had with *The Warriors*. While Paramount never publicized incidents of cinema violence, they replied quickly to press inquiries and thereby maintained media coverage of their film. Thanks to their efforts, *The Warriors* was the top-grossing film in the country in March 1979.[63] After *Boulevard Nights'* failure, however, the 1979 gang film cycle collapsed, as did panicked reception culture around gang violence in movie theaters. The issue received no further attention until 1988, when Dennis Hopper's middling gangsploitation movie *Colors* jump-started another cycle of audience panic around violence at films by and about Black men.

BLAMING THE *BOYZ*

Colors was not the first film afflicted with cinema violence after *Boulevard Nights*, but it was the first to inspire a panicked reception culture. Indeed, the panic began before the movie came out, because of its subject matter. During the 1980s, Los Angeles experienced a surge in gang violence, and Hopper's film capitalized on related fears and prejudices. *Colors* pits two white Los Angeles policemen against Black and Latino gangs selling crack cocaine. Hopper hired local gang members to serve as extras during filming, leading police and community members to worry that those gangs would seek out the film and bring violence to theaters. The Los Angeles Police Department (LAPD) became so alarmed that they held a private screening one month before the film's release to evaluate its potential impact.[64] Afterward, Sheriff's Sargent Wes McBride publicly predicted that the movie would "leave dead bodies from one end of this town to the other. . . . I wouldn't be the least surprised if a shooting erupted in a movie theater."[65] Within days, news of the screening and the police reaction had spread across the country; journalists and community activists condemned Hopper and star Sean

Penn for inciting violence that had not yet happened. The NAACP and the citizens' group Guardian Angels protested *Colors* at various sites across Los Angeles, including the sixtieth annual Academy Awards ceremony. The Guardian Angels "carried picket signs and coffins"; they tried to present the film's distributors with "blood money" and left "Hall of Shame" awards on Hopper's and Penn's front lawns: pictures of the celebrities framed by toilet seats.[66] They even pressured the insurers of local movie theaters to require that that the film be dropped, predicting violence and vandalism.[67]

Despite the controversy—or maybe because of it—*Colors* opened big, wide, and without incident on April 15, 1988. In its opening weekend, it grossed over $4.8 million at 422 theaters, accompanied "by only minor scuffles that led to thirteen arrests" in the Los Angeles area.[68] Then on April 24, David Dawson was fatally shot while standing in line to purchase a ticket to the film outside a theater in Stockton, California. The assailant was Charles Queen, a member of the Bloods. Dawson was a member of the Crips, reportedly identifiable to Queen because of the blue bandana he was wearing.[69] Queen was arrested in Mississippi two months after the shooting, but in the interim, the incident received international attention.[70] Queen allegedly shot Dawson because he was "upset with the way his gang was depicted in the movie."[71] As the Toronto *Globe and Mail* explained to its readers, "the main rule of gangland is retaliation. The film depicts one fictional gang called the Coup-de-Ville Crips attacking a gang called Bloods. But the Bloods never get their revenge in the film." "'That's what's gonna ruffle the feathers, that's what's gonna bother the brothers,'" reported one of its sources.[72] After Dawson's death, some theater chains cancelled *Colors* at the request of local law enforcement, but it still became number one at the box office.[73] The film's notoriety overcame its mediocrity, earning it far more attention and revenue than it merited. It also created a precedent for predicting violence at premiers of African American urban dramas, notably Spike Lee's *Do the Right Thing* (1989)—where no violence occurred—and John Singleton's *Boyz N the Hood*, where some did.[74] After *Colors*, simply depicting urban Black communities on film was enough to inspire a panicked reception culture.

The 1990s brought a renaissance in Black filmmaking, including a cycle of low-budget films by African American men about the problems afflicting Black inner-city communities. When violence broke out at three such movies—Mario Van Peebles's *New Jack City* (1991), *Boyz N the Hood*, and *Juice*—the films and their makers were blamed for inciting violence despite their anti-violence messages of personal responsibility.

These messages—which ironically downplay the larger social forces undergirding gang violence in the United States—were not mentioned in the cinema violence coverage, but their individualism did inflect reporters' analyses. That is, reporters blamed the assailants for their actions without considering the conditions of dispossession influencing their choices, the very conditions depicted in these films. Accordingly, the press never described cinema violence at the films of the "ghetto action cycle"—as S. Craig Watkins calls them—as "random"; that label would be reserved for incidents where white victims were attacked at movies aimed at white audiences.[75]

The panicked reception of New Jack City had everything to do with the movie's subject matter, but the violence that marked its opening night did not. The film premiered on March 8, 1991, only four days after the Los Angeles television station KTLA broadcast George Holliday's video of Rodney King being beaten by LAPD officers.[76] To call the Holliday video incendiary is, of course, insufficient; it provided documentation of the LAPD's long-term, systemic brutality toward African Americans. Yet most journalists failed to appreciate the significance of Holliday's video when reporting on a riot outside of one New Jack City screening. At the Mann Westwood Fourplex in Los Angeles, ticket holders became upset when denied entry to an evening show. Police Sargent Nicholas Barbara asserted that the theater oversold the show, a charge its representatives vehemently denied. They blamed the seat shortage on people sneaking in without a ticket. In any event, six hundred to eight hundred disgruntled individuals congregated outside the theater; when patrol officers ordered them to disperse, the crowd began shouting "Black Power" and "Fight the Power!"[77] A riot ensued, wherein King's name became a rallying cry against police racism. When protestors began "looting stores, throwing beer cans, vandalizing cars and tearing branches off of trees to smash store windows," one hundred officers in riot gear were called in.[78]

Most reporters did not take the connection to King's beating seriously, and an anti-Black film panic ensued.[79] Subsequent articles only associated the Westwood riot with other cinema violence, including the death of Gabriel Williams at a Brooklyn screening of New Jack City.[80] The New York Times translated these incidents into a fear-mongering think-piece about how a "Film on Gangs Becomes Part of the World It Portrays."[81] In fact, what happened in Westwood and to Williams bears not even the slightest resemblance to New Jack City. Van Peebles's movie uses the conventions of neo-noir to fictionalize the rise and fall of drug lord Leroy "Nicky" Barnes and dramatize the devastating effects of crack cocaine on poor Black communities. It has nothing in common with the political unrest in Westwood or the fatal scuffle between teenagers in Brooklyn, except that Black men are involved. Eventually, the *New York Times* granted producers Doug McHenry and George Jackson an op-ed to argue that "*New Jack City* doesn't cause riots," but by then a paradigm had been established.[82] After *New Jack City*, journalists associated ghetto action films with cinema violence; as Singleton put it, they were "lying in wait" when *Boyz N the Hood* came out on July 12.[83]

Boyz N the Hood has been regarded as the apogee of the early 1990s ghetto action film cycle, both for its exceptional quality and because of the exceptional violence that accompanied its premiere. The panicked reception culture around Black gang films, combined with the advance marketing for *Boyz N the Hood*, influenced the media's perception of these events, which occurred during the film's opening weekend but were predicted before that. *Boyz N the Hood* did not induce violence any more than *The Warriors*, *New Jack City*, or any other film at which an altercation occurred. However, cinema violence has shaped its reception and legacy more than those of any other film, including *The Dark Knight Rises*, which currently has the dubious distinction of accompanying the biggest mass shooting at any US cinema. *Boyz N the Hood* and its representation of Black masculinity in South Central Los Angeles have been understood almost entirely in terms of violence. This includes Singleton's message of personal responsibility, which helped the film court a white, "crossover" audience but also encouraged that audience's fear of Black men.[84] The result was that when violent incidents did occur, they provided confirmation bias for further racist prejudice.

Like other ghetto action films, *Boyz N the Hood* was preceded by a deceptively violent marketing campaign. In her book on American film cycles, Amanda Ann Klein shows how the campaigns for *Boyz N the Hood* and *Juice* in particular "sought to confirm an image of authentic or realistic 'blackness' . . . synonymous with aggressive masculinity, random violence, and gang culture."[85] These films premiered in the wake of *New Jack City* and in the midst of another panicked reception culture around gangsta rap.[86] Both featured famous rap artists, namely Ice Cube (Doughboy in *Boyz N the Hood*) and Tupac Shakur (Bishop in *Juice*). While the films themselves denounce gang violence and challenge the racist assumption that all young Black men must be gang members, their trailers and posters belie such intentions. As Klein observes, "the theatrical trailer for *Boys N the Hood* opens with warlike imagery" and "culminates in a series of brief images of angry African American males shooting their guns directly at the viewer."[87] Another trailer begins with the narrator intoning, "This is Los Angeles: gang capital of the nation" and prominently features Ice Cube's song "How to Survive in South Central."

In addition to violence and gangsta rap, social realism and personal responsibility were also prominent elements of Columbia's marketing campaign for *Boyz N the Hood* and furthered its pursuit of a white audience. To bolster the film's claim to social realism, its theatrical trailer introduces three young protagonists through their contrasting responses to the dire underdevelopment of South Central L.A.: "Tre wanted to work his way up. . . . Ricky was looking for a better life. . . . Doughboy was living by the laws of the street." The trailer acknowledges that "In South Central L.A., it's tough to beat the streets"—as Doughboy pulls out his gun and loads the chamber—but such phrasing suggests an individual's responsibility to rise above rather than, say, a demand that state agencies intervene.[88] Individualism absolves the spectator of doing anything about the world they see on screen, while social realism rewards them for taking an interest at all. Columbia exploited the latter strategy in its home video trailer for *Boyz N the Hood*, which begins with footage from the Vietnam War and a narrator intoning, "Five minutes away from your nice, safe neighborhood, there's a war going on. And the news isn't covering it. *Boyz N the Hood*. It's the kind of news that usually gets buried."[89] This trailer presumes a "safe" audience physically and psychically distant from the turmoil of the inner city and uses that distance to sell Singleton's film as a realistic exploration of an underreported crisis. It counters the cynicism of *Boyz N the Hood*'s first poster, where the original taglines "Once upon a time in South Central L.A." and "It ain't no fairy tale," imply that Singleton's film will serve as a wake-up call to apathetic or ignorant audiences. After violence marred the movie's opening weekend, Columbia changed the film's tagline to "Increase the Peace," its concluding title card message and a bromide for fearful audiences. For while the imperative tense might seem confrontational, it reinforces the notion of personal—not state or social—responsibility to reduce gang violence.

Columbia's advertising strategies reflected and inadvertently provided fodder for the moral panic that took off after people started getting hurt at screenings of *Boyz N the Hood*. The weekend that *Boyz N the Hood* opened, there were shots fired at 16 of its 829 locations. Over thirty people were injured, and two died: Michael Booth and Jitu Jones.[90] Booth saw the film at the Halstead Twin Drive-In in Riverdale, Illinois, with his girlfriend and young son. As they waited in line to leave, Timothy Turner, "a reputed gang member," walked up to their car and asked for a light.[91] Booth refused, and Turner shot him. Jones was shot outside the Skyway 6 Theatre in downtown Minneapolis, Minnesota, after fleeing a gun battle inside the theater. Police noted that Jones was not involved in the fracas and that the bullet "apparently was intended for someone else."[92]

Reporters did little to commemorate Booth or Jones, instead sensationalizing the weekend's violence. Their articles brought together unrelated incidents to suggest that *Boyz N the Hood* was causing mayhem from coast to coast. These included non-lethal shootings in Los Angeles, Upland, Pinole, Chino, and Sacramento, California; Las Vegas, Nevada; Texas City, Texas; Detroit, Michigan; Tuscaloosa, Alabama; Akron, Ohio; Miami, Florida; Brooklyn, New York; and West Springfield, Massachusetts.[93] In addition, a "gun-toting band of black youths" in Hollywood reportedly started shooting in a screening of *Boyz N the Hood*, then chased their targets into *Terminator 2: Judgment Day* (James Cameron, 1991) before heading outdoors, where five more shots were fired.[94] People were also stabbed at or outside screenings in Detroit; Miami; New Bern, North Carolina; and Commack, New York.[95] "Melees" were reported in Tukwila, Washington, and Orlando, Florida; the latter allegedly ended in "full-scale pandemonium" as police "were pelted with bottles."[96] Eleven people were arrested at the Tukwila incident, which began with a brawl inside the theater and grew to "more than 100" people fighting outside the theater.[97] The LAPD set up defensive barricades in Westwood, fearing a riot similar to the one that accompanied *New Jack City* (and evidently in denial about the latter's correlation with King's assault). Newspapers hyperbolized all of these events with headlines like "Trail of Trouble for *Boyz*" and "Film Opens with Wave of Violence."[98] One article quotes an Atlanta theater manager scoffing, "Frankly, I'm surprised they haven't banned the movie."[99] One *Washington Post* reporter erroneously lamented, "there has never been anything like the kind of trouble now being associated with black movies."[100] These protestations stem from a dubious, and highly racialized, fantasy of the cinema as a safe, homogenized space—a fantasy only made possible by ignorance of actual cinema history and an expectation of de facto segregation in movie theaters.

Even after the bloodshed ended, newspapers continued to run stories and quote sources condemning Singleton's movie as "just an excuse for getting rowdy."[101] Many journalists noted that nineteen theaters dropped *Boyz N the Hood* in response to or in fear of theater violence; few mentioned that another eighty added it.[102] International newspapers began to pick up the story too, alleging that "in Los Angeles watching movies can be hazardous to your health."[103] *London Sunday Times* reporter Mark Graham claimed that at one LA theater, "young black men imitated the characters on screen, fired shots in the air, and pushed and shoved each other, while frightened security guards and ushers watched helplessly."[104] He also informed readers that "attending a showing of the film in Times Square is like taking a step into the lives depicted on screen."[105] While some journalists—mostly Australian—observed that *Boyz N the Hood* was being scapegoated for a much broader social problem, the film nonetheless became internationally notorious.[106]

Much as McHenry and Jackson were for *New Jack City*, Singleton was called to publicly defend his film against the charge that it incited violence. On July 13, Singleton met with reporters in Los Angeles and reminded them that cinema violence does not justify censorship but is rather an "indication of the degradation of American society . . . a society that breeds illiteracy, economic deprivation, and doesn't educate its kids, and then puts them in jail."[107] Speaking to and then about Black audiences, he observed, "There is a certain segment of the population that wants you to do what you are doing to each other. You have to think before you do it. Those people are my family. I am not going to turn my back on them and I don't want them to turn their backs on me by causing trouble while my film is playing."[108] This last request sounds defensive, but then Singleton was defending himself. He reminded reporters that he "didn't create the conditions in which people just shoot each other. . . . This happens because there's a whole generation of people who are disenfranchised."[109] Singleton also criticized reporters for drawing attention to the violence at *Boyz N the Hood* screenings but failing to investigate "where the root of the problem lies." "There are a lot of other films where things happen around the corner and nothing is reported," he said. "But when my film comes out, it's all reported. I call that artistic racism."[110]

Singleton's words went unheeded, as the mainstream white press continued to predict cinema violence at subsequent ghetto action movie premiers, including that of Ernest R. Dickerson's *Juice*. *Juice*—which depicts a group of friends struggling to come of age in Harlem—opened on January 17, 1992. The day before, the *St. Petersburg Times* ran a story recapping incidents at *New Jack City* and *Boyz N the Hood* and assuring readers that area theaters "will employ extra security guards as a means of dissuading potential violence," even though "no incidents occurred locally with either movie."[111] Some theaters that had become sites of violence during *New Jack City* or *Boyz N the Hood* declined to show *Juice*, including Mann's Westwood Fourplex.[112] *Juice* nevertheless opened at over one thousand theaters in the United States. When violence occurred near some of them, the press immediately blamed *Juice*. In Chicago, sixteen-year-old Tyesa Cherry was shot and killed when two teenage gang members got in a fight outside the Chestnut Station Cinemas.[113] Although there were other movies showing at Chestnut Station that night, reporters attributed her death to *Juice*. Eight other theaters reported cinema violence the night of January 17. Guns were fired at theaters in Lansing, Michigan, and Cheltenham, Pennsylvania; someone was stabbed at a theater in New York City. Some journalists admitted that the violence "may have been coincidental" to the screening, yet the tone of their reports belied such disclaimers.[114] The Cheltenham police stated that *Juice* "was showing and the shooting was in the parking lot. That's all we know," but *Washington Post* reporter Thomas Lippman buried that observation under a litany of violent incidents purportedly related to *Juice*. Lippmann concludes by reminding readers of the Westwood riot at *New Jack City*, which he blithely summarizes as "hundreds of disappointed moviegoers . . . on a rampage after being turned away from a sold-out showing."[115] The Westwood riot was entirely unrelated to what happened in Cheltenham, except within a panicked reception culture seeking confirmation for its biased assumptions about violence at Black films.

The panic over violence at ghetto action films fueled a backlash against African American films throughout the 1990s, a backlash that compromised the careers of many promising African American filmmakers. In February 1992, McHenry, Jackson, Singleton, and fellow filmmakers Warrington Hudlin and Robert Townsend spoke at the ShoWest exhibitors' convention to combat anti-violence (which is to say anti-Black) sentiment among theater owners. There they argued that "the media is laying the foundation for an argument to ban or censor" Black films with each "pre-release 'witch hunt' as to whether or not there will be violence."[116] William Fartozian, president of the National Association of Theater Owners, then "revealed that exhibitors have been put under pressure by patrons, community leaders and landlords to pull some of the films" predicted to incite violence.[117] The session ended with Jackson and McHenry leading attendees in a promise to support a series of anti-violence public service announcements, but no such announcements were ever screened.

Instead, US exhibitors generated new scheduling policies for films predicted to inspire cinema violence—that is, Black films. Within two weeks of the *Boyz N the Hood* premiere, General Cinema started intentionally "lengthening breaks between screenings . . . to cut down on gatherings outside the cinema."[118] As *Variety* reporter Mark Becker observed, theater executives also began "pre-screening films for their off-screen violence potential," a move Charles Acland compares to racial profiling, as "detecting the negative social impact of a film has as much to do with an assessment of populations as with texts themselves."[119] At the same time, exhibitors began releasing so-called "urban films" aimed at African American audiences on Wednesdays rather than Fridays.[120] The practice commenced in October 1991 with *House Party* 2 (Doug McHenry and George Jackson). In July 1993, the Los Angeles Cineplex Odeon postponed the opening of *Poetic Justice*—John Singleton's second film—from a Friday to the subsequent Wednesday to avoid violence, even after the Los Angeles City Council denounced the delay as racist.[121] Such "preventative measures" prevented big opening weekends for these movies, reducing their ticket sales and their filmmakers' career prospects.

It may seem ironic that reporters and exhibitors were so panicked over violence at films that advocated personal responsibility in the face of public violence. In fact, the films' individualist philosophies provided discursive models for reception rhetoric that blamed Black men for bloodshed in their communities. *New Jack City*, *Boyz N the Hood*, and *Juice* all depict Black men struggling against the drug trade, poverty, and gang violence, and each shows one man creating a meaningful life by adopting an individualist ideology wherein no one can save you but yourself. This ideology guides all the characters in *New Jack City*, but only Detective Scotty Appleton (Ice T) survives his encounter with the drug trade by channeling his rage and frustration into his work with the New York City Police Department. In *Juice*, Q (Omar Epps) is able to resist the thrills of theft and murder that entice his friends because he has higher aspirations as a DJ. Yet none of the ghetto action films advocate personal responsibility more overtly than *Boyz N the Hood*, a distinction that contributed to its panicked reception.

Boyz N the Hood embeds its philosophy of individual uplift in its ideal of Black masculinity, Furious Styles (Laurence Fishburne). The movie begins with Furious teaching his young son, Tre (Cuba Gooding Jr.), how to be a man, which amounts to lessons in individual sovereignty: "I'm trying to teach you how to be responsible. Your friends across the street, they don't have anybody to show them. You're gonna see how they end up too." This seemingly idle threat in fact portends the film's outcome. Before Tre graduates from high school, his friend Ricky (Morris Chestnut) will be shot by gang members for being in the

FIGURE 25. Furious sells Los Angeles on the importance of Black autonomy in *Boyz N the Hood* (John Singleton, 1991).

wrong place at the wrong time. Ricky's brother Doughboy will be killed two weeks later. Furious does not literally foresee their deaths, but he surmises that young Black men need personal accountability to avoid becoming the one out of twenty-one African American men who "will be murdered in their lifetime," per the film's preface.

Throughout *Boyz N the Hood*, Furious serves as an idol and sage for his entire community (except for Tre's mother, his ex-partner and the only character to call him out on his androcentrism). Nowhere is Single-ton's veneration of the character clearer than in his lecture on gentrifica-tion. It begins when Furious takes Tre and Ricky to "see something" in Compton, a lower-income Black neighborhood that visibly intimidates both boys. Furious admonishes Ricky, "we can't afford to be afraid of our own people anymore," as the camera frames him against a billboard for "Seoul to Seoul Real Estate" offering "cash for your home" (figure 25). Furious then expounds on the importance of community ownership while passersby cross the street to listen. Just as Jesus delivered the prin-ciples of Christian discipleship during his Sermon on the Mount, Furious stands on a hill above his audience explaining, "What we need to do is keep everything in our neighborhood, everything, Black: Black-owned with Black money." "They want us to kill ourselves," he reminds his listeners, to which one replies, "What am I supposed to do? Fool roll up and try to smoke me, I'm going to shoot the motherfucker if he don't kill me first." "You're doing exactly what they want you to do," Furious retorts. "You have to think, young brother, about your future."

Furious's tone is neither condescending nor demeaning, but it suggests that every man is responsible for how he responds to racism and dispossession—precisely the attitude journalists would take toward cinema violence at Boyz N the Hood. Furious is not indifferent to the effects of deterritorialization and imminent violence, but he nevertheless espouses an individualist philosophy of social uplift reminiscent of Booker T. Washington and W. E. B. Du Bois.[122] With Furious lionized by his own community and the film itself—in glamor shots that routinely emphasize Fishburne's strong jaw and muscular physique—he serves as the mouthpiece of the film's philosophy. The solution to Black suffering will not come from schools, the police, or social services but from Black men assuming the individualist morality of bourgeois capitalism. Anyone who doesn't assimilate can be held responsible for failing themselves, be they drug dealers like Doughboy or teenagers shooting other teenagers in movie theaters.

Boyz N the Hood advocates a politics of personal responsibility to discourage violence against Black men, but the panicked reception culture around ghetto action films deployed this politics as a means of victim-blaming. One position was antiracist and the other deeply racist, yet both implied that the violence happening in Black communities and among Black audiences was not random. As mentioned, the media almost never referred to cinema violence as "random" until it started happening in white communities. Of the dozens of filmmakers, exhibitors, policemen, journalists, and pundits who commented on early 1990s cinema violence, only two—from the white or Black press, domestic or international—ever described it as "random." These exceptions occur in:

- a short statement from Columbia Pictures in July 1991 acknowledging that "Random violence exists not only in Los Angeles but all over the country. It predated the opening of Boyz N the Hood and sadly it almost certainly will continue well into the future."[123]
- a September 1997 article in the Ottawa Citizen whose author mentions Boyz N the Hood while satirizing cinema violence.[124]

Columbia employs the term random to minimize recent incidents while the Ottawa Citizen deploys it in a cavalier and thoughtless attempt at humor. In all other press about Boyz N the Hood, cinema violence was implicitly presented as the specific, even logical outcome of exhibiting films by and about young Black men.[125] Not one single journalist acknowledged that the violence at *Boyz N the Hood*—or any other ghetto action film—might have been random, meaning arbitrary, senseless, and heartbreaking.

THE WHITE SHOOTER RISES

In the twentieth century, cinema violence was so closely associated with African American gangs and gang violence that reporters treated theater shootings and stabbings by non-Black assailants as anomalies rather than a troubling trend. Cinema violence wasn't limited to Black audiences during this period, nor to movies aimed at Black audiences. But that was the only kind of violence that induced panicked reception cultures. After *Colors*, *New Jack City*, *Boyz N the Hood*, and *Juice*, the media inextricably associated cinema violence with gangs—and hence with African Americans. Despite incidents at white films—including at *Cocktail* (Roger Donaldson, 1989) and *Schindler's List* (Steven Spielberg, 1993)—panicked reception cultures were limited to Black films. It was only when mentally disturbed white men started instigating cinema violence in the twenty-first century that the press began to foment panics about "random" tragedies in theaters. Noticeably, though, these panics focused on violations of cinema space, and white films and filmmakers were never blamed for drawing violent audiences to the cinema.

The first national panic around "random" cinema violence at a white Hollywood blockbuster occurred in 2012, after James Eagan Holmes opened fire on approximately four hundred viewers at a midnight premiere of Christopher Nolan's *The Dark Knight Rises* in Aurora, Colorado, on July 20 of that year.[126] Holmes wounded seventy and killed twelve. Within hours, commentators on Reddit and CNN had begun to refer to the event as the "Aurora massacre." This epithet distinguished the incident among mass shootings and also among incidents of cinema violence, as it divorced the attack from the film it accompanied by tying it to a location instead. Over the next few weeks, more information about Holmes's assault and its victims would fuel anxiety about "random" violence, mass shootings, and gun control. Journalists and industry pundits would repeatedly venerate the movie theater as a safe, even sacred space—despite all evidence to the contrary. The mainstream media never compared Holmes's attack with 1990s cinema violence, yet differences in the tenor and quantity of its coverage show how deeply race and class are imbricated in US cinema culture. Not only did the media frame the Aurora massacre as random, they also lamented it as "tragic." This rhetoric retroactively reveals popular distress over cinema violence as limited to white victims, given that only their deaths—and not the previous deaths of people of color—were hailed as tragedies.

While reporters never blamed *The Dark Knight Rises* or its director for Holmes's assault, some suggested that he may have been attracted to the hype around its opening weekend. Advance marketing had created huge anticipation for *The Dark Knight Rises* that summer; Warner Bros. advertised its premiere as a "movie event," a moniker intimately tied to the tradition of midnight screenings in the United States.[127] At midnight on July 20, *The Dark Knight Rises* was playing in 4,404 theaters—just over 11 percent of all US cinema screens at that time.[128] *The Dark Knight* (2008), Christopher Nolan's previous Batman movie, had grossed over $1 billion in worldwide ticket sales, then a record for superhero movies. *The Dark Knight Rises* was expected to do even better, thanks in part to the critical prominence of its predecessor.[129] *The Dark Knight* had also been nominated for eight Academy Awards—the most for any movie based on a comic book—with Heath Ledger posthumously winning Best Supporting Actor for his work as the Joker. All of these exploitable elements were mobilized to promote *The Dark Knight Rises*, which would not feature Ledger but would conclude one of the most popular and prestigious trilogies of the new century.

Holmes bought his ticket for *The Dark Knight Rises* at Aurora's Century 16 megaplex almost two weeks in advance, a fact that prosecutors and pundits would later cite as evidence of premeditation. Security footage shows him entering the building, lingering by the concession stand, and entering Theater Nine slightly before midnight. Approximately twenty minutes later, Holmes left the auditorium through an emergency exit to change into defensive apparel (including a gas mask, ballistics helmet, and bullet-resistant clothing). He then reentered the theater carrying gas canisters and a handgun, shotgun, and semiautomatic rifle. According to the *New York Times* and other sources, "witnesses told police that Mr. Holmes said something to the effect of 'I am the Joker,'" before tossing his gas canisters and opening fire.[130] Victims began calling emergency services right away, and the police arrived within ninety seconds. At 12:45 a.m., Officer Jason Oviatt noticed a man in the theater parking lot wearing atypical tactical gear and apprehended him. During the arrest, Holmes reportedly identified himself as the Joker again and asked, "There weren't any children hurt, were there?"[131] There were four: Veronica Moser-Sullivan (six years old), her cousin Kaylin Bailey (thirteen years old), Prodeo Patria (fourteen years old), and Catherine Streib (sixteen years old). The youngest, Moser-Sullivan, died of her wounds at the scene.

As Holmes's question anticipates, juvenile victims would contribute significantly to panicked reactions to the shooting, although race and mental illness played a more important role. The media almost exclusively invoke tragedy for cinema violence with middle-class white victims; Black and working-class victims are not mourned in the same way, especially if their murders were associated with gang activity (e.g., Marvin Eller and Martin Yakubowicz). Loss of life alone does not constitute tragedy in a society where some lives are grieved more than others. Because affluent white Americans presume themselves insulated from social violence, its "random" appearance disrupts the social order, making its victims "tragic." This is why mental illness provides such a convenient framework for interpreting white-on-white cinema violence; it explains the event without challenging the system.

James Eagan Holmes was certainly mentally ill, but the panicked cinema culture that developed in the Aurora massacre had less to do with his diagnosis than with the sensationalized threat of mental illness. While some media personalities (including President Barak Obama) condemned Holmes as "evil," the courts and the press focused on his alleged madness.[132] Insanity explained the event without challenging the broader cultural supposition that white audiences should, indeed deserved to, be insulated from public violence that was assumed to be an inevitable part of Black and Latinx culture. If Holmes was insane, then his massacre did not have to be, could not be, explained. It was "random," its victims "tragic," whereas prior panicked reception cultures implicitly or explicitly blamed the victims for going to dangerous films.[133]

In the wake of the shooting and during Holmes's trial, reporters indulged a morbid fascination with every symptom of his derangement. Intricacies of the Colorado constitution buoyed this fascination as well. Colorado is one of the few states where, after a defendant pleads not guilty by reason of insanity, prosecutors may subpoena their medical and mental health records, as District Attorney George Bouchard did for James Eagan Holmes on August 29, 2013. His subpoena ensured that graphic descriptions of Holmes's mental decline would become part of the public record. Reporters churned out story after story about Holmes's past, emphasizing any signs of a monster in the making. They discovered that Homes, a doctoral student in neuroscience at the University of Colorado, had emailed a colleague about "dysphoric mania" in advance of the shooting, that he took drugs (including LSD), and that he saw three mental health professionals at the University during his year there.[134] When Holmes's pre-shooting diary was introduced into court proceedings, journalists poured over "pages of runic symbols; nonsensical equations about life and death, infinity and 'negative infinity'"; and ruminations on his "broken" mind.[135] The madder Holmes seemed, the more random his crime seemed—and the more innocent his victims, who were of course no more or less innocent than any others affected by cinema violence.

Focusing on Holmes's mental illness also allowed the mainstream media to ask and answer the question "Why?"—a question that never previously entered their discourse about cinema violence. To put it bluntly: journalists did not question why African American and Latinx men were shooting, stabbing, and assaulting movie theater patrons because it was presumed that "those people" are violent. But white people supposedly are not; consequently, national newspapers never linked Holmes's race to his murders, even euphemistically, as they did with Black and Latinx cinema assailants. "Mental illness" thus functioned as a sanitizing discourse, preventing whiteness from generating the same panic that Blackness and Brownness did in previous reception cultures. It facilitated relentless media attention to Holmes's crime while also rendering it exceptional and anomalous, in contrast to the allegedly gang-related theater shootings and stabbings of the twentieth century.

This is where the panic around the "Aurora massacre" so crucially departs from those that surrounded *The Warriors*, *Colors*, and *Boyz N the Hood*. The press and the public blamed those films for inciting violence because they presumed the inevitability of violence and death for the characters they depicted and the audiences they targeted. No one blamed *The Dark Knight Rises*, though, because Holmes was insane and an insane gunman is outside the social order, beyond the system's capacity to regulate.[136] Holmes's madness could not be predicted or prevented, only isolated and contained—or so the story goes. Nolan's previous Batman movie, *The Dark Knight*, provided an uncanny narrative precedent for Holmes's criminal exceptionalism in the Joker. Because witnesses thought that Holmes alluded to the villain during his massacre, Nolan's film provided a template for making sense of his crime. *The Dark Knight* suggests that anarchist villains like the Joker (and Holmes) complete the logic of, and are thus an inevitable result of, Batman's conservative vision of law and order.[137] They are burdens that have to be tolerated as well as combatted, for to question their appearance would be to question the system of white supremacy itself.

The Dark Knight follows Bruce Wayne (Christian Bale), a member of the US corporate aristocracy, as he disciplines his fellow citizens under the name and mask of Batman. The movie begins as Batman encounters "a better class of criminal," namely the Joker, a self-proclaimed "agent of chaos" who wants to show Batman, Police Commissioner Gordon (Gary Oldman), and District Attorney Harvey Dent (Aaron Eckhart) "how pathetic their attempts to control things really are." After making his debut by stealing the collected savings of every gang in the city, the Joker announces that he wants to end Batman's reign of righteousness. He publicly vows to kill one of Gotham's citizens every day until Batman reveals his true identity. Batman and his fellow agents of justice try but fail to derail the Joker's plans, because—as Wayne's butler, Alfred Pennyworth (Michael Caine), explains—they cannot understand that "some men just want to watch the world burn." Alfred comes the closest to understanding the Joker's philosophy, but he still assumes that the Joker wants something, that he wants *for* something. In fact, he lacks nothing, because, as he tells Batman, "you complete me." Moreover, the Joker completes Batman: he is the unstoppable—because unmotivated—engine of destruction that gives Batman a reason for existing. Just as Gotham produced Batman—the elite white vigilante enforcing law and order where the state cannot—so too Batman produced the Joker, an anarchist who exists for no reason except to threaten law and order. Without the Joker, Batman might eventually defeat Gotham's crime syndicates and retire to his house in the country with the ostensible love of his life, Assistant District Attorney Rachel Dawes (Maggie Gyllenhaal). The Joker keeps Batman relevant, which is why, as he so lovingly reminds his caped crusader, "you have nothing to threaten me with."

Of course, Batman roundly rejects the Joker's insights, just as the US media refused to consider that James Eagan Holmes might be a foreseeable product of US policies on gun control and mental health care. Nolan's film clearly depicts the Joker as both the scourge and the apotheosis of its white world. All of Nolan's Batman movies construct bastions of whiteness—viz., their casting and their commitment to law and order at any price—but *The Dark Knight* epitomizes this trend.[138] Although *The Dark Knight Rises* includes three supporting characters played by actors of color, all the agents of power, both good and bad, are white, as they are in all of Nolan's Batman films. The Joker represents the horror of whiteness turning on itself. In his white clown makeup and bespoke three-piece suit, he is a caricature of Wayne's corporate cronies. He also understands white privilege far better than any other character; as he explains to Batman, "No one panics when the expected people get killed. . . . If I tell the press that tomorrow a gang banger will get shot, or a truckload of soldiers will be blown up, nobody panics. . . . But when I say that one little old mayor will die, everyone loses their minds!" The Joker terrifies because he exploits white privilege to torment its enforcers (albeit without naming it as such). To that end, he drives Gotham's "white knight," Harvey Dent, insane by reminding him of the arbitrary nature of the universe. Randomness is fair, they agree, but it also fundamentally incompatible with US (racialized) ideals of justice. Hence Dent abandons the latter forthwith, joining the Joker to expose the perversions within Batman's idea of justice.

At length, Dent threatens to kill Commissioner Gordon's young son, thereby invoking the trilogy's superlative icon of innocence: the threatened white boy, always a stand-in for Bruce Wayne himself.[139] That white boy metonymizes—and racializes—victimhood during the climactic face-off between Dent (now Two-Face) and Batman. The boy's death would be the most tragic, exceeding even that of superlative white woman Rachel Dawes, since the boy might be the next Batman, the next enforcer of law and order. Hence Nolan deploys images of terrorized white boys throughout his Batman trilogy to convey the immorality of Batman's nemeses (figures 26–28). These youngsters bestow innocence on all of the villains' victims, absolving them—and whiteness more broadly—of instituting and perpetuating the system of violence to which they have become suddenly, unexpectedly vulnerable. In a culture organized around the veneration of whiteness, unmotivated attacks on white children represent the ultimate random tragedy.

Holmes's massacre also imperiled white children and so threatened the hegemonic principle of white insularity undergirding Nolan's Batman trilogy and white cinema culture. The day of the attack, Nolan issued a statement lamenting "the senseless tragedy" at the Century 16 cinema: "the movie theatre is my home, and the idea that someone would violate that innocent and hopeful place in such an unbearably savage way is devastating."[140] Nolan was not alone in regarding the Century 16 as a haven; the *New York Times* described it as "a place of seeming safety, if not sanctuary."[141] As spaces of entertainment, movie theaters often cultivate impressions of protection and security, but, as exhibition historians have shown, those impressions are historically blinkered fantasies.[142] During the first decade of the twentieth century, movie theaters were regarded with suspicion; they were seen as "crime breeders" where immigrants, women, and children might be hurt or led

FIGURES 26–28. The terrorized moppets of Christopher Nolan's Dark Knight Trilogy: an unnamed street urchin in *Batman Begins* (Christopher Nolan, 2005), James Gordon Jr. in *The Dark Knight* (Christopher Nolan, 2008), and a busload of unidentified orphans from *The Dark Knight Rises* (Christopher Nolan, 2012).

astray.[143] People have been getting shot, stabbed, and otherwise assaulted at movie theaters for decades. Indeed, it would require a willful act of naiveté to consider the cinema an "innocent and hopeful place" were it not for the ahistoricism with which the press addresses such violence. The "Aurora massacre" was represented as an appalling anomaly in part because the film that it accompanied presented violence that way, particularly white intra-racial violence. Nolan's Batman movies advocated top-down law and order. In contrast, the 1970s gang movies and 1990s ghetto action films espoused anti-violence via individualism. As a result, when cinema violence happened at their screenings, they were censured. Given the consistency of this pattern, I argue that cinema violence is not limited to who did what to whom at which movie; it includes the cultural violence of racism and white privilege in its reporting. That is why cinema violence is always white violence, even and especially when it was being dismissed as a Black problem.

CONCLUSION: AFTER AURORA

The "Aurora massacre" was not the last cinema shooting in the United States. Cinema violence isn't common, but it isn't going away either. On January 13, 2014, Curtis Reeves shot and killed Chad Oulson at a Tampa, Florida, screening of *Lone Survivor* (Peter Berg, 2014) after a dispute about texting during the previews.[144] On January 21, 2016, Dane Gallion accidentally shot Michelle Mallari at a Renton, Washington, screening of *13 Hours: The Secret Soldiers of Benghazi* (Michael Bay, 2016) with a gun he brought for self-protection.[145] And on July 23, 2015, John Russell Houser shot and killed Mayci Breaux and Jillian Johnson at a Lafayette, Louisiana, screening of the Amy Schumer comedy *Trainwreck*. The latter shooting occurred in the midst of the Holmes trial, which no doubt accelerated the moral panic it inspired. This incident never engendered a panicked reception culture, however, possibly because the shooter was a vocal white supremacist and male chauvinist.[146] Journalists speculated that Houser may have chosen the movie because of its feminist themes, but they did not blame the movie, because the shooter was targeting its target audience but was not himself a member of it.[147] Consequently, Schumer was never called upon to defend her film. Instead, she was able to use her familial connection to Senator Chuck Schumer to advocate for gun control while maintaining the randomness of public violence at her film.[148]

Between the Aurora massacre and the Houser shooting, US exhibitors also took steps to attenuate the perceived threat of cinema violence.

FIGURE 29. AMC tries to inject fun into an injunction, circa 2015.

Specifically, they turned the responsibility for cinema violence back on viewers. Between 2012 and 2015, AMC gradually introduced a new series of pre-roll videos that suggested that audiences monitor themselves for potential assailants.[149] Pre-rolls play before the previews at movie theaters and typically urge viewers to purchase concessions and refrain from talking during the film. Each video in AMC's pre-roll series used the protocols of a different genre (e.g., comedy, action, mystery, or horror) to encourage viewers to turn off their cell phones, be courteous to other guests—oh, and keep an eye out for "suspicious characters." These were serious warnings couched in film culture levity, such as science-fiction genre references: "Let's start this mission with a few safety tips. Keep track of your stuff. Report suspicious characters. And in case of angry robots or other emergencies, watch your step and walk to the nearest exit, which may be in front of you, behind you, or on either side. Then exit the building and move far away from the angry robot."[150] Other pre-rolls warned of "suspicious characters with masked agendas" (romance), "unusual characters with suspicious agendas" (indie drama), "slimy characters with questionable agendas" (comedy, timed to coincide with the release of Paul Feig's *Ghostbusters* remake [2016]), and "shady characters with strange agendas" (mystery) (figure 29).[151] The pre-rolls teach viewers that being vigilant is part of the routine of multiplex moviegoing, part of the excitement a viewer chooses along with the genre of movie they see. In these pre-rolls, cinema violence is no longer exceptional but conventional, an element of classical Hollywood storytelling and industry hospitality.

Cutesy warnings about cinema violence may make viewers more alert, even safer, but they obscure the panicked reception cultures such incidents have historically engendered. In fact, these warnings subtly perpetuate the same racist suppositions about cinema as a white idyll that undergirded those panics. AMC advised its patrons to beware of suspicious characters, as if what counts as suspicious was not historically and culturally specific.[152] The American Civil Liberties Union has confirmed that citizen vigilance campaigns of the "If you see something, say something" variety lead to grassroots racial profiling.[153] AMC avoids using human figures in its pre-roll animations, but that does not neutralize the impact of the initiative. Rather it reproduces the euphemistic racism of prior panicked reception cultures. Both the pre-rolls and the press remove cinema violence from its sociohistorical and political contexts. Both subtly craft connections between the movie being screened and any proximate violence to support fantasies of the cinema as a safe place. Both obscure the foundational roles that white privilege and anti-Black prejudice play in US cinema culture and its reactions to cinema violence.

Cinema violence shapes viewers' perceptions of movies, their makers, and their audiences, not because of the material violence itself but because of how the press represents that violence. For the past forty years, race has been the dominant factor determining media reactions to cinema violence. Some movies afflicted by cinema violence have met with panicked reception cultures; some have not. In each case, the races of the assailants, victims, film characters, and filmmakers have determined which films were blamed for inciting violence and which were not; which assailants were reduced to stereotypes and which profiled as individuals; which audiences were assumed to be constitutive of US cinema culture and which spurned as threats to it. Cinema violence is an enduring and pervasive force of US cinema culture; its influence far exceeds the actual incidents of material violence to feed white supremacist fantasies about cinema space. Cinema violence also is not likely to end anytime soon, and until we account for the ways that our reactions to it perpetuate a white cinematic hegemony, we cannot bring justice to its many victims.

This chapter is dedicated to the memory of John Singleton (1968–2019).

Conclusion

Expanding the Scene of the Screen

This just in: film and television scholars are people too. As media consumers, we eat the popcorn, buy the T-shirts, and relax into the luxurious cinema recliners just like everybody else. But you would never know it from reading our articles and monographs, where somehow these creature comforts rarely come up. Most media scholars continue to analyze "the scene of the screen" as if it involved nothing more than viewers, technologies of exhibition, and media texts.[1] Why is that? Are we ashamed of our commoditized material engagements with media, the same way we were once reluctant to write about the bodily sensations that cinema elicits?[2] Maybe we are. Respectability politics still circumscribe certain topics and methodologies in our field, alienating scholars from their own viewerly practices. Critics working in porn studies, fan studies, and piracy studies have all faced such impediments; so too will scholars of material media cultures. It feels risky, scary even, to pin your career on analyzing the stuff most people consider beneath notice: classic Hollywood coasters and robot dogs, disintegrating videocassettes and movie-themed cocktails, rock'n'roll riots and strains of cannabis named after television shows. But if we don't take risks, we never grow, and material culture studies offers film and media critics multiple avenues for growth.

First, material culture studies provides film and media scholars with new approaches to historiography and ideology critique, approaches that can contribute to a broader institutional defense of the humanities and social sciences. Second, material culture studies can resolve out-moded divides within film and media studies, such as the one between apparatus theorists and reception historians.[3] Third, it generates a new purpose and rationale for textual analysis, a long-esteemed methodology of film and media studies that has fallen out of favor in the twenty-first century. Collectively, these interventions suggest that material media culture provides a new frame for considering both film and television and film and television criticism, one that will, I hope, prove useful to other scholars.

The Stuff of Spectatorship models the disciplinary interventions listed above through its heterogeneous mix of case studies, which demonstrate that film and television culture involves not just media and viewers but consumer goods, intoxicating substances, physical violence, and many other things of this world. Its first three chapters consider how viewers' perceptions of television and film history are affected by various commodity forms, from (deteriorating) home video formats to branded merchandise and consumer experiences. These chapters explore how viewers access classic media and how they are interpellated as spectators of classic media by the material cultures around it. Hence, they are also about historiography, since these materials shape fans' and scholars' impressions of film history. Historically, media scholars have framed "access" as an issue of distribution and circulation, but it also includes the broader commodity cultures that media industries generate around their content. These paratexts teach consumers how to interpret and value what they are being given access to. Turner Classic Movies (TCM) is one of the most influential distributors of classic cinema in the twenty-first century, in large part because of the extensive material network they have developed to promote their brand. Many fans rely on TCM as "the ultimate destination for classic film" and embrace its transformation of cinephilia into a trademarked identity that one inhabits by purchasing TCM goods and services.[4] Material media cultures like TCM's are historiographic because they change how viewers perceive media history. Writing about these material practices of historiography allows film and television scholars to reconsider their own relations to the classic texts they write about, how their investigations are also shaped by material culture.

Material culture studies also offers film and media scholars new ways to think about the circulation of ideology within media cultures. As anthropologists have shown, material culture always involves social politics, including cultural biases around gender, race, class, and sexuality.[5] That is why, and how, exhibitors use the material presence of alcohol in cinemas to construct specific viewing experiences and entice desired demographics; viewers' preconceptions about alcohol, class, and ethnicity influence their perception of businesses that serve alcohol, including movie theaters. The material presence of cinema violence in theaters likewise influences public reactions to affected films, particularly when the films are by or about African Americans. As these examples demonstrate, attending to the material cultures around film and other media enables new perspectives on their ideological positioning and thus new ways of doing ideology critique. For the past few decades, ideology critique has been a disparaged methodology within film and media studies; scholars assumed that it meant—and could only mean—"deal[ing] with films as ideological symptoms" and condemning prejudiced representations of marginalized communities.[6] Material culture studies revitalizes the project of ideology critique by extending it to consider the objects and institutions around the screen and how they influence political perceptions of film and television. It reveals that the meanings audiences attach to texts come not just from the texts themselves but from a vast network of physical objects and forces, none of which are ideologically neutral.

Exploring how material media cultures change viewers' relation to film and television (not to mention radio, video games, and other media) can place media scholarship in conversation with other humanities disciplines as they face common institutional challenges. In the wake of the global financial crisis of 2007–2008 and the novel corona virus pandemic of 2020, college and university administrators routinely promoted and rewarded the so-called STEM fields (science, technology, engineering, and mathematics) over the humanities and social sciences. Many scholars of arts and culture now find themselves called upon to explain why their programs are valuable when their research cannot be monetized or their methods taught as professional skills. Material culture studies will not align media studies with such corporatized objectives, but it can enhance scholars' struggle against them. Thinking in terms of material culture can illuminate the social politics embedded in the material objects that institutions adopt or discard. Analyses of material media cultures thus have applications in the classroom and faculty senate, where they can support arguments against the ableism of many "smart" classroom technologies, such as clickers.[7] Scholars of material media cultures can also help university librarians think about the pedagogical implications of maintaining different media platforms. The language of material culture studies has helped me explain to colleagues why it is still important to teach students how to project celluloid film (even though most cinemas no longer use it) and why it's worth preserving aging videocassettes and even (gasp!) the boxes they came in. To be sure, many film and television scholars are already engaged in interdisciplinary resistance to neoliberal reforms at their institutions. Material culture studies can be one more weapon in the arsenal we use to defend the humanities as meaningful and necessary to our students, colleagues, and administrators.

Studying material media cultures also exposes long-standing divisions within film and media studies as illusory and unnecessary, particularly the discord between spectatorship theorists and reception historians. Since the 1970s, these groups have represented their specialties as diametrically opposed, with spectatorship theorists asserting the power of ideology and reception historians maintaining the individual's capacity to resist or negotiate with ideology. The historians have accused the theorists (especially apparatus theorists) of transhistoricism and of universalizing the hegemonic white male subject, not to mention doctrinaire pessimism. The theorists correspondingly have dismissed the historians (especially those in fan studies) as overly optimistic, even naive, for refusing to recognize how capitalism defines viewers' relation to the culture industries. Neither perception is fair, but attending to material culture pushes the fields together and reveals their common ground. For starters, it impels spectatorship theorists to reconsider the geohistoric specificity of their object(s) of inquiry. When one investigates the physical condition of any media apparatus—be it a third-generation Apple iPad with Retina Display or the oldest continuously operating movie theater in the world (the State Theater in Washington, Iowa)—one cannot ignore its situation in time and space. Also relevant are its particular production histories and materials, which inform the meaning of the medium for the cultures that use it. Material culture studies makes it impossible (or at least counterintuitive) to consider an apparatus out of its sociohistorical context; it also encourages apparatus theorists to consider how different media engage and complicate theoretical concepts like interactivity or immersion at different historical junctures.[8] Addressing material cultures is not a failsafe, of course; there are certainly ways to dehistoricize the material world, if that's what a scholar really wants to do. But focusing on material culture at least impels them to make a case for transhistoricism and universalism, as I have made a case for historicization here.

By the same token, material culture studies invites reception historians to reflect on how physical conditions inform different reception communities' relation to media. Complicating reception narratives to include nonhuman influences pushes historians toward a theory of spectatorship by disestablishing their focus on human agency. Too often, ethnographies of media reception reproduce rather than challenge informants' stories about how they use and relate to media texts. Rarely do informants argue that their actions and attitudes were colored by their physical environment, and yet anthropologists have shown that such influence is inevitable. To fully understand a reception phenomenon or community, therefore, scholars must consider the material culture shaping it. Describing that interrelation means theorizing it, since one can hardly count upon a glass of wine or a cruise ship to explain how it affects viewers' interpretations of the media they encounter.

Here the concept of the actant and Karan Barad's theory of intra-action are helpful, as they provide vocabulary for understanding the agency of material objects and forces within media cultures. In actor-network theory, *actant* describes anything "that acts or to which activity is granted by others."[9] Importantly (and controversially), the term divorces action from human agency, making it possible to recognize and analyze the sovereignty of nonhuman forces. One way inanimate entities act is by transforming or otherwise affecting the entities around them; hence cannabis acts on its consumers through its physiological and psychotropic effects. Barad takes the concept of the actant further, arguing that animate and inanimate entities contain and produce meaning equally, as "mattering is simultaneously a matter of substance and significance."[10] Material objects generate meaning when they *intra-act*, or co-constitute each other through mutual engagement. Hence Barad understands "knowing [as] a matter of part of the world making itself intelligible to another part."[11] Meaning emerges through mutual intra-action, then, and not merely as a result of human agency. My opinions, beliefs, and theories are the result of the intra-action of my material body (including but not limited to my brain) and the physical world, including but not limited to books, VHS cassettes, movie theaters, wine, TCM cruises, a riot outside a screening of *New Jack City* in March 1991 . . . the list could go on indefinitely. Applied to media cultures, intra-action suggests that the scene of the screen consists of an almost infinitely complex network of actants that co-determine meaning within the scene. Reception historians can enrich their accounts of media audiences by analyzing the vectors of intra-action in the scenes they write about. As *The Stuff of Spectatorship* demonstrates, ignoring all the other actants in the world in favor of humans is an unsustainable, even dangerous, critical position. It blinkers scholars to the way politics permeates viewers' environments and their lives.

To model the value of Barad's theory for reception history, I return to my introductory analysis of *TV Guide*. *TV Guide* performed key actions within twentieth-century US television culture, such as affirming the industry's ideology of abundance and shepherding viewers through its possibilities. The journal was granted other powers by its consumers, including myself. I responded to its distinctive size and glossy cover with unmitigated class envy, assuming that friends who possessed it were richer and more sophisticated than I was. *TV Guide* does not itself confer class distinction, but as a child, I responded to its material sumptuousness by according it that authority. This was part of our intra-action, how the matter of *TV Guide* became intelligible and attained meaning in Lincoln, Massachusetts, in the mid-1980s. That intra-action still partially determines how I make myself intelligible to *TV Guide*, or at least to US television culture. In response to my encounters with the little digest, I wrote this book, trying to explain how intra-actions with material media cultures changed me and other film and television viewers. In sum, *TV Guide* and I historically co-constituted each other. Nevertheless, I cannot fully understand the kind of reception culture that *TV Guide* inspired among my buddies and me without theorizing the subject position that my intra-actions with it generated.

Finally, studying material media cultures reinvigorates film and media studies by providing scholars with an opportunity to reimagine and reinvest in textual analysis. Many academics have informed me that after enjoying decades as a (if not the) privileged methodology of the field, close reading has fallen from favor. Since the 1980s, interest in industries and audiences has driven film and media studies toward other critical approaches, including but not limited to ethnography, economic and policy analysis, cognitive science, and computational approaches to historiography. Regardless of how a given scholar feels about the disciplinary decentering of textual analysis, they can no longer assume that their close readings will necessarily be valued in the field. (By valued, I mean published or accepted for conferences or symposia.) Film and media studies no longer seems to desire another formal or thematic breakdown of *The Dark Crystal* (Jim Henson and Frank Oz, 1982), however insightful it might be. Conversely, material culture studies provides fresh rationales and objects for textual analysis. Considering the material function of puppets in *The Dark Crystal* and their remediation in toys and action figures might offer compelling insight into the tension between aesthetic experimentation and commercial imperatives in Jim Henson's Creature Shop during the years leading up to its canceled merger with the Walt Disney Company. In this context, textual analysis provides a means of exploring how material culture gets invested with social significance, while material culture studies enriches the stakes of textual analysis. Is it possible to do film and media studies—even material media culture studies—without analyzing media as texts? Certainly. But material culture reminds scholars of how important texts are to the societies in which they circulate; it reminds us that matter and meaning are inextricable in this world. To study material media cultures without addressing how texts use them to make meaning blinkers our understandings of both. Thus, material culture studies offers a new future for textual analysis, one in which its hermeneutic can acknowledge and embrace both meaning and matter.

To make the interventions I discuss here, material media culture studies does not need to become its own subfield or method; in fact, it should not. At its best, it provides a new way of regarding extant subfields and practicing extant methods. It is, in other words, a frame. Frames have been a structuring discourse of film and television theory since their inception. The frame, we know, bestows order and meaning on the images that appear within it. Its borders define the field of vision.[12] In *Stuff*, Daniel Miller argues that material culture is best understood as a frame because it constitutes the environment for (and later provides interpretive clues to) human activity.[13] When material culture becomes the frame for understanding media cultures, then nothing is out-of-frame—only out of focus. Media cultures are inextricable from material culture; we simply cannot encounter film, television, radio, or video games without also encountering objects, things, and stuff. When we expand the scene of the screen to include that stuff, we recognize it as comprised of actants with which we intra-act to coproduce meaning. Framed in this way, it is no longer clear where any given material media culture ends, what objects it does not include. And that's the point. Expanding the scene of the screen expands the potential of film and media studies and overrides its divisions. It opens our discipline to the world and vice versa.

Appendix

Date	Film Title	Location of Screening	Inside or Outside Theater	# of People Hurt	# of People Killed	Details of Incident
February 1910	unknown	Coney Island, NY	Inside	1	0	Martha Blair shot her date, John Hutchinson.
September 1910	unknown	Los Angeles, CA	Inside	0	1	Rudolph Gastelum was shot by unknown assailant.
September 1911	unknown	Bartlesville, OK	Inside	2	1	C. R. Richardson fatally shot Maggie Sprague and shot and injured M. Bennett and Charles Music.
May 1913	unknown	Los Angeles, CA	inside	0	1	An usher (Israel Gore) was shot after shushing a rowdy group of viewers.
April 1915	The Birth of a Nation	Boston, MA	Inside	0	0	Protestors threw an "acid bomb" and an egg during a screening of Griffith's film.
August 1915	unknown	New Bedford, MA	Inside	0	0	Leon Ethier shot at and missed May Holland.
n.dat. 1920	unknown	Washington, DC	Inside	0	1	An unnamed young man killed his date for refusing his sexual advances.
April 1923	unknown	Pittsburgh, PA	Inside	0	2	Gustave Lieson shot his wife (name unknown) and her lover, Edward Weigner.
October 1923	unknown	Nashville, TN	Inside	0	1	Mary Martin slit Lizze Evans's throat with a razor for reading intertitles aloud.
February 1927	n/a	Davenport, IA	Outside	0	1	R.D. Draper shot at and missed box office cashier Rosemary Donohoe, then shot himself.

Date	Film	City	Location			Description
March 1928	n/a	Allentown, PA	Outside	1	1	Gustave Weber shot and injured box office cashier Ida Kemmerer then chased her into the theater and shot himself in the head.
July 22, 1933	Manhattan Melodrama	Chicago, IL	Outside	0	1	John Dillinger was shot after exiting the theater after an FBI manhunt.
August 17, 1955	The Road to Denver	Chicago, IL	Inside	1	0	Officer Clarence Kerr was shot while apprehending a criminal.
n.dat. 1955	Blackboard Jungle	London, Dublin, and other cities	Inside	0	0	Police were called when teenagers began dancing to "Rock Around the Clock"; vandalism ensued. The press referred to these incidents as "rock'n'roll riots."
n.dat. 1956	Rock Around the Clock	Boston, MA; Hartford, CT; Atlanta, GA; Newport, RI; Manchester, England; Sydney, Australia; Oslo, Norway.	Inside and outside	Unknown	.	Teenagers allegedly rioted in and outside screenings of the film, vandalizing furniture, breaking bottles, throwing rocks and lit cigarettes, and overturning cars.
January 22, 1972	Hair	Memphis TN	Box-office	0	1	Mary Mildred Pierce was shot and killed during a robbery attempt at the downtown Malco Theater.
February 12, 1979	The Warriors	Palm Springs CA	Drive-in snack bar	0	1	Marvin Kenneth Eller was shot during a dispute with an unknown assailant.
February 12, 1979	The Warriors	Ventura, CA	Lobby	3	1	Timothy Gitchel was stabbed during a dispute with an unknown assailant.

(continued)

Appendix (continued)

Date	Film Title	Location of Screening	Inside or Outside Theater	# of People Hurt	# of People Killed	Details of Incident
February 15, 1979	The Warriors	Dorchester, MA	Subway station	0	1	Martin Yakubowicz was stabbed during a fight between two white gangs.
n.dat. 1979	The Warriors	New York City	Subway station	Unknown	Unknown	A "subway rampage" was attributed to the film.
n.dat. 1979	The Warriors	Pasadena, CA	Unknown	Unknown	Unknown	A theater manager was beaten.
March 4, 1979	The Warriors	Boston, MA	In a car, on a local highway	1	0	A hitchhiker, Charles Eltringham, was picked up and beaten by three men who called themselves the Warriors.
March 23, 1979	The Warriors	San Juan Capistrano, CA	Drive-in snack bar	1	0	Eddie Rosenbaum was stabbed; there may have been another victim.
March 23, 1979	Boulevard Nights	Ontario, CA	Drive-in	3	0	One teen was shot and two stabbed outside the restroom.
March 23, 1979	Boulevard Nights	San Francisco, CA	Outside	5	0	Four people were stabbed and one, Jocelyn Vargas, shot in a fight between rival gangs.
December 18, 1987	Eddie Murphy: Raw	Monrovia, CA	Outside	1	0	A man was stabbed in the chest during a sixty person fight and "gang-related incident" in the theater.
December 18, 1987	Eddie Murphy: Raw	Paramount, CA	Drive-in	Unknown	1	Raymond Espinoza was shot in the chest during a fight.
December 18, 1987	Eddie Murphy: Raw	Los Angeles, CA	Outside	Unknown	0	Approximately 1,500 people were involved in "a violent crowd fracas in Westwood," according to press reports.
April 17, 1988	Colors	Stockton, CA	Outside	0	1	David Dawson was shot in a drive-by assault while waiting to buy a ticket.

Date	Film	Location				Description
November 17, 1989	*Harlem Nights*	Detroit, MI	Inside	1	2	Two men were shot in the theater. One woman panicked and ran out of the theater and into traffic. One police officer was also shot.
November 17, 1989	*Harlem Nights*	Sacramento, CA	Inside, then outside	2	0	No details available.
November 17, 1989	*Harlem Nights*	Richmond, CA	Unknown	0	1	An hour-long riot occurred when police stopped the movie to investigate a shooting in which teenager Marchel Thompson died.
November 17, 1989	*Harlem Nights*	Boston, MA	Outside	Unknown	Unknown	Mayor Raymond Flynn threatened to have a Boston theater closed due to fistfights as the crowd left the movie. Flynn blamed the film for the "riot" because it "glorifies violence."
December 15, 1989	*Blaze & Cocktail* (double feature)	Carson, CA	Drive-in	1	2	After a carjacking and kidnapping, three men attacked Jesus Martinez and Irene Franco and later raped and killed her.
February 23, 1990	*Angel Town*	Westminster, CA	Outside	1	0	In an outdoor brawl, baseball bats were used to smash car windows.
December 25, 1990	*The Godfather Part III*	Valley Stream, NY	Inside	3	1	Four people were shot during a dispute between two groups of teenagers; Tremain Hall died.
March 8, 1991	*New Jack City*	Los Angeles, CA	Outside	n/a	n/a	600–800 people protested outside a Westwood theater.
March 8, 1991	*New Jack City*	Brooklyn, NY	Outside	0	1	Gabriel Williams was shot in a gun fight with Shawn Curry.

(continued)

Appendix *(continued)*

Date	Film Title	Location of Screening	Inside or Outside Theater	# of People Hurt	# of People Killed	Details of Incident
March 8, 1991	*New Jack City*	Sayreville, NJ	Outside	4	0	Three police officers and one civilian were injured in a "melee."
March 8, 1991	*New Jack City*	Las Vegas, NV	Unknown	Unknown	0	Fifteen people were arrested during two "gang disturbances."
March 9 and 10, 1991	*New Jack City*	Chicago, IL	Outside	2	0	One man was stabbed and another shot outside different theaters showing the film.
March 10 and 12, 1991	*New Jack City*	San Francisco, CA	Outside	1	0	A man was shot outside New Mission Theater in a drive-by assault. There was also an unrelated fight between two gangs.
July 12, 1991	*Boyz N the Hood*	Riverdale, IL	Drive-In, in line to leave	0	1	Michael Booth was shot by Timothy Turner after declining to light his cigarette.
July 12, 1991	*Boyz N the Hood*	Minneapolis, MN	Outside	0	1	Jitu Jones was shot outside the cinema after fleeing a shooting inside; he was only a bystander to the initial incident.
July 12, 1991	*Boyz N the Hood*	Los Angeles, CA	Unknown	Unknown	0	Shooting; no details available.
July 12, 1991	*Boyz N the Hood*	Upland, CA	Unknown	Unknown	0	Shooting; no details available.
July 12, 1991	*Boyz N the Hood*	Pino, CA	Unknown	Unknown	0	Shooting; no details available.
July 12, 1991	*Boyz N the Hood*	Chino, CA	Unknown	Unknown	0	Shooting; no details available.
July 12, 1991	*Boyz N the Hood*	Sacramento, CA	Unknown	Unknown	0	Shooting; no details available.
July 12, 1991	*Boyz N the Hood*	Las Vegas, NV	Unknown	Unknown	0	Shooting; no details available.
July 12, 1991	*Boyz N the Hood*	Texas City, TX	Unknown	Unknown	0	Shooting; no details available.
July 12, 1991	*Boyz N the Hood*	Detroit, MI	Unknown	Unknown	0	Shooting; no details available.
July 12, 1991	*Boyz N the Hood*	Tuscaloosa, AL	Unknown	Unknown	0	Shooting; no details available.

Date	Film	Location	Location detail			Description
July 12, 1991	*Boyz N the Hood*	Akron, OH	Unknown	Unknown	0	Shooting; no details available.
July 12, 1991	*Boyz N the Hood*	Miami, FL	Unknown	Unknown	0	Shooting; no details available.
July 12, 1991	*Boyz N the Hood*	Brooklyn, NY	Unknown	Unknown	0	Shooting; no details available.
July 12, 1991	*Boyz N the Hood*	West Springfield, MA	Unknown	Unknown	0	Shooting; no details available.
July 12, 1991	*Boyz N the Hood*	Detroit, MI	Unknown	Unknown	0	Stabbing; no details available.
July 12, 1991	*Boyz N the Hood*	New Bern, NC	Unknown	Unknown	0	Stabbing; no details available.
July 12, 1991	*Boyz N the Hood*	Commack, NY	Unknown	Unknown	0	Stabbing; no details available.
July 12, 1991	*Boyz N the Hood*	Tukila, WA	Inside, then outside	Unknown	0	A riot ended with over 100 people fighting.
July 12, 1991	*Boyz N the Hood*	Orlando, FL	Unknown	Unknown	0	During a melee, police were pelted with bottles.
July 13, 1991	*Boyz N the Hood*	Memphis TN	Unknown	1	0	A shooting occurred "during a Saturday night fracas."
August 2, 1991	*Boyz N the Hood*	San Bernardino, CA	Outside	3	1	Two patrons left the theater, walked to their car, removed rifles, and started shooting; the victims' names were not released.
January 17, 1992	*Juice*	Chicago, IL	Outside	0	1	Tyesa Cherry was a bystander when two gang members exchanged shots outside the theater.
January 17, 1992	*Juice*	Lansing, MI	Unknown	Unknown	0	A teen was injured during a shooting.
January 17, 1992	*Juice*	Cheltenham, PA	Outside	Unknown	0	A teen was injured during a shooting.
January 17, 1992	*Juice*	New York, NY	Inside	Unknown	0	Stabbing; no details available.
January 17, 1992	*Juice*	multiple/unknown	Unknown	Unknown	Unknown	There was violence at eight theaters "from Anchorage to New York," according to press reports.
January 6, 1994	*Schindler's List*	San Diego, CA	Inside	1	0	Ellen Campbell was shot by James Michael Kirby, who said he pulled the trigger "to test God."

(continued)

Appendix (*continued*)

Date	Film Title	Location of Screening	Inside or Outside Theater	# of People Hurt	# of People Killed	Details of Incident
December 24, 2004	*Meet the Fockers*	Queens, NY	Outside	2	1	Three teens were stabbed and assaulted; Davey Adams died.
November 10, 2005	*Get Rich or Die Tryin'*	Philadelphia, PA	Lobby	0	1	Sheldon Flowers was shot during a fight with unknown others.
December 16, 2005	*King Kong*	Hamilton Township, NJ	Parking lot	0	1	Cindy Cade was shot by Walter Dille; the prosecutor cited his "hatred of minorities" as a reason for the incident.
June 15, 2006	*X-Men: The Last Stand*	Owings Mills, MD	Inside	0	1	Paul Schrum was shot by Mujtaba Rabbani Jabbar, who was later diagnosed as schizophrenic.
February 24, 2008	*The Signal*	Fullerton, CA	Inside	2	0	Two people were shot by a stranger during the movie.
December 25, 2008	*The Curious Case of Benjamin Button*	Philadelphia, PA	Inside	0	1	Wofford Lomax Jr. was shot by a stranger for talking during the movie.
January 16, 2009	*Notorious*	Greensboro, NC	Inside	1	0	Clive O'Connor was stabbed by an unidentified assailant.
January 19, 2009	*My Bloody Valentine 3D*	Valley Stream, NY	Inside	1	0	Stabbing; no details available.
April 6, 2009	*The Watchmen*	Eugene, OR	Inside	0	1	A man committed suicide by shooting himself in the head in the theater.
February 27, 2010	*Shutter Island*	Lancaster, CA	Inside	3	0	A man was stabbed with a digital thermometer after a fight with another man whose fiancée was talking on her cell phone during the movie. Two others were also injured.

Date	Movie	Location	Place			Description
August 29, 2010	unknown	Riverside, CA	Drive-in	3	0	Three people were hurt in an incident police said "may have been gang related."
May 15, 2012	unknown	Atlanta, GA	Drive-in	0	1	Mitt Lenix was shot by Quentric Williams after asking Williams for help with car trouble.
July 20, 2012	The Dark Knight Rises	Aurora, CO	Inside	70	12	Mass shooting by James Eagan Holmes.
January 13, 2014	Lone Survivor	Tampa, FL	Inside	0	1	Chad Oulson was shot by Curtis Reeves, Jr. in a dispute about texting during the previews.
December 23, 2014	Finesse	Atlanta, GA	Lobby	2	0	One man was shot in the buttocks, while a woman was grazed by a bullet.
July 23, 2015	Trainwreck	Lafayette, LA	Inside	9	3	John Russell Houser shot eleven people, killing Mayci Breaux and Jillian Johnson, in an unexplained rampage that ended with his suicide.
August 5, 2015	Mad Max: Fury Road	Nashville TN	Inside	3	1	Vincente David Montano was shot by SWAT officers after assaulting other audience members with a pellet gun, hatchet, and pepper spray.
January 16, 2016	13 Hours	Renton, WA	Inside	1	0	Dane E. Gallion accidently shot Michelle Mallari; he brought a gun to the theater to protect himself against public violence.
March 24, 2019	Us	Concord, NC	Inside	1	0	Bryant Gregory Eaves Jr. shot William Weldon in a dispute over seating.
May 2, 2019	Us	Washington, PA	Inside theater, then in hallway	1	0	Chris Williams attacked six teens, punching then shooting one of them.

Notes

INTRODUCTION

1. When I say "little attention," I do not mean no attention; rather, the books and essays on material media cultures have not cohered into an ongoing conversation. However, I strongly recommend the work on material culture done by home video scholars, feminist film theorists, media archaeologists, and exhibition historians. Material culture may not have been their sole concern, but the scholars listed here greatly informed my own approach to it. See Joshua M. Greenberg, *From Betamax to Blockbuster: Video Stores and the Invention of Movies on Video* (Cambridge, MA: MIT Press, 2008); Amelie Hastie, *Cupboards of Curiosity: Women, Recollection, and Film History* (Durham, NC: Duke University Press, 2007); Daniel Herbert, *Videoland: Movie Culture at the American Video Store* (Berkeley: University of California Press, 2014); Jussi Parikka, *A Geology of Media* (Minneapolis: University of Minnesota Press, 2015); Chuck Tryon, *On-Demand Culture: Digital Delivery and the Future of Movies* (New Brunswick, NJ: Rutgers University Press, 2013).

2. Regarding apparatus theory, see Jean-Louis Baudry, "Ideological Effects of the Basic Cinematographic Apparatus," trans. Alan Williams, in *Narrative, Apparatus, Ideology: A Film Theory Reader*, ed. Philip Rosen (New York: Columbia University Press, 1986), 286–98; Jean-Louis Baudry, "The Apparatus: Metapsychological Approaches to the Impression of Reality in Cinema," trans. Bertrand Augst, in Rosen, *Narrative, Apparatus, Ideology*, 299–318; Jean-Louis Comolli, *Cinema against Spectacle: Technique and Ideology Revisited*, ed. and trans. Daniel Fairfax (Amsterdam: Amsterdam University Press, 2015); Christian Metz, *The Imaginary Signifier: Psychoanalysis and the Cinema*, trans. Celia Britton, Annwyl Williams, Ben Brewster, and Alfred Guzzetti (Bloomington: Indiana University Press, 1982); Laura Mulvey, "Visual Pleasure and Narrative Cinema," in *Visual and Other Pleasures*, 2nd ed. (New York:

Palgrave Macmillan, 2009), 14–29. For more on ideology in television design, see Sheila C. Murphy, *How Television Invented New Media* (New Brunswick, NJ: Rutgers University Press, 2011); Susan Murray, *Bright Signals: A History of Color Television* (Durham, NC: Duke University Press, 2018); Lynn Spigel, *Make Room for TV: Television and the Family Ideal in Postwar America* (Chicago: University of Chicago Press, 1992).

3. See Jennifer M. Barker, *The Tactile Eye: Touch and the Cinematic Experience* (Berkeley: University of California Press, 2009); Ann duCille, *Technicolored: Reflections on Race in a Time of TV* (Durham, NC: Duke University Press, 2018); Alison Griffiths, *Carceral Fantasies: Cinema and Prison in Early Twentieth-Century America* (New York: Columbia University Press, 2019); Anna McCarthy, *Ambient Television: Visual Culture and Public Space* (Durham, NC: Duke University Press, 2001); Vivian Sobchack, *The Address of the Eye: A Phenomenology of Film Experience* (Princeton, NJ: Princeton University Press, 1992).

4. See Lisa Parks, *Cultures in Orbit: Satellites and the Televisual* (Durham, NC: Duke University Press, 2005); Lisa Parks and Nicole Starosielski, eds. *Signal Traffic: Critical Studies of Media Infrastructures* (Urbana: University of Illinois Press, 2015); Nicole Starosielski, *The Undersea Network* (Durham, NC: Duke University Press, 2015); Tung-Hui Hu, *A Prehistory of the Cloud* (Cambridge, MA: MIT Press, 2015).

5. Daniel Miller, *Stuff* (Cambridge, UK: Polity, 2010), 51.

6. Miller, *Stuff*, 50.

7. Vivian Sobchack, "The Scene of the Screen: Envisioning Photographic, Cinematic, and Electronic 'Presence,'" in *Carnal Thoughts: Embodiment and Moving Image Culture* (Berkeley: University of California Press, 2004), 136.

8. In the mid-1980s, *TV Guide* cost fifty cents per issue, or $23.40 for an annual subscription.

9. David Lachenbruch, quoted in Jeremy Gerard, "*TV Guide*'s Power over the Air," *New York Times*, August 11, 1988, D1.

10. "News in the Advertising and Marketing Fields," *New York Times*, October 26, 1954, 45.

11. "National TV Guide—The First Years," TV History, accessed September 7, 2019, http://www.tvhistory.tv/tv_guide1.htm.

12. Michael Dann, quoted in Gerard, "*TV Guide*'s Power," D1.

13. Kent A. MacDougall, "A Magazine Prospers by Mixing TV Listings with 'Inside' Articles," *Wall Street Journal*, June 13, 1967, 1.

14. Gerard, "*TV Guide*'s Power," D1.

15. Brian Selter, "Six Days and 23 Hours to Read *TV Guide*," *New York Times*, September 27, 2007, https://mediadecoder.blogs.nytimes.com/2007/09/27/six-days-and-23-hours-to-read-tv-guide/.

16. *Paper Tiger Television*, episode 21, "Brian Winston Reads *TV Guide*: Journal of the Waste-land," aired April 28, 1982 accessed October 20, 2019, http://papertiger.org /brian-winston-reads-tv-guide-journal-of-the-wasteland/.

17. Glenn C. Altschuler and David I. Grossvogel, *Changing Channels: America in TV Guide* (Urbana: University of Illinois Press, 1992), xi.

18. Caetlin Benson-Allott, *Killer Tapes and Shattered Screens: Video Spectatorship from VHS to File Sharing* (Berkeley: University of California Press, 2013).

19. Hu, *A Prehistory of the Cloud*.

20. Daniel Herbert, Amanda D. Lotz, and Aswin Punathambekar, *Media Industry Studies* (Medford, MA: Polity, 2020), 5.

21. While Havens, Lotz, and Tinic argue convincingly for the importance of the word *critical* in the name and epistemological commitments of this nascent field, the term ultimately faded from popular use. Timothy Havens, Amanda D. Lotz, and Serra Tinic, "Critical Media Industry Studies: A Research Approach," *Communication, Culture & Critique* 2, no. 2 (2009): 234.

22. See for example Amanda D. Lotz, *We Now Disrupt This Broadcast: How Cable Transformed Television and the Internet Revolutionized It* (Cambridge, MA: MIT Press, 2018); Parks, *Cultures in Orbit*.

23. Notably, many media retail and merchandise scholars characterize their work as a reaction to media industry studies' prior emphasis on production. As Daniel Herbert and Derek Johnson observe, focusing on production "overlooks how media culture is similarly informed by the beliefs, norms, and practices of retail professionals and countless media shoppers." Nevertheless, Herbert, Johnson, and the authors in their anthology "embrace critical media industry studies as a way of linking concerns for the political economy of media retail to the everyday experiences of those who participate in the media cultures constituted by retail contexts." Daniel Herbert and Derek Johnson, "Introduction: Media Studies in the Retail Apocalypse," in *Point of Sale: Analyzing Media Retail*, ed. Daniel Herbert and Derek Johnson (New Brunswick, NJ: Rutgers University Press, 2020), 3, 7. See also Elisabeth Affuso and Avi Santo, "Mediated Merchandise, Merchandisable Media: An Introduction," *Film Criticism* 42, no. 2 (2018): http://dx.doi.org/10.3998/fc.13761232.0042.201; Erin Hanna, "Ret(ail)con: From Dealers' Room to Exhibit Hall," in *Only at Comic-Con: Hollywood, Fans, and the Limits of Exclusivity* (New Brunswick, NJ: Rutgers University Press, 2020), 124–59.

24. Jonathan Gray, *Show Sold Separately: Promos, Spoilers, and Other Media Paratexts* (New York: New York University Press, 2010), 175, 176. See also Affuso and Santo, "Mediated Merchandise, Merchandisable Media."

25. See Herbert, Lotz, and Punathambekar, *Media Industry Studies*; Havens, Lotz, and Tinic, "Critical Media Industry Studies"; Jennifer Holt and Alisa Perren, "Introduction: Does the World Really Need One More Field of Study?" in *Media Industries: History, Theory, and Method*, ed. Jennifer Holt and Alisa Perren (Malden, MA: Wiley-Blackwell, 2009), 1–16; Jennifer Holt and Alisa Perren, "Media Industries: A Decade in Review," in *Making Media: Production, Practices, and Professions*, ed. Mark Deuze and Mirjam Prenger (Amsterdam: Amsterdam University Press, 2019), 31–42.

26. Stuart Hall, "Encoding/Decoding," in *Culture, Media, Language*, ed. Stuart Hall, Dorothy Hobson, Andrew Lowe, and Paul Willis (London: Hutchinson, 1980), 128–38.

27. Michael Aronson, *Nickelodeon City: Pittsburgh at the Movies, 1905–1929* (Pittsburgh: University of Pittsburgh Press, 2008); Richard Abel, *Menus for Movieland: Newspapers and the Emergence of American Film Culture, 1913–1916* (Oakland: University of California Press, 2015).

28. Daniel Biltereyst, Richard Maltby, and Philippe Meers, "Introduction: The Scope of New Cinema History," in *The Routledge Companion to New*

Cinema History, ed. Daniel Biltereyst, Richard Maltby, and Philippe Meers (New York: Routledge, 2019), 2.

29. Richard Maltby, "New Cinema Histories," in *Explorations in New Cinema History: Approaches and Case Studies*, ed. Richard Maltby, Daniel Biltereyst, and Philippe Meers (Malden, MA: Wiley-Blackwell, 2011), 4; Richard Maltby, Daniel Biltereyst, and Philippe Meers, "Acknowledgements," *Explorations in New Cinema History*, xii.

30. Maltby, "New Cinema Histories," 3.

31. For more on memory and digital humanities approaches to cinema studies, see Annette Kuhn, *An Everyday Magic: Cinema and Cultural Memory* (London: I. B. Tauris, 2002), and Eric Hoyt, "Arclights and Zoom Lenses," in Biltereyst et al., *The Routledge Companion to New Cinema History*, 83–95.

32. Douglas Gomery, *Shared Pleasures: A History of Movie Presentation in the United States* (Madison: University of Wisconsin Press, 1992); Ross Melnick and Andreas Fuchs, *Cinema Treasures: A New Look at Classic Movie Theaters* (St. Paul, MN: MBI, 2004); Jocelyn Szczepaniak-Gillece, *The Optical Vacuum: Spectatorship and Modernized American Theater Architecture* (New York: Oxford University Press, 2018).

33. Jocelyn Szczepaniak-Gillece and Stephen Groening, "Afterword: Objects in the Theater," *Film History* 28, no. 3 (2016): 140, 139–40.

34. Here I do not mean to slight scholars "bound to film in film studies," as Jon Lewis puts it, or committed to the rich technological or cultural histories of particular platforms. But I do want to insist that there are more cases to be made for medium promiscuity than there are for medium specificity. Media arise from, and we encounter them in, "the messiness of the world." I for one like the mess; I am more interested in what happens if we cross boundaries than if we erect them. Jon Lewis, "Parting Glances," *Cinema Journal* 43, no. 3 (2004): 99; Szczepaniak-Gillece and Groening, "Afterword: Objects in the Theater," 139.

35. See N. Katherine Hayles, *How We Became Posthuman: Virtual Bodies in Cybernetics, Literature, and Informatics* (Chicago: University of Chicago Press, 1999); Sherry Turkle, *The Second Self: Computers and the Human Spirit*, 20th anniversary ed. (Cambridge, MA: MIT Press, 2005).

36. See Bill Brown, ed., *Things* (Chicago: University of Chicago Press, 2004); Diana Coole and Samantha Frost, eds., *New Materialisms: Ontology, Agency, and Politics* (Durham, NC: Duke University Press, 2010); Graham Harman, *Object-Oriented Ontology: A New Theory of Everything* (New York: Pelican, 2018); Miller, *Stuff*.

37. Cultural materialism holds that artistic and popular texts reflect the physical, economic, and social conditions of their production; scholars of cultural materialism thus read books, films, and other creative work to understand "the material character of the production of a cultural order," as Raymond Williams put it when he introduced the concept in 1977. Since then, many scholars have embraced cultural materialism's imperative to read "texts as inseparable from the conditions of their production and reception," as Jonathan Dollimore and Alan Sinfield explain. *The Stuff of Spectatorship* certainly reflects cultural materialism's investment in politicized historiography, yet it is more interested

in how other material entities influence media consumption than in the demographic details of specific media producers or consumers. For that reason, I consider *The Stuff of Spectatorship* a work of material culture studies rather than cultural materialism, although it is certainly deeply influenced by the latter. Raymond Williams, *Marxism and Literature* (New York: Oxford University Press, 1977), 93; Jonathan Dollimore and Alan Sinfield, "Cultural Materialisms," foreword to *The Shakespeare Myth*, ed. Graham Holderness (New York: St. Martin's Press, 1988), ix.

38. Anna Malinowska and Karolina Lebek, "Introduction: The Popular Life of Things," in *Materiality and Popular Culture: The Popular Life of Things*, ed. Anna Malinowska and Karolina Lebek (New York: Routledge, 2016), 18.

39. Andrew F. Smith, *Popped Culture: A Social History of Popcorn in America* (Columbia: University of South Carolina Press, 1999), 20.

40. Smith, *Popped Culture*, 97.

41. Karen Barrow, "Popcorn's Dark Secret," *New York Times*, November 19, 2009, https://well.blogs.nytimes.com/2009/11/19/popcorn/.

42. Ian Hodder, *Entangled: An Archaeology of the Relationships between Humans and Things* (Malden, MA: Wiley-Blackwell, 2012), 1.

43. Thom van Dooren, "Wild Seed, Domesticated Seed: Companion Species and the Emergence of Agriculture," *PAN: Philosophy Activism Nature* 9 (2012): 22–28.

44. See Grant Bollmer, *Materialist Media Theory: An Introduction* (New York: Bloomsbury, 2019), 3–7.

45. Hodder, *Entangled*, 38.

46. Eve Kosofsky Sedgwick, "Paranoid Reading and Reparative Reading, or, You're So Paranoid, You Probably Think This Essay Is About You," in *Touching Feeling: Affect, Pedagogy, Performativity* (Durham, NC: Duke University Press, 2003), 123–52.

47. Stuart Elliott, "TCM Moves to Lure Film Buffs Out of Their Living Rooms," *New York Times*, August 21, 2013, https://www.nytimes.com/2013/08/22/business/tcm-moves-to-lure-film-buffs-out-of-their-living-rooms.html.

48. John Fithian, quoted in Jen Yamato, "Produced By: Hispanics 'Most Important' Ticket Buyers; Theater Owners Testing In-Movie Language Translation App," *Deadline*, June 8, 2014, https://deadline.com/2014/06/hispanics-movies-in-theater-translation-john-fithian-nato-roberto-orci-742202/.

49. By poetics, I mean the formal and narrative principles that shape a work of art, such as a television series.

50. Maggie Hennefeld, "Cinema's First Epidemic: From Contagious Twitching to Convulsive Laughter," *Los Angeles Review of Books*, June 23, 2020, https://lareviewofbooks.org/article/cinemas-first-epidemic-from-contagious-twitching-to-convulsive-laughter/.

51. Hennefeld, "Cinema's First Epidemic"; Gary D. Rhodes, *The Perils of Moviegoing in America: 1896–1950* (New York: Bloomsbury, 2011), 86–103.

52. Joanne Cachapero, "Cannabis and Coronavirus: Sales Surge as the Industry Carries On," *MG Magazine*, August 27, 2020, https://mgretailer.com/cannabis-news/cannabis-and-coronavirus-sales-surge-as-the-industry-carries-on/.

CHAPTER 1. COLLECTING AND RECOLLECTING

1. "*Battlestar Galactica* (1978) promo segments," YouTube, accessed July 24, 2016, https://www.youtube.com/watch?v=VdRrfHWwpfc; "*Battlestar Galactica* 1978 Premiere Promo," YouTube, accessed July 24, 2016, https://www.youtube .com/watch?v=QfnqA1sU33U.

2. John Kenneth Muir, *An Analytical Guide to Television's "Battlestar Galactica"* (Jefferson, NC: McFarland, 2005), 19, 37.

3. Each of these key terms of television studies—liveness, flow, and ephemerality—has inspired decades of scholarship, but do see Jane Feuer, "The Concept of Live Television," in *Regarding Television: Critical Approaches—An Anthology*, ed. E. Ann Kaplan (Frederick, MD: University Publications of America, 1983), 12–22; Raymond Williams, *Television: Technology and Cultural Form* (New York: Schocken, 1975); Paul Grainge, ed., *Ephemeral Media: Transitory Screen Culture from Television to YouTube* (London: Palgrave Macmillan, 2011).

4. By "technologies of memory," Sturken means personal and mass-produced objects that trigger memories of past events or can be used to produce such triggers—for example, both photographs and cameras. Marita Sturken, *Tangled Memories: The Vietnam War, the AIDS Epidemic, and the Politics of Remembering* (Berkeley: University of California Press, 1997), 17.

5. The only video-on-demand platform that offers critical or historical bonus material as of 2019 is the Criterion Channel. That could change at any time, but the video-on-demand industry generally does not provide bonus materials.

6. Marshall McLuhan, "Understanding Media," in *Essential McLuhan*, ed. Eric McLuhan and Frank Zingrone (New York: Basic Books, 1995), 151.

7. Jeremy Wade Morris's thinking on commodity form has been deeply influential to my own, particularly his observation that "digitization creates a new set of materials through which the commodity form is manifest and through which value accrues." Jeremy Wade Morris, *Selling Digital Music, Formatting Culture* (Oakland: University of California Press, 2015), 6.

8. Constantine Verevis has done some very interesting research on how filmic adaptations of legacy television series extend those series' commercial and cultural life; while such "television features" are beyond the purview of this chapter, the "question of how [television] properties continue to circulate—as texts and as memories" through remakes is certainly related. Constantine Verevis, *Film Remakes* (Edinburgh: Edinburgh University Press, 2006), 38, 53.

9. Lucas Hilderbrand offers an outstanding analysis of *access* as a key term for video studies in *Inherent Vice: Bootleg Histories of Videotape and Copyright* (Durham, NC: Duke University Press, 2009), 3–27. Chuck Tryon continues to interrogate the ideology of access for digital video cultures in *On-Demand Culture: Digital Delivery and the Future of Movies* (New Brunswick, NJ: Rutgers University Press, 2013).

10. Frederick Wasser notes less than 2 percent of US households had VCRs in 1978, although Aaron Foisi Nmungwun notes that as of 1979, "approximately 1 million American households contained VCRs," which would be 1.3 percent of all US households. Frederick Wasser, *Veni, Vidi, Video: The Hollywood Empire and the VCR* (Austin: University of Texas Press, 2001), 95; Aaron

Foisi Nmungwun, *Video Recording Technology: Its Impact on Media and Home Entertainment* (New York: Routledge, 1989), 164.

11. "Domestic Grosses: Adjusted for Ticket Price Inflation," Box Office Mojo, accessed July 24, 2016, http://www.boxofficemojo.com/alltime/adjusted.htm.

12. For more on the innovations in US diplomatic strategy during the 1970s, see Barbara Zanchetta, *The Transformation of American International Power in the 1970s* (New York: Cambridge University Press, 2014).

13. In 1947, in the wake of World War II disputes over colonial occupation and the Jewish migration to Palestine, the United Kingdom announced that it would cede its governing powers over the Palestine territory. The United Nations proposed dividing the area, then known as Mandatory Palestine, into an Arab state and a Jewish state, with Jerusalem held under an international trusteeship. The Arab League and the Arab Higher Committee rejected the proposal, but the Jewish Agency for Palestine nonetheless declared independence for Israel on May 14, 1948. Egypt, Syria, Transjordan, and Iraq promptly invaded the territory to aid Palestinians in their uprising against the new state, resulting in the 1948 Arab-Israeli War. The war ended ten months later, but Egypt and Israel remained hostile for the next three decades, at times breaking into periods of armed combat such as the 1967 Six-Day War and the 1973 Yom Kippur War.

14. Jimmy Carter, "President Carter's Remarks on Joint Statement at Camp David Summit," September 17, 1978, Miller Center, University of Virginia, accessed July 24, 2016, https://millercenter.org/the-presidency/presidential-speeches/september-17-1978-president-carters-remarks-joint-statement.

15. MegoMan, April 27, 2006 (6:57 a.m.), comment on "ABC News Report (9-17-78)," Radio Discussions, http://www.radiodiscussions.com/showthread.php?470745-ABC-News-Special-Report(9-17-78)&p=4189300&viewfull=1#post4189300.

16. Jon Nichols, October 7, 2014, comment on "You're a Jackass, Jimmy Carter," *Esoteric Synaptic Events* (blog), http://esotericsynapticevents.blogspot.com/2014/09/youre-jackass-jimmy-carter.html.

17. David McDonnell, "John Colicos: 'Full Expression,'" Star Trek, March 10, 2015, http://www.startrek.com/article/john-colicos-full-expression.

18. Steven Hard, "A Cultural Moment," *The Opinion Mill* (blog), September 18, 2008, https://theopinionmill.wordpress.com/tag/camp-david-accords/.

19. Richard, August 27, 2015 (3:18 p.m.), comment on Woodsy, "*Battlestar Galactica* Paperback from Dinnington Near Sheffield," *Moonbase Central* (blog), http://projectswordtoys.blogspot.com/2015/08/battlestar-galactica-paperback-from.html.

20. To be more accurate, ABC has "no one that can help with a request" for past news break-ins. Whether or not they possess copies of the break-ins remains unclear. Ric Dispinseri, email message to author, October 20, 2015.

21. Sarah Mitchell, voicemail to the author, June 27, 2016.

22. buddhawood, "How many VHS/Beta/Laserdisc do you own?" DVD Talk, November 7, 2009, http://forum.dvdtalk.com/dvd-talk/564191-how-many-vhs-beta-laserdisc-do-you-own-3.html. All attempts to reach buddhawood went unanswered.

23. Hilderbrand, *Inherent Vice*, 64.

24. Gilles Deleuze, *The Logic of Sense*, ed. Constantin V. Boundas, trans. Mark Lester, rev. ed. (New York: Columbia University Press, 1990), 256.

25. Hilderbrand, *Inherent Vice*, 7. So too does digital video recording (DVR), although I will not discuss DVR separately in this chapter. Suffice it to note that DVR is more vulnerable to planned obsolescence than videocassette (especially its operating software) and far more vulnerable to external manipulation or erasure.

26. Hilderbrand, *Inherent Vice*, 180.

27. In the mid- and late 1970s, Hilderbrand argues, "attention to new videocassette formats contributed to this paradigm shift toward television as well: not only *should* television programming be saved, but now it *could* be." Hilderbrand, *Inherent Vice*, 15. See also Joshua Greenberg's investigation of home taping cultures in chapter one of *From Betamax to Blockbuster: Video Stores and the Invention of Movies on Video* (Cambridge, MA: MIT Press, 2008).

28. Kim Bjarkman, "To Have and to Hold: The Video Collector's Relationship with an Ethereal Medium," *Television and New Media* 5, no. 3 (August 2004): 225–26.

29. Bjarkman, "To Have and to Hold," 221.

30. Bjarkman, "To Have and to Hold," 221, 223, 226, 240.

31. André Bazin, "The Ontology of the Photographic Image," trans. Hugh Gray, *Film Quarterly* 13, no. 4 (Summer 1960): 4.

32. Bazin, "The Ontology of the Photographic Image," 4.

33. Bazin, "The Ontology of the Photographic Image," 6.

34. While television scholars showed immense and immediate interest in how DVD extras and box sets changed fans' relationships with classic and cult television series, even suggesting that DVD revolutionized television as a genre, few note the interim transformations wrought by VHS and Betamax. In his article on television DVD box sets, Matt Hills invokes the common claim that "Digital Versatile Disc (DVD) technology has led to a destabilisation of the 'object' of television," then distinguishes himself by noting that this "argument holds pretty well in relation to the DVD's 'predecessor' technology in the 1970s, 1980s and 1990s: video." Derek Kompare observes that until the early twenty-first century, television had not "established the same relationship with home video" as film, but he does not analyze the videotape remediations that did occur. These were comparatively few, which may be why the authors of "The Economics of the Prerecorded Videocassette Industry" do not address television's contributions to the field. As Kompare explains, "television's primary goal is selling potential audiences to advertisers, not selling products to consumers," so it was not immediately clear that audiences would embrace television as a material commodity. Matt Hills, "From the Box in the Corner to the Box Set on the Shelf," *New Review of Film and Television Studies* 5, no. 1 (2007): 41–42; Derek Kompare, "Publishing Flow: DVD Box Sets and the Reconception of Television," *Television & New Media* 7, no. 4 (November 2006): 337; Megumi Komiya and Barry Litman, "The Economics of the Prerecorded Videocassette Industry," in *Social and Cultural Aspects of VCR Use*, ed. Julia R. Dobrow (Hillsdale, NJ: Lawrence Erlbaum Associates, 1990), 25–44; Kompare, "Publishing Flow," 337.

35. Cassettes were also quite bulky for extensive home collection. When a single VHS cassette stores no more than two hours' content, an entire season can easily take up a couple of feet of shelf space. This helps explain why "virtually every series made available on home video during this period [the 1980s and 1990s] was only ever released in individual episode or incomplete configurations." Kompare, "Publishing Flow," 343. For a thorough analysis of the "architectures of classification" and material limits of video store shelving, see the "Architectures of Classification" section in Daniel Herbert, *Videoland: Movie Culture at the American Video Store* (Berkeley: University of California Press, 2014), 55–67.

36. Sturken, *Tangled Memories*, 24.

37. Muir, *An Analytical Guide to Television's* Battlestar Galactica, 29.

38. Muir, *An Analytical Guide to Television's* Battlestar Galactica, 29.

39. Michael Z. Newman, "From Beats to Arcs: Toward a Poetics of Television Narrative," *Velvet Light Trap* 58 (Fall 2006): 16.

40. Newman, "From Beats to Arcs," 16.

41. Newman, "From Beats to Arcs," 17.

42. Newman, "From Beats to Arcs," 18.

43. Newman, "From Beats to Arcs," 21.

44. The other narrative changes to *Battlestar Galactica—The Video* are relatively minor. The characters of Serina (Jane Seymour) and Athena (Maren Jensen) lose scenes that contribute to their character development, and there is slightly less exposition on the nature of the human-Cylon conflict, but the plot remains the same.

45. Newman, "From Beats to Arcs," 20.

46. Today *Battlestar Galactica—The Movie* is available to stream on Amazon Prime and other subscription video-on-demand (SVOD) platforms and is sold as part of various *Battlestar Galactica* box sets, so its phenomenological autonomy is not as defined. I will address box set and video-on-demand spectatorship in subsequent sections of this chapter.

47. For more on media paratexts, see Jonathan Gray, *Show Sold Separately: Promos, Spoilers, and Other Media Paratexts* (New York: New York University Press, 2010).

48. See, for instance, Deborah Parker and Mark Parker, "Directors and DVD Commentary: The Specifics of Intention," *The Journal of Aesthetics and Art Criticism* 62, no. 1 (Winter 2004): 13–22; Barbara Klinger, "The DVD Cinephile: Viewing Heritages and Home Film Culture," in *Film and Television after DVD*, ed. James Bennett and Tom Brown (New York: Routledge, 2008), 19–44; Gray, *Show Sold Separately*, 81–116. I too have argued that DVD bonus features fundamentally change the spectatorial experience, including the spectator's impression of historical value; see Caetlin Benson-Allott, *Killer Tapes and Shattered Screens: Video Spectatorship from VHS to File Sharing* (Berkeley: University of California Press, 2013), 147.

49. Derek Kompare, *Rerun Nation: How Repeats Invented American Television* (New York: Routledge, 2004), 132, 208. In the twenty-first century, he notes, "DVD box sets have become the ultimate bearers of televisual repetition, placing television programming in a more direct, repetitive, and acquisitive relationship with its viewers" (200).

50. Bob Schmolze, quoted in Larry Jaffee, "Special Editions Aim to Appeal to the 'Collector Gene,'" *Medialine* 10, no. 10 (October 2005): 28.

51. Kompare, "Publishing Flow," 349. Kompare also provides a list of series released as DVD season box sets between 2000 and 2003. Kompare, "Publishing Flow," 353–55.

52. Bjarkman, "To Have and to Hold," 232.

53. For more information on how DVD season box sets create and venerate the television auteur, see Hills, "From the Box in the Corner to the Box Set on the Shelf," 41–60.

54. Karl Marx, *Karl Marx: A Reader*, ed. Jon Elster (Cambridge: Cambridge University Press, 1986), 64.

55. Not that television itself is not a commodity, but as Eileen Meehan argues, commercial broadcast actually uses its programming to produce audiences that it sells to advertisers. The programming is a means to an end rather than an end in itself. Meehan, "Why We Don't Count: The Commodity Audience," in *Logics of Television: Essays in Cultural Criticism*, ed. Patricia Mellencamp (Bloomington: Indiana University Press, 1990), 117–37.

56. Noel Barrett, email message to author, June 27, 2016.

57. Susan Stewart, *On Longing: Narratives of the Miniature, the Gigantic, the Souvenir, the Collection* (Durham, NC: Duke University Press, 1992), xii.

58. Charlotte Brunsdon, "Bingeing on Box Sets: The National and the Digital in Television Crime Drama," in *Relocating Television: Television in the Digital Context*, ed. Jostein Griprud (New York: Routledge, 2010), 72.

59. The *Battlestar Galactica* reboot began with a two-episode mini-series on the Sc-Fi Channel in December 2003 then continued with full-season production between 2005 and 2009 (2004 and 2009 in the UK). *Battlestar Galactica— The Complete Epic Series* was released in February 2004, probably to fortify audience enthusiasm between the mini-series and the first season premiere.

60. Jacques Derrida, *Of Grammatology*, trans. Gayatri Chakravorty Spivak (Baltimore, MD: Johns Hopkins University Press, 1998), 154, 281.

61. Stewart, *On Longing*, 152.

62. Stewart, *On Longing*, 156.

63. Stewart, *On Longing*, 151.

64. Stewart, *On Longing*, 151.

65. Stewart, *On Longing*, 163.

66. Needless to say, *Remembering "Battlestar Galactica"* extends no such nostalgic consideration—or indeed any consideration at all—to the construction of race or gender on the show.

67. Eve Kosofsky Sedgwick, "Paranoid Reading and Reparative Reading, or, You're So Paranoid, You Probably Think This Essay Is About You," in Sedgwick, *Touching Feeling: Affect, Pedagogy, Performativity* (Durham, NC: Duke University Press, 2003).

68. Hills, "From the Box in the Corner," 51.

69. Hills, "From the Box in the Corner," 51. I make a similar point regarding DVD and film historical value in the next chapter.

70. Adrian Martin, "Stocking Up on Old Bones," *Film Quarterly* 61, no. 2 (Winter 2007): 68.

71. Thierry Jousse, "A Fish in the Aquarium," trans. Adrian Martin, *Rouge* 9 (2006): http://www.rouge.com.au/9/fish.html.

72. Martin, "Stocking Up on Old Bones," 68.

73. Amanda D. Lotz, *Portals: A Treatise on Internet-Distributed Television* (Ann Arbor: Michigan Publishing, 2017), 8. For more on internet distribution and contemporaneous television production, see Amanda D. Lotz, *The Television Will Be Revolutionized*, 2nd ed. (New York: New York University Press, 2014), 131–66, and M. J. Robinson, *Television on Demand: Curatorial Culture and the Transformation of TV* (New York: Bloomsbury Academic, 2017).

74. Jeremy Egner et al., "Your Streaming Guide, in 6 Easy Questions," *New York Times*, November 11, 2019, https://www.nytimes.com/interactive/2019/11/10/arts/television/what-to-stream.html.

75. Lotz, *Portals*, 39.

76. *Battlestar Galactica*, a Universal Television production, ended up on NBC.com, despite originally airing on ABC, because in 2003, General Electric—which has owned NBC since 1986—purchased an 80 percent share in Universal Entertainment, the media conglomerate that includes Universal Studios. General Electric merged the television network, the film studio, and their various subsidiaries to form NBCUniversal.

77. Amanda Lotz argues that curation is the "primary task" of VOD media services, but some services emphasize curation more than others. The relative promotion of curation is central to brand identity as well as the user's experience of the service's content. Lotz, *Portals*, 8.

78. "*Battlestar Galactica*," Netflix, accessed September 2, 2016, http://www.netflix.com.

79. Sheila C. Murphy, *How Television Invented New Media* (New Brunswick, NJ: Rutgers University Press, 2011), 86.

80. Murphy, *How Television Invented New Media*, 86.

CHAPTER 2. THE COMMERCIAL ECONOMY OF FILM HISTORY

1. This chapter is specifically concerned with the distribution practices of the Hollywood studios' home entertainment divisions, and I acknowledge that many independent video distributors do adhere to a preservationist logic. These include Kino Lorber, Vinegar Syndrome, and (to an extent) the Criterion Collection. Unfortunately, they comprise only a small share of the home entertainment market.

2. Other critics have already addressed more famous lost films—notably Disney's *Song of the South* (1946) and Todd Haynes's *Superstar: The Karen Carpenter Story* (1987)—but their analyses focus on the films' fame, on their continued cultural impact despite their disappearance, rather than on the role that distribution plays in the business of film history. See Jason Sperb, *Disney's Most Notorious Film: Race, Convergence, and the Hidden Histories of "Song of the South"* (Austin: University of Texas Press, 2013); and Lucas Hilderbrand, "Grainy Days and Mondays: *Superstar* and Bootleg Aesthetics," *Camera Obscura* 19, no. 3 (2004): 56–91.

3. See, for example, Daniel Herbert, "Distributing Value," in *Videoland: Movie Culture at the American Video Store* (Berkeley: University of California Press, 2014), 155–82; Eric Hoyt, *Hollywood Vault: Film Libraries before Home Video* (Oakland: University of California Press, 2014); Alisa Perren, *Indie, Inc.: Miramax and the Transformation of Hollywood in the 1990s* (Austin: University of Texas Press, 2013).

4. Nathan Carroll, "Unwrapping Archives: DVD Restoration Demonstrations and the Marketing of Authenticity," *Velvet Light Trap* 56, no. 1 (Fall 2005): 21. David Church argues that this logic applies to consumer taste as well, noting that "canons of great works . . . gain their traditional power as much through the force of exclusion as inclusion." David Church, *Disposable Passions: Vintage Pornography and the Material Legacies of Adult Cinema* (New York: Bloomsbury Academic, 2016), 3.

5. I estimate the video watch-by date for *Looking for Mr. Goodbar* based on its last LaserDisc and VHS release dates and the durability of these platforms given average storage conditions. *Looking for Mr. Goodbar* has become legendary among fans who have only heard about it or remember seeing it years ago and cannot access it now. Whenever un- or mis-licensed copies surface online, these fans post comments such as "The ending has been burned into my brain. . . . Definitely a must-see. . . . WHY has this not been released on DVD???" and "I don't want to live in a world where this movie is not universally recognized as brilliant." "*Looking for Mr. Goodbar*: Member Reviews," Netflix, accessed April 19, 2015, http://www.netflix.com/WiMovie/60010608?trkid=439131.

6. Eve Kosofsky Sedgwick, "Paranoid Reading and Reparative Reading, or, You're So Paranoid, You Probably Think This Essay Is About You," in Sedgwick, *Touching Feeling: Affect, Pedagogy, Performativity* (Durham, NC: Duke University Press, 2003), 123–52.

7. While I advocate sitting with as a spectatorial alternative to the savior complex, it is important to note that fear is not the only response one might have to a degraded media object. As David Church so compellingly argues, one might also respond with arousal, especially in the case of deteriorating pornographic media. He dubs this blend of cinephilic and necrophilic pleasures *cinecrophilia* and notes that both cinephilia and necrophilia are fundamentally narcissistic attractions, suggesting that *cinecrophilia* may be an alternative to paranoid or reparative reading. Church, *Disposable Passions*, 49–60.

8. Carroll, "Unwrapping Archives," 21.

9. Wes Haynes, Manuscript Report #740683 on "Looking for Mr. Goodbar," Memorandum to Paramount Studios, December 17, 1974, *Looking for Mr. Goodbar* Script, File #L671, Margaret Herrick Library, Los Angeles, CA. Gay and lesbian bars have a longer history in the United States that goes as far back as Prohibition-era speakeasies. See, for example, Reina Gattuso, "The Founder of America's Earliest Lesbian Bar Was Deported for Obscenity," *Atlas Obscura*, September 3, 2019, https://www.atlasobscura.com/articles/what-was-first-gay-bar.

10. Mary Jane Lupton, "Ladies' Entrance: Women and Bars," *Feminist Studies* 5, no. 3 (Fall 1979): 572.

11. Lawrence Van Gelder, "Long Islanders: His 'Intervention': The Singles Bar," *New York Times*, April 8, 1984, http://www.nytimes.com/1984/04/08

/nyregion/long-islanders-his-intervention-the-singles-bar.html; Chris Jones, "Chicago Invented Improv. Did Mother's Invent the Singles Bar?" *Chicago Tribune*, November 27, 2013, http://www.chicagotribune.com/entertainment/theater/ct-ae-1201-jones-division-street-bar-20131127-column.html.

12. Lupton, "Ladies' Entrance," 582–83.

13. Jones, "Chicago Invented Improv."

14. The film never specifies its setting but was shot in Chicago and Los Angeles.

15. Many critics have commented on the virgin/whore dichotomy between the daytime Theresa, a caring teacher, and the nighttime Theresa, who takes drugs and enjoys casual sex. Such polarization is hardly surprising given the era in which the film was made; what is remarkable is that the film suggests that Theresa is aware that she has internalized this misogynist binary and that it urges the viewer to care deeply about Theresa's death without representing her death as the necessary result of her sexual activity.

16. Some critics have argued that *Looking for Mr. Goodbar* presents a universally negative view of men, which is not true. Brooks's film might have a universally negative view of white men, but the two African American men in Theresa's life—the older brother of one of her students and the drug dealer she buys from—both treat her with kindness and respect. See Derek Nystrom, *Hard Hats, Red Necks, and Macho Men: Class in 1970s American Cinema* (New York: Oxford University Press, 2009), 129–56.

17. "*Goodbar* Good B.O.," *Variety*, December 14, 1977, n.p., in "*Looking for Mr. Goodbar*" File, Core Collection, Margaret Herrick Library, Los Angeles, CA; "*Looking for Mr. Goodbar*," *Box Office Mojo*, accessed January 12, 2015, http://www.boxofficemojo.com/movies/?id=lookingformrgoodbar.htm.

18. Stephen Farber, "*Looking for Mr. Goodbar* but Finding Disappointment," review of *Looking for Mr. Goodbar*, dir. Richard Brooks, *New West*, November 7, 1977, 97, in "*Looking for Mr. Goodbar*" File, Core Collection, Margaret Herrick Library, Los Angeles, CA. See also John Mariani, "A Man's Director, a Woman's Film," review of *Looking for Mr. Goodbar*, dir. Richard Brooks, *New York*, September 19, 1977, 12, in "*Looking for Mr. Goodbar*" File, Core Collection, Margaret Herrick Library, Los Angeles, CA; Richard Corliss, "A Morality Tale for Man Haters," review of *Looking for Mr. Goodbar*, dir. Richard Brooks, *New Times*, October 28, 1977, 74, in "*Looking for Mr. Goodbar*" File, Core Collection, Margaret Herrick Library, Los Angeles, CA.

19. Vincent Canby, "*Goodbar* Turns Sour," *New York Times*, October 20, 1977, 27, ProQuest Historical Newspapers.

20. Pauline Kael, "*Goodbar*, or How Nice Girls Go Wrong," in *When the Lights Go Down* (New York: Holt, Rinehart, & Winston, 1980), 317.

21. Kael, "*Goodbar*, or How Nice Girls Go Wrong," 318.

22. Robin Wood, *Hollywood from Vietnam to Reagan . . . and Beyond*, exp. and rev. ed. (New York: Columbia University Press, 2003), 42.

23. Fran Moira, Margie Crow, and Terri Poppe, review of *Looking for Mr. Goodbar*, dir. Richard Brooks, *Off Our Backs* 7, no. 10 (December 1977): 18.

24. Betsy Erkkila, review of *Looking for Mr. Goodbar*, dir. Richard Brooks, *Cineaste* 8, no. 3 (Winter 1977–78): 43.

25. Erkkila, review of *Looking for Mr. Goodbar*, 44.

26. Molly Haskell, "Exposing a Nerve," review of *Looking for Mr. Good-bar*, *New York*, October 31, 1997, 116.

27. Haskell, "Exposing a Nerve," 119.

28. Haskell, "Exposing a Nerve," 118.

29. Haskell, "Exposing a Nerve," 116.

30. Gary Arnold, "Ladies' Day at the Movies: Here's Looking at You, Sweethearts," *Washington Post*, August 7, 1977, G1, LexisNexis.

31. Jane Wilson, "Hollywood Flirts with the New Woman," *New York Times*, May 29, 1977, 47, ProQuest Historical Newspapers. See also Vincent Canby, "Who Keeps House in Those Women's Films?" *New York Times*, March 12, 1978, A1, B2, ProQuest Historical Newspapers.

32. Shari Nussbaum, letter to the editor, *Ms.* 6, no. 12 (June 1978): 12, in *"Looking for Mr. Goodbar"* File, Core Collection, Margaret Herrick Library, Los Angeles, CA.

33. Tracey Johnston, "Who Else Is *Looking for Mr. Goodbar?*" *Ms.* 6 (February 1978): 24, 26. See also Charlotte Brunsdon, "A Subject for the Seventies," *Screen* 23, nos. 3–4 (September–October 1982): 20–29; Susan Gubar, "Representing Pornography: Feminism, Criticism, and Depictions of Female Violation," *Critical Inquiry* 13, no. 4 (Summer 1987): 712–41; and Elaine Showalter, "Rethinking the Seventies: Women Writers and Violence," *Antioch Review* 39, no. 2 (Spring 1981): 156–70.

34. IMDb.com lists *Looking for Mr. Goodbar* as the eleventh-highest-grossing film of 1977 while The Numbers (a more reliable source) lists it as the twenty-ninth. "Top-US-Grossing Feature Films Released in 1977," IMDb.com, accessed June 15, 2016, http://www.imdb.com/search/title?sort=boxoffice_gross_us&title_type=feature&year=1977,1977; "Top 1977 Movies at the Domestic Box Office," The Numbers, accessed June 15, 2016, http://www.the-numbers.com/movie/records/domestic/1977.

35. *Looking for Mr. Goodbar* premiered at the start of the Format Wars, the competition among a half-dozen home video systems for a monopoly of that emerging market.

36. "*Looking for Mr. Goodbar*," WorldCat, accessed January 12, 2015, www.worldcat.org/title/looking-for-mr-goodbar/oclc/5816949; "Paramount Home Video," LaserVision Landmarks, accessed January 12, 2015, http://laservideodisc.tripod.com/LaserVision/id10.html; Philip Pullella, "Electronic TV Gadgets Alter Viewing Habits," *Reading Eagle*, December 18, 1978, http://news.google.com/newspapers?id=tN8hAAAAIBAJ&sjid=LaEFAAAAIBAJ&pg=3984%2C6410632.

37. ABC reportedly paid "around $200,000" for the rights to broadcast Brooks's film, much to the consternation of some of its more conservative affiliates. Others eagerly anticipated the film's broadcast, though; *People Magazine* recommended it as one of its Picks of the Week during that all-important May sweeps weekend. "Picks and Pans Review: *Looking for Mr. Goodbar*," *People* 13, no. 20 (May 19, 1980), http://www.people.com/people/archive/article/0,,20076482,00.html.

38. Paramount did license a digital remaster of *Looking for Mr. Goodbar* for television syndication in 2014, specifically to Escape, an Atlanta-based over-the-air broadcast network aimed specifically at women ages twenty-five to fifty-four

(operating as Court TV Mystery as of September 2020). Like Grit, its masculinist equivalent, Escape relied on back-catalog films and syndicated series to fill its schedule. *Looking for Mr. Goodbar* was among the first 200 films Escape licensed from Paramount, and it appeared on the network intermittently thereafter. Because Escape was not part of any digital cable packages, however, *Looking for Mr. Goodbar* remained unavailable for on-demand viewers and thus as ephemeral as ever. Someone could have recorded *Looking for Mr. Goodbar* during one of its Escape broadcasts. Fifty-eight percent of Americans still owned a VCR in 2014, and one can also record off-the-air broadcasts with digital video recorders from Tablo, TiVo, Nuvyyo, and others. Such recordings do not replace legal, licensed distribution for reviving public awareness of or scholarly interest in the film, however. "Escape and Grit Announce Licensing Agreement with Nearly 200 Feature Films," press release, July 22, 2014, https://www.grittv.com /escape-grit-announce-licensing-agreement-with-paramount-pictures-for-nearly -200-feature-films/; Andrew Dugan, "Americans' Tech Tastes Change with Times," Gallup, January 6, 2014, http://www.gallup.com/poll/166745/americans -tech-tastes-change-times.aspx?.

39. Encounters with damaged or poorly maintained VCRs, extreme temperatures, excess humidity, and poor storage conditions typically reduce a tape's lifespan to ten years or less. John W. C. Van Bogart, "Life Expectancy: How Long Will Magnetic Media Last?" Council on Library and Information Resources, June 1995, http://www.clir.org/pubs/reports/pub54/4life_expectancy.html.

40. Pioneer stopped making new LaserDisc players in 2009. Funai Electric, the last manufacturer of stand-alone VCRs, discontinued them in July 2016. As of September 2020, refurbished DVD-VHS players were still widely available, but I could not find any new units for sale. Lamarco McClendon, "The Last VCRs Ever Will Be Made This Month," *Variety*, July 21, 2016, https://variety .com/2016/biz/news/vcr-video-cassette-recorder-end-production-1201819406/.

41. Mark Quigley, email to author, August 20, 2014. Metrocolor may be responsible for much of this damage. Metrocolor was MGM's proprietary process for developing Eastman color film stock. Unfortunately, its dyes turned out to be unstable and prone to fading and yellowing. As Douglas Gomery notes, many films were ruined by Metrocolor fading before MGM improved the process in the 1980s. *Looking for Mr. Goodbar* was processed with Metrocolor, but there is no evidence that Metrocolor damage is the reason that Paramount has not rereleased this film, since prior video transfers of the movie still exist and since Paramount continues to rent a passable 35 mm print of it to repertory theaters. Douglas Gomery, *Shared Pleasures: A History of Movie Presentation in the United States* (Madison: University of Wisconsin Press, 1992), 245.

42. By poststructural critics, Sedgwick means followers of Marx, Nietzsche, and Freud—a group that includes many contemporary Western film scholars. Paul Ricoeur, quoted in Sedgwick, "Paranoid Reading and Reparative Reading," 124.

43. Diane Keaton, *Then Again* (New York: Random House, 2011), 129.

44. In fact, Paramount's copyright now extends to 2072, thanks to the Copyright Renewal Act of 1992 and the Sonny Bono Copyright Term Extension Act of 1998. *Catalog of Copyright Entries: Motion Pictures*, July–December 1977, 3rd

series, vol. 31, parts 12–13, no. 2 (Washington, DC: Library of Congress, 1978), 157, on Internet Archive, accessed January 12, 2015, www.archive.org/stream/19 77motionpictur3311213libr#page/157/mode/1up; United States Copyright Office, *How to Investigate the Copyright Status of a Work*, brochure no. 22 (Washington, DC: Library of Congress, 2012), 10, http://copyright.gov/circs/circ22.pdf.

45. Richard Redlich, email to author, October 21, 2014. All further queries went unanswered.

46. Greg Julian (Vice President of Legal Affairs, MGM), phone interview with Caetlin Benson-Allott, March 12, 2016.

47. Many classic television shows were delayed or never released on DVD or video on demand due to music licensing disputes, including *WKRP in Cincinnati* (CBS, 1978–1982) and *Ally McBeal* (Fox, 1997–2002). Others were reissued with new songs replacing unlicensed or unaffordable originals, including *Roswell* (WB, 1999–2002) and *Northern Exposure* (CBS, 1990–1995). See Katie Dean, "Copyrights Keep TV Shows Off DVD," *Wired*, March 1, 2005, https://www .wired.com/2005/03/copyrights-keep-tv-shows-off-dvd/; Emily VanDerWerff, "The Weird Legal Reason Many of Your Favorite Shows Aren't on DVD," *Vox*, March 26, 2015, https://www.vox.com/2014/11/3/7145231/shows-not-on-dvd -music-rights-wonder-years-wkrp.

48. Darren Richard, "Music Licensing 101: A Nuts and Bolts Guide for Filmmakers, Television Producers, Music Publishers, and Songwriters," *Entertainment and Sports Lawyer* 30, no. 4 (2012): 13.

49. Bradley Schauer, "The Warner Archive and DVD Collecting in the New Home Video Market," *Velvet Light Trap* 70 (Fall 2012): 35.

50. These include Criterion Channel, Fandor, and SnagFilms, all of which focus on independent and art cinema. Mainstream VOD platforms like Netflix and Hulu have had a detrimental effect on classic cinema distribution; see Zach Schonfeld, "Netflix, Streaming Video, and the Slow Death of the Classic Film," *Newsweek*, September 15, 2017, http://www.newsweek.com/2017/09/22/netflix -streaming-movies-classics-664512.html.

51. Paul Benzon, "Bootleg Paratextuality and Digital Temporality: Towards an Alternate Present of the DVD," *Narrative* 21, no. 1 (January 2013): 95.

52. Benzon, "Bootleg Paratextuality and Digital Temporality," 95.

53. Carroll, "Unwrapping Archives," 21.

54. Schauer's research suggests that most MOD consumers are over fifty years old and less comfortable downloading films than purchasing them in tangible form. Customers who do not download films legally are unlikely to download them *illegally*, suggesting that for this demographic, MOD is their only access to many back-catalog films. Schauer, "The Warner Archive," 35.

55. Schauer, "The Warner Archive," 35, 39–40.

56. "MOD Systems Signs Warner Brothers and Paramount Digital," Paramount Digital press release, Bloomberg, January 8, 2009, https://www.businesswire .com/news/home/20090108005478/en/MOD-Systems-Signs-Warner-Brothers- Paramount-Digital; Leonard Maltin, "Studio Vaults Open—on DVD," *Indie Wire*, April 25, 2013, accessed December 15, 2014, http://blogs.indiewire.com /leonardmaltin/studio-vaults-openon-dvd; Deadline Team, "Warner Bros & Paramount Announce Home Media Distribution Deal," Deadline News, October 4,

2012, http://deadline.com/2012/10/warner-bros-paramount-announce-home-media
-distribution-deal-348266/.

57. While some internet publications have begun running articles on the new
titles arriving on VOD services every month, particularly Netflix and Amazon
Prime, their short descriptive summaries do not constitute reparative reviews,
nor do they have the same industrial or cultural impact.

58. Peter J. Nichols, "'High Noon,' Frame by Frame," *New York Times*,
July 2, 1999, LexisNexis.

59. Peter Nichols, "New DVDs; Inspired by Good Books, Folkies and
Johnny Cash," *New York Times*, September 23, 2003, LexisNexis.

60. J. Hoberman, "Studies in Decay and Flamboyance," *New York Times*,
December 26, 2014, http://www.nytimes.com/2014/12/28/movies/the-picture-of
-dorian-gray-and-portrait-of-jason-on-blu-ray.html; J. Hoberman, "Inadvertently Baring Necessities," *New York Times*, February 23, 2014, http://www
.nytimes.com/2014/02/23/movies/homevideo/disneys-the-jungle-book-comes
-to-blu-ray.html.

61. D. A. Miller, "Second Time Around: Review of *Cruising*," *Film Quarterly* 61, no. 2 (Winter 2007): 73.

62. Vincent Canby, "Pacino Stars in Friedkin's *Cruising*," review of *Cruising*, dir. William Friedkin, *New York Times*, February 15, 1980, ProQuest Historical Newspapers; Roger Ebert, review of *Cruising*, dir. William Friedkin,
February 15, 1980, http://www.rogerebert.com/reviews/cruising-1980.

63. There were few articles written on *Cruising* between its theatrical release
and its 2007 DVD release, but in the years since, it has garnered hundreds of
pages of analysis and reflection: reparative criticism that corrects prior claims
about masculinity, class, and narrative incoherence in 1970s cinema. For pre-
2007 criticism of *Cruising*, see Guy Davidson, "'Contagious Relations': Simulation, Paranoia, and the Postmodern Condition in William Friedkin's *Cruising* and
Felice Picano's *The Lure*," *GLQ: A Journal of Lesbian and Gay Studies* 11, no. 1
(2005): 23–64; Gary Morris, "William Friedkin's *Cruising*," *Bright Lights Film
Journal*, April 1, 1996, http://brightlightsfilm.com/william-friedkins-cruising/#.
VKAGOsAwA. For post-2007 criticism of *Cruising*, see Michael Koresky,
"Return of the Repressed: William Friedkin's *Cruising*," IndieWire, September 4,
2007, http://www.indiewire.com/article/review_return_of_the_repressed_william_
friedkins_cruising; Trenton Straube, "Scent of a Man," *Slate*, September 11,
2007, http://www.slate.com/articles/arts/dvdextras/2007/09/scent_of_a_man.html;
and Nathan Lee, "Gay Old Time," *Village Voice*, August 28, 2007, http://www
.villagevoice.com/2007-08-28/film/gay-old-time/. For more on *Cruising*'s exclusion from previous heterocentric readings of narrative incoherence in 1970s
cinema, see Nystrom, *Hard Hats, Red Necks*, 129–56; R. Barton Palmer,
"Redeeming *Cruising*: Tendentiously Offensive, Coherently Incoherent, Strangely
Pleasurable," in *B Is for Bad Cinema: Aesthetics, Politics, and Cultural Value*, ed.
Claire Perkins and Constantine Verevis (Albany: State University of New York
Press, 2014), 85–104.

64. Miller, "Second Time Around," 73.

65. Miller, "Second Time Around," 73.

66. Sedgwick, "Paranoid Reading and Reparative Reading," 124.

67. For more on the political promise of reparative reading, see Tan Hoang Nguyen, *A View from the Bottom: Asian American Masculinity and Sexual Representation* (Durham, NC: Duke University Press, 2014), 24.

68. Elizabeth S. Anker and Rita Felski, eds., "Introduction" in *Critique and Postcritique* (Durham, NC: Duke University Press, 2017), 1. See also Robyn Wiegman, "The Times We're In: Queer Feminist Criticism and the Reparative 'Turn,'" *Feminist Theory* 15, no. 1 (April 2014):1–24.

69. Lucas Hilderbrand, *Inherent Vice: Bootleg Histories of Videotape and Copyright* (Durham, NC: Duke University Press, 2009), 13.

70. Of course, a viewer could rewind and rewatch a DVD or Blu-ray too; my points about video-assisted reparative reading is not limited to videocassette. However, no such editions currently exist, so all *Looking for Mr. Goodbar* viewers must watch like VHS viewers: without bonus materials or chapter breaks, directing their own progress through the film in response to their own interests and uncertainties.

71. See, for instance, Canby, "*Goodbar* Turns Sour"; Andrew Sarris, "The Divine Diane," *Village Voice*, October 17, 1977, 49; and Henry A. Giroux, review of *Looking for Mr. Goodbar, Film Quarterly* 31, no. 4 (Summer 1978): 54.

72. Wood, *Hollywood from Vietnam to Reagan*, 44.

73. See Alexander Doty, *Flaming Classics: Queering the Film Canon* (New York: Routledge, 2000).

74. See Allan Cameron, *Modular Narratives in Contemporary Cinema* (New York: Palgrave Macmillan, 2008), and Warren Buckland, ed., *Puzzle Films: Complex Storytelling in Contemporary Cinema* (Malden, MA: Wiley-Blackwell, 2009).

75. Sedgwick, "Paranoid Reading and Reparative Reading," 149.

76. Wiegman, "The Times We're In," 17.

77. Church, *Disposable Passions*, 49.

78. Cherchi Usai defines the Model Image as "a complete experience of the narrative and the pictorial character of the moving image." To be complete, it must exist outside of history and is therefore a Platonic ideal, never encountered by any viewer. Paolo Cherchi Usai, *The Death of Cinema: History, Cultural Memory, and the Digital Dark Age* (London: British Film Institute, 2001), 49.

79. This is where sitting with diverges from Church's cinecrophilia, which involves "a haptic visuality that blurs the phenomenological boundaries between viewing subject and object." Church, *Disposable Passions*, 52.

80. Iris Carlton-LaNey et al., "'Sitting With the Sick': African American Women's Philanthropy," *Affilia: Journal of Women and Social Work* 16, no. 4 (December 2001): 447–66.

81. Susan Exley, "The Tradition of Sitting Up with the Dead," *Effingham Herald*, November 15, 2007, https://www.effinghamherald.net/lifestyle/echoes -of-effingham/the-tradition-of-sitting-up-with-the-dead/; Dawn Scott, "Old Time Burial Customs," Mildred McConnell's Scrapbook Articles, Scott County Historical Society—Scott County, Virginia, Ancestory.com, accessed June 22, 2015, http://www.rootsweb.ancestry.com/~vaschs2/burial_customs.htm.

82. Dust patterns in the image suggest that only one transfer was used for all the video editions of *Looking for Mr. Goodbar*.

83. Artifacts of this averaging are known colloquially as color blocking or pixelation.

84. Theresa's death mask also challenges André Bazin's famous claim that film, being "change mummified," provides a "defense against the passage of time" and against death; Bazin, "The Ontology of the Photographic Image," trans. Hugh Gray, *Film Quarterly* 13, no. 4 (Summer 1960): 8, 4. As Laura Mulvey argues in *Death 24x a Second: Stillness and the Moving Image* (London: Reaktion, 2006), death is in fact the uncanny basis of film's imitation of life. Theresa's death mask confronts the viewer with that reality: film is a reminder of death as well as an escape from it.

85. Jane Bennett, *Vibrant Matter: A Political Ecology of Things* (Durham, NC: Duke University Press, 2010), 6.

86. Karen Barad, *Meeting the Universe Halfway: Quantum Physics and the Entanglement of Matter and Meaning* (Durham, NC: Duke University Press, 2007), 3.

87. I say "loss of visual information" because *Looking for Mr. Goodbar* used a monaural sound mix, suggesting a relatively simple original sound design. I also cannot claim to hear traces of any missing aural information, although others certainly might.

88. Caetlin Benson-Allott, "Looking for *Looking for Mr. Goodbar*: Or, Strategies for Sitting with the Abject Archive," *Feminist Media Histories* 1, no. 3 (Summer 2015): 156.

89. Anne Friedberg, *Window Shopping: Cinema and the Postmodern* (Berkeley: University of California Press, 1993), 8.

90. J.D. Connor, "Going Global," '77 (New York: Film Society of Lincoln Center, 2017), brochure.

91. Connor, "Going Global."

92. Michael Marder, "Dust, the Ledger of Past Existence," *Atlantic*, March 14, 2014, https://www.theatlantic.com/technology/archive/2014/03/dust -the-ledger-of-past-existence/284387/.

93. For those who might wonder, the print itself was in surprisingly decent condition, scratched here and there but only moderately faded.

CHAPTER 3. "LET'S MOVIE"

1. "Let's Movie: TCM Original Promo," Turner Classic Movies, accessed October 12, 2018, http://www.tcm.com/mediaroom/video/1118505/Let-s -Movie-TCM-Original-Promo-2015.html.

2. *Post-network era* denotes a few different changes in North American television culture that all began in the late 1990s and found fruition in the twenty-first century. These include the transition to digital distribution, which allowed cable subscribers to receive hundreds rather than dozens of channels. Channel proliferation weakened the industrial and cultural preeminence of the Big Three networks—ABC, NBC, and CBS—and allowed other networks to embrace identity- and interest-based "niche-casting." For more on the post-network era and the history of the US television industry, see Amanda Lotz, *The Television Will Be Revolutionized*, 2nd ed. (New York: New York University Press, 2014).

3. Jonathan Ronzio, "Brand Activations Work: Here's How," Cramer: A Brand Experience Agency, accessed July 16, 2018, https://cramer.com/story /brand-activations-work-heres-how/.

4. As Elizabeth Affuso and Avi Santo explain in the introduction to their special issue of *Film Criticism* on "Film and Merchandise," "Media-inspired merchandise is often presented to consumers as opportunities to link their 'self-brand' to a life-style brand with whom they supposedly share a brand story." Elizabeth Affuso and Avi Santo, "Mediated Merchandise, Merchandisable Media: An Introduction," *Film Criticism* 42, no. 2 (2018): http://dx.doi.org/10.3998/fc.13761232 .0042.201.

5. Stuart Elliott, "TCM Moves to Lure Film Buffs out of Their Living Rooms," *New York Times*, August 21, 2013, https://www.nytimes.com/2013/08/22/business /tcm-moves-to-lure-film-buffs-out-of-their-living-rooms.html.

6. Kristen Welch (integrated brand manager, Turner Classic Movies), interview with Caetlin Benson-Allott, Atlanta, GA, June 20, 2018.

7. Welch, interview with Benson-Allott. To be sure, branded "product" has been a critical component of the film and television industries for years; as Neal Gabler has shown, Disney opened its consumer products division in 1932 and has relied on it ever since. Neal Gabler, *Walt Disney: The Triumph of the American Imagination* (New York: Vintage, 2007).

8. Genevieve McGillicudy (vice president of Brand Activation and Partnerships, Turner Classic Movies), interview with Caetlin Benson-Allott, Atlanta, GA, June 20, 2018.

9. McGillicudy, interview with Benson-Allott.

10. Pierre Bourdieu, *Distinction: A Social Critique of the Judgment of Taste*, trans. Richard Nice (Cambridge, MA: Harvard University Press, 1984), 511.

11. Bourdieu, *Distinction*, 2.

12. Bourdieu, *Distinction*, 174–75.

13. Albert M. Muniz Jr. and Thomas C. O'Guinn, "Brand Community," *Journal of Consumer Research* 27 (2001): 412, 426.

14. Muniz and O'Guinn, "Brand Community," 412, 426.

15. See "The TCM Movie Database," Turner Classic Movies, accessed July 12, 2018, http://www.tcm.com/tcmdb/; "Welcome to TCM Backlot," TCM Backlot, accessed October 12, 2018, https://www.tcmbacklot.com/; "TCM Big Screen Classics," Fathom Events, accessed October 12, 2018, https://www .fathomevents.com/series/tcm-big-screen-classics.

16. Patrick R. Parsons, *Blue Skies: A History of Cable Television* (Philadelphia: Temple University Press, 2008), 380–84.

17. Robert Goldberg and Gerald Jay Goldberg, *Citizen Turner: The Wild Rise of an American Tycoon* (San Diego: Harcourt, 1995), 351.

18. Goldberg and Goldberg, *Citizen Turner*, 362.

19. Turner was also the owner and operator of CNN (or Cable News Network), launched in 1980, and CNN2, later CNN Headline News and now known simply as HLN, launched in 1982. While these networks arguably recycle stories to fill their twenty-four-hour news cycle, they do not rely on libraries of previously aired programming—for all the obvious reasons.

20. Megan Mullen, *The Rise of Cable Programming in the United States: Revolution or Evolution?* (Austin: University of Texas Press, 2003), 155.

21. Mullen, *Rise of Cable Programming*, 9.

22. Alan Citron, "MGM/UA Blasts Insurers' Offer to Settle Lawsuit," *Los Angeles Times*, September 12, 1990, http://articles.latimes.com/1990-09-12/business/fi-251_1_turner-broadcasting.

23. Frederick M. Winship, "Turner Opens All-Movie TV Channel," UPI Archives, April 14, 1994, https://www.upi.com/Archives/1994/04/14/Turner-opens-all-movie-TV-channel/8198766296000/.

24. Mike Barnes, "Robert Osborne, Beloved Host of Turner Classic Movies, Dies at 84," *Hollywood Reporter*, March 6, 2017, https://www.hollywoodreporter.com/news/robert-osborne-dead-turner-classic-movies-host-was-84-727070.

25. "TCM Host Robert Osborne's First Movie Introduction," YouTube, accessed September 5, 2020, https://youtu.be/s4iPLnAvI6I.

26. Elliott, "TCM Moves to Lure."

27. John Voland, "Turner Defends Move to Colorize Films," *Los Angeles Times*, October 23, 1986, http://articles.latimes.com/1986-10-23/entertainment/ca-6941_1_black-and-white-films; Tony Frazier, "Colorization: Views Differ on Its Value," *News OK*, January 11, 1987, https://newsok.com/article/2171898/colorization-views-differ-on-its-value. See also Peter Brunette, ed., *Martin Scorsese: Interviews* (Jackson: University of Mississippi Press, 1999).

28. "In Cult of Turner Classic Movies, Front Row Is Lined with Filmmakers," *Denver Post*, June 18, 2016, https://www.denverpost.com/2016/06/18/in-cult-of-tcm-front-row-is-lined-with-filmmakers/.

29. Antoine de Baecque and Thierry Frémaux, "La cinéphile ou l'invention d'une culture," *Vingtième siècle* 46 (1995): 136; translated by and quoted in Christian Keathley, *Cinephilia and History, or The Wind in the Trees* (Bloomington: Indiana University Press, 2005), 12.

30. Thomas Elsaesser, "Cinephilia or the Uses of Disenchantment," in *Cinephilia: Movies, Love, and Memory*, ed. Marijke de Valck and Malte Hagener (Amsterdam: Amsterdam University Press, 2005), 27.

31. Keathley, *Cinephilia and History*, 15.

32. Keathley, *Cinephilia and History*, 19.

33. Turner Classic Movies, "Research: TCM Brand Health," PowerPoint slide presentation by Jennifer Dorian, June 20, 2018.

34. Jennifer Dorian (general manager, Turner Classic Movies), interview with Caetlin Benson-Allott, Atlanta, GA, June 20, 2018. Dorian left TCM in January 2020.

35. American Marketing Association, quoted in Chandra Sekhar Patro and Madhu Kishore Raghunath Kamakula, "Emotional Branding as a Strategy in Promoting Customer Loyalty," in *Brand Culture and Identity: Concepts, Methodologies, Tools, and Applications* (Hershey, PA: IGI Global, 2019), 184.

36. Paul Grainge, *Brand Hollywood: Selling Entertainment in a Global Media Age* (New York: Routledge, 2008), 26.

37. See Sarah Banet-Weiser, *Authentic™: The Politics of Ambivalence in a Brand Culture* (New York: New York University Press, 2012), 24; David Ogilvy, *Ogilvy on Advertising* (New York: Random House, 2013), 18.

38. Jack Neff, "Ten Years in, Dove's 'Real Beauty' Campaign Seems to Be Aging Well," *Ad Age*, January 22, 2014, https://adage.com/article/news/ten-years -dove-s-real-beauty-aging/291216/.

39. "History of Cable," California Cable and Telecommunications Association, accessed September 17, 2018, https://www.calcable.org/learn/history-of-cable/.

40. Celia Lury, *Brands: The Logos of the Global Economy* (New York: Routledge, 2004), 6.

41. Lury, *Brands*, 1.

42. Lury, *Brands*, 26; Phil Knight, quoted in Lury, *Brands*, 49.

43. Lury, *Brands*, 8.

44. "Turner Classic Movies (TCM) Unveils Brand New Campaign with New Network Tagline 'Let's Movie,'" press release, WarnerMedia, August 31, 2015, accessed September 17, 2018, https://pressroom.warnermediagroup.com/us.

45. Dorian, interview with Benson-Allott.

46. McGillicuddy, interview with Benson-Allott.

47. Jonathan Gray, *Show Sold Separately: Promos, Spoilers, and Other Media Paratexts* (New York: New York University Press, 2010), 25.

48. Gray, *Show Sold Separately*, 3.

49. Gray, *Show Sold Separately*, 7.

50. Here it is important to note that TCM fans also generate their own expressions of affection for the network through grassroots organizations like the TCM Knitting Club. However, this chapter addresses corporate merchandizing and its effects on television spectatorship and cable-era cinephilia. Nitrate Diva, "Sign Up for the TCM Knitting Club!" accessed September 25, 2018, https://us14.campaign-archive.com/home/?u=ccb883223b28a4566e1675a80& id=283b47a4c2; Sabina Stent, "The Return of the #TCMKnittingClub," Sabina Stent.com, March 2, 2018, https://sabinastent.com/2018/03/02/the-return-of -tcmknittingclub/.

51. Stefania Saviolo and Antonio Marazza, *Lifestyle Brands: A Guide to Aspirational Marketing* (New York: Palgrave Macmillan, 2013), 3.

52. Gray, *Show Sold Separately*, 45.

53. *The Wizard of Oz: Original Motion Picture Soundtrack* (Atlanta, GA: Turner Entertainment Co., 1995), cassette.

54. *Showboat: Original Motion Picture Soundtrack* (Atlanta, GA: Turner Entertainment Co., 1995), CD; *Gigi: Original Motion Picture Soundtrack* (Atlanta, GA: Turner Entertainment Co., 1996), CD.

55. This CD was marked "for promotional use only, not for sale," although it is now widely for sale on resale sites like eBay. *The Sounds of TCM* (Atlanta, GA: Turner Entertainment Co., 1997), CD.

56. *Totally Classic: A Bluffer's Guide to Classic Movies*, director unlisted (Total Film & TCM, 1999), VHS.

57. Iain Chapman, "TCM Encrypts on Satellite," Digital Spy, January 6, 2004, http://www.digitalspy.com/tech/satellite/news/a12924/tcm-encrypts-on -satellite/.

58. Jeffrey Richards, "Turner Classic Movies British Film Guides," in Christine Geraghty, *My Beautiful Launderette* (London: I. B. Tauris, 2005), no page.

59. Jeremy Arnold, *The Essentials: 52 Must-See Movies*, foreword by Robert Osborne (Philadelphia: Running Press, 2016); "Turner Classic Movies: The Essentials—2007 Wall Calendar" (Woburn, MA: Graphique De France, 2006).

60. Max Weber, quoted in Bourdieu, *Distinction*, 174.

61. Tenaya Darlington and André Darlington, *Turner Classic Movies: Movie Night Menus—Dinner and Drink Recipes Inspired by Films We Love* (Philadelphia: Running Press, 2016), 7.

62. While most of the recipes in the book are original or derive from the public domain, some, like the Beet Red Devil Cake, are credited to other sources—*The Moosewood Restaurant Book of Desserts*, in this case. Darlington and Darlington, *Movie Night Menus*, 18.

63. Darlington and Darlington, *Movie Night Menus*, back cover.

64. TCM staff and staff at the TCM Shop itself could not confirm when the site launched; however, the Internet Archive's WayBack Machine suggests that the shop opened for business in March 2011; Internet Archive WayBack Machine, accessed September 27, 2018, https://web.archive.org/web/*/www.tcm.com/shop/index.html; Turner Classic Movies Shop Digital Catalogue, July 2018, accessed October 18, 2018, http://console.virtualpaper.com/turner-classic-movies/tcm_07_2018/?az=37-12718#66/.

65. "Shop," AMC, accessed October 18, 2018, https://www.amc.com/shop.

66. Dorian, interview with Benson-Allott; "HGTV Personal Shopper," HGTV, accessed September 28, 2019, https://www.hgtv.com/design/packages/shopping; "HGTV Home: Products for Your Home," HGTV, accessed October 18, 2018, https://www.hgtv.com/design/decorating/design-101/HGTV-HOME-products-for-your-home; "Food Network," Kohl's, accessed October 18, 2018, https://www.kohls.com/catalog/food-network.jsp?CN=Brand:Food%20Network.

67. See "Shop PBS," PBS, accessed October 18, 2018, https://shop.pbs.org/.

68. "About the Festival," TCM Classic Film Festival Hollywood 2018, accessed September 28, 2018, http://2018.filmfestival.tcm.com/about/.

69. "TCM Movie News," quoted by hlywdkjk, "*TCM Classic Film Festival Hollywood 2010," TCM Message Boards: Classic Film Forum, November 4, 2009, http://forums.tcm.com/topic/27446-tcm-classic-film-festival-hollywood-2010/; Genevieve McGillicuddy, quoted in Monica Castillo, "Why Young People Go Nuts for the TCM Classic Film Festival," *LA Weekly*, April 27, 2016, http://www.laweekly.com/arts/why-young-people-go-nuts-for-the-tcm-classic-film-festival-6857252.

70. McGillicuddy, quoted in Castillo, "Why Young People Go Nuts."

71. Rebecca Keegan, "TCM Classic Film Festival: Comic-Con for the Martini Set," *Vanity Fair*, April 27, 2010, https://www.vanityfair.com/hollywood/2010/04/tcm-classic-film-festival-comic-con-for-the-martini-set.

72. Miss Goddess, "*TCM Classic Film Festival Hollywood 2010," TCM Message Boards: Classic Film Forum, November 4, 2009, http://forums.tcm.com/topic/27446-tcm-classic-film-festival-hollywood-2010/.

73. hlywdkjk, "*TCM Classic Film Festival Hollywood 2010," TCM Message Boards: Classic Film Forum, November 4, 2009, http://forums.tcm.com/topic/27446-tcm-classic-film-festival-hollywood-2010/.

74. lzcutter, "*TCM Classic Film Festival Hollywood 2010," TCM Message Boards: Classic Film Forum, November 6, 2009, http://forums.tcm.com /topic/27446-tcm-classic-film-festival-hollywood-2010/?page=2.

75. michaelb4, "*TCM Classic Film Festival Hollywood 2010," TCM Message Boards: Classic Film Forum, November 18, 2009, http://forums.tcm.com /topic/27446-tcm-classic-film-festival-hollywood-2010/?page=2.

76. In response to fan complaints, TCM also made a concerted effort to follow up with smaller, less costly screening events around the country, including their 2011 "Road to Hollywood" series. "Road to Hollywood," TCM, accessed October 18, 2018, http://www.tcm.com/2011/roadtohollywood/index.html.

77. Erin Hanna, *Only at Comic-Con: Hollywood, Fans, and the Limits of Exclusivity* (New Brunswick, NJ: Rutgers University Press, 2020), 16.

78. Michael Nordine, "TCM Classic Film Festival: Watching Hollywood's Greatest Films on Its Most Annoying Boulevard," *LA Weekly*, April 29, 2013, http://www.laweekly.com/arts/tcm-classic-film-festival-watching-hollywoods -greatest-films-on-its-most-annoying-boulevard-4178795.

79. Mimi Pond, "Ready for Our Closeup: The 2017 TCM Classic Film Festival," *New Yorker*, May 5, 2017, https://www.newyorker.com/culture/culture -desk/ready-for-our-closeup-the-2017-tcm-film-festival.

80. The winning answer was *Hello, Dolly!* (Gene Kelly, 1969), and it was one of the first US films released on VHS and Betamax, although Frederick Wasser credits Magnetic Video's releases of *The Sound of Music* (Robert Wise, 1965), *Patton* (Franklin J. Schaffner, 1970), and *M*A*S*H* (Robert Altman, 1970) as coming out even earlier. Frederick Wasser, *Veni, Vidi, Video: The Hollywood Empire and the VCR* (Austin: University of Texas Press, 2001), xx.

81. Full disclosure: TCM generously gave me a Classic Pass to attend the 2019 TCM Classic Film Festival, valued at $649.

82. "TCM and Bonhams Add Costumes, Comedy Team Memorabilia, Portraits, Posters from Robert Osborne's Private Collection and More to November Auction," press release, Bonhams, accessed September 18, 2018, https:// www.bonhams.com/press_release/17583/.

83. Not all forms of auction require that the winner have the highest bid, but the open ascending-bid model used by Bonhams and most US auction houses does.

84. René Girard, *Violence and the Sacred*, trans. Patrick Gregory (Baltimore, MD: Johns Hopkins University Press, 1979), 170.

85. Robert Osborne, "Introduction," in *What Dreams Are Made Of: A Century of Movie Magic at Auction as Curated by Turner Classic Movies* (New York: Bonhams & Butterfields Auction Corp., 2013), 8.

86. "TCM & Bonhams Auction—(TCM Original) What Dreams Are Made Of," Turner Classic Movies, accessed July 14, 2018, http://www.tcm .com/mediaroom/video/770498/TCM-Bonhams-Auction-TCM-Original-What -Dreams-Are-Made-Of.html.

87. "The Iconic Lead Statuette of the Maltese Falcon from the 1941 Film of the Same Name," Bonhams, accessed July 14, 2018, http://www.bonhams.com /auctions/21427/lot/225/.

88. "TCM & Bonhams Auction."

89. Every TCM Classic Film Festival also has a memorabilia display where fans can ogle props from popular film and television series of yore.

90. Walter Benjamin, "The Work of Art in the Age of Mechanical Reproduction," in *Illuminations: Essays and Reflections*, ed. Hannah Arendt, trans. Harry Zohn (New York: Schocken Books, 2007), 221; Vivian Sobchack, "Chasing the Maltese Falcon: On Fabrications of a Film Prop," *Journal of Visual Culture* 6, no. 2 (2007): 219–46.

91. Sobchack, "Chasing the Maltese Falcon," 240.

92. *What Dreams Are Made Of*, 125.

93. Sobchack, "Chasing the Maltese Falcon," 223.

94. Bryan Burrough, "The Mystery of the Maltese Falcon, One of the Most Valuable Movie Props in History," *Vanity Fair*, February 19, 2016, https://www.vanityfair.com/hollywood/2016/02/mystery-of-the-maltese-falcon.

95. It is worth noting that *The Maltese Falcon* was among the many classic films that Turner Broadcasting colorized in 1986. Turner's claim at the time—"The last time I checked, I owned the films that we're in the process of colorizing [and] I can do whatever I want with them"—is symptomatic of the same capitalist logic underpinning memorabilia auctions. John Voland, "Turner Defends Move to Colorize Films," *Los Angeles Times*, October 23, 1986, http://articles.latimes.com/1986-10-23/entertainment/ca-6941_1_black-and-white-films.

96. Richard Edwards, phone interview with Caetlin Benson-Allott, June 28, 2018.

97. Edwards, interview with Benson-Allott.

98. Edwards, interview with Benson-Allott.

99. Edwards, interview with Benson-Allott.

100. Edwards, interview with Benson-Allott.

101. Edwards, interview with Benson-Allott.

102. Steven Denker, email to author, October 8, 2018; Katy Jordan, "MOOC Completion Rates: The Data," June 12, 2015, http://www.katyjordan.com/MOOCproject.html.

103. Steven Denker (director of marketing, Turner Classic Movies), interview with Caetlin Benson-Allott, Atlanta, GA, June 20, 2018.

104. Steven Denker, email to author, October 8, 2018.

105. Vanessa Theme Ament, phone interview with Caetlin Benson-Allott, June 28, 2018.

106. Edwards, interview with Benson-Allott.

107. "TCM Presents Mad About Musicals! Boutique," TCM Shop, accessed July 19, 2018. https://shop.tcm.com/promotions/mad-about-musicals.

108. "TCM Melody: Chainmail Statement Necklace," TCM Shop, accessed July 13, 2019, https://shop.tcm.com/tcm-melody-chainmail-statement-necklace/685650057965.

109. Susan Stewart, *On Longing: Narratives of the Miniature, the Gigantic, the Souvenir, the Collection* (Durham, NC: Duke University Press, 1992), xii.

110. Jennifer Dorian, quoted in "Turner Classic Movies (TCM) Launches TCM Wine Club to Help Consumers Discover Wine through the Lens of Movies," press release, October 27, 2015, https://www.prnewswire.com/news-releases/turner-classic-movies-tcm-launches-tcm-wine-club-to-help-consumers

-discover-wine-through-the-lens-of-the-movies-300166247.html. TCM now partners with Laithwaite's for its wine club service.

111. TCM Wine Club, accessed July 14, 2019, http://tcmwineclub.com/.

112. Dorian, interview with Benson-Allott.

113. Denker, interview with Benson-Allott.

114. "Silver Puffs Sauvignon Blanc 2016," TCM Wine Club tasting notes; "Ridgerider Cellars Chardonnay 2016," TCM Wine Club tasting notes.

115. Douglas Gomery, *Shared Pleasures: A History of Movie Presentation in the United States* (Madison: University of Wisconsin Press, 1992), 79–80.

116. James Lyons, "What about the Popcorn? Food and the Film-Watching Experience," in *Reel Food: Essays on Food and Film*, ed. Anne L. Bower (New York: Routledge, 2004), 320.

117. Hastie builds on Sobchack's observation that when watching a movie, "meaning, and where it is made, does not have a discrete origin in either spectators' bodies or cinematic representation but in their conjunction." That conjunction necessarily includes the things viewers put into their bodies while watching cinematic representations. Amelie Hastie, "Eating in the Dark: A Theoretical Concession," *Journal of Visual Culture* 6, no. 2 (2007): 295; Vivian Sobchack, *Carnal Thoughts: Embodiment and Moving Image Culture* (Berkeley: University of California Press, 2004), 67, quoted in Hastie, "Eating in the Dark," 295.

118. Hastie, "Eating in the Dark," 286.

119. See "TCM Classic Film Tour," On Location Tours, accessed October 19, 2018, https://onlocationtours.com/tour/tcm-classic-film; "TCM Movie Locations Tour," TCM, accessed October 19, 2018, http://www.tcm.com/tours/tour_la.html.

120. "TCM Classic Film Tour," TCM, accessed October 9, 2018, http://www.tcm.com/tours/tour_ny.html.

121. Dennis Adamovich, quoted in Jane Levere, "Robert Osborne of TCM Hosts New Bus Tour of New York City Film Locations," *Forbes*, August 30, 2013, https://www.forbes.com/sites/janelevere/2013/08/30/robert-osborne-of-tcm-hosts-new-bus-tour-of-new-york-city-film-locations/#1c3270374d19.

122. Elliott, "TCM Moves to Lure Film Buffs."

123. TCM's 2018 Italian vacation cost $9,769 for a single-occupancy room ($6,979 with double-occupancy), plus airfare, gratuities, the occasional lunch or dinner, and any alcohol or souvenirs purchased over the course of the trip. My university, generous as it is, does not offer any faculty research grants sufficient to cover such an expense.

124. See "Daily Itinerary," TCM Destinations Presented by Adventures by Disney, accessed April 13, 2018, http://tcmdestinations.com/; "Frequently Asked Questions," TCM Destinations Presented by Adventures by Disney, accessed April 13, 2018, http://tcmdestinations.com/; "See the Reel New York," 2019 TCM Cruise, accessed October 17, 2019, https://2019.tcmcruise.com/seethereel/.

125. Stanley Cavell, *The World Viewed: Reflections on the Ontology of Film*, enlarged ed. (Cambridge, MA: Harvard University Press, 1979), 40.

126. Cavell, *The World Viewed*, 41.

127. Jonathan Culler, "The Semiotics of Tourism," in *Framing the Sign: Criticism and Its Institutions*, ed. Jonathan Culler (Norman: University of Oklahoma Press, 1988), 167.

128. The Celebrity Millennium can actually hold 2,138 passengers, but TCM claims that cruise sold out. It remains unclear what happened to three hundred-odd passenger spots, although presumably some of those stateroom facilities were needed for TCM staff and talent. Sixthman, "TCM Classic Cruise 2011 Recap," YouTube, October 19, 2012, https://youtu.be/eGD6Xl4vbpo; Debra Levine, "Hitchcock Stars Add Glamour to Film-Buff Cruise," *Huffington Post*, December 14, 2011, https://www.huffingtonpost.com/debra-levine/turner -classic-movies-cruise_b_1146026.html#s541610&title=Cruisers_Laurel_.

129. Gene Sloan, "Film Stars of Old to Sail on Movie-Themed Cruise," *USA Today*, May 31, 2013, https://www.usatoday.com/story/cruiselog/2013/05/31 /classic-movie-cruise-disney-tcm/2375107/.

130. Richard Tribou, "This Year's TCM Classic Cruise Will Be the Last," *Orlando Sentinel*, September 7, 2016, http://www.orlandosentinel.com/travel /florida-cruise-guide/os-last-tcm-classic-cruise-20160910-story.html#.

131. Dorian, interview with Benson-Allott.

132. Dorian, interview with Benson-Allott.

133. As a fellow guest pointed out to me, all of the films screening on the ship were also available on TCM as well as multiple video-on-demand services.

134. David Foster Wallace, "A Supposedly Fun Thing I'll Never Do Again," in *A Supposedly Fun Thing I'll Never Do Again: Essays and Arguments* (Boston: Little, Brown and Company, 1997), 261.

135. André Bazin, "The Ontology of the Photographic Image," trans. Hugh Gray, *Film Quarterly* 13, no. 4 (1960): 8.

136. Bourdieu, *Distinction*, 175, 174.

137. Theme parks mark an interesting exception to this rule. Disney introduced Disneyland in 1955, followed by Disney World in 1971. Universal began offering tours of its lot in 1915, adding theme park rides and other attractions beginning in 1965. Warner Brothers opened its Movie World in Queensland, Australia, in 1991. These parks create a world around famous properties produced by the studio in question (or one of its corporate partners) and train visitors to adore the studio qua studio, albeit through the intellectual properties the studio produces.

138. Marshall McLuhan, "Understanding Media," in *Essential McLuhan*, ed. Eric McLuhan and Frank Zingrone (New York: Basic Books, 1995), 151.

139. Mike Fleming Jr., "PTA, Cuaron, Streisand, Del Toro, Edgar Wright, Inarritu, DiCaprio, Chazelle, Nolan among Directors Appealing to Warner Bros to Save FilmStruck," *Deadline Hollywood*, November 14, 2018, https:// deadline.com/2018/11/filmstruck-alfonso-cuaron-barbra-streisand-guillermo -del-toro-edgar-wright-alejandro-gonzalez-inarritu-leonardo-dicaprio-damien -chazelle-christopher-nolan-toby-emmerich-1202502251/.

140. Ann Hornaday, "The Death of FilmStruck: Erasing Cinema's History Will Only Have a Negative Effect on Its Future," *Washington Post*, November 1, 2018, https://www.washingtonpost.com/lifestyle/style/the-death-of-filmstruck

-erasing-cinemas-history-will-have-only-a-negative-effect-on-its-future/2018
/11/01/05e3de50-ddd4-11e8-b3f0-62607289efee_story.html?utm_term=.2b150
bd2d942.

141. Jean-Louis Baudry, "Ideological Effects of the Basic Cinematographic Apparatus," trans. Alan Williams, in *Narrative, Apparatus, Ideology: A Film Theory Reader*, ed. Philip Rosen (New York: Columbia University Press, 1986), 286–98.

142. Frank Kessler, "The Cinema of Attractions as *Dispositif*," in *The Cinema of Attractions Reloaded*, ed. Wanda Strauven (Amsterdam: Amsterdam University Press, 2006), 61.

CHAPTER 4. SPIRITS OF CINEMA

1. John Fithian, quoted in Jen Yamato, "Produced By: Hispanics 'Most Important' Ticket Buyers; Theater Owners Testing In-Movie Language Translation App," *Deadline*, June 8, 2014, https://deadline.com/2014/06/his-panics -movies-in-theater-translation-john-fithian-nato-roberto-orci-742202/.

2. Jéssica Bruna Santana Silva et al., "Effects of Acute Alcohol Ingestion on Eye Movements and Cognition: A Double-Blind, Placebo-Controlled Study." *PLos One* 12, no. 10 (2017): https://www.ncbi.nlm.nih.gov/pmc/articles/PMC5638320/; Nicole Monico, "Alcohol Consumption and Blurred or Double Vision," Alcohol. org, updated June 1, 2020, https://www.alcohol.org/effects/double-vision/.

3. Christine Woodworth and Amy E. Hughes, "Audience Appetites: Food, Class, and Consumption in New York City's Theaters," in *Food and Theatre on the World Stage*, eds. Dorothy Chansky and Ann Folino White (New York: Routledge, 2016), 266.

4. As the novelist and historian Susan Cheever notes, "one of the things many of our modern historians miss are the effects of alcoholism. I have read hundreds of indexes and tables of contents, and dozens of books on American history, and few historians even mention drinking and its effects on the events they write about." The same is very much true in film studies. I found many scholarly studies on the representation of alcohol in film, but almost no historical, phenomenological, or empirical studies of inebriated reception. However, Jocelyn Szczepaniak-Gillece's forthcoming monograph, *Movies Under the Influence*, promises to address this oversight. Susan Cheever, *Drinking in America: Our Secret History*, reprint ed. (New York: Twelve, 2016), 218.

5. Douglas Gomery, *Shared Pleasures: A History of Movie Presentation in the United States* (Madison: University of Wisconsin Press, 1992), 79–82.

6. Moneytips staff, "When You Buy a Movie Ticket, Where Does That Money Go?" *The Week*, September 8, 2016, https://theweek.com/articles/647394 /when-buy-movie-ticket-where-does-that-money.

7. Jessica Toomer, "A Little Booze and a Lot of Big Ideas Are Keeping Movie Theaters Relevant," Uproxx, March 17, 2017, https://uproxx.com/movies /movie-theater-alcohol-laws/.

8. Amelie Hastie, "Eating in the Dark: A Theoretical Concession," *Journal of Visual Culture* 6, no. 2 (2007): 296.

9. Every national drinking culture generates a different relation between cinema and alcohol. France, for instance, is far less ambivalent than the United States in its attitudes toward drinking, particularly drinking wine. There cinema was born and remains in the company of strong drink. Specifically, the Lumière brothers' first commercial film exhibition was held in the basement Salon Indien of Paris's Grand Café Capucines on December 28, 1895.

10. Quoted in Woodworth and Hughes, "Audience Appetites," 255.

11. Woodworth and Hughes, "Audience Appetites," 259.

12. Woodworth and Hughes, "Audience Appetites," 260.

13. Woodworth and Hughes, "Audience Appetites," 260.

14. In his textbook *American Film: A History*, Jon Lewis maintains that "films in those early days were also shown in saloons (over and over again, in some cases)." Michael Aronson argues that by the turn of the twentieth century, "local taverns, according to some scholars, were likely a popular site for early movie exhibition." Neither names his sources, however. Jon Lewis, *American Film: A History* (New York: Norton, 2007), 15; Michael Aronson, *Nickelodeon City: Pittsburgh at the Movies, 1905–1929* (Pittsburgh: University of Pittsburgh Press, 2008), 174.

15. Woodworth and Hughes, "Audience Appetites," 260–61.

16. Cynthia Baron, "Dinner and a Movie: Analyzing Food and Film," *Food, Culture & Society* 9, no. 1 (Spring 2006): 108.

17. Ross Melnick, *American Showman: Samuel "Roxy" Rothafel and the Birth of the Entertainment Industry, 1908–1935* (New York: Columbia University Press, 2012), 43.

18. Melnick, *American Showman*, 42.

19. Formalized via the Volstead Act in October 1919, Prohibition went into effect on January 20, 1920.

20. Robin Room, "The Movies and the Wettening of America: The Media as Amplifiers of Cultural Change," *British Journal of Addiction* 83 (1988): 12.

21. Room, "The Movies and the Wettening of America," 12.

22. This agenda was especially important given that many reformers also characterized movie theaters as dens of sexual iniquity and vice. See Gary D. Rhodes, *The Perils of Moviegoing in America, 1896–1950* (New York: Bloomsbury, 2011). Aronson, *Nickelodeon City*, 174.

23. Bill Higgins, "Hollywood Flashback: 100 Years Ago, Prohibition Led to Gangster Movies," *The Hollywood Reporter*, January 17, 2019, https://www.hollywoodreporter.com/news/100-years-prohibition-led-gangster-movies-1176028.

24. Michael Lerner, "Prohibition: Unintended Consequences," PBS.org, accessed June 10, 2019, https://www.pbs.org/kenburns/prohibition/unintended-consequences/.

25. Lerner, "Prohibition."

26. Gomery, *Shared Pleasures*, 79–82; Andrew F. Smith, *Popped Culture: A Social History of Popcorn in America* (Columbia: University of South Carolina Press, 1999), 101.

27. Ross Melnick and Andreas Fuchs, *Cinema Treasures: A New Look at Classic Movie Theaters* (St. Paul, MN: MBI, 2004), 96–97.

28. Smith, *Popped Culture*, 102

29. Melnick and Fuchs, *Cinema Treasures*, 96–97.

30. Smith, *Popped Culture*, 120.

31. Kerry Segrave, *Drive-In Theaters: A History from Their Inception in 1933* (Jefferson, NC: McFarland, 1992), 4.

32. Segrave, *Drive-In Theaters*, 9.

33. Segrave, *Drive-In Theaters*, 82.

34. At least it did during the 1950s. Segrave, *Drive-In Theaters*, 82.

35. Segrave, *Drive-In Theaters*, 64.

36. John Durant, "The Movies Take to the Pasture," *Saturday Evening Post* 223, October 14, 1950, 24, quoted in Segrave, *Drive-In Theaters*, 192.

37. Andrew Horton, "Turning On and Tuning Out at the Drive-In: An American Phenomenon Survives and Thrives," *Journal of Popular Film*, 5, nos. 3–4 (1976): 233. On a similar score, see Grant Lobban, "The Great Outdoor Movies: The Story of the Drive-In—Part One: From Passion Pits to Family Entertainment Centres," *Cinema Technology* 9, no. 2 (1996): 8–11.

38. Vikki Ortiz, "Flashback to Drive-In's Heyday," *Chicago Tribune*, June 19, 2009, https://www.chicagotribune.com/news/ct-xpm-2009-06-19-0906170586 -story.html.

39. See Erin Blakemore, "Why Drive-Ins Were More Than Movie Theaters," *JSTOR Daily*, March 18, 2017, https://daily.jstor.org/why-drive-ins-were-more -than-movie-theaters/; "When the Drive-In Theater Was King," *Detroit News*, October 7, 2003, http://blogs.detroitnews.com/history/2003/10/07/when-the -drive-in-theater-was-king/; Gena Hiemenz, "St. Cloud Area Then and Now: St. Cloud Drive In," *St. Cloud Times*, accessed May 3, 2019, http://sctimesapps .com/news/thennow/pages/marcus.php.

40. Ben Davis, *Repertory Movie Theaters of New York City: Havens for Revivals, Indies, and the Avant-Garde, 1960–1994* (Jefferson, NC: McFarland, 2017), 7.

41. Davis, *Repertory Movie Theaters*, 21.

42. Davis, *Repertory Movie Theaters*, 7.

43. Davis, *Repertory Movie Theaters*, 39.

44. J. Hoberman and Jonathan Rosenbaum, *Midnight Movies* (New York: Harper & Row, 1983), 43. Hoberman and Rosenbaum go on to note that "Dope, particularly marijuana, has been a recurring subject of, as well as a perennial accoutrement to, midnight movies" at US cinemas; *Midnight Movies*, 260.

45. Carter Moulton, "Midnight Movies," in *The Routledge Companion to Cult Cinema*, ed. Ernest Mathijs and Jamie Sexton (New York: Routledge, 2019), 211.

46. Toby Talbot, *The New Yorker Theater and Other Scenes from a Life at the Movies* (New York: Columbia University Press, 2009), 55.

47. Jack Stevenson, *Land of a Thousand Balconies: Discoveries and Confessions of a B-Movie Archaeologist* (Manchester, UK: Headpress, 2003), 76, 137.

48. Stevenson, *Land of a Thousand Balconies*, 139.

49. Stevenson, *Land of a Thousand Balconies*, 140.

50. Stevenson, *Land of a Thousand Balconies*, 141.

51. Samuel R. Delany, *Times Square Red, Times Square Blue* (New York: New York University Press, 1999), 34.

52. Delany, *Times Square Red, Times Square Blue*, 36.

53. Paul Siebenand, "The Beginnings of Gay Cinema in Los Angeles: The Industry and the Audience" (PhD diss., University of Southern California, 1975), 298.

54. Ryan Bowles Eagle, "Ambient XXX: Pornography in Public Spaces," in *New Views on Pornography: Sexuality, Politics, and the Law*, ed. Lynn Comella and Shira Tarrant (Santa Barbara, CA: Praeger, 2015), 409.

55. Nicholas Mancall-Bite, "The 7 Sexiest Bars in the Country You'll Actually Want to Go To," *Thrillist*, October 2, 2017, https://www.thrillist.com/culture/best-adults-only-bars.

56. Paul Glantz, quoted in Bruce Weber, "Liked the Movie, Loved the Megaplex," *New York Times*, August 17, 2005, https://www.nytimes.com/2005/08/17/movies/liked-the-movie-loved-the-megaplex.html.

57. James Duffy (co-founder, Cinema 'N' Drafthouse), interview with Caetlin Benson-Allott, Atlanta, GA, September 20, 2019.

58. Philip Shaikun, "Bring Down the Lights, Bring Out the Pizza," *St. Petersburg Times*, July 19, 1987, 1I.

59. John Duffy, quoted in Shaikun, "Bring Down the Lights," 1I.

60. Duffy, interview with Benson-Allott.

61. Jeremy Lang, "Drafthouses Mix Movies with Snacks, Beer and Wine," *Fort Lauderdale Sun Sentinel*, June 19, 1987, https://www.sun-sentinel.com/news/fl-xpm-1987-06-19-8702230297-story.html.

62. "Annual Average U.S. Ticket Price," National Organization of Theater Owners, accessed June 10, 2019, http://www.natoonline.org/data/ticket-price/. During the late 1980s, Reef Plaza Cinema 'N' Drafthouse in Lauderdale Lakes, Florida, also hosted midnight screenings of *The Rocky Horror Picture Show* (Jim Sharman, 1975). Theater manager Chris Pritchard priced tickets for those shows at $4 "because of the cleaning up that's necessary." Chris Pritchard, quoted in Lang, "Drafthouses Mix Movies," 40.

63. Ken Berg, "Movie Draft House Taps Into Varied Crowds," *Orlando Sentinel*, August 19, 1990, F7; Shaikun, "Bring Down the Lights," 1I.

64. Shaikun, "Bring Down the Lights," 1I.

65. "Cinema N' Drafthouse Taps Profits," *Fort Lauderdale Sun Sentinel*, September 30, 1985, https://www.sun-sentinel.com/news/fl-xpm-1985-09-30-8502110376-story.html. In 1987, some Cinema 'N' Drafthouse locations began adding weekend matinées aimed at families with young children. As one Drafthouse manager noted, "It's just like going to a restaurant and ordering wine with your children at the table," albeit in the middle of the day. Chris Pritchard, quoted in Lang, "Drafthouses Mix Movies," 40.

66. Duffy, interview with Benson-Allott.

67. Lang, "Drafthouses Mix Movies," 40.

68. "Cinema N' Drafthouse Taps Profits."

69. Shaikun, "Bring Down the Lights," 1I.

70. "Cinema N' Drafthouse Taps Profits."

71. Cinema 'N' Drafthouse, Advertisement, *The Orlando Sentinel*, October 24, 1975, 61, https://www.newspapers.com/newspage/224568247/.

72. Duffy, interview with Benson-Allott.

73. "Cinema N' Drafthouse Taps Profits."

74. Shaikun, "Bring Down the Lights," 1I.

75. Shaikun, "Bring Down the Lights," 1I.

76. Quoted in Clark, "Behind the Closing Curtains."

77. Matt Clark, "Behind the Closing Curtains," *Naples Daily News*, August 21, 2011, 1A, 13A–16A; Roger Moore, "Naples Newspaper Tracks Onetime Plaza Cinema Cafe Operator James T. Duffy's History of 'Fraud' and 'Forgery,'" *Orlando Sentinel*, August 22, 2011, https://www.orlandosentinel.com/entertainment/os-xpm-2011-08-22-os-movie-story-duffy-plaza-naples-story.html.

78. Clark, "Behind the Closing Curtains."

79. Clark, "Behind the Closing Curtains."

80. Moore, "Naples Newspaper Tracks."

81. Sumner Rand, "Screen Plays," *Orlando Sentinel*, April 25, 1980, 8-E.

82. Berg, "Movie Draft House Taps."

83. John Duffy, quoted in Peter Waldman, "Silver Screens Lose Some of the Their Luster," *Wall Street Journal*, February 9, 1989, B1. As Waldman reports elsewhere in his article, the problem was that the number of movie screens in the United States had gone up by almost 25 percent between 1979 and 1985—from 17,095 to 21,097—while number of tickets sold dropped from 1.12 billion to 1.05 billion, taking the average per screen admission from 65,575 to 49,936.

84. There are really too many craft breweries running theater pubs these days to provide anything like a comprehensive list, so I'll simply mention a few personal favorites: the Asheville Brewing Company's Two Moons Brew and View in Asheville, North Carolina; the Phantom Carriage Brewery and Blendery of Carson, California, which includes a small theater that screens classic horror movies; and the Peddler Brewing Company of Seattle, Washington, which hosts outdoor screenings in its beer garden every summer. And then there's the Flix Brewhouse chain, "the only first run movie theater in the world to incorporate a fully functioning microbrewery." The first Flix Brewhouse opened in Round Rock, Texas in 2011; it plans to have ten locations up and running by late 2019, offering "authenticity and connectedness" to a variety of Midwestern urban communities. Greg Johnson, quoted in Aaron Wells, "Flix Brewhouse Is Besting the Competition with a Microbrewery in Every Location," *Boss Magazine*, April 2018, 29, https://thebossmagazine.com/magazine/april18/#28-29.

85. "Hillsdale Brewery & Public House," McMenamins, accessed June 10, 2019, https://www.mcmenamins.com/hillsdale-brewery-public-house.

86. "Mission Theater & Pub," McMenamins, accessed June 10, 2019, https://cms.mcmenamins.com/files/History/Mission/history.mission.pdf.

87. McMenamins corporate history specifically cites the Mission Theater's "Bogart Extravaganza" as an early repertory festival that failed to draw crowds. The author presumes that the McMenamins drew inspiration for their Bogart series from the Brattle Theatre's famous annual Bogart series, which began in 1953 and has become a tradition among exam-weary Harvard students. John

Engstrom, "Essential Art House: 50 Years of Janus Films," Brattle Theatre, accessed June 10, 2019, https://www.brattlefilm.org/brattlefilm/series/2006 /janus/first_100.html.

88. Tim Jones, "A Case of Pub Cinema: Changing Neighborhoods, Craft Beer, and Creative Consumption" (paper presented at the Society for Cinema and Media Studies annual conference, Seattle, March 13, 2019).

89. Gomery, *Shared Pleasures*, 116.

90. In fact, James Duffy identifies TGI Friday's—the early singles bar—as an inspiration for the Cinema 'N' Drafthouse. Baron, "Dinner and a Movie," 108–9; Duffy, interview with Benson-Allott.

91. See Anna McCarthy, *Ambient Television: Visual Culture and Public Space* (Durham, NC: Duke University Press, 2001).

92. External wall plaque, The Commodore Theatre, Portsmouth, VA.

93. Fred Schoenfeld (owner, Commodore Theatre), interview with Caetlin Benson-Allott, Portsmouth, VA, January 19, 2019.

94. Schoenfeld, interview with Benson-Allott.

95. Schoenfeld, interview with Benson-Allott.

96. It is quite surprising, given the age of the theater and the racist culture of the southern United States in the 1940s, that the murals are explicitly integrationist. Whether they were so when first painted, or whether Johnson improved their politics while updating them, I cannot say. However, I can attest to the enthusiastic multiracial audience I saw at the Commodore the night I was there, which convinced me that it does not convey white cinema culture as much as other high-end cine-bistros I have attended.

97. Schoenfeld, interview with Benson-Allott.

98. Alissa Wilkinson, "Why Movie Theaters Are Trading Popcorn and Soda for Chimichangas and Custom Cocktails," *Vox*, updated September 23, 2018, https://www.vox.com/the-goods/2018/9/20/17870760/movie-theater -concessions-dinner-movie-alamo-regal-amc-metrograph.

99. Nate Jackson, "How a Guy from Fort Worth Influenced the New York Cinema Scene," *Dallas Observer*, December 13, 2017, https://www .dallasobserver.com/arts/fort-worths-matthew-viragh-paved-the-way-for-alamo -drafthouse-to-open-in-new-york-city-10160741.

100. Jackson, "How a Guy from Fort Worth." In 2017, New York Governor Andrew Cuomo proposed another bill that would have allowed exhibitors to sell beer and wine without a full kitchen on site, but only at movies rated PG-13, R, or NC-17. The bill did not pass the state senate. Toomer, "A Little Booze and a Lot of Big Ideas."

101. "Alcohol at the Movie Theater? New Law Allows New York Moviegoers to Have a Few," *Huffington Post*, updated November 26, 2011, https:// www.huffpost.com/entry/alcohol-at-the-movie-thea_n_980954.

102. Rick Fogel, quoted in Daniel Loria, "Happy Hours: Alcohol Service Emerges as Hot Trend in U.S. Moviegoing," *Box Office Pro*, July 4, 2017, https://www.boxofficepro.com/happy-hours-alcohol-surges-hot-trend-u-s -cinemagoing/. Fogel further advises theater owners, "As you build your signature drink development, you'll have core drinks that will be part of your menu and popular drinks that will be exclusive to your location. Then you get into a

second tier, limited-time offers (LTOs), which allow you to build feature cocktails for specific movies coming up." LTOs help cinemas distinguish their presentation of a given title from those of their competitors and strengthen their
brand. Menu engineering is not new, however; as Richard Nowell documents,
the practice extends back to exploitation marketing in 1970s US drive-ins.
Richard Nowell, "Cars and Girls (and Burgers and Weed): Branding, Main-
streaming, and Crown International Pictures' SoCal Drive-In Movies," in
Grindhouse: Cultural Exchange on 42nd Street, and Beyond, ed. Austin Fischer
and Johnny Walker (New York: Bloomsbury, 2016), 120.

103. "Dining and Bar," Nighthawk Cinema, accessed May 25, 2019, https://
nitehawkcinema.com/williamsburg/dining-bar/. Cannabidiol (CBD) ostensibly
does not have any psychoactive effects but is noted for its relaxing qualities.
Following its federal decriminalization in December 2018, it began to appear in
a number of items on the Nighthawk's menu, especially those related to movies
in which cannabis plays a prominent role.

104. I would imagine that the Nighthawk does engineer menus around films
with minority leads; I just never found an example of them doing so. The closest
instance would be *John Wick 3: Parabellum*, as lead actor Keanu Reeves has
always identified as mixed race.

105. Emma Balter, "Surround Sound? IMAX? Chardonnay? Movie Theaters
Look to Alcoholic Beverages," *Wine Spectator*, February 24, 2017, https://
www.winespectator.com/articles/movie-theaters-look-to-alcoholic-beverages.

106. By 2019, the Michelin website no longer referenced Commissary, and I
could find no evidence of such a review in the Internet Archive's Wayback
Machine. So my source for this alleged review—other than friends' breathless
assurances—is Miriam Kreinin Souccar, "The Indie-Film Boom Is Fueling a Rise
in Art-House Theaters," *Crain's New York Business*, September 25, 2017, https://
www.crainsnewyork.com/article/20170925/ENTERTAINMENT/170929944
/the-indie-film-boom-is-fueling-a-rise-in-art-house-theaters.

107. "About," Metrograph, accessed June 10, 2019, http://metrograph.com
/about.

108. "Movie Ticket Prices Inside New York City's Five Boroughs," Val-
uePenguin, accessed August 10, 2019, https://www.valuepenguin.com/2015/04
/movie-ticket-prices-inside-new-york-citys-five-boroughs.

109. "The CinéBistro Experience," CinéBistro, accessed August 10, 2019,
https://cinebistro.com/about-cinebistro/index.php.

110. "CinéBistro at Town Brookhaven," CinéBistro, accessed August 10,
2019, https://cinebistro.com/brookhaven/menu.php.

111. Mike Barstow and Bill Barstow, quoted in Micah Mertes, "More
Details on the New Movie Theater Coming Soon-ish to West Omaha," *Omaha
World-Herald*, May 31, 2018, https://www.omaha.com/go/more-details-on
-the-new-movie-theater-coming-soon-ish/article_4a3b6339-4ad4-5055-a2a5
-1bc2b1d92e9c.html.

112. Paul Glantz, quoted in Melnick and Fuchs, *Cinema Treasures*, 189.

113. As Ted Ostrow, a former house manager of the Bleecker Street Theater,
explains, concessions weren't originally part of the business model for rep
houses, in part because they emerged from French and American film apprecia-

tion movements that went out of their way to regard films as art. Ted Ostrow, quoted in Ben Davis, "The Bleecker Street Cinema: From Repertory Theater to Independent Film Showcase," *Cinéaste* 38, no. 1 (Winter 2012): 17.

114. Tim League applied for a liquor license before reopening Bakersfield's Tejon Theater but was denied. Jason Heid, "An Oral History of Alamo Drafthouse," *Austin Monthly*, May 1, 2017, https://www.austinmonthly.com/AM/May-2017/An-Oral-History-of-Alamo-Drafthouse/.

115. Elijah Wood, quoted in Heid, "An Oral History"

116. "About," Alamo Drafthouse, accessed June 10, 2019, https://drafthouse.com/austin/about.

117. Richard Linklater, quoted in Heid, "An Oral History."

118. Donna de Ville, "The Persistent Transience of Microcinema (in the United States and Canada)," *Film History* 27, no. 3 (2015): 2.

119. Tim League, quoted in Heid, "An Oral History." For examples of Alamo Drafthouse pre-rolls cautioning viewers against talking or texting during a screening, see "Alamo Drafthouse," YouTube, accessed June 10, 2019, https://www.youtube.com/channel/UC5hYQ9a_QgTFnOCqHBzlX4g.

120. Dan Solomon, "Alamo Drafthouse's Long History of Minimizing Sexual Assault and Harassment," *Splinter*, February 8, 2018, https://splinternews.com/alamo-drafthouses-long-history-of-minimizing-sexual-ass-1822816916.

121. "Building a Safer, More Inclusive and Better Alamo Drafthouse," Alamo Drafthouse, February 8, 2018, https://drafthouse.com/austin/news/building-a-safer-more-inclusive-and-better-alamo-drafthouse. See also Abby Olcese and Brock Wilbur, "Projecting Innocence: Years after Promised Reforms, Alamo Drafthouse Theaters Still Breed Harassment," *The Pitch*, August 12, 2020, https://www.thepitchkc.com/drafthouse-abuse-kansas-city-mainstreet/.

122. Justin LaLiberty (creative manager, Alamo Drafthouse Yonkers), interview with Caetlin Benson-Allott, Skype, March 26, 2019.

123. LaLiberty, interview with Benson-Allott.

124. LaLiberty, interview with Benson-Allott.

125. Jones, "A Case of Pub Cinema."

126. Brian Mendelson, quoted in Jones, "A Case of Pub Cinema."

127. Jim Lane, "Critical and Cultural Reception of the European Art Film in 1950s America: A Case Study of the Brattle Theatre (Cambridge, Massachusetts)," *Film & History* 24, nos. 3–4 (1994): 50, 54.

128. Lane, "Critical and Cultural Reception," 56.

129. Rebecca J. Mazur, "Past Tense: The Brattle Theatre," *Harvard Crimson*, February 14, 2013, https://www.thecrimson.com/article/2013/2/14/brattle-theater-past-tense/.

130. Mazur, "Past Tense"; Valerie J. Macmillan, "Kendall Sq. Cinema Set to Open," *Harvard Crimson*, August 15, 1995, https://www.thecrimson.com/article/1995/8/15/kendall-sq-cinema-set-to-open/.

131. "A Timeline of Recent Brattle History," Brattle Theatre, accessed June 10, 2019, https://www.brattlefilm.org/calendar/previously-at-the-brattle/a-timeline-of-recent-brattle-history/.

132. "Annual Report 2009," Brattle Theatre, accessed June 10, 2019, https://www.brattlefilm.org/brattlefilm/pdf/2009/2009-annual-report.pdf.

133. Marc Levy, "How Can a 'Restaurant' Have No Kitchen?" *Cambridge Day*, updated May 25, 2017, https://www.cambridgeday.com/2017/05/09/how -can-a-restaurant-have-no-kitchen-when-officials-deny-appropriate-licenses/.

134. Levy, "How Can a 'Restaurant.'"

135. See de Ville, "Persistent Transience of Microcinema."

136. Daniel Maurer, "A Hidden Theater and Underground Cruising Spot Has Left the East Village," *Bedford and Bowery*, May 1, 2019, https://bedfordand bowery.com/2019/05/a-hidden-movie-theater-and-underground-cruising-spot -has-left-the-east-village.

137. Lance Richardson, "Cruising the Bijou, a Hidden Underground Cinema and Sex Den, *Bedford and Bowery*, June 27, 2014, https://bedfordandbowery .com/2014/06/discovering-the-bijou-a-hidden-underground-cinema-and-cruising -den/.

138. de Ville, "Persistent Transience of Microcinema," 115.

139. de Ville, "Persistent Transience of Microcinema," 124; Graham Rock-ingham, "Welcome to Trash Palace," *Hamilton Spectator*, January 12, 2016, https://www.thespec.com/whatson-story/6227862-welcome-to-trash-palace-a -connoisseur-s-collection-of-bad-movies/.

140. de Ville, "Persistent Transience of Microcinema," 106.

141. David Cabrera (co-owner, Suns Cinema), interview with Caetlin Benson-Allott, Washington, DC, May 23, 2019.

142. Cabrera, interview with Benson-Allott.

143. Cabrera, interview with Benson-Allott.

144. Cabrera, interview with Benson-Allott.

145. Motion Picture Association of America, *Theatrical Market Statistics 2010*, 8, accessed December 19, 2019, https://wikileaks.org/sony/docs/03_03 /Mktrsch/Market%20Research /MPAA%20Reports/2010/2010%20Theatrical% 20Market%20Statistics.pdf.

146. Weber, "Liked the Movie."

147. Fithian, quoted in Yamato, "Produced By."

148. Juan Llamas-Rodriguez, "A Global Cinematic Experience: Cinépolis, Film Exhibition, and Luxury Branding," *JCMS: Journal of Cinema and Media Studies* 58, no. 3 (2019): 57.

149. Wilkinson, "Why Movie Theaters."

150. Llamas-Rodriguez, "A Global Cinematic Experience," 51.

151. "Investor Day: April 17, 2019," AMC, accessed June 10, 2019, http:// investor.amctheatres.com/Cache/1500119352.PDF?O=PDF&T=&Y=&D=& FID=1500119352&iid=4171292; Ayanna Julien, "Booze and Snacks Are Com-ing to the Rescue for Regal Cinemas," *Cinema Blend*, accessed June 10, 2019, https://www.cinemablend.com/new/Booze-Snacks-Coming-Rescue-Regal -Cinemas-71225.html.

152. "AMC History," AMC, accessed June 10, 2019, https://www.amctheatres .com/corporate/amc-history.

153. "AMC History."

154. Jennifer Douglass, quoted in J. Sperling Reich, "CJ Interview: Dining-In with Jennifer Douglass of AMC Theaters," *Celluloid Junkie*, September 7, 2017,

https://celluloidjunkie.com/2017/09/07/cj-interview-dining-in-with-amcs
-jennifer-douglass/.

155. AMC Entertainment Holdings, "Registration Statement under the Securities Act of 1933," August 30, 2013, https://www.sec.gov/Archives/edgar /data/1411579/000104746913008773/a2216396zs-1.htm, 97.

156. Buster Coen, "Movie Theaters Are Turning to Booze to Solve Their Problems," *The Street*, July 8, 2017, https://www.thestreet.com/story/14216745 /1/theater-chains-turn-to-booze-to-solve-woes.html; Ari E. Lebowitz, "AMC Steps Up the Movie Game," *Sioux City Journal*, December 6, 2018, https:// siouxcityjournal.com/weekender/amc-steps-up-the-movie-game/article_ 929fde9e-e899-59c5-9c60-4e210f0d8445.html.

157. "AMC Theatres 'Now Serving' at More than 250 Locations," *Celluloid Junkie*, accessed June 10, 2019, https://celluloidjunkie.com/wire/amc-theatres -now-serving-at-more-than-250-locations/.

158. Asian American filmgoers also buy a disproportionate number of movie tickets, comprising 8 percent of frequent moviegoers yet only 6 percent of the US population. *2017 THEME Report*, Motion Picture Association of America, accessed June 10, 2019, https://www.mpaa.org/wp-content/uploads/2018/04 /MPAA-THEME-Report-2017_Final.pdf.

159. AMC Holdings, "Registration Statement," 8.

160. Austin Alonzo, "AMC's Lopez, Execs Talk Hispanic Marketing, Hiring," *Kansas City Business Journal*, July 14, 2015, https://www.bizjournals .com/kansascity/blog/2015/07/amc-theatres-gerry-lopez-hispanic-marketing -hiring.html.

161. AMC Holdings, "Registration Statement," 8.

162. George Patterson, quoted in Richard Verrier, "Theater Chains Boost Bottom Line with Booze Sales," *Los Angeles Times*, October 28, 2014, https://www .latimes.com/entertainment/envelope/cotown/la-et-ct-alcohol-movie-theaters -20141018-story.html.

163. John Fithian, quoted in Yamato, "Produced By."

164. Lucas Shaw, "Booze, Better Food and Indies—How Theaters Are Luring More Hispanics," *The Wrap*, July 17, 2014, https://www.thewrap.com/booze -better-food-and-indies-how-theaters-are-luring-more-hispanics/.

165. Ryan Noonan, quoted in Shaw, "Booze, Better Food and Indies."

166. Shaw, "Booze, Better Food and Indies."

167. "Pantallas AMC," AMC, accessed August 27, 2019, https://www .amctheatres.com/programs/pantallas; Rob Cain, "Indian Movies Are Booming in America," *Forbes*, May 5, 2017, https://www.forbes.com/sites/robcain/2017/05 /05/these-are-the-best-of-times-for-indian-movies-in-america/#11da32da2b97.

168. Shaw, "Booze, Better Food and Indies."

169. Chris Aronson, president of Domestic Distribution at Fox, quoted in Lucas Shaw, "How Hispanics Became Hollywood's Most Important Audience," *The Wrap*, July 14, 2014, https://www.thewrap.com/how-hispanics-became -hollywoods-most-important-audience/.

170. Hastie, "Eating in the Dark"; Lena Wilson, "'I Found a Half-Pint of Seafood Salad': How Movie Theater Employees Feel about All the Weird

Snacks People Smuggle In," *Slate*, April 17, 2018, https://slate.com/human-interest/2018/04/how-movie-employees-feel-about-bringing-snacks-from-outside.html.

171. Emily Bell, "The Definitive Guide to Smuggling Booze into a Movie," *VinePair*, December 16, 2015, https://vinepair.com/wine-blog/how-to-smuggle-booze-into-a-movie-like-a-baller/.

172. Wil Fulton, "How to Sneak Booze into Any Place, Any Time," *Thrillist*, April 8, 2016, https://www.thrillist.com/drink/nation/how-to-sneak-booze-into-8-very-specific-locations.

173. Jelisa Castrodale, "Mom Arrested after Allegedly Sneaking Booze into Movies via Her Kid's Sippy Cup," *Vice*, October 5, 2018, https://www.vice.com/en_us/article/8xjdeb/mom-arrested-after-allegedly-sneaking-booze-into-movies-via-her-kids-sippy-cup.

174. Cheever, *Drinking in America*, 218.

CHAPTER 5. BLUNT SPECTATORSHIP

1. Approximately one half of US adults smoke cannabis at some point in their lives and 7.5 percent smoke cannabis regularly. Martin Lee, *Smoke Signals: A Social History of Marijuana—Medical, Recreational, and Scientific* (New York: Scribner, 2013), 369, 3; Wynne Armand, "Marijuana: Health Effects of Recreational and Medical Use," Harvard Health Publishing, August 19, 2016, https://www.health.harvard.edu/blog/the-health-effects-of-marijuana-from-recreational-and-medical-use-2016081910180.

2. There are television shows that explore a Black poetics of inebriation, and this chapter analyzes one of them, *Atlanta* (FX, 2016–). However, the sketch-comedy series *Chapelle's Show* (Comedy Central, 2003–2006), *Key & Peele* (Comedy Central, 2012–2015) and *Random Acts of Flyness* (HBO, 2018–) also address a Black spectator while cultivating stoner affects, and I strongly recommend them.

3. In August 1937, Congress passed the Marihuana Tax Act, making it illegal to buy, sell, transfer, or possess cannabis sativa in the United States without paying an excise tax on the product. Because the tax stamps that the act created were (almost) never issued, the act represented an effective prohibition on cannabis. Some states had already outlawed cannabis before the Marihuana Tax Act, and in the late twentieth century, some began decriminalizing or legalizing it. As of January 2020, consuming cannabis for medical purposes is legal in thirty-three states and the District of Columbia. It is legal or decriminalized for recreational consumption in eleven states and the District of Columbia.

4. Bruce Horovitz and Julie Appleby, "Prescription Drug Costs Are Up: So Are TV Ads Promoting Them," *USA Today*, March 16, 2017, https://www.usatoday.com/story/money/2017/03/16/prescription-drug-costs-up-tv-ads/99203878/.

5. Marie Winn, *The Plug-In Drug: Television, Children, and the Family* (New York: Viking, 1977).

6. Here it might be helpful to explain how I use the terms *spectator* and *viewer*. *Spectator* refers to the subject position constructed by a text for its *viewers*, the individuals who comprise its audience. These individuals may occupy,

reject, or negotiate a complex relationship to that position while watching. Viewers may or may not resemble the spectatorial position they are asked to occupy; such alignment is not necessary for a text to hail a viewer as its spectator.

7. OED Online, s.v. "intoxicate, v." (Oxford University Press), accessed April 30, 2018, http://www.oed.com.proxy.library.georgetown.edu/view/Entry/98572?.

8. OED Online, s.v. "sobriety, n." (Oxford University Press), accessed January 13, 2018, http://www.oed.com.proxy.library.georgetown.edu/view/Entry/183726?redirectedFrom=sobriety.

9. David Lenson, *On Drugs* (Minneapolis: University of Minnesota Press, 1999), 3.

10. Pabst Blue Ribbon Beer was also an early television sponsor. Charles L. Ponce de Leon, *That's the Way It Is: A History of Television News in America* (Chicago: University of Chicago Press, 2015), http://press.uchicago.edu/books/excerpt/2015/De_Leon_Thats_Way_It_Is.html.

11. Lee, *Smoke Signals*, 6. See also Norman E. Zinberg and Andrew T. Weil, "The Effects of Marijuana on Human Beings: A Scientific Report," *New York Times*, May 11, 1969, 28–29, 79, 82–83, 89, 92–93.

12. While "sativas are said to produce a soaring, cerebral high" and indicas "a more sedative, dreamy, body-oriented buzz," there are also hundreds of hybrid strains bred for distinctive therapeutic uses and experiences. Eating the drug also produces a more intense and sustained high than smoking it. Lee, *Smoke Signals*, 176.

13. Michael Pollan, *The Botany of Desire: A Plant's-Eye View of the World* (New York: Random House, 2002), 150–51.

14. Zinberg and Weil, "The Effects of Marijuana," 29, 92.

15. Zinberg and Weil, "The Effects of Marijuana," 29.

16. Allan Ginsberg, quoted in Lee, *Smoke Signals*, 74.

17. Pollan, *Botany of Desire*, 158, 170, 168.

18. Pollan, *Botany of Desire*, 164.

19. Lenson, *On Drugs*, 106.

20. Lee, *Smoke Signals*, 6.

21. Michelle Alexander, "The New Jim Crow," *Ohio State Journal of Criminal Law* 9, no. 1 (2011): 18.

22. Dziga Vertov, quoted in Robert Stam, *Film Theory: An Introduction* (Malden, MA: Blackwell, 2000), 29; Dziga Vertov, "From a Kino-Eye Discussion," in *Modernism: An Anthology of Sources and Documents*, ed. Vassiliki Kolocotroni, Jane Goldman, and Olga Taxidou (Chicago: University of Chicago Press, 1998), 237.

23. Siegfried Kracauer, *Theory of Film: The Redemption of Physical Reality* (New York: Oxford University Press, 1960), 159.

24. Kracauer, *Theory of Film*, 160.

25. René Clair, *Réflexion faite: Notes pour server à l'histoire de l'art cinématographique de 1920 à 1950* (Paris: Gallimard, 1951), quoted in Laura Rascaroli, "Oneiric Metaphor in Film Theory," *Kinema: A Journal for Film and Audiovisual Media* (Fall 2002): https://doi.org/10.15353/kinema.vi.982.

26. For more on the history of dream imagery in spectatorship theory, see Rascaroli, "Oneiric Metaphor in Film Theory."

27. Kracauer, *Theory of Film*, 163, 165; Roland Barthes, "Leaving the Movie Theater," in *The Rustle of Language*, trans. Richard Howard (New York: Hill and Wang, 1986), 346.

28. Like Kracauer, Clair, and others before them, Baudry presumes a spectator in the grip of a powerful fascination, but he does not imagine the spectator to be incapacitated or impaired by drugs or dreams, only ideology. Jean-Louis Baudry, "Ideological Effects of the Basic Cinematic Apparatus," trans. Alan Williams, in *Narrative, Apparatus, Ideology: A Film Theory Reader*, ed. Philip Rosen (New York: Columbia University Press, 1986), 286–98.

29. John Ellis, *Visible Fictions: Cinema, Television, Video*, rev. ed. (New York: Routledge, 1992), 25. For rare examples of past scholarship on inebriated spectatorship, see David Church, "The Doors of Reception: Notes Towards a Psychedelic Film Investigation," *Senses of Cinema* 87 (June 2018), http://sensesofcinema.com/2018/feature-articles/the-doors-of-reception-notes-toward-a-psychedelic-film-investigation/; Jocelyn Sczcepaniak-Gillece, "Black to Light: Aldo Tambellini, Psychedelica, Widescreen, Space," *Cultural Critique* (forthcoming).

30. See, for example, E. Ann Kaplan, ed., *Regarding Television: Critical Approaches—An Anthology* (Frederick, MD: University Publications of America, 1983); Robert C. Allen, ed., *Channels of Discourse: Television and Contemporary Criticism* (Chapel Hill: University of North Carolina Press, 1987); Ellen Seiter, Hans Borchers, Gabriele Kreutzner, and Eva-Maria Warth, eds., *Remote Control: Television, Audiences, and Cultural Power* (New York: Routledge, 1989); Patricia Mellencamp, ed., *Logics of Television: Essays in Cultural Criticism* (Bloomington: Indiana University Press, 1990).

31. Robert Stam, "Television News and Its Spectator," in *Regarding Television*, 27.

32. Lynn Spigel, *Make Room for TV: Television and the Family Ideal in Postwar America* (Chicago: University of Chicago Press, 1992), 75. See also Tania Modleski, "The Rhythms of Reception: Daytime Television and Women's Work," in *Regarding Television*, 67–75.

33. Quoted in Spigel, *Make Room for TV*, 80. Of course, television also threatened to divert women from their chores; see Spigel, *Make Room for TV*, 86–89.

34. Ellis, *Visible Fictions*, 50. Janet Staiger offers a fuller genealogy of glance theory in *Perverse Spectators: The Practices of Film Reception* (New York: New York University Press, 2000), 25–26n8.

35. Ellis, *Visible Fictions*, 24, 128.

36. Ellis, *Visible Fictions*, 25, 137.

37. John Thornton Caldwell, *Televisuality: Style, Crisis, and Authority in American Television* (New Brunswick, NJ: Rutgers University Press, 1995), 25.

38. Caldwell, *Televisuality*, 25, 26.

39. Caldwell, *Televisuality*, 27.

40. Jason Mittell, *Complex TV: The Poetics of Contemporary Television Storytelling* (New York: New York University Press, 2015), 38.

41. Richard Nixon, "Remarks about an Intensified Program for Drug Abuse Prevention and Control," June 17, 1971, https://www.presidency.ucsb.edu/documents/remarks-about-intensified-program-for-drug-abuse-prevention

-and-control; see also Stephen Siff, "'Why Do You Think They Call It Dope?': Richard Nixon's National Mass Media Campaign Against Drug Abuse," *Journalism and Communications Monographs* 20, no. 3 (2018): https://journals.sagepub.com/doi/10.1177/1522637918787804.

42. Ronald Reagan claimed that Nancy Reagan came up with the maxim "Just Say No" herself while talking to school children in 1982, but evidence suggests that it was actually coined by Robert Cox and David Cantor, advertising executives at the firm of Needham, Harper & Steers. Ronald Reagan, "Remarks at the Nancy Reagan Drug Abuse Center Benefit Dinner in Los Angeles, California," January 4, 1989, https://www.reaganlibrary.gov/research/speeches/010489a; Sam Roberts, "Robert Cox, Man Behind the 'Just Say No' Antidrug Campaign, Dies at 78," *New York Times*, June 22, 2016, https://www.nytimes.com/2016/06/23/business/media/robert-cox-man-behind-the-just-say-no-antidrug-campaign-dies-at-78.html.

43. The Communications Act of 1934 requires radio and television broadcasters to operate in "the public interest, convenience, and necessity." What *public interest* means has always been up to the FCC to determine. US Congress, House, *Communications Act of 1934*, 47 U.S.C. § 307(a) (1982 and Supp. V 1987).

44. Sharon Bernstein, "That's Not All, Folks—Cartoons Join the Drug War," *Los Angeles Times*, http://articles.latimes.com/1990-04-20/entertainment/ca-1433_1_drug-abuse.

45. Daniel Forbes, "Prime-Time Propaganda: How the White House Secretly Hooked Network TV on Its Anti-Drug Message," *Salon*, January 13, 2000, https://www.salon.com/2000/01/13/drugs_6/.

46. Ariel Berschadsky, "White House Anti-Drug Policy and Government Manipulation of Media Content," *Entertainment and Sports Lawyer* 18, no. 2 (Summer 2000): 3.

47. Only one show was rejected from the ONDCP program, *Buffy the Vampire Slayer* (WB, 1997–2001; UPN, 2001–2003), for being "immune to the drug office's world view." In all, thirty-nine episodes of twenty-three different series received ONDCP money for antidrug content. Forbes, "Prime-Time Propaganda"; see also Berschadsky, "White House Anti-Drug Policy," 4.

48. While most television producers "knew nothing of the money involved" in the ONDCP deal, they did work with the ONDCP in tailoring their content to its mission. Forbes, "Prime-Time Propaganda."

49. Berschadsky, "White House Anti-Drug Policy," 4–5.

50. Dylan Scott, "The Untold Story of TV's First Prescription Drug Ad," *STAT News*, December 11, 2015, https://www.statnews.com/2015/12/11/untold-story-tvs-first-prescription-drug-ad/.

51. Scott, "The Untold Story."

52. Megan Angelo, "The Sneak-Attack Feminism of *Broad City*," *Wall Street Journal*, February 14, 2011, http://on.wsj.com/17dJT3N.

53. Ellis, *Visible Fictions*, 112.

54. John Fiske, *Television Culture* (London: Methuen, 1987), 105.

55. Raymond Williams, *Television: Technology and Cultural Form* (New York: Schocken, 1975), 93.

56. Williams, *Television*, 92.

57. Williams, *Television*, 69.

58. Mittell, *Complex TV*, 58.

59. Some colleagues have suggested that this sequence appropriates Black culture. Ilana certainly does appropriate Black and Latina culture in the show, but the visual allusions to the Williams video and Minaj's star image suggest more pointed references to me.

60. Some scholars take a less favorable view of television's poetics of distraction. Jonathan Crary, for instance, abjures the "patterns of consumption" imposed by (commercial) TV and "psychoactive drugs, both legal and illegal." He sees them as colonizing the individual for global capitalism, while I see them as modes of perception that can encourage hegemony or resistance. Jonathan Crary, *24/7: Late Capitalism and the Ends of Sleep* (London: Verso, 2013), 55, 54.

61. As David Lenson observes, "drugs of the cannabis family seem to heighten the user's sense of humor. Objects become funny (that adjective of play) as their estrangement from mechanical cognition is accentuated by the drug. They seem awkward and out of place in their momentary oneness." *On Drugs*, xvii, 74.

62. *Atlanta* explores inebriation as resistance in ways specific to Black culture. In its second season in particular, *Atlanta* explores how weed's distanciation helps characters accept arbitrary events in their lives (some but not all related to racial prejudice).

63. As mentioned, Ilana frequently appropriates Black and Latina slang and fashion, but her drug use seems to exceed her cultural colonization.

64. See Jennifer L. Pozner, *Reality Bites Back: The Troubling Truth about Guilty Pleasure TV* (New York: Seal Press, 2010).

65. Conjunctival injection, or vasodilation of blood vessels in the sclera (the white part of the eye), is the most common side effect of smoking marijuana. Lenson, *On Drugs*, 65.

66. Casey Glynn, "Drug Found on Friend of *Jersey Shore* Cast Member Identified as Ketamine," *CBS News*, August 16, 2011, https://www.cbsnews.com/news/drug-found-on-friend-of-jersey-shore-cast-member-identified-as-ketamine/; Kendall Fischer, "*Jersey Shore*'s Mike 'The Situation' Sorrentino Reveals He Was 'Heavily Using' on the Show," E News, May 18, 2017, http://www.eonline.com/news/854388/jersey-shore-s-mike-the-situation-sorrentino-reveals-he-was-heavily-using-on-the-show.

67. Derek Kompare, *Rerun Nation: How Repeats Invented American Television* (New York: Routledge, 2004), xi.

68. "Ad-Break Double-Take," TV Tropes, accessed January 20, 2018, http://tvtropes.org/pmwiki/pmwiki.php/Main/AdBreakDoubleTake.

69. Modleski, "The Rhythms of Reception," 73.

70. Amanda Ann Klein, "Abject Femininity and Compulsory Masculinity on *Jersey Shore*," in *Reality Gendervision: Sexuality and Gender on Transatlantic Reality Television*, ed. Brenda R. Weber (Durham, NC: Duke University Press, 2014), 159–60.

71. Importantly, it seems that Ferro and his friends first began to harass and steal drinks from the *Jersey Shore* cast because they recognized—and resented—them as television personalities, even though the series itself was as yet unknown.

72. Brian Moylan, "The Most Annoying Thing About Reality TV," *Gawker*, March 14, 2011, http://gawker.com/5781717/the-most-annoying-thing-about-reality-tv.

73. Moylan, "The Most Annoying Thing."

74. See Joseph V. Del Raso, "Official Statement: MTV's *Jersey Shore*," National Italian American Foundation, press release, n.d., accessed January 21, 2018, http://www.niaf.org/niaf_event/national-italian-american-foundation-official-statement-mtvs/; "Ratings Juggernaut *Jersey Shore* Helps MTV to Best Summer Ratings in Three Years," TV By the Numbers, September 1, 2010, accessed January 21, 2018, http://tvbythenumbers.zap2it.com/network-press-releases/ratings-juggernaut-jersey-shore-helps-mtv-to-best-summer-ratings-in-three-years/.

75. Bailey Rahn, "The Best Cannabis Strains for Focus and ADD/ADHD," Leafly, January 12, 2016, https://www.leafly.com/news/strains-products/best-cannabis-strains-for-focus-and-addadhd.

76. Emily Steiner and Kun Xu, "Binge Watching Motivates Change: Uses and Gratifications of Streaming Video Viewers Challenge Traditional TV Research," *Convergence* (January 9, 2018) (published online: https://doi.org/10.1177/1354856517750365): 8.

77. Sony, Advertisement, "Beta Ads," accessed April 18, 2018, http://www.betainfoguide.net/betaads.html; Chuck Tryon, *On-Demand Culture: Digital Delivery and the Future of Movies* (New Brunswick, NJ: Rutgers University Press, 2013).

78. Jonathan Crary, *Suspensions of Perception: Attention, Spectacle, and Modern Culture* (Cambridge, MA: MIT Press, 2001), 78.

79. Ri Pierce-Grove, "Just One More: How Journalists Frame Binge Watching," *first monday* 22, no. 1 (January 2017): http://firstmonday.org/ojs/index.php/fm/article/view/7269/5792. Many critics use the term "marathon" to refer to streaming multiple episodes of a series back to back, but I find this metaphor more troublesome than helpful. Historically, "television marathon" refers to a programming strategy of scheduling multiple episodes of a syndicated series successively, a practice that began in 1985 on the cable channel Nick at Night. Furthermore, as Michael Z. Newman notes, "'marathon' suggests endurance rather than indulgence" and "seems almost masochistic" in contrast to the "pleasure sprees" of binge-watching. As a distance runner, I could not agree with him more. Marathons hurt—both the running of them and the months of training leading up to them. Binge-watching is what I do after running a marathon and requires no training at all. Michael Z. Newman, January 25, 2009, comment on Michael Z. Newman, "TV Binge," *FLOW: A Critical Forum on Media and Culture*, (January 23, 2009), https://www.flowjournal.org/2009/01/tv-binge-michael-z-newman-university-of-wisconsin-milwaukee/.

80. Pierce-Grove, "Just One More."

81. James Poniewozik, "Streaming TV Isn't Just a New Way to Watch: It's a New Genre," *New York Times*, December 16, 2015, https://www.nytimes.com/2015/12/20/arts/television/streaming-tv-isnt-just-a-new-way-to-watch-its-a-new-genre.html.

82. Tanya Horeck, Mareike Jenner, and Tina Kendall, "On Binge-Watching: Nine Critical Propositions," *Critical Studies in Television* 13, no. 4 (2018): 501.

83. Todd Spangler, "Binge Racing: *Gilmore Girls, Fuller House* Are Top Netflix Series that Viewers Finish in First 24 Hours," *Variety*, October 18, 2017, http://variety.com/2017/digital/news/binge-racing-netflix-gilmore-girls-fuller-house-1202593449/.

84. Dorothy Pomerantz, "Netflix, *Breaking Bad*, and the Business Triumph of Quality Television," *Forbes*, September 27, 2013, https://www.forbes.com/sites/dorothypomerantz/2013/09/27/breaking-bad-and-the-triumph-of-quality-television/#195d95af48df.

85. Pomerantz, "Netflix, *Breaking Bad*, and the Business Triumph of Quality Television."

86. Mittell, *Complex TV*, 10.

87. Andrew Romano, "Why You're Addicted to TV," *Newsweek*, May 15, 2013, https://www.newsweek.com/2013/05/15/why-youre-addicted-tv-237340.html.

88. John Jurgensen, "Binge Viewing: TV's Lost Weekends," *Wall Street Journal*, July 13, 2012, D1.

89. Angela Watercutter, "*Breaking Bad* Creator Vince Gilligan on Why Binge-Watching Saved His Show," *Wired*, June 4, 2013, https://www.wired.com/2013/06/breaking-bad-season-5-dvd/.

90. Anna Gunn, "I Have a Character Issue," *New York Times*, August 23, 2013, https://www.nytimes.com/2013/08/24/opinion/i-have-a-character-issue.html.

91. Poniewozik, "Streaming TV Isn't Just."

92. Poniewozik, "Streaming TV Isn't Just."

93. Poniewozik, "Streaming TV Isn't Just."

94. Vince Gilligan, quoted in Jurgensen, "Binge Viewing," D1.

95. Here it is worth noting that not all critics privilege the series' narrative above all else. In *"Breaking Bad" and Cinema Television*, Angelo Restivo analyzes these show's structural and visual allusions to cinema history, arguing these references are "sounding alarms at the state of American culture." It's a compelling analysis but does not address the show's alarming reproduction of American racism and sexism. Angelo Restivo, *"Breaking Bad" and Cinematic Television* (Durham, NC: Duke University Press, 2019).

96. Stephen Bowie, "The Case against *Breaking Bad*," *The A.V. Club*, August 12, 2013, https://tv.avclub.com/the-case-against-breaking-bad-1798239855; Gunn, "I Have a Character Issue."

97. Silpa Kovvali, "*Breaking Bad*'s Big Critique of the Macho (and Its Problems with Women)," *Atlantic*, October 1, 2013, https://www.theatlantic.com/entertainment/archive/2013/10/-em-breaking-bad-em-s-big-critique-of-the-macho-and-its-problem-with-women/280171/.

98. See for example Rebecca Price Wood, "Breaking Bad Stereotypes about Postpartum: A Case for Skyler White" in *The Methods of Breaking Bad: Essays on Narrative, Character, and Ethics*, ed. Jacob Blevins and Dafydd Wood (Jefferson, NC: McFarland, 2015), 132–46; Stuart Joy, "Sexual Violence in Serial Form: *Breaking Bad* Habits on TV," *Feminist Media Studies* 19, no. 1 (2019): 118–29.

99. Mittell, *Complex TV*, 256, 257.

100. Paul Elliott Johnson, "Walter White(ness) Lashes Out: *Breaking Bad* and Male Victimage," *Critical Studies in Media Communication* 34, no. 1 (2017): 23.

101. Mittell, *Complex TV*, 155; emphasis mine. The euphemism "nonconsensual encounter" belies the fact that sexual assault and rape are felonies in New Mexico, where *Breaking Bad* is set; the erectile joke implied by "perks up" is so offensive that I sincerely hope it was unintentional.

102. I do not have room to name all the names in this footnote. However, one might reasonably expect books about *Difficult Men* or *Television and Masculinities in the 21st Century* to mention attempted rape when it comes up in one of their key case studies. Brett Martin, *Difficult Men: Behind the Scenes of a Creative Revolution: From "The Sopranos" and "The Wire" to "Mad Men" and "Breaking Bad"* (New York: Penguin Books, 2014); Amanda D. Lotz, *Cable Guys: Television and Masculinities in the 21st Century* (New York: New York University Press, 2014).

103. Emily VanDerWerff, "*Breaking Bad*'s Racial Politics: Walter White, Angry White Man," *Salon*, September 22, 2013, https://www.salon.com/2013/09/22 /breaking_bads_racial_politics_walter_white_angry_white_man/.

104. Malcolm Harris, "*Breaking Bad*: White Supremacist Fable?" *Salon*, September 13, 2012, https://www.salon.com/2012/09/12/breaking_bad_white_ supremacist_fable/; Maitri Mehta, "Is It Fair to Accuse *Breaking Bad* of Racism?" *Bustle*, September 24, 2013, https://www.bustle.com/articles/5604-accusations-that-breaking-bad-is-racist-but-is-it-really. See also Curtis Marez's *Critical Inquiry* blog post on *Breaking Bad*, where readers' comments reveal a racist resistance to considering the representation of Latinx characters on the show. Curtis Marez, "From Mr. Chips to Scarface, or Racial Capitalism in *Breaking Bad*," *Critical Inquiry* (blog), September 25, 2013, https://critinq.wordpress.com/2013/09/25 /breaking-bad/#more-487.

105. Some scholars point to Walter's last name, White, as evidence that the show is singularly focused on white masculinity, which some also characterize as "toxic" or "under threat." But observing how the series investigates whiteness is not the same as critiquing its treatment of racial minorities. Only a handful of the dozens of scholarly books and articles on *Breaking Bad* analyze its racist treatment of Latinx characters. See for example Johnson, "Walter White(ness) Lashes Out"; Jason Ruiz, "Dark Matters: Vince Gilligan's *Breaking Bad*, Suburban Crime Dramas, and *Latinidad* in the Golden Age of Television," *Aztlan* 40, no. 1 (2015): 37–62. Andrew Howe argues that Latino characters of *Breaking Bad* are all villainized but are sufficiently heterogenous to count as humanized; I disagree. Andrew Howe, "Not Your Average Mexican: *Breaking Bad* and the Destruction of Latino Stereotypes," in *"Breaking Bad": Critical Essays on the Contexts, Politics, Style, and Reception of the Television Series*, ed. David R. Pierson (Lanham, MD: Lexington Books, 2013), 87–102.

106. Seasons three and four do concentrate more on the Guy than seasons one and two or the preceding webseries. However, he never becomes the show's sole narrative engine.

107. See, for example, Emily Nussbaum, "Taster's Choice," *New Yorker*, June 9 and 16, 2014, https://www.newyorker.com/magazine/2014/06/09/tasters

-choice; Rachel Syme, "The Surprising Compassion of *High Maintenance*," *New Yorker*, September 23, 2016, http://www.newyorker.com/culture/culture -desk/the-surprising-compassion-of-high-maintenance; David Sims, "*High Maintenance* Is TV's Most Compassionate Cult Comedy," *Atlantic*, September 16, 2016, http://www.theatlantic.com/entertainment/archive/2016/09/high-maintenance -is-a-shaggy-empathetic-triumph/500306/.

108. Syme, "Surprising Compassion of *High Maintenance*."

109. Caetlin Benson-Allott, "What It Means to Be *High Maintenance*," *Film Quarterly* 71, no. 4 (Summer 2018): 52–57.

110. Daniel Freeman and Jason Freeman, "Cannabis Really Can Cause Paranoia," *Psychology Today*, July 6, 2014, https://www.psychologytoday.com /blog/know-your-mind/201407/cannabis-really-can-cause-paranoia.

111. Freeman and Freeman, "Cannabis Really Can Cause Paranoia."

112. Brian Carr, "Paranoid Interpretation, Desire's Nonobject, and Nella Larsen's *Passing*," *PMLA*, 119, no. 2 (March 2004): 282.

113. Rita Felski, "Suspicious Minds," *Poetics Today* 32, no. 2 (Summer 2011): 228.

114. Rita Felski, "After Suspicion," *Profession* (2009): 33.

115. Felski, "Suspicious Minds," 230.

116. *The X-Files* is a notable forerunner in the inebriated poetics of paranoia. Not coincidentally, "X-Files" is also the name of a hybrid strain of cannabis produced by Pheno-Type Seeds and noted for its high THC concentration. Leafly, accessed April 18, 2018, https://www.leafly.com/hybrid/x-files.

117. Susan Sontag, "Against Interpretation," in *Against Interpretation and Other Essays* (London: Picador, 2001), 5.

118. Mittell, *Complex TV*, 51–54.

119. Chris Andrews, "Paranoid Interpretation and Formal Encoding," *Poetics Today* 30, no. 4 (2009): 673n5.

120. Eve Kosofsky Sedgwick, "Paranoid Reading and Reparative Reading, or, You're So Paranoid, You Probably Think This Essay Is About You," in Sedgwick, *Touching Feeling: Affect, Pedagogy, Performativity* (Durham, NC: Duke University Press, 2003), 124.

121. To be fair, Jason Mittell finds the color symbolism of *Breaking Bad* to be quite enriching to his experience of the series. See Jason Mittell, "Walter's Whiteness," Vimeo, accessed April 26, 2020, https://vimeo.com/346469126.

122. *Atlanta* is a quality show, but it is not "quality TV." As multiple critics have pointed out, the poetics and values of the quality TV genre are deeply racialized. In their book *Horrible White People*, Taylor Nygaard and Jorie Lagerway explicitly assert "that 'quality' aesthetics are *white* aesthetics." They build on Alfred R. Martin Jr.'s argument that "quality television (and its demographic) is white." Taylor Nygaard and Jorie Lagerway, *Horrible White People: Gender, Genre, and Television's Precarious Whiteness* (New York: New York University Press, forthcoming); Alfred R. Martin Jr., "Notes from *Underground*: WGN's Black-Cast Quality TV Experiment," *Los Angeles Review of Books*, May 31, 2018, https://lareviewofbooks.org/article/notes-from-underground-wgns -black-cast-quality-tv-experiment/.

123. Bijan Stephen, "*Atlanta* Dreaming," *Dissent* 53, no. 3 (2018): 8.

124. Anthony Reed, telephone conversation with Caetlin Benson-Allott, May 5, 2020.

125. 1-260-33QUEST is a functioning telephone number; four years after the episode first aired (on October 11, 2016), one could still call to hear the following recording: "Salutations, and welcome to Free Your Mind. I'm unavailable right now due to a brief incarceration. Please, type your number and a member of the brotherhood will contact you shortly. Enjoyable day to you."

126. Tad Friend, "Donald Glover Can't Save You," *New Yorker*, February 26, 2018, https://www.newyorker.com/magazine/2018/03/05/donald-glover-cant-save-you; Stephen, "*Atlanta* Dreaming," 7.

127. Terri Francis, "The No-Theory Chant of Afrosurrealism," *Black Camera* 5, no. 1 (Fall 2013): 104.

128. Francis, "No-Theory Chant," 101.

129. Amiri Baraka, quoted in Francis, "No-Theory Chant," 100.

130. Wesley Morris, "*Atlanta* Skips a Grade," *New York Times*, May 11, 2018, https://nyti.ms/2G8dK4H.

131. Donald Glover, quoted in Friend, "Donald Glover Can't Save You."

132. See Shervin Assari et al., "Perceived Racial Discrimination and Marijuana Use a Decade Later: Gender Difference among Black Youth," *Frontiers in Pediatrics* 7, no. 78 (March 19, 2019): https://doi.org/10.3389/fped.2019.00078.

133. Donald Glover, quoted in Rembert Browne, "Donald Glover's Community," *Vulture*, August 22, 2016, https://www.vulture.com/2016/08/donald-glover-atlanta.html.

134. Glover, quoted in Friend, "Donald Glover Can't Save You."

135. Here it is important to note that *Atlanta* has a strong white following; in fact, only half of its viewership is Black. "TV Programs with Black Stars, Storylines Drawing Diverse Eyes, Nielsen Reports," PRWeb, February 8, 2017, http://www.prweb.com/releases/2017/02/prweb14054224.htm.

136. Glover, quoted in Friend, "Donald Glover Can't Save You."

137. For more on the social significance of trap, see Jesse McCarthy, "Notes on Trap," *n+1* 32 (Fall 2018): https://nplusonemag.com/issue-32/essays/notes-on-trap/.

138. See "B.A.N." In as much as *Atlanta* induces racialized paranoia through cultural references unintelligible to white folks, I defer to Black critics of Black humor and digital media for analyses of its contemporary cultural references. Joshua Adams praises Spectro's work for the series while noting that "*Atlanta* elevates discussions within black culture in smaller, less overt details." I didn't know who Spectro was until I looked him up—and that's the point. Joshua Adams, "'Double Talk' and the Black Comedic Tradition in FX's *Atlanta*," *Medium*, October 29, 2016, https://medium.com/@journojoshua/double-talk-and-the-black-comedic-tradition-in-fx-s-atlanta-28a9a9dda8do.

139. Danielle Fuentes Morgan, *Laughing to Keep from Dying: African American Satire in the Twenty-First Century* (Champaign: University of Illinois Press, 2020), 69.

140. Adams, "'Double Talk.'"

141. The televisual metaphor "window on [or to] the world" was popularized by Thomas Hutchinson in 1946 with his book *Here Is Television, Your Window to the World*. *Window on the World* was also the name of a 1949 variety show on the DuMont network in the United States, but the phrase was used internationally to promote television as far back as the 1930s. Thomas H. Hutchinson, *Here Is Television, Your Window to the World* (New York: Hastings House, 1946); Andreas Fickers, "Presenting the 'Window on the World' to the World: Competing Narratives of the Presentation of Television at the World's Fairs in Paris (1937) and New York (1939)," *Historical Journal of Film, Radio and Television* 28, no. 3 (2008): 291–310.

142. Donald Glover, quoted in Joe Coscarelli, "The Cast of *Atlanta* on Trump, Race and Fame," *New York Times*, February 27, 2018, https://nyti.ms/2sWiJ7e.

143. Kara Keeling, *Queer Times, Black Futures* (New York: New York University Press, 2019), x–xi.

144. Erin Nyren, "*Disjointed, Bojack Horseman* Get Their Own Branded Weed for Netflix Pop-Up," *Variety*, August 25, 2017, http://variety.com/2017/tv/news/netflix-weed-cannabis-hollywood-1202539276/.

145. Netflix press release, quoted in Nyren, "*Disjointed, Bojack Horseman*."

146. Alexander, "The New Jim Crow."

CHAPTER 6. SHOT IN BLACK AND WHITE

1. Albert D. Kirwan, *Revolt of the Rednecks: Mississippi Politics 1876–1925* (Lexington: University of Kentucky Press, 1951), 222.

2. Gary D. Rhodes, *The Perils of Moviegoing in America: 1896–1950* (New York: Continuum, 2012). Blair is one of only two female perpetrators of cinema violence ever noted in the US press.

3. For a detailed case study of geographical cinema segregation and cinema violence, see Laura Baker, "Screening Race: Responses to Theater Violence at *New Jack City* and *Boyz N the Hood*," *Velvet Light Trap* 44 (Fall 1999): 4–19.

4. Dan Frosch and Kirk Johnson, "Gunman Kills 12 in Colorado, Reviving Gun Debate," *New York Times*, July 20, 2012, http://www.nytimes.com/2012/07/21/us/shooting-at-colorado-theater-showing-batman-movie.html.

5. Mark Kurlansky, *Ready for a Brand New Beat: How "Dancing in the Street" Became the Anthem for a Changing America*, reprint ed. (New York: Riverhead Books, 2013), 21.

6. Ellen Barnes, "Riots, Rebellion, and Rock and Roll: The Story of 'Rock Around the Clock,'" Gibson, November 25, 2010, http://es.gibson.com/News-Lifestyle/Features/en-us/bill-haley-1125.aspx.

7. Joseph Marshall, "Rock and Roll Riots Sweep thru Anglo-Saxon World," *New Journal and Guide*, October 13, 1956, 14.

8. Kurlansky, *Ready for a Brand New Beat*, 21.

9. R. Serge Denisoff and William Romanowski, "Katzman's *Rock Around the Clock*: A Pseudo-Event?" *Journal of Popular Culture* 24, no. 1 (Summer 1990): 69–70.

10. "Alltime B'Klyn 204G B.O. High on Rock 'n' Roll," *Variety*, April 11, 1956, 60, quoted in Denisoff and Romanowski, "Katzman's *Rock Around the Clock*," 69.

11. Douglas L. Rathgeb, *The Making of "Rebel Without a Cause"* (Jefferson, NC: McFarland, 2004), 159.

12. See Glen C. Altschuler, *All Shook Up: How Rock'n'Roll Changed America* (New York: Oxford University Press, 2004).

13. James C. Howell, *The History of Street Gangs in the United States: Their Origins and Transformations* (Lanham, MD: Lexington Books, 2015), 9–10.

14. Howell, *History of Street Gangs*, 10.

15. Pictures of the Savage Skulls and the Young Skulls' colors are available in John Bradshaw, "Savage Skulls," *Esquire*, June 1977, 76, 78–79; H. Craig Collins, "New York Street Gangs of the '70s: A Decade of Violence" *Law and Order* 28 (December 1980): 23.

16. Notably, the Riffs' costumes and discipline resemble and may well have been modeled on the militant Black empowerment gangs of the 1960s, including the Black Panthers, the Blackstone Rangers, and the Devil's Disciples. For more on gangs and community empowerment in the 1960s and 1970s, see Walter B. Miller "American Youth Gangs: Fact and Fantasy" in *Deviance and Liberty: Social Problems and Public Policy*, ed. Lee Rainwater (Piscataway, NJ: Transaction, 1974), 267; and James Alan McPherson, "Chicago's Blackstone Rangers," *Atlantic*, May 1969, http://www.theatlantic.com/magazine/archive/1969/05/chicagos-blackstone-rangers-i/305741/.

17. Glenn Fowler, "Desperate Battle against Growing Urban Blight," *New York Times*, August 11, 1974, https://timesmachine.nytimes.com/timesmachine/1974/08/11/99178092.html.

18. Susan Chira, "At Coney Island, Symbols of Heyday Fading Away," *New York Times*, August 20, 1983, http://www.nytimes.com/1983/08/20/nyregion/the-talk-of-coney-island-at-coney-i-symbols-of-heyday-fading-away.html.

19. Leslie Maitland, "Air of Uncertainty Dogs Coney Island," *New York Times*, November 3, 1975, https://timesmachine.nytimes.com/timesmachine/1975/11/03/78260699.html; Joshua Glick, "Nostalgia, Nightmares, and the Spirit of Resilience: 1971–2008," in *Coney Island: Visions of an American Dreamland 1861–2008*, ed. Robin Jaffee Frank (New Haven, CT: Yale University Press: 2015), 252. See also Marcia Chambers, "New York, after 10 Years, Finds a Plan to Create a Coney Island Park Is Unsuccessful," *New York Times*, April 3, 1977, https://timesmachine.nytimes.com/timesmachine/1977/04/03/80290972.html.

20. "The Flick of Violence," *Time* 113, no. 12 (March 19, 1979): 39

21. Specifically, *People* magazine suggests that "during an intermission a white girl drew comment from blacks belonging to a youth gang called the Blue Coats. Their white counterparts, the Family, came to her rescue." "A Street-Gang Movie Called *The Warriors* Triggers a Puzzling, Tragic Wave of Audience Violence and Death," *People* 11, no. 10 (March 12, 1979), http://www.people.com/people/archive/article/0,,20073115,00.html.

22. Louise Sweeney, "Does Violence on the Screen Mean Violence on the Street?" *Christian Science Monitor*, April 3, 1979, B26 (emphasis mine).

23. Robin Herman, "Ads Resumed for a Gang Movie after Sporadic Violence at Theaters," *New York Times*, February 23, 1979, A18.

24. Here it is worth noting that the *Warriors* murders were not covered in any of the nation's major Black newspapers, although they were addressed extensively in the regional and national white press. "The Flick of Violence"; Sweeney, "Does Violence on the Screen," B26; "Youth Fatally Stabbed, 2 Injured in Theater Fracas," *Los Angeles Times*, February 13, 1979, A1.

25. "Youth Fatally Stabbed."

26. Ed Trieberg, quoted in "A Street-Gang Movie."

27. "Youth Fatally Stabbed"; Sweeney, "Does Violence on the Screen."

28. Megan Rosenfeld, "Violence in the Wake of *Warriors*," *Washington Post*, February 22, 1979, C1.

29. Douglas Crocket, "Death Ends a Gentle Kid's Dream," *Boston Globe*, February 18, 1979, 25.

30. Alan Sheehan, "'Warrior Case' Defendant Guilty," *Boston Globe*, October 26, 1979, 21.

31. "Rite Held for Slain Boy; DA Aids View Movie," *Boston Globe*, February 21, 1979, 31.

32. Alan H. Sheehan, "12-Year Term Ordered in Dorchester Stabbing," *Boston Globe*, October 27, 1979, 20.

33. William V. Yakubowicz, administrator v. Paramount Pictures Corp. 404 Massachusetts 624 (December 8, 1988–April 18, 1989), http://masscases.com/cases/sjc/404/404mass624.html.

34. Yakubowicz v. Paramount.

35. Marguerite Guidice, "Tough Luck: Playing to Lose in the Game of Violence," *Boston Globe*, July 29, 1979, D9.

36. Guidice, "Tough Luck," D9.

37. Rosenfeld, "Violence in the Wake," C1; Charles Schreger, "Keeping an Eye on *Warriors*," *Los Angeles Times*, February 26, 1979, E1.

38. The exception to the rule is San Juan Capistrano, California, where Eddie Rosenbaum was stabbed while seeing *The Warriors* at a local drive-in, although racism plays a part in the Rosenbaum story as well. The *Los Angeles Times* reports that "Rosenbaum was walking to the rest room at the theater when he encountered a group of eight to ten Mexican-Americans ready for a fight." "San Juan Hits Screening of *The Warriors*," *Los Angeles Times*, April 8, 1979, B10.

39. Guidice, "Tough Luck," D9.

40. "Hitchhiker Says 3 Youths Tortured Him," *Boston Globe*, March 5, 1979, 16.

41. Bruce McCabe and Gary McMillan, "Hitchhiker's Desperate Ride: 'I Thought I Was Going to Die,'" *Boston Globe*, March 6, 1979, 21.

42. McCabe and McMillan, "Hitchhiker's Desperate Ride," 21.

43. Chris Black, "Beating Victim Speaks Out; Film People Defend *Warriors*," *Boston Globe*, March 13, 1979, 15.

44. Black, "Beating Victim Speaks Out," 15.

45. Unfortunately, the Saxon Theater in Boston did not receive Paramount's offer until the morning after Martin Yakubowicz was attacked. It is unlikely

that extra theater security would have saved him, however, given that his death did not occur anywhere near the Saxon Theater and was probably not related to *The Warriors*. Robin Herman, "Ads Resumed."

46. Gene Siskel and Michael Hirsley, "Ads Halted for *The Warriors* after 3 Deaths Tied to Film," *Chicago Tribune*, February 18, 1979, 52.

47. Pauline Kael, "Rumbling," review of *The Warriors*, *New Yorker*, March 5, 1979, 108.

48. Herman, "Ads Resumed."

49. It's clear from the rest of the article that Smith had not actually seen *The Warriors*, which he describes as "actually racist" while also praising the quality of its sound track, "which utilizes a musical form known as Punk Rock." In fact, *The Warriors* employs disco covers, a synthesized score, and a closing theme song by the Eagles that's about as far from punk as one can get. "Gang Film Draws Community Protest," *Los Angeles Sentinel*, February 22, 1979, A2.

50. Bruce McCabe, "There's No Debate on *Warriors*," *Boston Globe*, February 25, 1979, D1.

51. "A Call to Arms," *Boston Globe*, March 4, 1979, A4.

52. David Wilson, "1st Amendment Not a License to Profit," *Boston Globe*, March 11, 1979, A7. See also "Letters to the Editor: Should *The Warriors* Be Banned?" *Boston Globe*, March 7, 1979, 18; "Letters to the Editor: *Warriors*, Violence, the First Amendment," *Boston Globe*, March 21, 1979, 16; "Letters to the Editor: Good *Warriors* Reaction," *Boston Globe*, April 3, 1979, 18.

53. "Film and Social Responsibility," *Variety*, February 21, 1979.

54. See Lee Margulies, "Halloween Furor over *Warriors*," *Los Angeles Times*, November 1, 1980, C8; Joanne Ball, "*Warrior* TV Airing Raises Bitter Specter," *Boston Globe*, February 25, 1983, 47.

55. "Hollywood's Year of the Gang," *Baltimore Sun*, March 21, 1979, B6.

56. Grant Lee, "New *Warriors* Ad Campaign," *Los Angeles Times*, February 22, 1979, E15.

57. Lee, "New *Warriors* Ad Campaign," E15.

58. Charles Schreger, "Gang Movies Stir Controversy," *Los Angeles Times*, March 28, 1979.

59. The *Chicago Tribune* was willing to be more overt; it uses the *Boulevard Nights* incidents as a hook before observing, "In the 1920s, there were the Irish gangs. . . . After them came the Italians. . . . The turbulence of the 1960s saw the rise of huge black youth gangs, the source of seemingly unending death and destruction before they, too, began to dissipate. Now most big-city street gangs are Hispanic, a minority group near the lowest rung on the nation's economic ladder." Michael Coakley, "The Gangs: A Continuing Menace," *Chicago Tribune*, May 25, 1979, 6.

60. Tony Bill, quoted in "*Boulevard Nights* Not Responsible for Violence, Says Bill," *Hollywood Reporter*, March 29, 1979, 4.

61. Bill v. Superior Court, 187 Cal. Rptr. 625, 634 (1982), https://law.justia .com/cases/california/court-of-appeal/3d/137/1002.html.

62. Bill, quoted in "*Boulevard Nights* Not Responsible," 4.

63. Jesse Walker, ". . . And Now a Word," *Baltimore Afro-American*, March 17, 1979, 11.

64. "LAPD Says: Gang Movie *Colors* Will Trigger Violence," *Los Angeles Sentinel*, March 31, 1988, A1.

65. Wes McBride, quoted in "LAPD Says," A1.

66. Sheena Lester, "*Colors*: Controversial Film Met with Protest," *Los Angeles Sentinel*, April 14, 1988, A3; Bill Girdner, "Movie Stirs Wave of Protest in Gang-Ridden Los Angeles," *Globe and Mail*, April 15, 1988, C3.

67. Lester, "*Colors*," A3.

68. John Voland, "Big—but Quiet—*Colors* Opening," *Los Angeles Times*, April 19, 1988, H1; "Gang Reaction to *Colors* Appears Pale," *Orlando Sentinel*, April 17, 1988, http://articles.orlandosentinel.com/1988-04-17/news /0030270109_1_gang-guardian-angels-violence.

69. "Stockton *Colors* Killer Sought Here," *Los Angeles Sentinel*, April 28, 1988, A1.

70. "*Colors* Shooter Arrested in South," *Los Angeles Sentinel*, June 30, 1988, A3; see also "Gang Rivalry Blamed in *Colors* Slaying," *Chicago Tribune*, April 26, 1988, 3.

71. While the police strongly implied that Queen had seen *Colors*, they never offered any evidence to that effect. In other words, Queen may have shot Dawson for reasons that had nothing to do with any movie. "Gang Rivalry Blamed," 3.

72. T. Rogers, quoted in Girdner, "Movie Stirs Wave of Protest," C3.

73. "Burbank Bans *Colors* Movie," *Los Angeles Sentinel*, May 12, 1988, A3.

74. See David Denby, "He's Gotta Have It," review of *Do the Right Thing* (Universal film), *New York Magazine*, June 26, 1989, 53, 54; Joe Klein, "The City Politic: Spiked?" *New York*, June 26, 1989, 14.

75. S. Craig Watkins, "Ghetto Reelness: Hollywood Film Production, Black Popular Culture, and the Ghetto Action Film Cycle," in *Genre and Contemporary Hollywood*, ed. Steve Neale (London: British Film Institute, 2002), 236–50.

76. Baker, "Screening Race," 7.

77. Elaine Woo and Irene Chang, "Rampage in Westwood," *Los Angeles Times*, March 10, 1991, http://articles.latimes.com/1991-03-10/news/mn-388_ 1_police-department.

78. Woo and Chang, "Rampage in Westwood."

79. A couple of early articles did note that "Friday night's violence was fueled, at least in part, by tensions created by the highly publicized beating of a black motorist by Los Angeles police officers last week," but that was all. Woo and Chang, "Rampage in Westwood"; see also John L. Mitchell and David J. Fox, "Theater Pulls Movie Linked to Rampage," *Los Angeles Times*, March 12, 1991, http://articles.latimes.com/1991-03-12/local/me-152_1_theater-chain.

80. Mitchell and Fox, "Theater Pulls Movie."

81. Seth Mydans, "Film on Gangs Becomes Part of the World It Portrays," *New York Times*, March 13, 1991, A16.

82. Doug McHenry and George Jackson, "Missing the Big Picture," *New York Times*, March 26, 1991, A23.

83. John Singleton, quoted in Robert Reinhold, "Near Gang Turf, Theater Features Peace," *New York Times*, July 15, 1991, A13.

84. As Daniel Herbert notes, "crossover" is a potentially offensive industry term for audience identification "only used when there is a white cis audience

for films about minoritized subjects." It fails to capture the promiscuous pleasures of media identification while also speaking to popular perceptions of audience biases, particularly in regard to race. I used it advisedly in this instance to consider how Columbia marketed *Boyz N the Hood* to white viewers. Daniel Herbert, personal correspondence to author, March 4, 2020.

85. Amanda Ann Klein, *American Film Cycles: Reframing Genres, Screening Social Problems, and Defining Subcultures* (Austin: University of Texas Press, 2011), 142.

86. See Michael Eric Dyson, "Gangsta Rap and American Culture," in *Between God and Gangsta Rap: Bearing Witness to Black Culture*, reprint ed. (New York: Oxford University Press, 1997), 176–86.

87. Klein, *American Film Cycles*, 157.

88. "Trailer (*Boyz N the Hood*)," IMDb, accessed June 4, 2017, http://www.imdb.com/video/screenplay/vi3989046041.

89. "*Boyz N the Hood* VHS Trailer," YouTube, accessed June 4, 2017, https://youtu.be/it5J9jzhK1I.

90. John Lancaster, "Film Opens with Wave of Violence," *Washington Post*, July 14, 1991, A1; "Minneapolis Youth Second Victim of Violence at Film Showing," *New York Times*, July 19, 1991, http://www.nytimes.com/1991/07/19/us/minneapolis-youth-2d-victim-of-violence-at-film-showing.html.

91. Cheryl W. Thompson, "Man Guilty in Killing at Drive-In," *Chicago Tribune*, May 14, 1993, https://www.chicagotribune.com/news/ct-xpm-1993-05-14-9305140315-story.html; Jerry Thomas and Andrew Gottesman, "Violence Distorting Message in *Boyz*," *Chicago Tribune*, July 17, 1991, https://www.chicagotribune.com/news/ct-xpm-1991-07-17-9103200457-story.html.

92. "Minneapolis Teen Shot at *Boyz* Debut Dies," AP News Archive, July 18, 1991, http://www.apnewsarchive.com/1991/Minneapolis-Teen-Shot-at-Boyz-Debut-Dies/id-855edc7a392f840f79db239c70173f1d; "Minneapolis Youth Second Victim."

93. "Trail of Trouble for *Boyz* Screenings across the Nation," *Hollywood Reporter*, July 15, 1991, 6; "Gunfire Mars Opening of *Boyz*," *St. Louis Post-Dispatch*, July 14, 1991, 4A; "*Boyz N the Hood* Violence Ebbs," United Press International, July 15, 1991, http://www.upi.com/Archives/1991/07/15/Boyz-N-the-Hood-violence-ebbs/6905679550400/.

94. Mike Graham, "Black Cinema Born in the Blood of the Ghettos," *London Sunday Times*, July 21, 1991, LexisNexis.

95. "Trail of Trouble for *Boyz*."

96. Mike Williams, "*Boyz N the Hood* Violence Subsides," *Atlanta Journal and Constitution*, July 15, 1991, A3; "*Boyz N the Hood* Showings Turn Violent," *Tampa Bay and State*, July 14, 1991, 4B.

97. David Landis, "Is the Message Lost?" *USA Today*, July 15, 1991, 1D.

98. "Trail of Trouble for *Boyz*"; Lancaster, "Film Opens with Wave."

99. Leslie Gibson (assistant manager, CNN Center theaters), quoted in Norma Wagner, "Atlanta-Area Theaters Beef Up Security for *Boyz*' Showings," *Atlanta Journal and Constitution*, July 14, 1991, A6.

100. Courtland Milloy, "Screening Out Violence," *Washington Post*, July 16, 1991, D3.

101. Jeff Harris (officer, Winter Park Police Department), quoted in Williams, "*Boyz N the Hood* Violence Subsides," A3.

102. "An Anti-Gang Movie Opens to Violence," *New York Times*, July 13, 1991, A10; "Gunfire Mars Opening of *Boyz*"; Charles R. Acland, *Screen Traffic: Movies, Multiplexes, and Global Culture* (Durham, NC: Duke University Press, 2003), 147; David Landis, "Violence Doesn't Hurt *Boyz* Gate," *USA Today*, July 15, 1991, 1A; Aleene MacMinn, "*Boyz* Death," *Los Angeles Times*, July 19, 1991, http://articles.latimes.com/1991-07-19/entertainment/ca-2279_1_columbia-pictures.

103. Christopher Weitz, "A History of Violence," *London Independent*, July 29, 1991.

104. Graham, "Black Cinema Born in the Blood."

105. Graham, "Black Cinema Born in the Blood."

106. See, for instance, Alex McGregor, "Films That Kill," *Sydney Morning Herald*, October 5, 1991, 34, ProQuest; Carolyn Ford, "Big, Bad *Boyz*," *The Advertiser*, February 1, 1992, ProQuest.

107. Andrea King, "Columbia Backing Up Its *Boyz*," *Hollywood Reporter*, July 15, 1991, 6.

108. George Hill, "John Singleton's Oscar Nod Surprises Him," *Los Angeles Sentinel*, March 18, 1992, ProQuest.

109. John Singleton, quoted in Dan McDonnell, "Lights, Action . . . War," *Herald Sun*, September 4, 1991, LexisNexis.

110. Singleton is likely referring to a Christmas night incident at *The Godfather Part III* (Francis Ford Coppola, 1990) at the Valley Stream Sunrise Cinema on Long Island. Four bystanders were shot during a dispute between two groups of teenagers watching the movie. One—fifteen-year-old Tremain Hall—died the next day. Residents of Valley Stream continued to refer to the Sunrise Cinema as the "murderplex" until it closed in January 2015, but beyond Long Island, the story of Tremain Hall and the *Godfather Part III* shooting has been overlooked or forgotten. So, while there were more shootings associated with *Boyz N the Hood* than with other films, Singleton's point remains: no one accused Coppola of inspiring cinema violence. John Singleton, quoted in John Hartl, Bill Dietrich, and Carlton Smith, "Violence Mars Film Premiere," *Seattle Times*, July 14, 1991, http://community.seattletimes.nwsource.com/archive/?date=19910714& slug=1294273; Sarah Lyall, "Patron Slain as 4 Are Shot at Mafia Film," *New York Times*, December 26, 1990, http://www.nytimes.com/1990/12/27/nyregion/patron-slain-as-4-are-shot-at-mafia-film.html; Sid Cassese, "Sunrise Multiplex Theater Offers Last Picture Show," *Newsday*, January 22, 2015, http://www.newsday.com/long-island/towns/sunrise-multiplex-theater-in-valley-stream-closing-for-mall-expansion-1.9819778.

111. Hal Lipper, "Extra Security at Movie Premiere," *St. Petersburg Times*, January 16, 1992, 8B.

112. Carla Hall, "Jittery over *Juice*," *Washington Post*, January 16, 1992, C1.

113. Teresa Wiltz, "Teen Slain Outside North Side Theater Showing Movie *Juice*," *Chicago Tribune*, January 19, 1992, https://www.chicagotribune.com/news/ct-xpm-1992-01-19-9201060135-story.html.

114. Thomas W. Lippman, "Outbreaks of Violence Mar Opening of *Juice*," *Washington Post*, January 19, 1992, https://www.washingtonpost.com/archive /politics/1992/01/19/outbreaks-of-violence-mar-opening-of-juice/c3851eef-e491 -481e-83e5-6cc9aa194c4d/.

115. Lippmann, "Outbreaks of Violence Mar Opening."

116. "Filmmakers on Violence," *Black Film Review* 7, no. 2 (1992): 3; George Jackson, quoted in "Filmmakers on Violence," 2.

117. "Filmmakers on Violence," 3.

118. Acland, *Screen Traffic*, 147.

119. Mark Becker, "Stepping Up Cinema Security," *Variety*, July 22, 1991, 13, quoted in Acland, *Screen Traffic*, 147; Acland, *Screen Traffic*, 148, 150.

120. Linda Lee, "A Midweek Opening Pattern in Urban Black Films," *New York Times*, March 10, 1997, http://www.nytimes.com/1997/03/10/business /a-midweek-opening-pattern-in-urban-black-films.html.

121. The Cineplex Odeon reached this decision before *Poetic Justice* came out, but unfortunately two people were shot, one fatally, outside screenings of the film. Needless to say, both incidents were reported as though there were some connection between the film and the violence even though a police officer associated with the latter incident averred that his department did not consider them related. Army Archerd and Suzan Ayscough, "'Poetic' Violence Surfaces," *Variety*, August 9, 1993, 14.

122. See Thomas Doherty, "Two Takes on *Boyz N the Hood*," *Cinéaste* 18, no. 4 (1991): 18.

123. David Landis, "Is the Message Lost?" *USA Today*, July 15, 1991, 1D.

124. James Surowiecki, "Shooting Film," *Ottawa Citizen*, September 14, 1997, M6.

125. It may go without saying, but not one single article referred to any of the violence at screenings of *The Warriors* or *Boulevard Nights* as "random." Rather, the popular interpretation held that "gang movies will inevitably attract gang members as an audience," which will inevitably lead to violence. Aljean Harmetz, "Gang Film Is Cancelled in Some Areas," *New York Times*, April 8, 1979, 45.

126. Holmes was not the first white cinema shooter, nor the first to open fire at a white Hollywood blockbuster. In the years immediately prior to Holmes's assault, Mujtaba Rabbani Jabbar shot Paul Schrum inside a screening of *X-Men: The Last Stand* and Walter Dillie Jr. shot Cindy Cade in a parking lot outside a screening of *King Kong*. However, the incidents never led to panicked reception cultures, although the Jabbar-Schrum murder was the first time the term *random* was employed in connection with cinema violence. Nick Shields and Josh Mitchell, "He Was the First and Closest Target," *Baltimore Sun*, June 17, 2006, https:// www.baltimoresun.com/news/bs-xpm-2006-06-17-0606170092-story .html; "White Supremacist Gets Life for Black Murder," *BET*, April 6, 2009, https://www.bet.com/news/news/2009/04/06/newsarticleracistgetslifeformurder .html.

127. Richard Corliss, "*The Dark Knight Rises* Survives the Darkest Night in U.S. Movie History," *Time*, July 24, 2012, http://entertainment.time.com/2012 /07/24/the-dark-knight-rises-survives-the-darkest-night-in-u-s-movie-history/;

David Church, "Liveness and Death at Midnight: Notes on the Aurora Theater Shooting" (paper presented at the annual meeting of the Society for Cinema and Media Studies, Montréal, Quebec, March 25, 2015).

128. Brooks Barnes, "Batman Sales High Despite Shootings," *New York Times*, July 23, 2012, https://mobile.nytimes.com/2012/07/23/movies/dark-knight -leads-at-box-office-in-the-shadow-of-massacre.html; "Number of U.S. Movie Screens," National Association of Theater Owners, accessed June 1, 2017, http:// www.natoonline.org/data/us-movie-screens/.

129. Ray Subers, "Forecast (cont.): 'The Dark Knight Rises' Prediction," Box Office Mojo, July 18, 2012, http://www.boxofficemojo.com/news/?id=3491.

130. Frosch and Johnson, "Gunman Kills 12 in Colorado, Reviving Gun Debate."

131. It was later confirmed that Holmes never mentioned the Joker; Oviatt and the other witnesses made the connection because Holmes had dyed his hair orange and Ledger dyed his hair green to play the Joker. Jack Healy, "Colorado Killer James Holmes's Notes: Detailed Plan vs. 'a Whole Lot of Crazy,'" *New York Times*, May 28, 2015, https://www.nytimes.com/2015/05/29/us/james-holmes -notebook-and-insanity-debate-at-aurora-shooting-trial.html; Jack Healy and Serge F. Kovaleski, "Pain and Puzzles in Wake of Deadly Colorado Attack," *New York Times*, July 22, 2012, http://www.nytimes.com/2012/07/22/us/pain-and -puzzles-in-wake-of-deadly-colorado-attack.html.

132. Gregg Kilday, "*Dark Knight Rises* Director Christopher Nolan: Colorado Shooting 'Devastating,'" *Hollywood Reporter*, July 20, 2012, LexisNexis.

133. Of the many articles on *The Warriors* murders, only one—the write-up in *People* magazine—deems them "tragic." One Paramount executive, Gordon Weaver, did describe the murders as "a truly tragic episode" to the *Chicago Tribune*, but authors Gene Siskel and Michael Hirsley buried the quote in the third-to-last paragraph of their article, and it was never cited again in any other article. A few US reporters called the plot of *Boyz N the Hood* tragic, but only one considered the violence at its screenings to be so. Jerry Thomas and Andrew Gottesman, writing for the *Chicago Tribune*, note that Michael Booth's trip to see *Boyz N the Hood* "brought tragedy" to his family after he was shot exiting the Halstead Twin Outdoor Theater, and Dan McDonnell, writing for the Brisbane *Courier-Mail* and the Melbourne *Herald Sun*, called the violence "routine if tragic" in both of his articles, a formula that all but disavows the devastation and injustice implied by the term *tragic*. "A Street-Gang Movie Called *The Warriors*"; Siskel and Hirsley, "Ads Halted for *The Warriors*"; Jerry Thomas and Andrew Gottesman, "Violence Distorting Message in *Boyz*," *Chicago Tribune*, July 17, 1991, https://www.chicagotribune.com/news/ct-xpm-1991-07-17-9103200457-story. html; Dan McDonnell, "Blood on the Screen Sparks More Blood on the Streets," *Courier-Mail*, July 17, 1991, LexisNexis; McDonnell, "Lights, Action . . . War." For examples of reporters describing the events of, but not the loss of life associated with, *Boyz N the Hood* as tragic, see Courtland Milloy, "Screening Out Violence," *Washington Post*, July 16, 1991, https://www.washingtonpost.com /archive/local/1991/07/16/screening-out-violence/2f2518b2-1a91-4512-b0d7 -07d5b03fc25a; Danny R. Cooks, "*Boyz* Is a Crying Shame Not Worthy of a Tear," *Michigan Citizen*, August 10, 1991, ProQuest.

134. Erica Goode et al., "Before Gunfire, Hints of 'Bad News,'" *New York Times*, August 26, 2012, http://www.nytimes.com/2012/08/27/us/before-gunfire -in-colorado-theater-hints-of-bad-news-about-james-holmes.html; Rick Sallinger, "James Holmes Saw Three Mental Health Professionals before Shooting," *CBS News*, September 19, 2012, http://www.cbsnews.com/news/james-holmes-saw -three-mental-health-professionals-before-shooting/.

135. Jack Healy, "Diary's Pages May Help Jurors Decide If Colorado Gunman Was Methodical or Mad," *New York Times*, May 26, 2015, https://www .nytimes.com/2015/05/27/us/diarys-pages-may-help-jurors-decide-if-james-holmes -theater-gunman-was-methodical-or-mad.html.

136. Some politicians did call for more thorough background checks for gun sales, but gun sales also spiked in Colorado in the wake of the Aurora massacre. Because Holmes had never been involuntarily committed and had no criminal record, it is unlikely that any background check would have prevented him from legally procuring firearms.

137. In the United States, "law and order" (from the Latin expression *lex et ordo*) has long been "the cry that the people in charge have raised to confront the threat of violence bubbling up from below." Since Richard Nixon's 1968 presidential campaign, it has particularly conveyed anti-Black prejudice. Geoff Nunberg, "Is Trump's Call for 'Law and Order' a Coded Racial Message?" *National Public Radio*, July 28, 2016, http://www.npr.org/2016/07/28/487560886/is-trumps -call-for-law-and-order-a-coded-racial-message.

138. See Martin Fradley, "What Do You Believe In? Film Scholarship and the Cultural Politics of the *Dark Knight* Franchise," *Film Quarterly* 66, no.3 (Spring 2013): 15–27.

139. In *Batman Begins* (Christopher Nolan, 2005), one learns that young Bruce Wayne's parents were both murdered in front of him during a mugging gone awry. Their deaths set Wayne on the path to cleaning up Gotham, making it the kind of town his father wanted it to be.

140. Christopher Nolan, quoted in Kilday, "*Dark Knight Rises* Director."

141. Years later, the *New York Times* would describe the Century 16 premiere as "a cheerful suburban screening"—at least until Holmes interrupted it. Frosch and Johnson, "Gunman Kills 12 in Colorado"; Jack Healy, "Colorado Shooting Trial of James E. Holmes Pits a Calculated Killer against an Erratic Mind," *New York Times*, April 28, 2015, https://www.nytimes.com/2015/04/28/us/families -steel-themselves-for-trial-of-aurora-theater-killer-in-colorado.html.

142. See Douglas Gomery, *Shared Pleasures: A History of Movie Presentation in the United States* (Madison: University of Wisconsin Press, 1992); and Rhodes, *Perils of Moviegoing*.

143. Lee Grieveson, *Policing Cinema: Movies and Censorship in Early-Twentieth-Century America* (Berkeley: University of California Press, 2004), 59, 15.

144. Mark Memmott, "'Absolutely Crazy': Man Killed in Movie Theater for Texting?" *NPR*, January 14, 2014, https://www.npr.org/sections/thetwo-way/2014 /01/14/262369211/absolutely-crazy-man-killed-in-movie-theater-for-texting.

145. Ángel González, "Man Who Says He Feared Mass Shootings Accidentally Shoots Stranger in Movie Theater, Police Say," *Seattle Times*, January 23, 2016,

http://www.seattletimes.com/seattle-news/crime/suspect-in-renton-theater
-shooting-says-he-feared-random-attacks/; Hana Kim, "Woman Shot Inside Renton
Theater Blames Regal Cinemas," *Q13 Fox*, January 29, 2016, http://q13fox.com
/2016/01/29/woman-shot-inside-renton-movie-theatre-blaming-regal-cinema/.

146. Campbell Robertson, Richard Pérez-Peña, and Alan Blinder, "Lafayette
Shooting Adds Another Angry Face in the Gunman's Gallery," *New York Times*,
July 24, 2015, https://www.nytimes.com/2015/07/25/us/lafayette-theater-shooting
-john-houser.html.

147. Lorena O'Neil, "Did the *Trainwreck* Shooter Purposefully Target a Feminist Movie?" *Hollywood Reporter*, July 27, 2015, http://www.hollywoodreporter
.com/news/lafayette-shooting-anti-feminist-john-811119.

148. "Amy Schumer, Chuck Schumer Urge Lawmakers to Back Gun Control
Bill," *MSNBC*, October 26, 2015, http://www.msnbc.com/msnbc/amy-schumer
-chuck-schumer-urge-lawmakers-back-gun-control-bill.

149. Loren Korn, "Central Florida Theaters Issue Message on Safety,"
WKMG News 6, July 30, 2015, http://www.clickorlando.com/news/central
-florida-theaters-issue-message-on-safety-measures.

150. "AMC Theatres: Pre-Rolls (2013–2015)," YouTube, accessed June 6,
2015, https://youtu.be/Hp_2NH5qABk.

151. "AMC Theatres: Coming Soon Bumper, Romance," YouTube, accessed
June 6, 2015, https://youtu.be/LRJUeFklizo; "AMC Theatres: Coming Soon
Bumper, Drama/Indie/Foreign (2015)," YouTube, accessed June 6, 2015, https://
youtu.be/R-3s2ML6kBs; "AMC Theatres Pre-Roll: Adult Comedy," YouTube,
accessed June 6, 2015, https://youtu.be/M_tbklfpzyo; "AMC Theatres Pre Show
Super Hero," YouTube, accessed June 6, 2015, https://youtu.be/JTyw4NiQ1LI.

152. In 2017, AMC introduced a revised line of pre-roll videos that urge
viewers to "report suspicious behavior" rather than characters.

153. See Steve Gorman, "ACLU Faults 'Suspicious Activity' Reporting by Law
Enforcement," *Reuters*, September 19, 2013, https://www.reuters.com/article
/us-usa-security-profiling/aclu-faults-suspicious-activity-reporting-by-law
-enforcement-idUSBRE98J01N20130920.

CONCLUSION

1. Vivian Sobchack, "The Scene of the Screen: Envisioning Photographic,
Cinematic, and Electronic 'Presence,'" in *Carnal Thoughts: Embodiment and
Moving Image Culture* (Berkeley: University of California Press, 2004). It bears
noting that Sobchack introduced the idea of "the scene of the screen" in 1987
at the "Materialität der Kommunikation" (Materiality of Communication) conference in Dubrovnik and first published on the concept in English in 1990. Her
work thus reflects a specific moment in the histories of film and media studies
and communications technology.

2. Fortunately, we got over that. See, as exemplars, Jennifer M. Barker, *The
Tactile Eye: Touch and the Cinematic Experience* (Berkeley: University of California Press, 2009); Linda Williams, *Hard Core: Power, Pleasure, and the
"Frenzy of the Visible,"* expanded ed. (Berkeley: University of California Press,
1999).

3. This acrimony began during the so-called "theory wars" between post-structuralists and new historicists during the 1970s and 1980s. For more on that fight, see D. N. Rodowick, *Elegy for Theory* (Cambridge, MA: Harvard University Press, 2015).

4. Genevieve McGillicudy (vice president of Brand Activation and Partnerships, Turner Classic Movies), interview with Caetlin Benson-Allott, Atlanta, GA, June 20, 2018.

5. See Daniel Miller, *Stuff* (Cambridge, UK: Polity, 2010).

6. Matthew Flisfeder, "Ideology Critique and Film Criticism in the New Media Ecology," *Film Criticism* 40, no. 1 (2016): http://dx.doi.org/10.3998/fc.13761232.0040.110; see also Nico Baumbach, *Cinema/Politics/Philosophy* (New York: Columbia University Press, 2018).

7. Jay T. Dolmage, *Academic Ableism: Disability and Higher Education* (Ann Arbor: University of Michigan Press, 2017), 167.

8. Newer theoretical approaches to spectatorship also have much to gain from considering material culture. Affect theorists can broaden their accounts of the zones of intensity they study by considering how architecture and interior design influence such interpersonal feelings. Cognitive film theorists could consider how material factors, including intoxicants, alter the body's reaction to audiovisual stimuli.

9. Bruno Latour, "On Actor-Network Theory: A Few Clarifications Plus More Than a Few Complications," 7, http://www.bruno-latour.fr/sites/default/files/P-67%20ACTOR-NETWORK.pdf.

10. Karen Barad, *Meeting the Universe Halfway: Quantum Physics and the Entanglement of Matter and Meaning* (Durham, NC: Duke University Press, 2007), 3.

11. Barad, *Meeting the Universe Halfway*, 185.

12. See Edward Branigan, "How Frame Lines (and Film Theory) Figure," in *Film Style and Story: A Tribute to Torben Grodal*, ed. Lennart Højbjerg and Peter Schepelern (Copenhagen: Museum Tusculanum Press, 2003), 59–86.

13. Miller, *Stuff*, 50.

Selected Bibliography

Acland, Charles R. *Screen Traffic: Movies, Multiplexes, and Global Culture.* Durham, NC: Duke University Press, 2003.

Affuso, Elizabeth, and Avi Santo. "Mediated Merchandise, Merchandisable Media: An Introduction." *Film Criticism* 42, no. 2 (2018): http://dx.doi.org/10.3998/fc.13761232.0042.201.

Alexander, Michelle. "The New Jim Crow." *Ohio State Journal of Criminal Law* 9, no. 1 (2011): 7–26.

Allen, Robert C., ed. *Channels of Discourse: Television and Contemporary Criticism.* Chapel Hill: University of North Carolina Press, 1987.

Anker, Elizabeth S., and Rita Felski, eds. *Critique and Postcritique.* Durham, NC: Duke University Press, 2017.

Aronson, Michael. *Nickelodeon City: Pittsburgh at the Movies, 1905–1929.* Pittsburgh: University of Pittsburgh Press, 2008.

Baker, Laura. "Screening Race: Responses to Theater Violence at *New Jack City* and *Boyz N the Hood.*" *Velvet Light Trap* 44 (Fall 1999): 4–19.

Barad, Karen. *Meeting the Universe Halfway: Quantum Physics and the Entanglement of Matter and Meaning.* Durham, NC: Duke University Press, 2007.

Baron, Cynthia. "Dinner and a Movie: Analyzing Food and Film." *Food, Culture & Society* 9, no. 1 (2006): 93–117.

Baudry, Jean-Louis. "Ideological Effects of the Basic Cinematographic Apparatus." Translated by Alan Williams. In *Narrative, Apparatus, Ideology: A Film Theory Reader*, edited by Philip Rosen, 286–98. New York: Columbia University Press, 1986.

Bazin, André. "The Ontology of the Photographic Image." Translated by Hugh Gray. *Film Quarterly* 13, no. 4 (1960): 4–9.

Benjamin, Walter. "The Work of Art in the Age of Mechanical Reproduction." In *Illuminations: Essays and Reflections*, edited by Hannah Arendt, translated by Harry Zohn, 166–95. New York: Schocken Books, 2007.

Bennett, Jane. *Vibrant Matter: A Political Ecology of Things*. Durham, NC: Duke University Press, 2010.

Benzon, Paul. "Bootleg Paratextuality and Digital Temporality: Towards an Alternate Present of the DVD." *Narrative* 21, no. 1 (2013): 88–104.

Biltereyst, Daniel, Richard Maltby, and Philippe Meers. "Introduction: The Scope of New Cinema History." In *The Routledge Companion to New Cinema History*, edited by Daniel Biltereyst, Richard Maltby, and Philippe Meers, 1–12. New York: Routledge, 2019.

Bjarkman, Kim. "To Have and to Hold: The Video Collector's Relationship with an Ethereal Medium." *Television and New Media* 5, no. 3 (2004): 217–46.

Bourdieu, Pierre. *Distinction: A Social Critique of the Judgment of Taste*. Translated by Richard Nice. Cambridge, MA: Harvard University Press, 1984.

Caldwell, John Thornton. *Televisuality: Style, Crisis, and Authority in American Television*. New Brunswick, NJ: Rutgers University Press, 1995.

Carr, Brian. "Paranoid Interpretation, Desire's Nonobject, and Nella Larsen's *Passing*." *PMLA*, 119, no. 2 (2004): 282–95.

Carroll, Nathan. "Unwrapping Archives: DVD Restoration Demonstrations and the Marketing of Authenticity." *Velvet Light Trap* 56, no. 1 (2005): 18–31.

Cavell, Stanley. *The World Viewed: Reflections on the Ontology of Film*. Enlarged ed. Cambridge, MA: Harvard University Press, 1979.

Cheever, Susan. *Drinking in America: Our Secret History*. Reprint ed. New York: Twelve, 2016.

Cherchi Usai, Paolo. *The Death of Cinema: History, Cultural Memory, and the Digital Dark Age*. London: British Film Institute, 2001.

Church, David. *Disposable Passions: Vintage Pornography and the Material Legacies of Adult Cinema*. New York: Bloomsbury Academic, 2016.

Crary, Jonathan. *Suspensions of Perception: Attention, Spectacle, and Modern Culture*. Cambridge, MA: MIT Press, 2001.

Culler, Jonathan. "The Semiotics of Tourism." In *Framing the Sign: Criticism and Its Institutions*, edited by Jonathan Culler, 155–67. Norman: University of Oklahoma Press, 1988.

Davis, Ben. "The Bleecker Street Cinema: From Repertory Theater to Independent Film Showcase." *Cinéaste* 38, no. 1 (Winter 2012): 14–19.

———. *Repertory Movie Theaters of New York City: Havens for Revivals, Indies, and the Avant-Garde, 1960–1994*. Jefferson, NC: McFarland, 2017.

de Ville, Donna. "The Persistent Transience of Microcinema (in the United States and Canada)." *Film History* 27, no. 3 (2015): 104–36.

Delany, Samuel R. *Times Square Red, Times Square Blue*. New York: New York University Press, 1999.

Eagle, Ryan Bowles. "Ambient XXX: Pornography in Public Spaces." In *New Views on Pornography: Sexuality, Politics, and the Law*, edited by Lynn Comella and Shira Tarrant, 395–416. Santa Barbara, CA: Praeger, 2015.

Ellis, John. *Visible Fictions: Cinema, Television, Video*. Rev. ed. New York: Routledge, 1992.

Elsaesser, Thomas. "Cinephilia or the Uses of Disenchantment." In *Cinephilia: Movies, Love, and Memory*, edited by Marijke de Valck and Malte Hagener, 27–44. New York: Amsterdam University Press, 2005.

Felski, Rita. "After Suspicion." *Profession* (2009): 28–35.

———. "Suspicious Minds." *Poetics Today* 32, no. 2 (2011): 215–34.

Fiske, John. *Television Culture*. London: Methuen, 1987.

Flisfeder, Matthew. "Ideology Critique and Film Criticism in the New Media Ecology." *Film Criticism* 40, no. 1 (2016): http://dx.doi.org/10.3998/fc .13761232.0040.110.

Fradley, Martin. "What Do You Believe In? Film Scholarship and the Cultural Politics of the *Dark Knight* Franchise." *Film Quarterly* 66, no. 3 (2013): 15–27.

Francis, Terri. "The No-Theory Chant of Afrosurrealism." *Black Camera* 5, no. 1 (Fall 2013): 95–111.

Friedberg, Anne. *Window Shopping: Cinema and the Postmodern*. Berkeley: University of California Press, 1993.

Girard, René. *Violence and the Sacred*. Translated by Patrick Gregory. Baltimore, MD: Johns Hopkins University Press, 1979.

Gomery, Douglas. *Shared Pleasures: A History of Movie Presentation in the United States*. Madison: University of Wisconsin Press, 1992.

Grainge, Paul. "Branding Hollywood: Studio Logos and the Aesthetics of Memory and Hype." *Screen* 45, no. 4 (Winter 2004): 344–62.

Gray, Jonathan. *Show Sold Separately: Promos, Spoilers, and Other Media Paratexts*. New York: New York University Press, 2010.

Grieveson, Lee. *Policing Cinema: Movies and Censorship in Early-Twentieth-Century America*. Berkeley: University of California Press, 2004.

Hanna, Erin. *Only at Comic-Con: Hollywood, Fans, and the Limits of Exclusivity*. New Brunswick, NJ: Rutgers University Press, 2020.

Hastie, Amelie. "Eating in the Dark: A Theoretical Concession." *Journal of Visual Culture* 6, no. 2 (2007): 283–302.

Havens, Timothy, Amanda D. Lotz, and Serra Tinic. "Critical Media Industry Studies: A Research Approach." *Communication, Culture & Critique* 2, no. 2 (2009): 234–53.

Herbert, Daniel. *Videoland: Movie Culture at the American Video Store*. Berkeley: University of California Press, 2014.

Herbert, Daniel, and Derek Johnson, eds. *Point of Sale: Analyzing Media Retail*. New Brunswick, NJ: Rutgers University Press, 2020.

Herbert, Daniel, Amanda D. Lotz, and Aswin Punathambekar. *Media Industry Studies*. Medford, MA: Polity, 2020.

Hilderbrand, Lucas. *Inherent Vice: Bootleg Histories of Videotape and Copyright*. Durham, NC: Duke University Press, 2009.

Hills, Matt. "Cult TV, Quality, and the Role of the Episode/Programme Guide." In *The Contemporary Television Series*, edited by Michael Hammond and Lucy Mazdon, 190–206. Edinburgh: Edinburgh University Press, 2005.

———. "From the Box in the Corner to the Box Set on the Shelf." *New Review of Film and Television Studies* 5, no. 1 (2007): 41–60.

Hodder, Ian. *Entangled: An Archaeology of the Relationships between Humans and Things*. Malden, MA: Wiley-Blackwell, 2012.

Holt, Jennifer, and Alisa Perren. "Introduction: Does the World Really Need One More Field of Study?" In *Media Industries: History, Theory, and Method*, 1–16. Malden, MA: Wiley-Blackwell, 2009.

Horeck, Tanya, Mareike Jenner, and Tina Kendall. "On Binge-Watching: Nine Critical Propositions." *Critical Studies in Television* 13, no. 4 (2018): 499–504.

Kaplan, E. Ann, ed. *Regarding Television: Critical Approaches—An Anthology*. Frederick, MD: University Publications of America, 1983.

Johnson, Catherine. "Quality/Cult Television: *The X-Files* and Television History." In *The Contemporary Television Series*, edited by Michael Hammond and Lucy Mazdon, 57–72. Edinburgh: Edinburgh University Press, 2005.

Jones, Tim. "A Case of Pub Cinema: Changing Neighborhoods, Craft Beer, and Creative Consumption." Paper presented at the Society for Cinema and Media Studies annual conference, Seattle, Washington, March 2019.

Keathley, Christian. *Cinephilia and History, or The Wind in the Trees*. Bloomington: Indiana University Press, 2005.

Keeling, Kara. *Queer Times, Black Futures*. New York: New York University Press, 2019.

Kessler, Frank. "The Cinema of Attractions as *Dispositif*." In *The Cinema of Attractions Reloaded*, edited by Wanda Strauven, 57–70. Amsterdam: Amsterdam University Press, 2006.

Klein, Amanda Ann. "Abject Femininity and Compulsory Masculinity on *Jersey Shore*." In *Reality Gendervision: Sexuality and Gender on Transatlantic Reality Television*, edited by Brenda R. Weber, 149–69. Durham, NC: Duke University Press, 2014.

———. *American Film Cycles: Reframing Genres, Screening Social Problems, and Defining Subcultures*. Austin: University of Texas Press, 2011.

Kompare, Derek. "Publishing Flow: DVD Box Sets and the Reconception of Television." *Television and New Media* 7, no. 4 (2006): 335–60.

———. *Rerun Nation: How Repeats Invented American Television*. New York: Routledge, 2004.

Kracauer, Siegfried. *Theory of Film: The Redemption of Physical Reality*. New York: Oxford University Press, 1960.

Lane, Jim. "Critical and Cultural Reception of the European Art Film in 1950s America: A Case Study of the Brattle Theatre (Cambridge, Massachusetts)." *Film & History* 24, nos. 3–4 (1994): 51–64.

Lee, Martin. *Smoke Signals: A Social History of Marijuana—Medical, Recreational, and Scientific*. New York: Scribner, 2013.

Lenson, David. *On Drugs*. Minneapolis: University of Minnesota Press, 1999.

Lewis, Jon. "Parting Glances." *Cinema Journal* 43, no. 3 (2004): 98–101.

Llamas-Rodriguez, Juan. "A Global Cinematic Experience: Cinépolis, Film Exhibition, and Luxury Branding." *JCMS: Journal of Cinema and Media Studies* 58, no. 3 (2019): 49–71.

Lotz, Amanda D. *Portals: A Treatise on Internet-Distributed Television*. Ann Arbor: Michigan Publishing, 2017.

———. *The Television Will Be Revolutionized*. 2nd ed. New York: New York University Press, 2014.

Lury, Celia. *Brands: The Logos of the Global Economy*. New York: Routledge, 2004.

Maltby, Richard. "New Cinema Histories." In *Explorations in New Cinema History: Approaches and Case Studies*, edited by Richard Maltby, Daniel Biltereyst, and Philippe Meers, 3–40. Malden, MA: Wiley-Blackwell, 2011.

Marez, Curtis. "From Mr. Chips to Scarface, or Racial Capitalism in *Breaking Bad*." *Critical Inquiry* (blog), September 25, 2013. https://critinq.wordress.com/2013/09/25/breaking-bad/#more-487.

Martin, Alfred R. Jr. "Notes from *Underground*: WGN's Black-Cast Quality TV Experiment." *Los Angeles Review of Books*, May 31, 2018. https://lareviewofbooks.org/article/notes-from-underground-wgns-black-cast-quality-tv-experiment/.

McCarthy, Anna. *Ambient Television: Visual Culture and Public Space*. Durham, NC: Duke University Press, 2001.

McLuhan, Marshall. "Understanding Media," in *Essential McLuhan*, edited by Eric McLuhan and Frank Zingrone, 149–74. New York: Basic Books, 1995.

Mellencamp, Patricia, ed. *Logics of Television: Essays in Cultural Criticism*. Bloomington: Indiana University Press, 1990.

Melnick, Ross, and Andreas Fuchs. *Cinema Treasures: A New Look at Classic Movie Theaters*. St. Paul, MN: MBI, 2004.

Miller, Daniel. *Stuff*. Cambridge, UK: Polity, 2010.

Mittell, Jason. *Complex TV: The Poetics of Contemporary Television Storytelling*. New York: New York University Press, 2015.

Morgan, Danielle Fuentes. *Laughing to Keep from Dying: African American Satire in the Twenty-First Century*. Champaign: University of Illinois Press, 2020.

Morris, Jeremy Wade. *Selling Digital Music, Formatting Culture*. Oakland: University of California Press, 2015.

Mullen, Megan. *The Rise of Cable Programming in the United States: Revolution or Evolution?* Austin: University of Texas Press, 2003.

Mulvey, Laura. *Death 24x a Second: Stillness and the Moving Image*. London: Reaktion, 2006.

Newman, Michael Z. "From Beats to Arcs: Toward a Poetics of Television Narrative." *The Velvet Light Trap* 58 (2006): 16–28.

———. "TV Binge." *FLOW: A Critical Forum on Media and Culture*, last modified January 23, 2009. https://www.flowjournal.org/2009/01/tv-binge-michael-z-newman-university-of-wisconsin-milwaukee/.

Nystrom, Derek. *Hard Hats, Red Necks, and Macho Men: Class in 1970s American Cinema*. New York: Oxford University Press, 2009.

Parsons, Patrick R. *Blue Skies: A History of Cable Television*. Philadelphia: Temple University Press, 2008.

Pierce-Grove, Ri. "Just One More: How Journalists Frame Binge Watching." *first monday* 22, no. 1 (2017): http://firstmonday.org/ojs/index.php/fm/article/view/7269/5792.

Rascaroli, Laura. "Oneiric Metaphor in Film Theory." *Kinema: A Journal for Film and Audiovisual Media* (2002): https://doi.org/10.15353/kinema.vi.982.

Restivo, Angelo. *"Breaking Bad" and Cinematic Television*. Durham, NC: Duke University Press, 2019.

Rhodes, Gary D. *The Perils of Moviegoing in America, 1896–1950*. New York: Bloomsbury, 2011.

Room, Robin. "The Movies and the Wettening of America: The Media as Amplifiers of Cultural Change." *British Journal of Addiction* 83 (1988): 11–18.

Schauer, Bradley. "The Warner Archive and DVD Collecting in the New Home Video Market." *Velvet Light Trap* 70 (2012): 35–48.

Sedgwick, Eve Kosofsky. "Paranoid Reading and Reparative Reading, or, You're So Paranoid, You Probably Think This Essay Is About You." In *Touching Feeling: Affect, Pedagogy, Performativity*, 123–52. Durham, NC: Duke University Press, 2003.

Segrave, Kerry. *Drive-In Theaters: A History from Their Inception in 1933*. Jefferson, NC: McFarland, 1992.

Seiter, Ellen, Hans Borchers, Gabriele Kreutzner, and Eva-Maria Warth, eds. *Remote Control: Television, Audiences, and Cultural Power*. New York: Routledge, 1989.

Smith, Andrew F. *Popped Culture: A Social History of Popcorn in America*. Columbia: University of South Carolina Press, 1999.

Sobchack, Vivian. "Chasing the Maltese Falcon: On Fabrications of a Film Prop." *Journal of Visual Culture* 6, no. 2 (2007): 219–46.

———. "The Scene of the Screen: Envisioning Photographic, Cinematic, and Electronic 'Presence.'" In *Carnal Thoughts: Embodiment and Moving Image Culture*, 135–62. Berkeley: University of California Press, 2004.

Sontag, Susan. "Against Interpretation." In *Against Interpretation and Other Essays*, 3–14. London: Picador, 2001.

Spigel, Lynn. *Make Room for TV: Television and the Family Ideal in Postwar America*. Chicago: University of Chicago Press, 1992.

Stam, Robert. "Television News and Its Spectator." In *Regarding Television: Critical Approaches—An Anthology*, edited by E. Ann Kaplan, 23–43. Frederick, MD: University Publications of America, 1983.

Stevenson, Jack. *Land of a Thousand Balconies: Discoveries and Confessions of a B-Movie Archaeologist*. Manchester, UK: Headpress, 2003.

Stewart, Susan. *On Longing: Narratives of the Miniature, the Gigantic, the Souvenir, the Collection*. Durham, NC: Duke University Press, 1992.

Sturken, Marita. *Tangled Memories: The Vietnam War, the AIDS Epidemic, and the Politics of Remembering*. Berkeley: University of California Press, 1997.

Szczepaniak-Gillece, Jocelyn. *The Optical Vacuum: Spectatorship and Modernized American Theater Architecture*. New York: Oxford University Press, 2018.

Szczepaniak-Gillece, Jocelyn, and Stephen Groening. "Afterword: Objects in the Theater." *Film History* 28, no. 3 (2016): 139–42.

Tryon, Chuck. *On-Demand Culture: Digital Delivery and the Future of Movies*. New Brunswick, NJ: Rutgers University Press, 2013.

Verevis, Constantine. *Film Remakes*. Edinburgh: Edinburgh University Press, 2006.

Wiegman, Robyn. "The Times We're In: Queer Feminist Criticism and the Reparative 'Turn.'" *Feminist Theory* 15, no. 1 (2014): 1–24.

Williams, Raymond. *Marxism and Literature*. New York: Oxford University Press, 1977.

———. *Television: Technology and Cultural Form*. New York: Schocken, 1975.

Index

Founded in 1893,
UNIVERSITY OF CALIFORNIA PRESS
publishes bold, progressive books and journals
on topics in the arts, humanities, social sciences,
and natural sciences—with a focus on social
justice issues—that inspire thought and action
among readers worldwide.

The UC PRESS FOUNDATION
raises funds to uphold the press's vital role
as an independent, nonprofit publisher, and
receives philanthropic support from a wide
range of individuals and institutions—and from
committed readers like you. To learn more, visit
ucpress.edu/supportus.